Y0-CWT-364

.F63
K49
2019

Metropolitan College of NY
Library - 7th Floor
60 West Street
New York, NY 10006

Artificial Color

Artificial Color

Modern Food and Racial Fictions

CATHERINE KEYSER

UNIVERSITY PRESS

OXFORD
UNIVERSITY PRESS

Oxford University Press is a department of the University of Oxford. It furthers
the University's objective of excellence in research, scholarship, and education
by publishing worldwide. Oxford is a registered trade mark of Oxford University
Press in the UK and certain other countries.

Published in the United States of America by Oxford University Press
198 Madison Avenue, New York, NY 10016, United States of America.

© Oxford University Press 2019

All rights reserved. No part of this publication may be reproduced, stored in
a retrieval system, or transmitted, in any form or by any means, without the
prior permission in writing of Oxford University Press, or as expressly permitted
by law, by license, or under terms agreed with the appropriate reproduction
rights organization. Inquiries concerning reproduction outside the scope of the
above should be sent to the Rights Department, Oxford University Press, at the
address above.

You must not circulate this work in any other form
and you must impose this same condition on any acquirer.

Library of Congress Cataloging-in-Publication Data
Names: Keyser, Catherine, 1980– author.
Title: Artificial color : modern food and racial fictions / Catherine Keyser.
Description: New York : Oxford University Press, [2018] |
Includes bibliographical references and index.
Identifiers: LCCN 2018012411 (print) | LCCN 2018012898 (ebook) |
ISBN 9780190673130 (Updf) | ISBN 9780190673147 (Epub) |
ISBN 9780190673123 (hardcover : alk. paper)
Subjects: LCSH: Food in literature. | American fiction—20th century—History
and criticism. | Food habits in literature. | Race in literature. |
Whites—Race identity—In literature. | Ethnicity in literature.
Classification: LCC PS374.F63 (ebook) | LCC PS374.F63 K49 2018 (print) |
DDC 813/.5093559—dc23
LC record available at https://lccn.loc.gov/2018012411

1 3 5 7 9 8 6 4 2

Printed by Sheridan Books, Inc., United States of America

Chapter 1 includes excerpts of Jean Toomer's unpublished memoirs, with the permission of the
Jean Toomer Papers, James Weldon Johnson Memorial Collection in the Yale Collection of American
Literature, Beinecke Rare Book and Manuscript Library. ©Yale University. All rights reserved.

Chapter 2 includes excerpts of materials from the Schuyler Family Papers, located at the Schomburg
Center for Research in Black Culture, with the permission of Karen T. Hilliard Johnson. Part of Chapter 3
was published previously as "An All-Too-Moveable Feast: Ernest Hemingway and the Stakes of Terroir,"
Resilience: A Journal of the Environmental Humanities 2.1 (Winter 2014), with the permission of University
of Nebraska Press. Part of Chapter 1 was published previously as "Bottles, Bubbles, and Blood:
Jean Toomer and the Limits of Racial Epidermalism," Modernism/modernity 22.2 (April 2015):
279–302, copyright © 2015 The Johns Hopkins University Press.

CONTENTS

Acknowledgments vii

Introduction 1

1. "A Purple Fluid, Carbon-Charged": Jean Toomer's Mutable Materials 15

2. Genius in the Raw: The Schuyler Family and the Modern Mulatta 42

3. Eating Like a Local: Ernest Hemingway, Gertrude Stein, and the Stakes of Terroir 73

4. "A Beaker Full of the Warm South": The Fitzgeralds and Mediterranean Infusions 111

5. The Monstropolous Beast: Animacy and Industry in Zora Neale Hurston and Dorothy West 141

Notes 171
Index 213

ACKNOWLEDGMENTS

To my tireless and brilliant informal team of core readers, editors, and interlocutors, I owe a huge debt of thanks: Greg Forter, Anne Gulick, Barbara Keyser, Nadine Knight, Phil Nel, and Sara Schwebel. Always willing to read new material, to ask important questions, and to root me on, they demonstrate that scholarship is ideally a collaborative endeavor, even when it seems like a solo performance.

Generous and smart colleagues have made this project stronger at every turn. Glenda Carpio, Allison Carruth, Brooks Hefner, Michael Gibbs Hill, Lisa Mendelman, and Jake Ruddiman read and commented on sections of the book. Mary Chapman read an early version of my book proposal and helped me find the book's structure. Michelle Coghlan, Danielle Coriale, Brian Glavey, Barbara Green, and David Greven were patient and wise sounding boards for the project as a whole, discussing its scope and approach. Kate Adams, Debra Rae Cohen, Jean Lutes, Kyla Wazana Tompkins, and Scott Trafton asked key questions as I developed this project in presentations and inspired new and crucial directions for my research. Meredith Goldsmith introduced me to the works of Dorothy West. The English Department at the University of South Carolina is a vibrant intellectual community of which I am proud to be a part, and department chairs Nina Levine and Bill Rivers supported this project enthusiastically. David Shields shared his astonishing breadth of culinary and agricultural knowledge; Holly Crocker introduced me to *Gut Feminism*; Seulghee Lee insisted that pleasure matters; and Eli Jelly-Schapiro reminded me that sometimes we can find redemptive potential even at the heart of benighted worldviews. Qiana Whitted was my comrade-in-arms and co-conspirator as we both worked on major projects. Susan Courtney and Susan Vanderborg, my fifth-floor office neighbors, asked for progress reports and gave regular pep talks. From this project's inception, my graduate mentors, Larry Buell and Werner Sollors, have provided support and supplied ideas; their generosity is the ideal I strive for in my own teaching and advising. To all, I offer my heartfelt thanks and deep appreciation.

At each stage of this process, a talented research assistant aided me in my endeavors: many thanks to Ali Arant for initial forays into new material; to Jada Ach for deep exploration of chapter-based inquiries; and to Jennifer Blevins for permissions requests and eagle-eyed copy edits. Thanks are also due to Danielle Di Leo and Michele degli Esposti for sharing their expertise in Italian language and culture; to Gayle Rogers for his expertise in Spanish language and culture; to Matt Gassan for combing back issues of the *Crisis* children's number; to Richard Barclay for the Andre Wilder poster; and to Lance Hall for producing high-resolution scans.

Thanks to the organizations that sponsored the conferences where I developed these ideas through panel presentations: Modern Language Association (2018); the Modernist Studies Association (2015); the Society for the Study of American Women Writers (2015); the American Literature Association (2013); and the Harvard University English Department (2011, 2014). Thanks to the faculty who invited me to present this work-in-progress in talks at Wake Forest University (Melissa Jenkins) and Oregon State University (Lily Sheehan) and to the audiences there whose responses added so much to the project. Thanks also to Sunny Stalter-Pace for directing me to the Scott and Zelda Fitzgerald Museum during my visit to Auburn.

Thanks to Sarah Pirovitz at Oxford University Press for shepherding this project and to Brendan O'Neill for bringing it to the Press. Thanks also to editorial assistants Abigail Johnson and Alexa Marcon, copy editor Mary Becker, and indexer Bob Ellis The anonymous reviewers championed my work and improved the book's scope and style; I am immensely grateful for their enthusiasm and acumen.

An earlier version of Chapter 1 appeared as "Bottles, Bubbles, and Blood: Jean Toomer and the Limits of Racial Epidermalism," in *Modernism/modernity* 22.2 (April 2015): 279–302. An earlier version of part of Chapter 3 appeared as "An All-Too-Moveable Feast: Ernest Hemingway and the Stakes of *Terroir*," in *Resilience: A Journal of the Environmental Humanities* 2.1 (Winter 2014): 10–23. Thanks to these journals for permission to reuse these materials, as well as to the editors and anonymous reviewers for helpful comments and revision suggestions.

Thanks to the University of South Carolina for supporting this project through the Provost Humanities Grant Program (2011–12, 2014); a sabbatical semester (2014); the Institute for African-American Research (IAAR) Fellowship (2011–12); the Peter and Bonnie McCausland Fellowship (2013–18); and the English Department Morrison Fellowship (2017).

The Hartman Center Travel Grant (Duke University Libraries) supported this project at an early stage. Many thanks to Nelson Donegan and Jean Fox

O'Barr for my accommodations at Yale and Duke respectively. Thanks to archivists and staff members at the Beinecke Rare Book and Manuscript Library; the Hartman Center for Sales, Advertising & Marketing History; the Schomburg Center for Research in Black Culture; and the Irvin Department of Rare Books and Special Collections at the University of South Carolina. Thanks to Michael Weisenburg for chasing down a Zelda Fitzgerald photograph for me, even when I had only the vaguest recollection of what I was looking for, and for bibliographic information on the first edition of *Paris France*. The Interlibrary Loan staff at Thomas Cooper Library obtained and scanned innumerable sources for me; I am in their debt.

Many thanks to my students in Fast and Slow Foods in Modern U.S. Literature (Spring 2012), Devouring Books: Food in Modern U.S. Literature (Spring 2013), and Eat This! Food and Modern U.S. Literature (Fall 2017). Their enlivening conversation and sharp ideas have contributed to this book.

Thanks to Chloe Bohl, Michelle Brigman, Sherri Cammisa, Victoria Chandler, Meir Muller, Kelly Stanton, and the faculty and staff at the Cutler Jewish Day School for providing my daughter with loving care, without which work on this book would not have been possible.

I could not get by without a little help from my friends, many of whom have already been named. For meals and conversations shared, thanks to Ryan Abrecht, Sam Amadon, Alex Beecroft, Harry Brent, Kate Callahan, Dan and Mary Cammisa, Jane Carr, John Castleman, Liz Countryman, Kristin DeHahn, Eleni Delopoulos, Tom Dent, Michael Dowdy, Emilie Duck, Caitlin Dunning, Alisa and Dick Freed, Ed and Lisa Gieskes, Pelagia Horgan, Heidi Johnson, Louise Klusek, Evren Ozselcuk, Tara Powell, Andy and Sara Rajca, Ehren Remal, Jessica Rogers, Josh Rothman, Eleanor Stein, Greg Stuart, Lauryl Tucker, Jenn Tyburczy, Shelley Welton, and Sarah Williams. Thanks to my family—Abrechts, Baios, Bridges, Cheresnicks, Famolaris, McCans, and Yarbroughs—for their support and love.

As long as I can remember, my mother and father, Barbara and Les Keyser, have shown me that intellectual endeavor could be—indeed, should be—a passionate and wide-ranging adventure. As an adult, I count on their counsel and their camaraderie. Their wisdom and humor enrich my days, and I can never sufficiently thank them for their support and unconditional love—I can only reciprocate.

I have been working on this book for my daughter Sophia's entire life; I am grateful both for her forbearance and for her. My husband, Paul Famolari, lightens my heart effortlessly and supports my endeavors unstintingly. Their love and company make my life a feast, and to them, I offer thanksgiving.

Artificial Color

Introduction

In *The Great Gatsby* (1925), Nick Carraway gazes upon the New York City skyline:

> Over the great bridge, with the sunlight through the girders making a constant flicker upon the moving cars, with the city rising up across the river in white heaps and sugar lumps all built with a wish out of non-olfactory money. The city seen from the Queensboro Bridge is always the city seen for the first time, in its first wild promise of all the mystery and beauty of the world.[1]

The shimmering white city suggests sunlight glancing off a skyscraper. However, these metaphorical "white heaps and sugar lumps" also reflect the source of Gatsby's fortune "built with a wish," which he amassed as a confirmed bootlegger and implied rum runner: sugar was a critical ingredient in whiskey and rum production.[2] This spectacle of whiteness as "wild promise" also carries racial connotations; James Gatz can rename himself Jay Gatsby and gain access to "all the mystery and beauty of the world," as long as his fortune (and, by extension, his body) remains "non-olfactory" (68). The plasticity of whiteness, like refined sugar, is a technology of the modern age, one that relies upon the repression and expulsion of corporeal abjection. In *Quicksand* (1928), Nella Larsen describes a city scene with another alimentary metaphor: her protagonist, Helga Crane, "stepped out into the moving multi-colored crowd, [and] there came to her a queer feeling of enthusiasm, as if she were tasting some agreeable, exotic food—sweetbreads, smothered with truffles and mushrooms, perhaps."[3] Larsen draws upon French haute cuisine, popularized by upscale restaurants like Delmonico's in the mid-nineteenth century, for this simile that essentially turns the anonymous, diverse Chicago crowd into offal and fungi.[4] The defamiliarization of cuisine through restaurant culture, the translation of earthy sensations into cosmopolitan prowess, models the sublimation of erotic intensity into a signature style that Helga pursues throughout the novel.

The spectacle of the city as subtlety, a medieval sugar sculpture on the banquet table of the wealthy, contrasts sharply with the smorgasbord of the city street in *Quicksand*, its intimacy and excess.[5] These tropes—white sugar mounds and queer sweetbreads—offer two distinct accounts of race. The first is predicated on whiteness's simultaneous blankness and spectacle; the vehicle of this figure may be a food, but it is a food that does not smell and hence must have an impoverished taste.[6] Nick knows that white sugar is produced by a machine, that it is the result of a technological process that relies on the sacrifice of unseen bodies; indeed, during his unpleasant train commute to New York, he hears the "hot whistles of the National Biscuit Company," a literalization of the food industry that is merely metaphorical in this passage (114). In spite of these signs of a corporeal and laboring world denied by Gatsby's philosophy, all Nick sees from Gatsby's car is the beauty of this glittering white monument to power.[7]

For Helga, by contrast, the immersion in the city street brings up pleasures on the edge of disgust, devouring organs and truffles, an ingredient that Baudelaire refers to as the entrails of the earth.[8] For a character typically obsessed with her own appearance, this oral immersion and the openness it implies are a stark departure from her established standoffishness. This encounter is explicitly racial; though the "multi-colored crowd" may also sport motley fashions, Helga Crane has just been rebuffed by her white Uncle Peter and his racist new wife, and she will soon visit the South Side branch of the Young Women's Christian Association, dedicated, she reflects ruefully, to "the uplift [of] . . . poor, poor colored people" (30).[9] *Quicksand* follows Helga's desperate movement back and forth between racial and regional contexts, unable to establish a lasting sense of belonging. This "queer" experience of tasting the other temporarily arrests her naturalist trajectory in a moment of possibility that opposes the hierarchies of segregation with the erotics of incorporation.

Both examples demonstrate the artificiality of color through the metaphoric medium of modern food. In Gatsby's case, whiteness is a vehicle for social ascension liable to come crashing down, as his demise indicates. This interlude in *Quicksand*, a novel pessimistic about the impact of racial regimes on mixed-race bodies that don't fit its harsh binaries, temporarily suspends the visual policing of race. For a brief moment, both food and bodies are made unfamiliar, and the ingestive imaginary articulates the encounter with the other, not as assimilation, absorption, or disgust, but as an ecstatic, embodied acknowledgment of the meatiness and the rot that we share. With these two poles to guide me, in the pages that follow I explore modern fiction's movement between sweetness and umami, spectacle and olfaction, abstemiousness and appetite, individualism and enmeshment as writers on both sides of the color line interrogate the stuff that race is (or isn't) made of.

Recent critics register the scalar shifts made possible in "the literature of food," between individual bodies, foodstuffs or food systems, and cultural imaginaries on a global scale.[10] "Across genres," Allison Carruth argues, "literature is a vehicle attuned to the modern food system due to the capacity of imaginative texts to shuttle between social and interpersonal registers and between symbolic and embodied expressions of power."[11] This movement between registers facilitates, in the words of Parama Roy, "scrutiny of the mundane and embodied, the aesthetic, and the ethicopolitical."[12] *Artificial Color* follows this methodological approach, which Kyla Wazana Tompkins dubs "critical eating studies," to trace three levels of alimentary representation: direct allusions to food technologies and systems; embodied tropes of incorporation, abjection, and expulsion that structure these texts; and ambivalent cultural fantasies about racial difference mobilized by these meditations on ingestion.[13] Though many discourses surrounding food seem to be disciplinary, enforcing purity rather than enabling invention, many of these tropes, I discover, expose the mutability of the body and the insufficiency of the social categories that attempt to contain it.

Modern food is an organizing concept for this argument, a term that encompasses new technologies, global geographies, and dietary regimens. These rapid changes troubled long-held beliefs about the body and the nation, placing the consumer in surprising relation to other bodies, human and nonhuman. Global maps underscored the networks that connected variously raced bodies through the food chain. Nutrition science commingled with emergent race theory, sometimes going so far as to propose that food quality could transform racial categorization. Not only did new food maps and dietary speculations make the relationship between race and ingestion explicit, newly available food products, like carbonated soda and tropical fruits, were also associated with the allure of exotic, racialized bodies.

As a result of these associations, US literature between the world wars tests the boundaries of racial categorization and probes the dynamics of interracial exchange, desire and fear, through its figurative and narrative engagements with modern food. As Toni Morrison suggests in *Playing in the Dark*:

> The literature of the United States, like its history, represents commentary on the transformations of the biological, ideological, and metaphysical concepts of racial difference. But the literature has an additional concern and subject matter: the private imagination interacting with the external world it inhabits. Literature redistributes and mutates in figurative language the social conventions of Africanism.[14]

Andrew Warnes, Psyche Williams-Forson, and Doris Witt have developed a rich account of the construction of blackness through the idiom of food, particularly within the African American literary tradition.[15] This book draws upon their insights to explore moments in modern literature when race becomes recognizable as artificial thanks to its dynamic relationship with consumption. In my association of literary form with racial interrogation, I follow scholars like Michael North and Walter Benn Michaels who argue that racial categorization and its instability are central engines of modernist cultural production.[16]

For white US writers, eating often articulates a desire for sensory intensity connected with racial difference, what bell hooks calls "eating the other."[17] "Do I dare eat a peach?" T. S. Eliot's poet-speaker J. Alfred Prufrock asks as he dreams of "sea-girls" who will wreath him with "seaweed red and brown," recalling Gauguin's Breton kelp gatherers.[18] "The only Emperor is the emperor of ice-cream," Wallace Stevens concludes as he describes Cuban and black laborers in Key West whipping "concupiscent curds" for a funeral.[19] However exoticizing or nostalgic their terms, such literary encounters between white bodies and desirable foods evince but also alter a racial imaginary so often preoccupied with keeping bodies apart through mechanisms such as Jim Crow segregation and nativist immigration legislation. For black writers, comestibles also encapsulate sensuous possibility, but they betray structural inequities as well. In Zora Neale Hurston's "Story in Harlem Slang" (1942), the protagonist, a migrant to New York from Alabama who renames himself Jelly, dreams of brown sweetness in the form of a sugar mama: "But baby! . . . Dat shape you got on you! I bet the Coca Cola Company is paying you good money for the patent!"[20] Through Jelly's itineracy and poverty, Hurston exposes the present conditions of black life; he "feel[s] chewed" by the world.[21]

In a prior generation of American literature published during the Progressive era, adulteration anxieties inflected and supported racial hierarchies. Upton Sinclair uses racist characterization to convey the didactic message of *The Jungle* (1906). The reader is meant to suffer along with the virtuous Lithuanian immigrants when only "pale-blue milk" tainted with formaldehyde is available for their children and to recoil when "negroes and the lowest foreigners— Greeks, Roumanians, Sicilians, and Slovaks"—break the strike and work on the killing floor.[22] In this novel, racial others both represent metaphorical contamination and purvey adulterated products: "a negro . . . went out and drew off the old dregs of beer that lay in barrels set outside of the saloons and after he had doctored it with chemicals to make it 'fizz,' he sold it for two cents a can."[23] When the protagonist, Jurgis, drinks this beer, his body is imperiled, but in the process it is also defined as a body that could be imperiled.[24] This scene suggests the dynamism of such definitions; Sinclair constructs the purity of the Lithuanians by framing other groups as dirty and poisonous.[25] It is this aperture—between a unilateral conception of the black body as the conveyor of taint, the embodiment of adulteration, and a relational view of racial formations—that modern literature of the interwar generation widens. Embracing the sensuousness of literary and corporeal form, these writers follow the aesthetic and affective possibilities of the "fizz" that Sinclair scorns.

Artificial Color explores an archive of mostly narrative literature—with a few forays into verse—that views modern food not as a synecdoche for intractable encompassing systems but rather as an imaginative vehicle for racial transformation.[26] For Jean Toomer, artificial color refuses the one-drop rule, while for George Schuyler, the deep freezer resurrects African vigor. F. Scott Fitzgerald fears that tropical infusions like coffee permeate and vitiate white male bodies, while Zelda Fitzgerald imagines syrupy stickiness as the racial adhesive connecting regional and global Souths. Modern food can also remap racial affiliations, as keenly evident in the fiction of Ernest Hemingway, where terroir grants the deracinated white American temporary belonging with the romanticized brown Basque, and in the works of Gertrude Stein, who uses gleaning and mushroom hunting as embodied figures for adopted citizenship. The phrase "Racial Fictions" in my subtitle refers not only to the literature of these and other writers, but also to the cultural field in which the literature emerged, which created equally fictitious if broadly influential and purportedly factual accounts of race. The decades between the two world wars saw the efflorescence of racial pseudo-science and nativist manifestos alongside advertising and consumer culture as well as exercise regimens, vitamania, and diet fads. The visual and textual artifacts of these movements create narratives about the origins, authenticity, hierarchy, and evolution of racial categories, sometimes explicitly (eugenics) and other times implicitly (advertising). The literature in my study speaks back to these other racial fictions, at points echoing their claims and at other points transforming, repurposing, or refuting them. My chapters thus consider literary examples alongside an extraliterary archive that also presumes an intimate relationship between the body, alimentation, and racial categorization.

Some of the book's nonliterary sources are prescriptivist and didactic, foretelling the fall of white masculinity thanks to the incursions of industrial food or urging readers to eat raw foods and regain the strength of primitive man. Others weave desirous fantasies about bodies, foods, and places: coca from South America and kola nuts from Africa, coffee from Brazil, peaches from the US South, bananas from Jamaica. Literature brings together these ideological strains, the disciplining and the idealizing, and places them in tension through narrative and imagery. Faced with such contradictions, the characters in these works aspire to liminal states and bodily transformations, whether by brewing cane syrup, eating raw meat, gathering mushrooms, or drinking coffee. As Anita Mannur argues, "The culinary idiom ... is both strategic and conjectural: the use of food is more than an a priori affirmation of palatable difference; it is also a way to undermine the racialized ideologies that culinary discourse is so often seen to buttress."[27]

The interwar fiction that I address reflects a range of genres and modes, often threaded together within the same text: experimental modernism, expatriate novel, bildungsroman, serial science fiction, and, in my concluding chapter, naturalism. The moments of imagistic suspension within these texts often counterbalance their plot trajectory, which tells a more pessimistic story about the nature of race relations. These decades of literary experimentation that *Artificial Color* charts coincided with the heightened classification and enforcement of racial categories. Anti-miscegenation laws and segregation policies strained to separate black and white; nativist immigration policies defined ethnic quotas; and in Europe, anti-Semitism shaped debates about the status of the foreigner. Though she confines her remarks to the "Africanist presence" in American literature—rather than, for example, the construction of Jewishness—Morrison illuminates the deep structural engagement with racialization in modern literary representation, which "often provides a subtext that either sabotages the surface text's expressed intentions or escapes them through a language that mystifies what it cannot bring itself to articulate but still attempts to register."[28] As the writers in my study consider what they should eat, how they should eat it, and the panoply of technologies changing the material form and geographical range of foods, they also investigate the failures of racial regimes of separation and purity. These modern writers register the profound instability of the category of whiteness, its impossible ephemerality and purity and its fluctuating boundaries.[29] *Artificial Color*, in developing this argument, further investigates a range of ethnicities—Italian, Greek, Irish, Jewish, Breton, and Basque—that vary in their relationship to whiteness and in their designation as legible categories. Sometimes romanticized, sometimes reviled, these classifications on the borders of whiteness highlight the fictitiousness of the category.[30]

Artificial Color focuses on Harlem Renaissance and Lost Generation writers and their relationship to food as consumers rather than producers, though the last chapter, on Zora Neale Hurston and Dorothy West, moves into the representation of agribusiness and the fruit import business. Thus, there is another story to be told about the alimentary histories and rhetorics of Asian America and interwar Orientalism as well as about Latino migrant workers in California and the Southwest who fade away in Steinbeckian narratives of the tragic (white) Okie.[31] In spite of my project's geographical list toward the East Coast and the Atlantic Ocean and toward Europe rather than Asia, fantasies and fears of Asian or Latin American bodies structure the racialization of other groups. While *Tender Is the Night* expresses anxieties about Latin masculinity in a Mediterranean context, Fitzgerald looks to Brazil to demonstrate this infiltrating influence, and West's protagonist, Cleo, defines black respectability against Chinese cannibalism. The construction of race is always relational and global.

In the fiction of this period, this global set of interrelationships is often understood climatologically. From early modern New World encounters to twentieth-century food industries, ideas of both tropicality and southernness threaten to transform white bodies, as medieval humoral theory finds new life in eugenics and related racial pseudo-sciences.[32] "The South" or "the tropics" spans a surprising set of landscapes, from Brazil to Cannes, from Alabama to Naples. Fulsome foods from these regions shape modern commodity culture, as scholars like Catherine Cocks, April Merleaux, Gary Okihiro, and Mimi Sheller persuasively argue, and modern fiction traces their global and digestive circulation.[33] The colonial conceit that the tropics transform the body also makes the transportation revolution of the early twentieth century an occasion for questioning race as a transhistorical, genealogical essence and confronting mutable corporeality. Though the white body infused with tropical goods could be enlisted to bear out a narrative of racial degeneration, *Artificial Color* focuses on moments in interwar fiction when the flow of goods and chemicals disrupts the coherence of the individual body as a metonym for racial category.

Some might charge this exercise with anachronism, particularly given the fabled political conservativism of some of my key players. Indeed, one of the most consistent features of racism is its disregard for apparent contradiction. The historian Helen Veit observes that euthenists of the period—that is, pseudo-scientists who explored the impact of environmental factors on race with a particular focus on hygiene and food—remained immune to the potential epistemological consequences of their beliefs about the changeable body: "Instead of debunking the notion of biological race itself . . . many interpreted diet's supposed physical and mental influences to mean that races could simply change more quickly than previously imagined."[34] Each writer in my study flirts with the fictitiousness or at least the radical mutability of biological race. I use the tools of contemporary theory to unearth the political potential of these imaginings and the stories that they have to tell about mutable forms—aesthetic, racial, social. Following the lead of Mel Y. Chen and Tompkins, who map the racialization of matter as well as bodies, I historicize the racialization of particular foodstuffs.[35] Modernist writers repurpose these resonant materials to reinvent affiliation, as Toomer embraces the mystical cane boil and Stein declares herself a mushroom hunter. They depict what Alexander Weheliye calls "racializing assemblages" as a site of both vulnerability and possibility, delving into food systems, unruly eating, and food's sensuousness to try to represent a self that is beyond individual—edible, eating, and enmeshed in extended ecologies, both social and biological.[36]

It behooves us, however, to recall how easy it is to drift from this posture of affiliation and invention to a dangerous political passivity or even racist retrenchment. F. Scott Fitzgerald, Ernest Hemingway, and Gertrude Stein, in spite of the networks of their expatriate imaginings, ultimately fall back upon characterological accounts of race, mouthing tragic narratives of white degeneration. Even Toomer and Schuyler, who write extensively about the artificiality of racial distinctions, from both a hereditary and a dietary point of view, ultimately depoliticize their interrogation of these categories, Toomer retreating into mysticism and Schuyler embracing the anti-communist Right. It seems perhaps that in the context of a social structure defined by binary racial divides, the construction of the in-between or the in-flux that is possible to imagine in literature becomes challenging if not impossible to sustain in life.

Modernism's aesthetic investments in form, technology, and the sensorium shape its perception of race as a labile form.[37] Colleen Lye proposes that "a focus on form may provide an initial bridge between the notion of race as a representation and the notion of race as constitutive of literary and other social formations."[38] This formal attunement, Lye opines, requires placing fetishistic accounts of the racial other (like primitivism) in conversation with articulations of racial affiliation (like the New Negro movement), as this project attempts to do: "we might describe race as the construction that emerges out of our theorization of the historically shifting relationship between these archives; for this reason, we cannot treat it as an *a priori* determinant of their boundaries."[39] Following Caroline Levine's methodological provocation that the critic consider the "collision" of multiple literary and social forms, I see technological transformation and geographical enmeshment as two forms that modern food systems made tangible, sometimes even tasteable.[40] These forms inspired literary experiment; Toomer plays with the aural texture of words to evoke effervescence, and through her surreal similes, Zelda Fitzgerald casts whiteness as an atomized essence like Chanel No. 5. These experiments in turn revealed alternatives to conceiving of race in terms of binary or hierarchy. Levine observes:

> Literary forms and social formations are equally real in their capacity to organize materials, and equally unreal in being artificial, contingent constraints. Instead of seeking to reveal the reality suppressed by literary forms, we can understand sociopolitical life as itself composed of a plurality of different forms, from narrative to marriage and from bureaucracy to racism.[41]

The connective accounts of matter and maps that dominate these texts unsettle the regnant divisions defined by the one-drop rule (Jim Crow) and country of origin (nativism). Formal heterogeneity categorizes the texts themselves—*Cane*'s combination of verse and prose, the surreal imagery in Zelda Fitzgerald's autobiographically inflected bildungsroman—and their dramatization of race as form.[42] In *Cane* (1923), artificial color as a trope of racial invention collides with segregation's spatial regimes; in *Save Me the Waltz* (1932), the dark stickiness that is whiteness's other provides a philosophical and phenomenological alternative to disembodied individualism. By close-reading these texts alongside contemporaneous racial representations—soda advertisements and Sayre family photographs—I aim both to historicize the racial forms they cite, their circulation beyond the boundaries of these texts, and yet also to underscore the transformation that those forms, and therefore their supposedly physiological or sociological underpinnings, undergo as they are digested by the text.

Several historical factors contribute to the simultaneous sense of confusion and urgency about racial etiology and trajectory in the interwar period. World War I brought new nationalisms to the explosive fore and exposed frictions between purportedly racial, ethnic, regional, and national identities. Along with raising substantial questions about affiliation and the racial component of citizenship, World War I expanded the technology and territory of industrial food, sparking the postwar rise of agribusiness and popularization of canned food.[43] In the early decades of the twentieth century, the United States also pursued a neo-imperialist agenda in Latin America and the Caribbean, so closely tied to the food industry that historians have dubbed this period and its conflicts the "Banana Wars."[44] The Great Migration brought African Americans who had been working in southern monocultures into northern cities, creating new diasporic affiliations and sparking racial tensions. In the 1920s, with European currency depressed, US expatriates went to France, Spain, and Italy, where they encountered regional food traditions and romanticized ethnicities, often at odds with national boundaries. At the same time that these mass migrations facilitated new encounters, a cultural tide of nativism, anti-Semitism, and renewed racism, including the resurgence of the Ku Klux Klan, variously attempted to legislate difference or to rout it out with violence. By the mid-1930s, Fascist leaders in Europe preached national superiority, racial purity, and agricultural territory.

Many defining elements of twentieth-century food culture—the chain store, the soda fountain, artificial flavors and colors, electric refrigeration—were developed at the turn of the century and first became ubiquitous in the 1920s and 1930s. Interwar fiction, then, trains special attention on these emergent phenomena, including US hemispheric imperialism. After World War II, as many historians have documented, the US food industry both expanded and consolidated with the rise of Monsanto and the food processors.[45] Perhaps as a result of this dominance, the textural, gustatory, commercial, and territorial novelties of the interwar period dulled into the backdrop of Cold War plenty.[46] In the interwar years, the close connection between world's fairs and futuristic visions of food remained vivid and exciting. For this reason, only one of the novels considered in *Artificial Color* comes from after World War II—Dorothy West's *The Living Is Easy* (1948)—and that text focuses on the earlier historical moment when all of this food culture was new or, at least, seemed novel, though much of it was continuous with a longer narrative of global imperialism.

The connection between food and racial categorization is easy to explain from the vantage point of historical materialism; global capital relies upon racialized labor to extract and process the raw materials of the food industry.[47] Euthenics and nutrition science lent ideological and purportedly clinical ballast to the hierarchy of the white consumer and the racialized laborer and monitored the boundaries between the two—fretting about undisciplined bourgeois consumption and attributing dietary deficits to racial predispositions. Nonetheless, their conception of the mutable body could be repurposed to alternative political ends, as evidenced by Toomer's investment in physical culture and Schuyler's embrace of raw foods as a medium of black advancement.[48] While white supremacists bemoaned the vitiation of Nordic bodies through the ingestion of industrial food, explaining the advance of the "brunet" races by their easy digestion of inferior products, some dietitians instead embraced primitivism, propounding the superior diets of isolated tribes.[49] The dentist Weston Price, for example, took photographs of tribal peoples from all over the world to show their strong, white teeth and to teach his US readers that they should obey the laws of nature rather than the dictates of the sweet tooth.[50] The Schuylers cited Price's work in their own dietary advice, published in the *Pittsburgh Courier* and *Opportunity* for black readers. While in recent years several exemplary historical studies have traced the intersection of diet and race in modern US culture, *Artificial Color* follows the consequences of these rationalized and racialized dietetics into literature.[51]

Modern writers noted a metaphorical and physical connection between transformed food systems and racial regimes. In *In the American Grain* (1925), William Carlos Williams complains about the energy that the United States expended on mechanical threshers and banana imports. He attributes the attenuated, technologized food chain to white racial panic:

> Do not serve another for you might have to TOUCH him and he might be a JEW or a NIGGER... Machines were not so much to save time as to save dignity that fears the animate touch. It is miraculous the energy that goes into inventions here. Do you know that it now takes just ten minutes to put a bushel of wheat on the market from planting to selling, whereas it took three hours in our colonial days? That's striking. It must have been a tremendous force that would do that. That force is fear that robs the emotions; a mechanism to increase the gap between touch and thing, *not* to have a contact.[52]

Ironically, arguably, the effect of Williams's minimalist poetics is to estrange the contact between objects and the social world, to depopulate the scene in a way that defers the deadly question of whether one "might be a JEW or a NIGGER." One of his most famous poems, "The Red Wheelbarrow," creates a tableau of white chickens and a wheelbarrow "glazed with rain / water" that presents an implicit argument for the philosophical and aesthetic sufficiency of such stark visual imagery. Recently, William Logan has unearthed historical evidence that this red wheelbarrow belonged to "Thaddeus Marshall, an African-American street vendor from Rutherford, N.J."[53] What does it mean to expel the black body, then, from a paradigmatic vision of the humble and, notably, agricultural sources of modern art? In a further twist, in *Yes, Mrs. Williams* (1959), Williams tells the story of his Puerto Rican grandmother, who concocted strawberry syrups for his grandfather to sell as street ices. It is tempting to see this creative feminine figure as a double for the poet, whose most celebrated poem describes the pleasures of a plum right out of the icebox, "so sweet and so cold."[54] Williams's ambivalence—caught between nativism and ethnic fetishism, between agricultural nostalgia and urban identification—infuses much of literary modernism, and to push its alimentary idiom beyond the immediate sense impression and into the larger context of racial imaginaries reveals more than minimalism cares to share but no less than it contains.

On the other end of the aesthetic spectrum from the minimalist impulse to clarify, distill, and decontextualize is the equally prominent pull of the grotesque, which muddies, mixes, and entangles. In Jim Crow America, the spatial logics of segregation belied the visceral intimacies of culinary labor; carnivalesque reversals could expose these flimsy fictions. In Claude McKay's *Home to Harlem* (1928), a black chef tries to fend off stereotype through self-denial: "The chef had a violent distaste for all the stock things that 'coons' are supposed to like to the point of stealing them. He would not eat watermelon, because white people called it 'the niggers' ice-cream.' Pork chops he fancied not. Nor corn pone. And the idea of eating chicken gave him a spasm."[55] He scorns his coworkers: "Cause you manicuring you' finger nails and rubbing up you' stinking black hide against white folks in that theah diner, you all think youse something" (167–68), and he threatens to spit in their food (172). The dark-skinned chef insults the light-skinned pantryman—"I'll throw this heah garbage in you' crap-yaller face" (168)—associating racial intermixture with excremental abjection. The pantryman takes his revenge, spiriting the fresh eggs away from the storeroom while the chef flirts with a "sweet yaller piece" on the platform (186). Unable to prepare the breakfast dishes requested by his white patrons, the chef is humiliated in front of the Irish steward who demotes him and has him moved to another train car. The vestibular space between whiteness and blackness demarcated by the dining car serves as a stage for both disgust and desire. The color yellow traverses tantalizing tastes (scrambled eggs) and revolting wastes (yolks sucked by rats) in a culture that both idealizes and abhors intermixture.

Social forms of disgust are often registered in a visceral idiom. Sharing food may consolidate social belonging, but eating also threatens to introduce what Mary Douglas calls "matter out of place" into the body.[56] When the chef spits in his coworkers' food, he symbolically equates them with effluvium and attempts to elevate himself above their abject blackness. He is the spitter, not the spit upon. As Douglas argues, the individual body, through dietary and hygienic regimens, performs a relationship to the social whole, the body politic "through the symbolic medium of the physical body."[57] Even when authors adopt an ethics of consumption to defend the wholeness of that body—Hemingway's aficion or Schuyler's raw foods regimen—the mechanism of disgust in these texts betrays the bodily intimacies it attempts to disavow. As Sara Ahmed points out, disgust requires having taken someone or something in before spitting the other out.[58] Thus, even when tracing a negative affect like anxiety, disgust, or even panic, *Artificial Color* pursues a productive politics of impurity.[59] As Alexis Shotwell observes, "Racialization . . . [is] centrally a project of purity" and "to be against purity is . . . not to be for pollution, harm, sickness, or premature death. It is to be against the rhetorical or conceptual attempt to delineate and delimit the world into something separable, disentangled, and homogenous."[60] The modern food system—especially as refracted in the literary imagination—makes manifest the impossibility of such disentanglement, necessarily multiplying imagined sources of impurity—artificiality, adulteration, intermixture, liminality, tropicality, and so on.

Abjection connects these ingestive imaginaries with racial ones. This point of intersection between psychoanalysis and postcolonial theory has been richly theorized by Frantz Fanon, Saidiya Hartman, Eric Lott, Hortense Spillers, and others.[61] Kristeva's category continues to animate feminist theory, queer of color critique, and critical race studies, all of which inform my approach here, as the fluidity and embodiment of abjection provide an alternative to homogeneity and alienation.[62] This modern fiction explores both the pain of identifying with the abject and the possibilities afforded by doing so. Weheliye observes that "partaking of the flesh . . . tenders flavors and textures found in lives of imprisoned freedom, desires for survival, and viscous dreams of life that awaken future anterior humanities, which exceed Man's inesculent culinary laws."[63] These flavors and textures can be nauseating and revelatory at the same time. In *Save Me the Waltz*, Alabama Beggs contracts blood poisoning and smells like "a soda fountain, thrown-up."[64] In *The Living Is Easy*, Cleo Judson calls her dark-skinned husband, Bart, "Mr. Nigger" and complains of the smell of rotting bananas that accompanies him wherever he goes.[65] The abject body throws into sharp relief the relation between white supremacy, segregation and colonialism, and the abstract, disembodied subject. Alabama's father is a southern judge, loosely based on Zelda Fitzgerald's father, Anthony Dickinson Sayre, author of the 1892 "Sayre Law," which, in his own words, "eliminate[d] the Negro from politics and in a perfectly legal way."[66] As Alabama's body breaks down, so too does her belief in his authority. And while Cleo's cruelty to Bart reflects her own indoctrination into a colorist system, she also recognizes—as he fails to—that his aspiration to the status of Man will always be saddled by the black body he hopes to transcend. In the conclusion of the novel, when she witnesses and shares in her husband's suffering, the possibility of empathy and resistance flickers into existence.

In spite of their unflinching depiction of entrenched power systems organized by race and their often tragic denouements, these narratives contain a kernel of potential. Even a paranoid text like *Tender Is the Night* harbors the fugitive dream that the disciplinary regimes of racialization, predicated on purification and heterosexuality, fail to define the horizon of embodiment and relationality. This potential is sometimes expressed through queer sexualities, explored by Stein and West, or utopian homosociality, championed by Hemingway. In these contexts, dining together, savoring the meal and the mouth, opens up the possibility of new intimacies, what Tompkins might call "queer alimentarity."[67]

The book has two parts, each with two chapters, and a final chapter that serves as a coda. The first part focuses on food technologies and mixed-race bodies as sites of racial ambiguity and cultural transformation in African American fiction. Chapter 1 addresses the experimental modernism of Jean Toomer and his use of cane syrup and soda pop as tropes for racial reinvention. Chapter 2 looks at George Schuyler's serialized science fiction, *Black Empire* and *The Black Internationale,* and its view of the light-skinned New Negro woman as an avatar of hybridity, connected to the hydroponic farms and deep freezers featured in these fictions. This science fiction advocates a raw foods diet as a way for black people to regain their primitive racial vigor. Schuyler and his white wife, Josephine Cogdell Schuyler, subscribed to this line of thinking and raised their mixed-race daughter, Philippa Schuyler, on this diet. This chapter considers Philippa's celebrity alongside Schuyler's fiction to point out the problems of purity in the construction of a utopian mixed-race ideal.

The second part of the book moves into the geographies of global food distribution in expatriate fiction by white writers of the Lost Generation. Chapter 3 follows the concept of terroir, or the taste of place, in expatriate fiction by Ernest Hemingway and Gertrude Stein, who were both drawn to the idea of romanticized localism, understood as ethnic particularity and belonging, but who also longed for cosmopolitan, transnational belonging through ingestion and connoisseurship. Hemingway's tragic fictions take up the figure of the American who might return to a premodern, European way of life and dining, and his inevitable failure to do so. Stein both dramatizes her Jewishness and explores the idea of transnational identity through the nomadic figures of the gleaner and the mushroom hunter. Chapter 4 considers the Mediterranean as simultaneously a setting for and fluid figure of southern circulation in novels by F. Scott and Zelda Fitzgerald. In *Tender Is the Night*, white women are all too comfortable ingesting the dark philters of the tropical South, while white men become addicted and degenerate from imbibing these infusions. *Save Me the Waltz*, by contrast, intimates that syrupy southernness might offer richer, sweeter possibilities for embodiment and affiliation than the fantasy of whiteness.

The final chapter moves into a later period, as Zora Neale Hurston and Dorothy West address the modern food supply chain more directly, Hurston through Florida agribusiness and West through Boston fruit importers. Hurston and West offer a corrective to earlier writers who thought modern food could be a sensuous medium for racial reinvention; in their naturalist fiction, they dramatize the implacability of systemic racism and the vulnerability of black bodies. At the same time, however, both writers explore the animacy that underwrites industry, the power of nonhuman bodies conflated with racialized bodies, and they use imaginative form to bring forth the political power of these associations between animals and people in *Their Eyes Were Watching God* and between fruit and women in *The Living Is Easy*. Thus, in an important way, Hurston and West continue the imaginative project of the other writers in my study who use food to recast received genres of racialization.

In their dramatization of catastrophe and their insistence on the precarity of black lives, Hurston and West bring out the nascent epistemological and physical violence in the earlier chapters: lynching as the outcome of miscegenation in Toomer; global attacks as the solution to white supremacy in Schuyler; masochism as the antidote to racialized abjection in Zelda Fitzgerald; Fascism as the preservation of regional ethnic purity in Stein. The stakes of racialization are life and death, and ingestive imaginaries dramatize the problem of the color line and indeed relocate it inside the body, in the mouth, throat, gut, and anus. While the tropological tools that these writers use to complicate and even flout racial epidermalism and the one-drop rule—soda bubbles, raw foods, wild mushrooms, leather wineskins, black caffeine, colorless Crisco, brown syrup—may seem whimsical, the modern body in flux faced a crisis of legibility that was also an opportunity. Into this fray stepped fiction, which could balance the microcosm and the macrocosm, the embodied self and the interconnected world. This literature unsettles the received notion of racial difference as raw material, a premise that supports white supremacy.[68] In its treatment of race as an artificial color or a culinary concoction, this fiction restores the role of imagination in social formations and advances the politics of the senses as a medium of resistance.[69]

1

"A Purple Fluid, Carbon-Charged"

Jean Toomer's Mutable Materials

While he was finishing his masterwork, *Cane* (1923), Jean Toomer wrote to Waldo Frank: "There is one thing about the Negro in America which most thoughtful persons seem to ignore: the Negro is in solution, in the process of solution. As an entity, the race is loosing [*sic*] its body."[1] In this letter propounding the inevitability of intermixture, Toomer employs multiple fluid figures: the "solution" that will dissolve blackness, simultaneously "losing" and "loosening" the body in Toomer's likely unconscious neologism; the "spirit saturate with folksong" that Toomer attributes to the "old Negro"; and the "buoyant" quality that he ascribes to "a new race."[2] Two states, one drenched with history and the other ascendant with expectation, provide potential fates for the body of "the Negro." This combination of liquid and gas, saturation and buoyance recalls carbonation, a process that the Enlightenment scientist Benjamin Priestly described as "Impregnating Water with Fixed Air," a suggestively reproductive locution.[3] Priestly believed that this elemental combination was salubrious, a concept that inspired the turn-of-the-century soda industry and its patent medicines. Toomer also assumes that the process of "solution" is healthful to the body politic, as "America needs these elements."[4] Carbonation provides an unexpected trope for miscegenation; it resists the visual and the epidermal logics of American racial categorization, retaining the scientific aura of racial biologism but imbuing it with the technological malleability of organic chemistry.

Carbonation is a "process of solution," whereby carbon dioxide is dissolved in water. However, rather than "loos[en]ing" as Toomer envisions, commercial carbonation uses pressure to maintain the rate of gas absorption.[5] If the pressure builds too high, the bottle could explode; if it is released, the beverage will go flat. Toomer's fiction pursues this volatile trope through characters who stray between categories, like Becky, the white mother who gives birth to black sons in *Cane*. She is impregnated by another element, but that act is suspect, the target of verbal and physical violence rather than a utopian intermediary state. Both black and white neighbors destroy her with their cruelty: "Taking their words, they filled her, like a bubble rising—then she broke."[6] The aspirations for chemical recombination that Toomer articulates in his private letter are deflated in his fictionalization of lives lived across the color line. As is so often the case, the fiction may have been wiser than the man.[7]

As this chapter will elaborate, Toomer found the soda fountain an inspiring vision of modernist recombination, one that could also be applied to racial forms. In his unpublished essay "On Being an American," Toomer insists that "in point of fact all of the main races are mixed races—and so mixed that no one can unravel them in all of their blended complexity."[8] This version of race as a "blended" solution that cannot be unmixed, and is in fact misrecognized thanks to obscuring and simplifying color labels, takes its cue from modern food technology. Toomer pursued an interest in dietetics and agricultural science throughout his life. In high school, he ate macerated wheat and followed the exercise and diet regimens prescribed by Bernarr Macfadden in *Physical Culture* magazine.[9] As a young man, he enrolled in the agricultural science program at the University of Wisconsin, hoping to experience "something new, even raw; with the tang of a sea-wind in it, with a touch of the earth."[10] Toomer recalled, "I wanted to be at the source of things, plowing, and planting and growing . . . I had an urge to use my mind body, close to the source of things, in direct contact with tangible necessities and their production. I hit upon farming."[11] After moving to Wisconsin and joining his class, Toomer admitted, "already there were grave doubts in me as to whether I really wanted an actual farm or if 'farm' were not a symbol."[12] He devised *Cane* during a stint as substitute principal at the Sparta Agricultural and Industrial School in Georgia. In 1923, the same year that he published *Cane*, Toomer became a follower of the Armenian philosopher and spiritualist Georges Gurdjieff, who viewed eating, sex, and intellectual impressions as three types of food, each requiring digestion and elimination for modern man to function properly.[13]

Toomer's ingestive imaginary probes the connection between the individual body and the outside world, between alimentation and racial categorization, between races and nation. Indeed, in an undated essay entitled "The Americans," Toomer casts America as a digesting stomach:

> The strength of a country can be measured by its ability to digest, assimilate, and transform all the diverse materials present in it. The health of a country is dependent upon the right flowing of its digestive processes . . . A country is like a huge stomach into which enters all kinds of materials, some unusable, some usable, and its existence is maintained, it is nourished, it grows and develops by subjecting these materials to the processes of digestion and assimilation, rejecting

unusable matters, incorporating usable materials into its structures and function.[14]

To a contemporary reader, this fantasy of assimilation into a nation-state, particularly with its stark utilitarian "reject[ion] of unusable matters," is troubling. As Kyla Wazana Tompkins has argued, narratives of nation-building in the nineteenth century constructed America as a white body that needed to expel and excrete racial others.[15] For Toomer, however, this symbolic cannibalism breaks down racial forms as a governing concept of social life within the nation, rebuilding the body politic through new assemblages:

> In America, the white race, the black race, the red race, the brown race must die before there can be a new race. They are dying. America is eating them. They are dead. America has eaten them. This is the tendency. The tending here is to break up all the old racial forms and incorporate their materials for the forming of a new racial form with new life. It has been said that America is a melting-pot. Rather I would view it as a stomach. Rather I would view it as the place where mankind, long dismembered into separate usually repellant groupings, long scattered over the face of the earth, is being re-assembled into one whole and undivided human race.[16]

This fantasy of eating and being eaten is simultaneously erotic and predatory, carnal and political. And while it may seem naive or even sinister for Toomer to believe in "one whole and undivided human race" predicated on the nation digesting difference, this metaphor reflects not a synecdochic understanding of the body politic, where a representative white citizen seamlessly mirrors the constitution of the whole, but rather a Frankensteinian conceit, where unlike forms "long dismembered" must find a way to achieve "new life" together.

Effervescence and Intermixture: The Soda Fountain

In an unpublished 1935 memoir, Jean Toomer reminisces about his job as a soda jerk in high school and exults in his hard-won expertise:

> I got my white coat. Under my friends [sic] guidance I learned to work the fountain, draw sodas, pile sundaes, brew special concoctions. Of course, I had imprinted upon me indelibly what my fellow-men consider tasty thirst-quenching drinks ... I was a serious youth at first, in every way an eager, earnest student of the job ... I soon became familiar

with the store's stock, the patent medicines, the chemicals in jars. Sime [*sic*] times I watched the doctor compound prescriptions and I had a feeling of fascination and mystery as if there were some magic about this and I were in—not the prosaic back of a modern drug store but in the work shop of an alchemist.[17]

Toomer's verbs animate the process of intermixture and especially his active role in that process: "work," "draw," "pile," "brew." While popular taste renders the soda jerk passive, even textual ("I had imprinted upon me indelibly"), the model of the doctor compounding prescriptions promises active and expert authorship. In this combination, we can see an alter ego for the literary modernist, reformulating the materials of popular culture with expertise. The audience for the work is meant to imbibe its results, to incorporate the concoction in the body and to experience the senses anew. The pharmacist thus models not only form as formula and bricolage as compounds but also the radical transformation of the consumer of this "magic." This alchemical metaphor for modernist practice suits Toomer's approach to race as well as his approach to art. Whalan observes that Toomer uses technological metaphors in *Cane* to represent a "dynamic process" of racial transformation: "At the centre of this exists the figure of the artist, transforming through a process of mechanical efficiency material forms which degrade or oppress into forms which offer liberation and agency."[18] When Toomer celebrates concoction and compounds at the soda fountain counter, he espouses the intermixture that he elsewhere champions in racial thought.

The outside world encroaches on this idyllic magician's workshop. Toomer's longed-for transformation of racial categorization was not so easily performed in the segregated spaces of the Jim Crow era, and the anecdote in his memoir bears this out. His grandmother disapproves of his ambition to work at a soda fountain: "I could not bring myself to ask my grandmother. I could hear her exclaim, 'My grandson a soda boy!'"[19] Her hesitation (and his) is telling. Washington, DC, a notoriously segregated city, had an anti-discrimination law on the books from 1872 stating that "keepers of ice-cream saloons or places where soda-water is kept for sale" would be fined for "refusing to sell or wait upon any respectable, well-behaved person, without regard to race, color, or previous condition of servitude," but in practice, this statute was ignored.[20] Toomer never specifies in his anecdote whether the soda fountain serves white patrons or black ones. It is unclear whether young Toomer could work behind the counter but not sit in front of it or if—perhaps equally distressing to his grandmother—it was a working-class establishment for black customers only. It is not a surprise that Toomer, frustrated at what he elsewhere calls "color labels," fails to mention the race of his friends, colleagues, or patrons at the soda fountain, but the fact that he does not do so draws attention to the racial politics that he tries to overlook.[21]

For many Harlem Renaissance writers, the segregated soda fountain represented social barriers rather than chemical recombinations.[22] In 1918, James Weldon Johnson wrote that "the denial of the privilege of drinking ice cream soda in certain places on account of race or color is a phase of the denial of full citizenship and common democracy."[23] In George Schuyler's *Black No More* (1931), his newly white protagonist learns about a local Klan rally at a soda fountain.[24] In *The Big Sea* (1940), Langston Hughes recalls stopping in St. Louis during a train trip in 1918 and being turned away from "the soda fountain where cool drinks were being served" because he was "colored." Hughes sardonically concludes, "I knew I was home in the U.S.A."[25]

Nonetheless, Toomer was not the only African American artist to find aesthetic inspiration in the intermixtures and effervescence of soda. A mere five years younger than Toomer, another teenage denizen of Washington, DC, Duke Ellington, named his first piece "The Soda Fountain Rag." "I was soda-jerking at the time," he later told an interviewer, "so that must have been the basis of inspiration."[26] When asked about the source of his songwriting, Ellington claimed, "It just bubbles out of me."[27] Later in the interview, he expanded upon this figure of effervescence: "If the guy, or the gal—if the person is a song writer—there are songs bubbling in him all the time; there are hundreds and hundreds of songs that want to get themselves written."[28] For Ellington, bubbles embody generative creativity.

For Toomer too, effervescence evinces an affect that both animates and exceeds the body. In "Bona and Paul," a crucial interracial encounter in the urban section of *Cane*, Toomer describes a white man going out to a jazz club at night as "a purple fluid, carbon-charged, that effervesces" (75). While I will return to "Bona and Paul" later in this chapter, it bears brief mention here that the body itself is "charged" and infused like the sodas that Toomer delighted in drawing and brewing in his soda fountain youth. Imaginative color ("purple fluid") and chemical kineticism provide a utopian alternative to the epidermal regimes of Jim Crow.

The hallucinatory nature of this imagery—purple bubbles appearing in front of a friend's face—also reflects sodas' pharmacological origins as patent medicines in drugstores.[29] Many of the ingredients in early sodas—whether coca or kola—were associated with colonial territories, racialized bodies, and communicable affects. White consumers both hoped they could imbibe primitive vigor and feared coca-crazed black bodies.[30] For Toomer, effervescence and intoxication, frequently associated with one another, offer an opportunity to burst the bubble of enlightenment autonomy in favor of modernist immersion. His characters long to imbibe the racialized affect of the other—the intellectual modernist drawn to the tragic mulatta, the white students fascinated by their "moony" friend Paul—but in spite of the limits of their consumer view of the other, they find that they are changed by the encounter.

With their provocative work, the cultural critics Sianne Ngai and Anne Anlin Cheng establish the importance of tracing the representation of race through modern technologies. As Cheng writes, "Not only do new visual technologies affect how we see racial difference, but, as I will suggest, racial difference itself influences how these technologies are conceived, practiced, and perceived."[31] The technologies of carbonation, bottling, and artificial coloration play a similarly shaping role in my account of Toomer's effervescent intermixtures, and these tropes shed light on Toomer's liminal aesthetic, the racialized discourses infusing soft drink production and marketing in the modern period, and the aspirant artificiality of experimental modernism. Toomer, unlike his peers in the Harlem Renaissance or in the white avant-garde, associated this last possibility with an overhaul of racial categorization and bodily experience.

While there has been a rich vein of criticism about modernist poetics, new technologies, and the mediated sensorium, as well as important work on race science, eugenics, and racial intermixture in modern American literature, Toomer's work demonstrates that these strands are interrelated rather than independent, that experimental modernists fascinated by new technologies and their sensory opportunities were also invested, however subtly, in racialization.[32] Like Toomer, prominent white modernists associate soda fountain intermixtures with the mixtures of blood imagined by contemporaneous race science. Unlike Toomer, however, these avant-garde writers are reluctant to move beyond received racial categories: decrying mass cultural and racial intermixtures (Ezra Pound), acknowledging colonial structures and fantasies without abandoning their indebtedness to them (John Dos Passos), stopping their critique at the point of parody (Hart Crane), or implying that the only possible cultural intermixture for a racialized subject is assimilation (Waldo Frank). A brief overview of these allusions to the modernist soda fountain—the transport through effervescence and artificial flavor to which they aspire and the recurring association between soda fountain syrups and racialized blood that they pursue—demonstrates the centrality of this fluid trope to representing the transformational relationship between modernist experiment and consuming body. Furthermore, each of the examples raises the possibility that race is an artificial structure or an intoxicating affect, but ultimately recapitulates the idea of race as a raw material, which Toomer would resist so memorably in his figuration of race as a solution in flux.

For Ezra Pound, soda seemed the perfect symbol for the insipidness, sweetness, and bubbly babble of American popular culture. In a 1917 letter to William Carlos Williams, Pound decried the "fizz, swish, and gabble of verbiage" as "echt Amerikanisch"; by contrast, he prized the "opacity" of Williams's work, a quality Pound attributed to his "Spanish blood," which refused to filter through the "blighted colander" of "current American ideation."[33] As he privileges sight over sound, Pound conflates experimental form (opacity) and heredity (Spanish blood). Both stand against the deceptive allures of immediate pleasure and promiscuous intermixture and confirm a hierarchical view of culture and race. In 1919, Pound wrote in the *New Age*, "The American people have sold [their liberties] for a mess of soda-water and walnut sundaes; each race as it likes, and always in the name of salvation."[34] Pound associates the seductions of mass culture with the collapse of racial hierarchies and the aesthetic categories that supported them.

By contrast, John Dos Passos, who like Toomer participated in Lola Ridge's literary salon, associated the technicolored qualities of modernist experiment with soda fountain bubbles. In *Manhattan Transfer* (1925), for example, Dos Passos uses effervescence as an objective correlative for the sensuous and even hallucinatory effects of modernist prose, as he describes Central Park at dusk: "great rosy and purple and pistachiogreen bubbles of twilight that swell . . . [and] bulge against the tall houses sharp gray as dead teeth."[35] The synesthetic moniker "pistachiogreen" recalls ice cream and soda syrup flavors, linking the modernist to the flavorist and opposing his work to the "sharp gray . . . dead teeth" of conventional realist literature, preoccupied with domesticity ("tall houses"). This revivifying capacity of form is in turn linked to the sensory immersion in the tropical and the primitive; earlier in the novel, before having this bubbly vision in the park, Ellen declared that she "love[s] to see people drink gin fizzes. It makes me feel like I'm in the tropics sitting in a jujube grove waiting for the riverboat to take us up some ridiculous melodramatic river all set about with fevertrees" (151). White urbanites long for the fizz and fever of the tropics, the fruit flavor of the jujubes. Indeed, the jujube signals the loss of the exotic and its replacement with the artificial, as two chemists lamented in their 1922 study *Food Products from Afar*: "But, alas! the jujube confection which is now on the market, especially in England, is made from gum-arabic, gelatin, sugar, and some artificial flavor, and is said to contain none of the real jujube pulp."[36] The artifice of experimental modernism tries to re-create the intensity of this tropical flavor.

Toomer's friend Hart Crane, the son of the inventor of Life Savers and a former soda jerk, associated artificial color and flavor with modernist form in a parody of e. e. cummings, an ode to laxatives entitled "America's Plutonic Ecstasies" (1923). With effulgent punctuation and choppy syntax, Hart extols the virtues of drugstore concoctions:

> unbelievably—Oh!
> HEADY!—those aromatic LEMONS!
> that make your colored syrup fairly
> PULSE! yes, PULSE!
> the nation's lips are thin and fast
> with righteousness . . .[37]

If the pulsing "colored syrup" were not enough to convey a conflation of race and sweet chemical transport, in the conclusion of the poem, Crane celebrates the "FREE-ER PASSAGE" facilitated by these lemon laxatives, associating, however playfully, the darkness of fantasized colonial subjects with the waste products of American consumerism.[38] The "thin"-lipped (presumably white) consumer wants both to imbibe and to jettison this "colored syrup."

From the perspective of the ethnic modernist, effervescence could seem equally alluring yet less promising as a vehicle for transcending the marked and othered body. Waldo Frank, who wrote the introduction to Toomer's *Cane*, published "Candy Cigar and Stationary" in *Broom* in January 1922. Several stories from *Cane*, including "Kabnis," "Karintha," and "Seventh Street," were published in *Broom*, and Toomer's letters suggest that he was a regular reader.[39] In Frank's story, a Jewish couple own a soda fountain, and they dream of their son achieving assimilation and success. For Lotte, his mother, the ethnically unmarked American children who enter their store represent glorious effervescence: "Children pouring from school, bubble and pelt and foam of children within the Block. They sparkled, they leaped, they clustered."[40] While Lotte is trapped in gray, black, and white ("Beneath my black dress, mark-meshed skin: beneath my gray skin is my body of white" [255]), she hopes that her son Herbert will escape this monochromatic otherness: "my hope runs red in his veins" (253). Unlike his "golden" classmates, however, Herbert "black[s]" his "whole face" with his favorite licorice candy (253–54). This language, which recalls minstrel makeup, associates Herbert's unrestrained appetites ("Give me another licorish stick," he demands [254]) with racial abjection.

The plot follows this implication. The golden-haired Miss Klaar, Herbert's teacher, comes to the soda fountain, feeling like a "heathen" in the Jewish family's home (256). Miss Klaar reports that she has been disturbed by Herbert's "dirty" behavior in school (257). She sends him for a medical examination, and the doctor informs the Rabinowiches that Herbert is "very backward, and will never be anything else" (259). The doctor explicitly associates Herbert's inferiority with racial difference, alluding to the biblical passage that consigns the descendants of Ham to being "drawers of water, hewers of wood" (259). Frank hints that the son's kineticism and spirit may outpace the school's eugenicist naysaying: "Herbert leaped ahead, lounged behind their black bent calm, glad of this adventure of moving through the city, far from home, with mother and father. Both!" (260). This ambiguous ending might be read as grim irony—Herbert blissfully ignorant of his own backwardness—or as affective rebellion.

Carbonation in ethnic modernism betrays the fragility of the bubbly spirit. In Toomer's "Carma," for example, a husband's harsh judgments deflate the spirit of an independent black woman: "Words like corkscrews, wormed to her strength. It fizzled out" (*Cane*, 13). For Frank and Toomer, the exterior threatens to prove implacable; perhaps the bubbles will not leap beyond the contours of the bottle (or body) in which they are housed, perhaps categorizations will overtake potential. However, while Frank associates the freedom of flow with the "sparkle" of whiteness, Toomer instead insists on the fluidity of racialized identities, questioning the conflation of embodiment and race in the first place. His work thus anticipates the recent critical-theoretical turn to "move beyond the concern with skin and boundary," as Tompkins enjoins, and "away from an investment in surfaces" that reproduces "the epidermal ontology of race."[41] Though Toomer's fellow modernists across the color line long for the affective transport extended by what Roy calls "the psychopharmacopoeia of empire—spices, opium, sugar, and tea"—and in this case, soda pop—they do not follow this dissolving and effervescing model of identity to its most radical conclusions, as Toomer does.[42] In *Cane*, I argue, we can find an author's nascent attempts to refuse confining skin by figuring identity as a bubbling fluid. This investment in effervescence is "neither purely metaphor nor purely luxury," as Omise'eke Natasha Tinsley puts it in her work on fluidity and the Middle Passage in black Caribbean literature.[43] As he tropes on the gaseous ascent from liquid states, Toomer also insistently registers the complex racial histories of the materials, not to mention the bodies, that are in flux in his figurations.

Southern Syrup and Modernist Immersion

The soda industry emerged in the post-Reconstruction South and belied the timeless pastoralism of this region that even Toomer sometimes mythologized. In 1958, a historian of the soft drink industry marveled at "the rapid progress the Southern States were to make, and the dominant position they were to take in the bottled refreshment field in the twentieth century."[44] Coca-Cola was developed by a pharmacist in Atlanta in 1886. By the turn of the century, Coca-Cola was sold at the (presumably segregated) soda fountain in Sparta, the Georgia town where Toomer lived for three months in 1921 while serving as substitute principal at the Sparta Agricultural and Industrial Institute.[45] Chero-Cola was founded in Columbus, Georgia (it would later become Royal Crown Cola), and had a bottling works in Sparta by 1918.[46] In *Cane*, "cardboard advertisements" for "Chero-Cola" are stacked in a store window in Sempter, the fictionalized version of Sparta (105).

Unlike the messy, creative soda fountain, soda bottles encapsulated mass production, uniform ingredients, and the careful containment of carbonation. In an August 1921 article, the *American Bottler* praised Chero-Cola for "unfailing uniformity, accuracy, and purity," the "mechanical perfection" of its bottling works, and the "highest possible degree of effervescence" found in its soda.[47] Advertising

Figure 1.1 In a postcard publicizing the Chero-Cola bottling works in Columbus, Georgia, the dark bodies of the workers stand out against their scrubs and the gleaming machines.
Source: C. T. American Art, author's collection.

postcards invited tourists to experience this modern marvel for themselves. For example, Figure 1.1 reproduces a 1920 postcard showing the "Interior" of the Chero-Cola Bottling Plant in Columbus. The factory floor, walls, and ceiling are all white; the workers wear white uniforms; and white lights gleam overhead. A white railing stands between the factory equipment and the viewer, as though even the photographer might contaminate the works. The bottles shuttle across a metal track in the center of the image, and on either side stands a dauntingly large bottling machine. Above each machine, a sign boasts of its astonishing productivity rate, calculated in "bottles per minute." The assembled scene is an ode to factory hygiene, mass production, and mechanical efficiency.

Against this backdrop of white, the black face of one of the plant workers stands out starkly. The composition of the image deemphasizes him. He is standing in the back and to the side, quite nearly obscured by metal track and white pillar. The other worker, whose race is indeterminate, has his back to the viewer and almost seems like a part of the machine he is operating. But the silhouetted black face in the backdrop of the image recalls both the African American labor that southern factories depended upon—and were increasingly losing to northern industry—and the implicit racial politics of the white-washing of industrial modernity. If progress is gleaming white, this image implies, then black bodies must be relegated to manual assistance or eventual obsolescence.

Toomer himself speculated that black culture would be subsumed into the impersonality of "mechanical civilization." He wrote about "Negroes" as though they were to be processed and packaged on the assembly line: "industrialism ... readily transforms them. A few generations from now, the Negro ... will be a conformist to the general outlines of American civilization."[48] In other polemical writings, Toomer used mass production as a metaphor for racial categorization: "we have labeled the bottle and forgotten its contents."[49] In either case, assimilation or stereotype, uniformity reigns and restricts. In *The Sacred Factory* (1927), Toomer mocks the modern spectacle of sameness: "Glory to the Drug Stores. See each bottle on the shelf. See the shelves row on row. Remember all you are familiar with."[50] As an antidote, Toomer recommends "great joys" that "burst" and "stream" (377), "a pleasure very subtly distilled in perfect Egoism" (399). Though this drama, written in his Gurdjieffian period, makes no mention of race, the conflict that he poses between the brittleness of the commercial container and the transport of fluid feeling recalls his earlier metaphors that describe the restriction of racial category.[51] Exuberant affects shatter "the perfection of cleanliness, purity, and sanitation" that supports racialization (368).

By connecting mass production and racialization in this way, Toomer recalls the genealogical relationship between industrial capitalism and slavery. In *Sweetness and Power*, Sidney Mintz argues that the cane plantation synthesized "field and factory" in an early example of "industrial enterprise."[52] The sugar mill developed two major features of industrialization, "scheduling and discipline," and slave bodies were treated as "interchangeable units."[53] Toomer addresses this history through lyrical redress rather than direct recollection. In *Cane*, a book that dramatizes black labor in the cotton fields and sawmills, sugar stands out for its association with pleasure rather than pain.[54] In their leisure hours, black laborers stay up all night brewing sugar syrup, "telling tales about the white folks ... and sweet nigger gals" (31). Toomer treats the cane boil not as a vestige of enslavement but as a form of resistance to it. While cane plantations and their sugar mills made racial violence constitutive of industrial modernity, the ritual of boiling the cane, along with the local economies it sustains, bespeaks autonomy, community, and pleasure.[55]

Toomer experimented with his mystical and exultant account of the cane boil in a short story, "Withered Skin of Berries," which he was working on as he composed *Cane*. This story is set in Washington, DC, and follows the romantic adventures of a light-skinned woman named Vera, who has been drained, like the berries of the title, in the process of conforming to modern life. Her desiccation seems to arise from three interrelated sources: office work, white culture, and sexual repression. Vera has been reduced to colorlessness because modernity has digested her: "Departmental buildings are grey gastronomic structures, innocuously coated with bile."[56] One potential suitor is a black man from the

South, suggestively named Art. He woos her with tales of the "syrup-man" and his art: "The syrup, toted in a barrel, is poured on the copper boiling stove. Then you begin to smell the cane. It goes to your head like wine" (151). The present tense and second person invite Vera's—and by extension, the reader's—participation. Though Vera does not end up choosing Art for a mate, she craves such intoxication and immersion to remedy her repressive relationship to her body and her race.

The cane boil counters each anhedonic element of Vera's draining life. A premodern and communal form of production, the cane boil affirms black culture through its amorphous eroticism. Solid individualism gives way to fluid community, as the human bodies around the boiling pot take on the liquid qualities of the cane syrup and steam:

> I saw my body there, seated with the other men. As I looked, it seemed to dissolve, and melt with the others that were dissolving too. They were a stream. They flowed up-stream from Africa and way up to a height where the light was so bright I could hardly see, burst into a multi-colored spraying fountain. (151)

This out-of-body experience inspires an ejaculatory vision of the "multi-colored" African diaspora. This ecstatic dissolution of self turns color into a "stream" and a "fountain" rather than a regulatory boundary. Here, racial identity is fluid, evolving, intoxicating—not a one-drop rule but a flood of possibility.

In *Cane*, Toomer revisits the trope of the cane boil in "Blood-Burning Moon." This ritual takes place in "a cleared spot on the edge of the forest," a wild space reclaimed from the incursions of industry (31). In the form of "steam," the "scent of cane" travels as far as "factory town" (31). Against the impoverished spectacle of "Negro shanties aligned along the single street of factory town" (30), smell and taste restore the sensuousness of the black experience:

> It drenched the men in circle seated around the stove. Some of them chewed at the white pulp of stalks, but there was no need for them to, if all they wanted was to taste the cane. One tasted it in factory town. And from factory town one could see the soft haze thrown by the glowing stove upon the low-hanging heavens. (31)

This circle of men is immersed in haze, engulfed by sweetness, "drenched" in a metaphorical baptism. Their sacred ritual in turn refigures the factory town. The workers who dwell there can taste this communion without participating in it directly and, like the magi in the nativity story, read the "low-hanging heavens" for this telltale "glow." The senses, stimulated by syrup and steam, supply a medium of escape from the relentlessness of cotton production, "working in the fields all day" (30).

Toomer shatters this intraracial unity and mystical transcendence with talk of miscegenation. Tom Burwell, who "chewed cane-stalk and laughed with the others," is brought up short by the rumors that his fiancée, Louisa, has been dallying with a white man, Bob Stone (31). Rage obliterates the softer affects of haze and glow upon which the ephemeral unity of the cane boil depends: "Blood ran up Tom's neck hotter than the glow that flooded from the stove" (31). Bob in turn gets wind of Tom's relationship with Louisa. Jealous, he questions his own desire for a black woman, recognizing that the flavor of difference is part of her appeal: "She was worth it. Beautiful nigger gal. Why nigger? Why not, just gal? Not it was because she was nigger that he went to her. Sweet . . ." (34, ellipses in original). In the midst of these meditations on Louisa's sweetness, derived from her blackness, Bob stumbles across "the scent of boiling cane" and "the rich glow of the stove" (34). This intrusion marks the collapse of the syrup circle as a utopian preserve from Jim Crow politics. In an altercation over Louisa, Tom slits Bob's throat, and a white mob lynches him for it.

In both "Withered Skin of Berries" and "Blood-Burning Moon," sexual rivalry across the color line symbolically exiles black men from the sanctuary of the syrup circle.[57] However surprisingly, given the genealogical terms in which it is often understood, diasporic affiliation turns out to be particularly vulnerable to the racial regimentation of heterosexuality.[58] It would be easy to construe Toomer's celebration of masculine homosociality as a condemnation of women, the weakest link in the production and protection of black community. Toomer's fluid renderings of the mixed-race woman in other chapters, however, further a queer fantasy of diaspora.[59] Tellingly, both the cane boil and mystical mulatta inspire lyrical imagery of solution and suspension, sweet steam and rippling foam. By emphasizing intermediate states in the material world, Toomer endorses fluctuating identities in the human one.[60]

The mixed-race title character in "Fern" embodies both the diasporic past and ongoing processes of intermixture. The narrator, a visitor from the North who becomes fascinated by this withdrawn light-skinned woman, sees in her face the geography and history of diaspora: "I follow the curves of her profile, like mobile rivers, to their common delta" (16). These "mobile rivers" evoke both the Babylonian Captivity and African slavery, as in Langston Hughes's poem "The Negro Speaks of Rivers" (1920). But the "flow" of Fern's face is no mere recollection of origin, hearkening back to a "common delta." Her features seem to constantly shift, as "Face flowed into her eyes. Flowed in soft cream foam and plaintive ripples" (16). Foam encloses gas in a liquid, and it flows under what is called "yield stress," pressure that threatens its formal integrity.[61] This intermediary state provides a productive analogy for Fern's liminal identity, which suspends multiple categories. The narrator variously views her as "virgin" and "concubine," "Semitic" and "black" (16–18). Under the pressuring gaze of the community and of the narrator himself, Fern, like foam, flows.

The "soft cream foam" and "plaintive ripples" of her features also recall the commercial allure of soda.[62] Flirting with Fern, the narrator tries to engage her with talk of "the new soft drink they had at old Pap's store," but she will not respond, giving "a yassur or nassur, without further comment" (18). By reducing syrupy solutions to mere commodities, the narrator misses the point. He must instead give in to the inarticulacy and the intimacy of desire, the "thing from her that made my throat catch" (19). Fern's fluidity grants her a mystical power that dissolves perceptual boundaries, much like the cane syrup in "Withered Skin of Berries" and "Blood-Burning Moon." If her lovely appearance makes her resemble a woman in a soft drink ad, Fern's mystical vision bears out the pharmacological promises of coca as a stimulant.

Fern's sensory perceptions turn solid land into shifting sea, distant vision into immediate absorption, sight into sound: "Like her face, the whole countryside seemed to flow into her eyes. Flowed into them with the soft listless cadence of Georgia's South" (17). The synesthetic effect here is deliberately mind-bending; the countryside speaks with a "soft listless cadence" as it enters Fern's eyes. Toomer melds eyes and palate by making speech into another "soft" liquid that traverses interior and exterior. This voice comes from the land and yet enters into Fern, anticipating her epiphanic mediumship in the encounter that follows. Fern's permeability underscores the narrator's perception of her gender, the femininity of "flow."

Once he gives in to this flow, the narrator's sensations are transformed, the boundaries between their bodies and between his mind and body breached. "I felt strange," he admits, and his physical actions overtake his conscious intentions: "From force of habit, I suppose, I held Fern in my arms—that is, without at first noticing it. Then my mind came back to her" (19). Arrested by her vision, the narrator cedes control, admitting that "her eyes, unusually weird and open, held me" (19). He and Fern are united in mystical vision: "[Her eyes] Held God. He flowed in as I've seen the countryside flow in. Seen men" (19). The narrator is now as "unusually weird and open" as Fern's eyes, and the increased fragmentation of his narration suggests his new susceptibility: "I must have done something—what, I don't know, in the confusion of my emotion" (19). The narrator has shifted from a local colorist, nostalgically recording the telling details of life in a small southern town, to a modernist, shaping his sentences to reflect unspeakable yet urgent psychic experiences.

The communicability of Fern's "weird" affect, infusing the narrator with its "flow," recalls the exoticism and primitivism of contemporaneous soda marketing. For example, in Figure 1.2, a black servant serves a group of well-dressed

Figure 1.2 In this newspaper advertisement for Chero-Cola, the black servant delivering sodas to white women stands in front of the palm tree, her body connected to the tropical ingredients.
Source: "Chero-Cola: There's None So Good," *Charlotte News,* August 2, 1914.

white women glasses of bubbling soda in a 1914 Chero-Cola advertisement. The copy promises that the soda "sharpens your wit—energizes your body and brain."[63] The tropical tree above the servant's head implies that the racialized body delivers this affect, both through the bubbling beverages on the tray and through her primitive person. Like the waitress conflated with the tropical tree in the Chero-Cola ad, Fern becomes indistinguishable from the sweet gum tree that she sits beneath, "swaying, swaying" (19).

Just as the waitress offers southern white women vicarious access to tropical reinvigoration, Fern grants the modernist narrator vicarious access to a fantasy of the South. "The sweet gum is probably more closely linked with plantation life in the South than any other tree," a 1914 tree guide opined. "It grows in the swamps, and many a slave hugged the slender shaft of a leafy gum tree while he waited all day for the north star to point him the way to freedom."[64] For the narrator, who is "from the North" and admits that he has "knocked about from town to town," the freedom of mobility is a fact of modern life, one that he associates with masculinity on both sides of the color line: "it makes no difference if you sit in the Pullman or the Jim Crow as the train crosses her road" (18). For Fern, however, the experience of embodied epiphany is quite painful, all the more so because she is rooted in one place: "Her body was tortured with something it could not let out. Like boiling sap it flooded arms and fingers till she shook them as if they burned her" (19).[65]

Through this "boiling sap," Toomer forces his narrator to confront the history of violence obscured by the exotic fantasy of the alluring mulatta. During this transformative epiphany, the urban modernist who had rhetorically distanced himself both from "black folks" and from "white men" now takes his immersive cue from the rural, mixed-race woman (17). Her experience of the epiphany, however, reveals that the stakes of racial classification are not merely aesthetic. The skin is permeable not only in its erotic openness to mystical revelation but in its terrifying receptiveness to pain, which in turn recalls the script of slavery written on racialized skin through whips, torture, and brands. Fern's suffering exceeds the bounds of her attractive body: it "boil[s]," "flood[s]," "burn[s]," and "spatter[s]" (19). This overwhelming force of negative feeling problematizes the modernist's elevation of the tragic mulatta as transcendent mystic because it suggests that he is exploiting her pain for his art. Sweet gum trees were also harmed in harvesters' search for its fragrant resin. One tree guide recommended "crushing a leaf," "bruising a twig," or "chip[ping] through the bark of a tree . . . [so that] an aromatic gum accumulates in the wound."[66] Personifying the sweet gum, a 1915 article in *Scientific American* calls the sap its "yellowish tears" and observes that "trees thus treated will die in the course of a year."[67] If the urban modernist avails himself of emotional and mystical transport through the vehicle of the racialized female body, he must also acknowledge, however metaphorically, the flow of blood and the physicality of suffering.

Sweet gum resin was renowned for its "mucilaginous and aromatic properties," as one southern Civil War–era medical botanist put it.[68] Two major forms of the resin's use seem inherently opposed; it could be used as expectorant or incense, to swallow or to burn, to clear the throat or to propitiate the gods.[69] These uses provide a suggestive symbolic parallel to the mind–body divide that plagues the narrator in its refusal to remain separate. The "boiling sap" that "found her throat, and spattered inarticulately in plaintive, convulsive sounds" evokes the racked body and the thwarted voice, the possibility of painful history choking off all expression (19). Toomer thus links pathology and pain with the fragmented and visceral aesthetic that characterizes literary modernism and its "plaintive, convulsive sounds." In this sense, literary modernism is both guttural (in sound) and of the gut, registering the pain of history on the body, providing one method of registering the unspeakable history of slavery. At the same time, the narrator experiences Fern's epiphany as sacred transport and even religious observance: "I felt that things unseen to men were tangibly immediate" (19). So too does experimental modernism attest to the power of imagination in mending (or aspiring to mend) a broken world. These antithetical qualities of the sweet gum resin melt together in Toomer's depiction of Fern: "A Jewish cantor singing with a broken voice" (19). Like the diasporic history of enslavement and racial violence, the sweet gum resin threatens to destroy the body but also renders its sensorium a crucial vehicle of protest and poetry.

The form that this artistry takes, then, is not in spite of the racialized body of the subject but because of the insistent somaticism of historical experience and even psychic interiority: "Her body was tortured with something she could not let out" (19). This image suggests the literary and cultural afterlife of the tragic mulatta, "tortured" by the curse of mixed blood. While Toomer jettisons the implications of biological determinism in this figure, he retains the tragic mulatta's often burdensome spectacularity and implies that modernist double consciousness, a masculin(ist) intellectual conceit, can trace its genealogy to a feminized and sexualized body.[70] The narrator seems uncomfortable with the proximity of his intellectual transcendence and Fern's physical vulnerability. Indeed, his encounter with her threatens to render him equally vulnerable and spectacular: "I got one or two ugly looks from town men who'd set themselves up to protect her. In fact, there was talk of making me leave town" (19).

The narrator concludes his tale of this epiphanic journey by attempting to sum up Fern's story, to name and hence to contain her: "Her name, against the chance that you happen down that way, is Fernie May Rosen" (19). Toomer creates a contrast between the liquidity and continuity of the "flow" associated with Fern—"Saw her face flow into them, the countryside and something that I call God, flowing into them"—and the action and finality of the verbs associated with the narrator: "Nothing ever really happened. Nothing ever came to Fern, not even I" (19). Toomer thus juxtaposes two ways of inhabiting experience: one that encompasses the "flow" of God and the other, a teleological view of history that prioritizes what happened and who won ("I came, I saw, I conquered"). The carbonation of soda's creamy foam and the exudation of sap's thick resin seem closer to Toomer's aesthetic of intermediates and fluidity than the narrator's historiographical declarations. Perhaps it is the intellectual seeking an authentic origin for a racialized self in the pastoral South—"When one is on the soil of one's ancestors, most anything can come to one"—who proves static and awkward amidst the shifting states of modernity, in spite of his claim to the last word (19).[71]

The (Artificial) Color Purple: Interracial Effervescence

In the southern section of *Cane*, the northern intellectual seeks proximity to the racialized feminine body, longing for eroticism and immersiveness that his "stuck-up" demeanor seems to lack (17). In the second section of *Cane*, entering the urban North, Toomer charts the interracial encounters of the Great

Migration, and in so doing, he articulates the white desire for color, imagined not simply as racialized skin but as communicable affect and enviable orality. Throughout the southern section of *Cane*, black, racially mixed, and ethnically marked characters—the "dusky, cane-lipped throngs"—are associated with song, sucking, laughter, banter, drinking, tobacco chewing, and other oral pleasures (15). In *Love and Theft*, Eric Lott argues that "matters of the body," particularly "gender anxieties, unconventional sexuality, and orality," provided the preoccupying subjects of blackface minstrelsy in order to "mediate and regulate" white masculinity.[72] They also inspired envy and desire, and "Bona and Paul" charts the longing of white characters for colorful speech and bodily immersion, which they associate with racially ambiguous Paul and his presumptive (yet well-hidden) primitivism.

First, a brief summary of "Bona and Paul": Light-skinned Paul is in a teacher training program in Chicago with southern white girl Bona. Suspecting that he is black, Bona is only more drawn to him. They go on a double date with Paul's white roommate, Art, and his girlfriend, Helen. Bona and Paul dance together at a jazz club and seem to experience a moment of connection in spite of the racial (and racist) frames that each superimposes on the other. They start to leave the club together, but then Paul sees the black doorman watching them. Frustrated, he goes back to try to explain to the doorman that this is not a sexual union to leer at but something beautiful that is about to happen. By the time he finishes confronting the doorman, Bona has disappeared without a trace. As even this bare-bones plot summary should suggest, "Bona and Paul" is at once about the desire to transcend race and to connect and about the way that discourses of race police boundaries both internal (the characters' thoughts about race) and external (the door of the club).

Walter Benn Michaels sees this tension as an indication of the failure of Toomer's racial imagination, a sign that in spite of the potential epistemological liberation of moving beyond prescriptive racial identity, Toomer ultimately recapitulates the logic of the one-drop rule: "both the sustained effort to imagine oneself belonging to a new American race and the occasional effort to imagine oneself belonging to no race at all are retroactively turned into the effort to conceal—even from oneself—one's 'real' race."[73] Toomer certainly mobilizes the potency of racist fantasy and stereotype to complicate the heady possibility of escaping categorization, but his treatment of color as an effervescent effect (and affect) complicates Michaels's view of the conclusiveness of racial authenticity in "Bona and Paul." Paul observes his white roommate, Art, and imagines his joy and confidence as color unloosed from racial signification:

> Art is happy and confident in the good looks that his mirror gave him. Bubbling over with a joy he must spend now if the night is to contain

it all. His bubbles, too, are curiously tinted purple as Paul watches them. Paul, contrary to what he had thought he would be like, is cool like the dusk, and like the dusk, detached. His dark face is a floating shade in evening's shadow. He sees Art, curiously. Art is a purple fluid, carbon-charged, that effervesces beside him. He loves Art. But is it not queer, this pale purple facsimile of a red-blooded Norwegian friend of his? (75)

Art's colorful and textural transformations embody a "joy" that Paul can watch and appreciate but not participate in. While Paul is haunted by the idea of blackness, a "floating shade" suggesting both shadow and ghost, Art can begin to transcend his ethnicity, a transcendence communicated by those bubbles and the way they exceed the bodily container ("bubbling over").[74] While "Paul" resembles a pall, Art enters the realm of artifice. As Michaels justly observes, "The alternative to being black in the story is not exactly being white ... What's being sporadically imagined here is not simply an alternative to being either 'nigger' or 'white,' but an alternative that, by disconnecting color from race and insisting on the priority of color over race, problematizes race by making it available only in 'facsimile.'"[75] Toomer's anxiety about the possibility of racial (re)invention comes through even in this lyrical passage; can a "facsimile" move beyond racial labels and become a vibrant aesthetic presence? Art's racial categorization as a "red-blooded Norwegian" may always win out over Paul's—and perhaps Toomer's—reimagining of his substance. Racial prescription drawn from purported biologism haunts the multicolored effervescence of "queer" vision. Michaels suggests that the truth of race is effectively the moral of the story—that Paul's racial identity proves essential and inescapable.[76] In my attention to effervescence in "Bona and Paul," however, I see a longed-for communicability of color and affect that bespeaks the limitations of whiteness. After all, Art's "good looks" may give him social confidence, but when he experiences burgeoning joy, it can only be expressed in a new color, "tinted purple." As Dyer observes, "The slippage between white as a colour and white as colourlessness forms part of a system of thought and affect whereby white people are both particular and nothing in particular, are both something and non-existent."[77] The threat of pallor, linking colorlessness, anhedonia, and immateriality, makes whiteness an impinging, even vampiric, presence in this story, metonymized in the undead skin: "Perhaps for some reason, white skins are not supposed to live at night." "Bona, would she be pale?" Paul wonders and fears (75).

While Art's name evokes the art and literature that Toomer hoped would help create a new American race, it also recalls "artificial color," a mandatory label on soda bottles of the period.[78] The description of Art as "a purple fluid, carbon-charged, that effervesces" suggests a soft drink, especially in an era when "artificially colored" grape sodas were popular, their purple color reproduced vividly in print ads.[79] Toomer's choice of soda as a trope for the shifting prism of color consciousness is an inspired one; synthetic colors sparked debates about their natural or artificial origins, a potent analogy for race as inheritance or invention that consumed Toomer's intellectual life. In May 1920, the *American Bottler* insisted that the required artificial color label misled consumers, implying an imitative function rather than an imaginative one: "The color is put in the soda for ornamental purposes and for no other reason. It does not conceal its character or make it look like something that it is not, for the simple reason that there is nothing else, either better or worse, that looks anything like bottled soda. If colored soda is an imitation, what is it supposed to be imitating?"[80] These anxieties about concealment and misleading appearance are soothed by the baselessness of color classification itself. The article goes on to celebrate inventive imagination; artificial color reflects "whatever hue fancy dictates."[81] Suggestively, the *American Bottler* considers the base of all beverages "water white," which could be infused with other colors.[82] This conflation of the transparent and the white, the assumption that "white" is the universal basis for all other colors, correlates suggestively with the racial ideology of unmarked whiteness. But the soda manufacturers take this assessment one step further, namely to lambast the affective and aesthetic emptiness of mere whiteness. The editorial bemoans what a "gloomy day" it would be if "all-day suckers and gum drops wore the pallid countenance that a niggardly nature gives them."[83] A "pallid countenance" would sap candies of flavor as well as color; whiteness has an inverse relationship to pleasure.

While the *American Bottler* mounted this defense of artificial color, the soda industry was plagued by controversy about contamination; in 1921, a suit was brought against the bottlers association for their use of coal tar to color their sodas (red, yellow, and purple).[84] These poles—water white and corrupting coal tar—play out in the racial dynamics of Toomer's story. Art's effervescence seems predicated upon his confidence as the master of public space; he can exceed bounded space because he can pass anywhere (Art urges Paul to "come on"; the dormitory matron invites him to "come right in" [74–75]). By contrast, Paul feels self-conscious when he passes the threshold of the club, fearful of blackness as a contaminating secret that will be exposed. The other patrons of the speakeasy stare at him over "ash-smeared tablecloths," and he imagines that they wonder about his racial origins (76).

Unlike the lively racialized subject described in Ngai's *Ugly Feelings*, Paul insists on his own melancholy, and it is this affect as much as Paul's dark appearance that discomfits Art: "he's getting moony. Its [sic] his blood. Dark blood: moony. Doesn't get anywhere unless you boost it. You've got to keep it going—" (74). Art complains about his roommate's dejection; so too does Bona expect vivacity and engagement from her would-be lover and resents their absence: "And then, for no tangible reason, her spirits drop. Without them, she is nervous, and slightly afraid. She resents this. Paul's eyes are critical. She resents Paul" (75). Their annoyance with Paul and his despondency recapitulates a long line of racist thought about African disposition and necessary chemical stimulation. In the sixteenth century, Caribbean slaveholders used kola leaves to offset the "attacks of constitutional despondency" that they imagined were a racial trait rather than a response to enslavement.[85] Early ads for Coca-Cola promised that it would be a brain tonic and a mood elevator. Here, the pressure to "boost" mood and tempo, to "keep it going" and elevate "spirits" is part of a racialized technology of self. As Ngai notes, "exaggerated emotional expressiveness . . . seems to function as a marker of racial or ethnic otherness in general" and "abet[s] [the racial other's] construction as unusually receptive to external control."[86] While Paul joins the others in ordering a highball, a carbonated cocktail, he remains self-contained; Helen complains that he is "so deep these days" (78).

Paul refuses to "set emotion flowing" in response to Art's invitation or even to Bona's romantic provocation (75); and his "fullness, and strength and peace" keep him viewing the club "Distantly" (77). This stillness finds an unexpected contrast in the jazzy movement and linguistic zing of his white companions. Art criticizes the waiter: "Make it snappy, will you?" (77). In a suggestive (though likely not intentional) link between Art's speech and his figuration as a charged liquid, the word "snappy" served as a term of art for fresh bubbles in the soda industry; one carbonator advertisement promised it was "like the Fountain of Youth when it comes to supplying fresh snappy soda at all times."[87] Art wants the drinks, the dancing, and the music to keep coming, and this cycle of pleasure requires a brisk tempo of service. As one pharmacist's journal quipped, "Everyone likes a snappy soda, no one likes a snappy dispenser."[88] This last jibe links the bite of bubbles with the sharpness of back talk, which Art clearly does not anticipate; while Art hails his server with "Say, waiter," his formulation implies that he (the customer) will say it all for him. In spite of this association between service and silence, speech and command, Paul fears that the words of pale people lack the tactility of colorful speech: "No doubt of it: her face is pale. She is talking. Her words have no feel to them" (76). White speech is insipid, does not appeal to the tongue, does not have a "feel" to it.

Inside the Crimson Gardens, the language of Paul's white companions becomes sharper, sexier, snappier. Art accuses his girl of getting "spiffy" (meaning offended, rather than dolled-up), while Helen (his girl) acknowledges that she is "snidy" to Paul in spite of her fascination with him (77–78). These slangy, neologistic word choices combine sibilance and bounce, the aural cognate of the effervescence of soda. Paul refuses this form of conversation, calling his coldness an imitation of "the first philosopher" and discussing "a priori" principles (79). By contrast, Bona wisecracks, "How do you know, Mr. Philosopher? . . . You talk well for a gym director" (79). Much like the jazz playing in the club (and the jazz that Art plays on the dorm piano before coming to the club), these forms of orality express an envy of the "snappy" culture of color by ventriloquizing what Art, Helen, and Bona all wish that Paul would be, namely sexy and funny. Art begrudges Paul's self-containment and tellingly complains, "What in hell's eating Paul?" (77). In this formulation, Paul's emotions are consuming him, thus rendering him unavailable for Art's consumption. In his internal monologue, Art transforms Paul's resistant affect into an appealing spice: "God, he's a good, straight feller, though. Only, moony. Nut. Nuttish. Nuttery. Nutmeg..." (77, ellipses in original). Even the wordplay here—riffing on "nut"—plays with the effervescence of language, the way that words can take on new, related but not identical shapes that tickle the tongue. Art turns light-skinned Paul into a light brown spice. Paul's white friends long for him as a refreshment, this kola "Nut" an infusion of exoticism much like the "crash of jazz from the palm-hidden orchestra" (79). Paul recognizes and sometimes enjoys this commodification and sexualization of his racial difference. When Bona is "a little stiff" in her dancing, Paul considers Helen instead, as she "wants every highball spoon her hands touch, for a souvenir" and is a "supple, perfect little dancer" (79). As Freud would say, sometimes a highball spoon is just a highball spoon, but in this case, it seems unlikely. Helen seems stirred by Paul, and he considers doing the stirring.

Bona and Paul come together on the dance floor, and erotic fluidity overcomes exotic objectification, transforming both of their bodies in the process. The club becomes "a body whose blood flows to a clot upon the dance floor" (79). Like two cells of this blood, Bona and Paul are now fluids that might solidify but, if so, will turn into a solid together, indistinguishable from one another. This metaphor resists phallic dominance, chooses red instead of the white and black of miscegenation, and replaces the eugenic discourse of "bloods" and inheritance with a rush of erotic desire. Indeed, the dance makes their bodies vessels of effervescence: "The dance takes the blood from their minds and packs it, tingling, in the torsos of their swaying bodies" (79). For a brief moment, pleasure promises to undo the illusory separation of skin: "They are a dizzy blood clot on a gyrating floor" (79).[89] The human body is turned inside out (blood clots on the dance floor), and intoxicating movement ("dizzy," "gyrating," "swaying") takes over. Temporarily, Bona casts off her white skin, as both Bona and Paul become hyper-embodied in this scene (blood clots) and also briefly escape the limitations of the racialized body. At the same time, Toomer's dance floor language cannot shed the unsettling connotation of injury; blood clots, after all, when it solidifies to stanch a wound.

When Bona and Paul head out of the door, the club appears to be a bubble of artificial color, a self-contained dream of purple: "[Paul] sees the [speakeasy] purple, as if he were way off" (79). But once they have left the club, Bona and Paul are confronted by blackness: "And a spot is in the purple. The spot comes furiously towards him. Face of the black man. It leers. It smiles sweetly like a child's" (79). In Paul's view of the black bouncer, Toomer articulates a dehumanizing stereotype, which he underscores with the pronoun "It." In a burlesque of the appealing orality and the vivacious affect that white characters associate with color throughout the story, the bouncer's mouth "leers." Barbara Foley points out that black bouncers were frequently hired by nightclubs in order to discern which patrons might be passing for white.[90] As much as Paul's white compatriots may enjoy imbibing a dream of color on the dance floor, they do so safely within enclaves that make that intoxication safe and temporary. Suggestively, in spite of his dreams of achieving a purple and red alternative to the black and white of racial binarism, Paul ultimately sees this doorman as a brother; he can clasp his hand in his own: "Paul and the black man shook hands" (80). The interracial union achieved with such fragile intensity inside the club is more difficult to maintain, as evanescent as it was effervescent: "When he reached the spot where they had been standing, Bona was gone" (80).

In *Cane*, Toomer treats fluidity and effervescence as modern figures of imagination and intoxication, solutions and infusions that convey to the doubting senses that the boundaries between bodies are permeable and perceptions of autonomy and self-containment illusory. In so doing, he makes an implicit argument for experimental modernism and its ambition to open "new sensory domains" and to "*intervene* in the body," but he also criticizes the racial fantasies that often accompany the desire for affective transport.[91] In Toomer's narratives, the desire to cross boundaries, to imbibe and incorporate the other, exposes the lack in the supposedly superior subject position that covets this sensualized immersion: the black modernist discovers that he needs the tragic mulatta to voice his fragmentary aesthetic of double-consciousness, the white spectator discovers that while trying to visualize the "candle that dances," the "autumn leaf" of vivid racial color, she has exposed her own alienation and envy (72). Through foaming cream and colored bubbles, which allow this too too solid flesh to melt, Toomer anticipates the theorization of the "epidermal racial schema" famously undertaken by Frantz Fanon in *Black Skin, White Masks* (1952). When Fanon writes of "Peeling, stripping my skin, causing a hemorrhage that left congealed, black blood all over my body" and claims that it is "not his idea," we might recall Toomer's dancers, "a dizzy blood clot" trying to concoct a new relationship to color.[92]

Coda: Crystal Apples and Flavorless Whiteness

Toomer's later work speculated that adaptive fluidity would give way to mechanical rigidity, reversing his earlier position on the collaborative relationship between novel technologies and liberatory forms of identity. In an unpublished science fiction sketch from 1933, "Man's Home Companion," Toomer describes a future man and woman, seated next to each other at a "high metal stand with a bright washable top, around which are grouped three high stools similar to those at bars and quick lunch counters" and "drinking from test tubes."[93] Toomer's soda fountain has returned, but this time as a sign of the abrogation of intimacy, the transformation of private space into public transaction, occasioned by modernity and its innovations. The couple shares nothing, not even a kiss; he "sort of beaks her as if begrudging the waste of his perfectly good emotions" (168). Ultimately, the husband crawls into "a sleeping contraption, itself resembling a test-tube," betraying solipsism and self-containment rather than the percolating possibilities of the dance floor in "Bona and Paul" (169).

In his own life, his fantasy of creating a new race became a desire to pass out of a marked one.[94] When he married Marjorie Lattimore, he commented to the press that he was not certain that his grandfather was black—that it might have been politically expedient for him to pass in order to achieve a position of influence in Reconstruction politics.[95] Toomer's view of food science also soured in the decades following the publication of *Cane*. Where soda fountains had provided a model for cultural invention, now the industrialization of food bore out the commodification and standardization that he saw more broadly in American culture. In his unpublished memoir, Toomer devoted several nostalgic pages to the recipes and fruits of yesteryear, praising local produce and regional recipes and lamenting the dislocations of the modern food system.[96]

Expounding his ideas about human character and the vitiations of modern culture, Toomer gave a talk on April 27, 1947, at the Westtown School entitled "The Flavor of Man." The notes for his speech indicate the sea change in Toomer's newly universalized understanding of identity, embodiment, and race. In his notes for the talk, Toomer clearly demarcated the interior and exterior that he blended in the fluid fashioning of bodies in *Cane*: "Flavor comes from true substance, and our true substance is inward." This turn toward interiority also prevented Toomer from acknowledging the continuing social force of Jim Crow. Instead, he exhorts the Quaker students, "Whatever racial group you [are] in, outgrow it." In this talk, rather than create his own array of compelling flavors in the chemist's workshop, Toomer adopts "real flavor" as the banner of existential authenticity: "In all of your choice and decisions . . . decide for which will increase your true substance and flavor."[97]

While Toomer had once understood the innovations of food science as an arena for racial reinvention, the next version of this lecture lays out the risks of scientific deception. In the William Penn Lecture in 1949, also entitled "The Flavor of Man," Toomer introduces his subject with an anecdote about seed hybrids:

> And once again, these being the days just before things start growing, catalogues arrive from the large houses that supply seeds for the gardens of America. Not long ago my wife was going through one of the catalogues that annually fascinate her . . . This is what she read: Crystal Apple. 65 days. An amazingly attractive cucumber, perfectly round, crystal-white at all stages, with a sweetness and lack of cucumber flavor that is remarkable. Produces a tremendous number of fruit about the size of a lemon when mature.[98]

Toomer is aghast: "Crystal Apple. It is not called a cucumber. It has neither the shape nor the size of a cucumber. And, to cap it all, it remarkably lacks the cucumber flavor! What ingenuity and labor went into the production of this cucumber that isn't a cucumber! Is this not typical of twentieth-century man?" (119). This product—"crystal-white at all stages"—is remarkable both for its "sweetness" and its "lack." In this combination, Toomer's Crystal Apple seems suggestively like the category of whiteness itself, which, Dyer argues, shows its paradoxical power in both its visual glamour and its uncanny invisibility.[99] On another sensory plane, the white Crystal Apple both appeals to the palate and remains "remarkably" flavorless.

It is tempting to speculate about Toomer's reasons for targeting this particular fruit of the modern food system.[100] His objections to the cucumber—its deceptive name and appearance, and the "ingenuity and labor" that went into producing "a cucumber that isn't a cucumber"—anticipate contemporary frustrations with light-skinned Toomer's decision to pass for white, as well as the critical impetus to define this decision as passing rather than an embrace of an array of identificatory possibilities, as young Toomer might have optimistically imagined the process of becoming a "new American."[101] The Crystal Apple provides a powerful metaphor for the reduction of hybridity into whiteness that Toomer had railed against and then capitulated to over the course of his life and career. Perhaps the pressure to achieve sweet flavorlessness ultimately proved more powerful than the affective pleasures of color. Certainly, Toomer's consideration of color in "Bona and Paul" suggests the risk of association with infusions of affect—the reduction to a stereotype and sensation. Nonetheless, his skepticism about the "amazingly attractive" cucumber might register a deeper misgiving about the cultural power of "crystal-white"-ness. Whatever the conscious or unconscious motives for castigating the Crystal Apple, the move away from "purple fluid, carbon-charged" is stark and uncompromising.

Toomer's talk goes on to criticize the bland, white products of the modern food system: "Consider the bread without the flavor of bread. In any restaurant you can get milk that hardly tastes like milk. Could it be that here in Philadelphia there is water that does not taste like water?" (119).[102] Extending the metaphor to American geopolitics, Toomer argues that an anodyne exterior disguises toxicity within: "Outstanding at this time is the fact that we have peace without the flavor of peace. But the wars we wage have the full horrible flavor of war. The bombs we make are not Crystal Apples" (119). This insight bears out the economic and structural relationship between the US industrial food system and its military might.[103] It also acknowledges inequities that Toomer tries to remedy through spirituality: "domestic antagonisms, racial conflicts, class wars, international wars—one party wanting to punish the other for its own frustration, one hoping to wrest from the other what neither possesses" (119). Toomer's discomfort with racial categorization, then, does not blind him to the cultural politics of whiteness as an emblem of nationalism and "a mechanized and commercialized society."[104] This hygienic fantasy of mass production, a fantasy that he noted in "The Sacred Factory" twenty years earlier, can be maintained only by the projection of waste into an undesirable elsewhere: "In cities there are slums and filth, and on the outskirts smoldering refuse."[105] Though Toomer insists that shared "human" problems subsume racial, religious, and political differences (124), he also speaks of "ghettos ... concentration camps and colonies," an invocation of de facto segregation, genocide, and the uneven process of postwar decolonization (123). Indeed, Toomer's strenuously avowed humanism may obscure the political implications of his discussion of pollution, which has racial as well as ecological connotations. Noting the "marks" that "vaunted lords of the earth" (presumably the captains of industry) leave on the land, Toomer turns the destruction of the earth and of other people into a kind of text: "gutted lives mak[ing] their miserable patterns upon the earth."[106] Herein lies the trouble with the "Crystal Apple," its empty-set loveliness the lie of consumer culture, the supposedly effortless, uninscribed now of American prosperity. The language of contamination, marking those in poverty, though their sufferings remain invisible within a white fantasy of prosperity, indirectly acknowledges the continuing power of race in American life.

Toomer lays the groundwork for more unabashed black intellectuals like James Baldwin, who writes memorably in "The Fire Next Time" (1962) about the cultural work performed by black people in America, as the focal point for white people's fears and desires. He too understands industrial food as evidence of the disavowal of the senses, the anhedonia of white culture:

White Americans . . . are terrified of sensuality and do not any longer understand it. The word "sensual" is not intended to bring to mind quivering dusky maidens or priapic black studs. I am referring to something much simpler and much less fanciful. To be sensual, I think, is to respect and rejoice in the force of life, of life itself, and to be present in all that one does, from the effort of loving to the breaking of bread. It will be a great day for America, incidentally, when we begin to eat bread again, instead of the blasphemous and tasteless foam rubber that we have substituted for it. And I am not being frivolous now, either. Something very sinister happens to the people of a country when they begin to distrust their own reactions as deeply as they do here, and become as joyless as they have become.[107]

Whether commenting on "Crystal Apples" or "tasteless foam rubber" bread, both Toomer and Baldwin, writing in the postwar period, see taste as a territory that has been ceded in the rush to embrace and promulgate the cult of whiteness—a capacious category encompassing commercialism, industrialism, nationalism, militarism, Anglo-Saxonism. This cultural afterlife of the pressure to bottle, standardize, and segregate that Toomer noted in his early essays renders *Cane*'s insistence on artificial color's vibrancy and carbonation's piquancy even more aesthetically and politically urgent to recuperate.

2

Genius in the Raw

The Schuyler Family and the Modern Mulatta

In 1864, a pamphlet entitled *Miscegenation*—it coined the term—pretended to advocate racial intermixture. The authors wax rhapsodic in their blazon of a mixed-race woman, comparing her to a hybrid strawberry:

> The most beautiful girl in form, feature, and every attribute of feminine loveliness that [the author] ever saw, was a mulatto. By crossing and improvement of different varieties, the strawberry, or other garden fruit, is brought nearest to perfection, in sweetness, size, and fruitfulness. This was a ripe and complete woman, possessing the best elements of two sources of parentage. Her complexion was warm and dark, and golden with the heat of tropical suns, lips full and luscious, cheeks perfectly moulded, and tinged with deep crimson.[1]

In this formulation, planned breeding, the "crossing and improvement of different varieties," would produce perfect beauty and the underlying superior qualities to sustain it. Although the pomological metaphor eroticizes this "beautiful girl," it also emphasizes her wholeness; she is "ripe and complete"—not fallen, bruised, bitten, or rotten. The tenderness of a gardener's care replaces the violent history of racial intermixture under slavery.

The authors did not intend to convince their readers of the superiority of this vision. On the contrary, Democrats David Goodman Croly and George Wakeman hoped that their pamphlet would alienate white voters, preventing Lincoln's reelection.[2] Even such fulsome descriptions of mixed-race beauty are meant to alarm readers; as Elise Lemire explains, "Croly and Wakeman knew full well, indeed counted on the fact, that most members of the middle class believed that attraction to such traits was a sign of very bad taste."[3] Nonetheless, their botanical metaphors for racial intermixture were so persuasive that they even made grape growers anxious about the implications of their breakthroughs.[4] As Tavia

Nyong'o argues, in spite of its racist aims, the *Miscegenation* pamphlet spurred speculation about "a hybrid future."[5]

The satirist George Schuyler is known for his speculative fiction about black futures. Like the *Miscegenation* pamphlet, his ironies are often difficult to read, embedded as they are in the conventions of science fiction. His landmark novel, *Black No More* (1931), speculates about what would happen if "electrical nutrition" could make black people white-skinned.[6] Schuyler concludes that people would darken their skins if they thought that whiteness had lost its exclusivity. Under the name "Samuel I. Brooks," he published two popular science fiction serials in the *Pittsburgh Courier*, *The Black Internationale: A Story of Black Genius Against the World*, from November 1936 until January 1937, and its sequel, *Black Empire: An Imaginative Story of a Great New Civilization in Modern Africa*, from October 1937 through April 1938.[7] In these installments, a black übermensch leads a global black underground to overthrow white supremacy. Schuyler scoffed at his own pseudonymous success, calling it "hokum and hack work of the purest vein," a combination of "race chauvinism and sheer improbability."[8]

Nonetheless, much as the *Miscegenation* pamphlet seems to get carried away by its own exaggerated rhetoric, Schuyler's fiction suggests a less skeptical view than he articulated in his personal correspondence. His futuristic visions of horticulture and nutrition intersect with the rational breeding and environmental control advocated in popular eugenics. In *The Black Internationale*, for example, the protagonist, Carl, a new recruit to the underground organization seeking global black supremacy, tours their hydroponic farms. On this tour, Carl is dazzled by two sights: enormous strawberries nourished by chemiculture and the beautiful woman with "strong white teeth" who eats them.[9] He marvels at their shared loveliness:

> A vine . . . was loaded with strawberries, but such strawberries as I had never seen, nor anybody else for that matter. They were fully as large as full-grown plums, bright red and as luscious a sight as I've ever witnessed. "White folks can't equal that," [the chemist] boasted. "We're sending a crop to market in New York and Philadelphia tomorrow." . . . Pat [took] a big bite out of one of the strawberries with her strong white teeth. (49)

Both berry and woman are the best of their kind; the fruit is "as luscious a sight as I've ever witnessed," and Patricia is "the prettiest colored girl I've ever seen" (40). When the chemist brags, "White folks can't equal that," speaking of the berry, he also implies that Pat is racially superior. Indeed, teeth were a charged cultural marker of racial decay or hygienic soundness in the 1930s.[10] Pat is an emblem of the Black Internationale movement as much as the strawberries are. Their superior bodies are the fruits of rational breeding and scientific nutrition and promise a better future for black people—one of prosperity and fertility.

With these hydroponic predictions, Schuyler speaks to the futuristic visions of his age. The New York World's Fair of 1939, which featured a piano concert by his daughter, Philippa, included a hydroponic farm sponsored by the Heinz Company. This exhibit was designed, as the food historian Warren Belasco explains, "less to lay out a workable blueprint for the future than to dramatize the sanitary purity of its ketchup and pickles."[11] This celebration of sanitation carried racial implications. In the Heinz exhibit brochure, a document the company denied permission to reproduce here, a trio that appears to be a nuclear family—father, mother, and son—watches a white-clad scientist replenish the transparent chemical food sustaining the plants. All four figures are blond, and the caption celebrates the "chemically-treated water" and the "pure-white sand" that nurture the tomatoes. They even call their tomatoes "aristocrat[s]," connecting human and botanical breeding.[12] The advertisement correlates racial whiteness with cleanliness and health and chemicultural purity with reproductive futurity.

In *The Black Internationale*, Schuyler also fetishizes cleanliness and control but in the name of black nationalism rather than white supremacy. The symbolism associating hydroponics with aspirational antisepticism is the same. The environment is carefully managed, "not a thing … left to chance" (49). Scientists eliminate the necessity for "dirt," which in turn obviates the risk of "soil erosion" (49); metaphorically, disorder and decline have been cast out of the planned garden. "Liquid chemical food" and "sunshine" infuse the plants with the "elements" that they need; though the farm is underground and could be imagined as a shadowy lair, these nutritional methods elevate transparency and light as tropes of progress (49). Ironically, transparency and light are often the very qualities of the modern visual landscape used to reinforce white supremacy. Pat declares, "We're using the weapons and knowledge of the white man against him" (50). Schuyler adapts the trope of hydroponics, a "perennial of agricultural futurism" and a standard of pulp science fiction, to apply not to a blond future but to a brown one.[13]

This fantasy of future agriculture makes no explicit mention of hybridization. The chemist does not indicate which strains of tomato went into the "bright red tomato as big as a full-size grapefruit" (50). Nutrition and environment are everything: "There is no plant disease, no poor distribution of food elements, no excess or lack of light" (49). Correspondingly, though Pat's teeth reflect her physical health, so often associated with racial hardiness during the period, Schuyler makes no mention of her likely mixed ancestry. In the 1920s and 1930s, the New Negro woman's light skin was adulated, but her interracial heredity went unremarked. As Nella Larsen wryly observes in *Quicksand*,

"Racial intermingling . . . was beyond definite discussion. For among black people, as among white people, it is tacitly understood that these things are not mentioned—and therefore they do not exist."[14] It was almost as if this iconic New Negro woman was born out of those clean, clear pools in the Black Internationale's underground farms.

Indeed, this choice—hydroponics over hybridization, white teeth over light skin, nutrition over eugenics—manages the anxieties about sexuality and racial intermingling piqued by the scandalous and seductive body of the mixed-race woman. Where pollination and cross-breeding promote sexual reproduction, and compost and fertilizer anticipate mortality and rot, "liquid chemical food" preserves distilled purity (49). The underground farm, protected from the vagaries of weather and wind, finely calibrates all environmental and nutritional inputs. Schuyler and his wife, Josephine, pursued a similar project of isolation and purification in raising their biracial daughter, Philippa. Attempting to shield Philippa from the contamination of industrial food, they raised her on raw foods and abjured refined sugars. They also kept her in the dark about Jim Crow and the politics of race in America. If a farm could be a laboratory, as the chemist proposes in *The Black Internationale*, so too could a New York apartment when a pair of like-minded parents strove to prove the superiority of racial intermixture in the face of a culture that abhorred miscegenation.

From toddlerhood, Philippa was heralded as a child prodigy, and the Schuylers eagerly advanced that characterization. Interviewed by the *New York Herald Tribune* on her third birthday, Philippa identified "continents and countries" on a globe; spelled words like "Cincinnati" and "rhinoceros"; and recited poetry—including Countee Cullen's lengthy poem "Heritage"—from memory.[15] A few months later, Josephine Schuyler introduced Philippa to the piano and enrolled her in lessons with a Juilliard alumna, Arnetta Jones. By the time she was five years old, Philippa had performed in a radio broadcast, a concert at the West 135th Street YMCA, and a music competition sponsored by the National Piano Teachers Guild. It was during the last of these three, Philippa's biographer, Kathryn Talalay, notes, "that, to even Jody's surprise, the judges discovered Philippa had perfect pitch."[16] Philippa also composed pieces of her own, "show[ing] a seemingly effortless ability to synthesize story and music, and to fashion a work far beyond her chronological age."[17] This aptitude for classical music and original composition distinguished Philippa from contemporaneous child stars who played the vaudeville circle or disported in Hollywood films.[18] Though one headline dubbed her the "Shirley Temple of American Negroes," her accomplishments bore out a narrative of cultivation rather than mere cuteness.[19]

From the Schuylers' point of view, such cultivation depended on alimentation. Thus, nutrition became a medium of negotiation between Philippa as a hybrid object and Philippa as a consuming subject. Eugenics' language of stocks and breeding stemmed from animal husbandry and horticulture, and the Schuylers espoused "hybrid vigor."[20] This agricultural association turns the mixed-race child into raw material, an improved cultivar. However, the very attractiveness of this offspring threatens her survival; the golden fruit might well be devoured, the delicate flower plucked. When Philippa was a baby, Schuyler wrote to his wife, "We must do everything to preserve her, like a hothouse flower, for she is a rare and exotic breed. There are few beings like her in the world."[21] As biographer Jeffrey Ferguson points out, the Schuylers "believed that the extraordinary efforts they put into shaping Philippa's environment gave her native gifts the best chance to develop."[22] A diet of raw foods would prevent the potential incursions of industrial life and racial degeneration.

In this sense, even a science diet could be a portal to the lost past or healthful wildness that had been regrettably superseded in the race to decadent civilization.[23] George Schuyler composed a strange but suggestive description of his infant child that casts her as a camouflaged forest creature, "[the color of] lightly done toast with dark liquid eyes of a fawn, and eyelashes like the black glistening stems of maiden hair ferns."[24] In this amalgamation of plant and animal categories, Schuyler signals the radicalism of racial intermixture, understood by so many as the combination of incompatible materials and life forms. However, for him, her variegated body is miraculous, even utopian. Philippa is an otherworldly creature of myriad and "glistening" surfaces. As "fawn" and "maiden hair fern," she is innocent and virginal. These forest similes suggest a wilder provenance than that "lightly done" breakfast toast, but all three comparisons evoke Philippa's fragility. Crunching jaws, a well-placed shot, or a trampling boot could destroy the wonder her parents wrought.

As Philippa got older, the Schuylers continued to celebrate the extraordinary purity of their daughter's body, but their emphasis shifted. Where the horticulture metaphor privileged parental planning, modern dietetics featured the child's virtue. By exhibiting to journalists her healthy appetite and willing abstinence from cooked foods and refined sugars, Philippa performed the role of the natural child preserved and maintained through artificial means. This regimen was continuous with "the discourse of child-rearing in the 1920s and 1930s," which cast "the middle-class home" as "the natural environment of the normal child" and the child's ability to adopt "middle-class, Protestant values of deferred gratification [and] self-control" as a sign of her likeliness to thrive.[25] Much of the developmental and educational research propounding these environmental theories, however, either excluded the "colored races" or skewed the results to support white supremacy.[26] This racist backdrop for Philippa's engineered childhood only heightens the symbolic significance of the mixed-race girl who carefully controls her ingestion.

This chapter brings together George Schuyler's science fiction, the Schuylers' published dietary advice, and Philippa's celebrity coverage to interrogate the relationship between nutritional purity and the sexual politics of the modern mulatta. Schuyler's science fiction builds upon a century of association between the mixed-race body and botany, Edenic fruit and scientific planning. As the biopolitical significance of racial intermixture shifted from debates over miscegenation and slavery in the mid-nineteenth century to eugenics and segregation in the twentieth, so too did this governing imagery evolve—from the tragic mulatta cast out of the garden to the modern mixed-race woman as revisionist Eve, refraining from temptation to regain paradisiacal harmony. Throughout this literary genealogy, the mulatta's eating—and her edibility—are crucially at stake.

Strange Fruit: The Literary Mulatta

Nineteenth-century literature turned to botany, chemistry, and nutrition to explore the potential perfectibility or inescapable corruption of the female body, a question intimately connected to racial politics.[27] In Nathaniel Hawthorne's stories "The Birth-Mark" (1843) and "Rappaccini's Daughter" (1844), scientists isolate young women from the world in order to infuse and transform their bodies with chemical influences. Their relationships are familial and implicitly reproductive. Aylmer experiments on his bride, Georgiana; Rappaccini on his daughter, Beatrice. Georgiana is "subjected to certain physical influences, either breathed in with the fragrant air or taken with her food," and Beatrice is "nourished with poisons from her birth upward" and as a result "herself had become the deadliest poison in existence."[28] In these laboratory experiments, where environment and ingestion reconstitute the female body, Hawthorne reflects the biochemical thought of his age. In 1840, Justus von Liebig published *Organic Chemistry*, advocating "new chemistry-based agriculture."[29] Soon thereafter, he applied his findings to "the relations of food consumption and human physiology . . . ultimately interested in how materials coursed around the earth and through bodies, and what effects that movement had on plants, animals, and people."[30] In Aylmer's laboratory, a plant sprouts, blooms, and withers in the space of a moment; in Rappaccini's garden, tropical plants thrive in an artificial pool and create a toxic miasma. The women's bodies undergo parallel processes.

Through botanical tropes, these stories articulate anxieties about racial intermixture.[31] Though Georgiana appears to be "the highest and purest of earthly mould," the birthmark "degrade[es] her into kindred with the lowest, and even with the very brutes" (120). Even the blossoming flower that dies in Aylmer's laboratory seems to allegorize the tragic mulatta trajectory: "The flower will wither in a few moments and leave nothing save its brown seed vessels; but thence may be perpetuated a race as ephemeral as itself. But Georgiana had no sooner touched the flower than the whole plant suffered a blight, its leaves turning coal-black as by the agency of fire" (124). The potential creator of a new and beautiful if ephemeral race, the tragic mulatta carries the mark of the "coal-black," which extinguishes racial futures in a "blight." In "Rappaccini's Daughter," the plants also reflect the scandal of miscegenation:

> Several also would have shocked a delicate instinct by an appearance of artificialness indicating that there had been such a commixture and, as it were, adultery of various vegetable species, that the production was no longer of God's making, but the monstrous offspring of man's depraved fancy, glowing only with an evil mockery of beauty. They were probably the result of experiment, which in one or two cases had succeeded in mingling plants individually lovely into a compound possessing the questionable and ominous character that distinguished the whole growth of the garden. (198)

This "questionable and ominous character" of these plants reflects the vexed status of the tragic mulatta, remarkable both for her loveliness and her fragility and also for the distressing possibility that she could pass unrecognized into white society. These two stories encapsulate the tragic mulatta convention: in spite of their innocence, these women are seductive, sensuous, infused with physical influences beyond their ken, and they die tragically as a result.

Abolitionist and anti-racist texts used horticultural figures to make mixed-race ancestry appealing rather than uncanny. Since these narratives typically followed the tragic mulatta from her protected childhood into ravished adulthood, their pomological imagery implied that emancipation could recuperate Eden, where sexual depredation and violence now reigned. In "The Quadroons" (1842), Lydia Maria Child compares Xarifa to "the sunny side of a golden pear."[32] In *Uncle Tom's Cabin* (1852), Cassy "play[s] hide and seek, under the orange trees, with [her] brothers and sisters."[33] In *Clotelle; or, the Colored Heroine: A Tale of the Southern States* (1867), William Wells Brown places his heroine amidst "rustling citron, lime, and orange, shady mango with its fruits of gold."[34] These effulgent heroines flourish within the protected garden of their childhood.[35] But when they reach adulthood and become the property of perverse white masters, this innocence is threatened or destroyed.

Adapting this Edenic imagery to scientific times, Progressive-era writers affirmed the successful self-management of the mixed-race woman. In Frances E. W. Harper's *Iola Leroy* (1892), the eponymous heroine experiences the "glad fruition of her hopes" and achieves the "calm loveliness of her ripened womanhood" thanks to her chastity and her temperance.[36] In Charlotte Perkins

Gilman's *Herland* (1915), the multihued denizens of this feminine utopia, vegetarians all, resemble the perfect fruits that they raise in their orchards: "Peaches! . . . Peacherinos—Apricot-nectarines! Whew!"[37] Though the male explorers would like to sample them, the women curb their appetites, reminding them that "mating" is for reproduction, not pleasure (124–25).[38] When one of the adventurers insists on his sexual prerogative, he uses racial subordination to excuse it, quoting Kipling: "I've taken my fun where I found it / I've rogued and I've ranged in my time, and / The things that I learned from the yellow and the black, / They 'ave helped me a 'eap with the white" (129). This marauding imperialist with his taste for the exotic is ultimately exiled from Herland's Eden. In these fictions, dietary and erotic restraint signal the virtue of the exemplary mulatta, holding fast against the tragedies that consumed her forebears.

In a grotesque afterlife of both of these strains—the mulatta as fruit and as dieter—the light-skinned daughter Peola in Fannie Hurst's *Imitation of Life* (1933) is repeatedly compared to a banana. This metaphor does not evoke lush tropicality, like the golden fruits of abolitionist fiction, but colorlessness and rigidity: "[her] pallor, the color of a pealed banana, lay over slim Caucasian features"; "now here was Peola, straight as a blade, her banana-colored pallor standing out."[39] In the denouement of the novel, Peola rejects her fat, dark-skinned mother, Delilah, who serves as the Aunt-Jemima-like trademark for a candy company and restaurant chain.[40] In this scene, the banana simile reaches its uncanny apotheosis as "the face of her child" becomes a hardened surface: "Rigid-eyed, it swung, the banana-colored mask, this way and that, away from the wetness" (242). Instead of a tempting, delicate fruit, the mulatta is now a surface that repels corporeality and sentiment, the abject "wetness" attributed to black womanhood. Peola experiences "a veritable nausea of revulsion" when she touches her mother's body (242).

Like the Progressive era mulatta, Peola models dietary and erotic abstention. As a child, she follows a science diet prescribed for the white girl with whom she is raised. As an adult, she passes over the color-line and undergoes sterilization so that she can wed her white fiancé with no fear of producing dark-skinned children: "There are millions to populate the world besides me. There is no shame in being sterilized in the name of the happiness of another" (247). Unlike Harper and Gilman, who endorse their heroines' self-control, Hurst undercuts Peola's project to restrict and refine the body through the pathos of Delilah's maternal grief. If both abolitionist and Progressive-era fiction use the fruit trope to project a better future for the mixed-race woman, then *Imitation of Life* reverses its tone and trajectory, following her into extinction.[41]

These contradictory but imbricated literary antecedents—the mulatta as a paradisiacal fruit or dangerous botanical experiment, filled with virtue or lacking sentiment—set the stage for Schuyler's light-skinned heroine, Patricia

Givens. Like Peola, Patricia resembles a "pale Indian" and wears a "cute modernistic hat" (40).[42] Like Philippa Schuyler, who was known as "Phil," Patricia goes by "Pat," a parallel that supports my reading of Patricia as significantly, though understatedly, of mixed race.[43] As Cherene Sherrard-Johnson observes, "Many illustrations, paintings, and photographs in New Negro periodicals chose identifiably mixed-race women to represent the positive and dignified face of the New Negro woman."[44] Schuyler invented Pat to appeal to magazine audiences; the *Courier* managing editor, W. G. Nunn, thought the serial would garner more women readers if protagonist Carl Slater had a love interest.[45] An uplift icon, Pat directs the Black Internationale's air force, manufacturing and flying planes (43).

From Carl's perspective, Pat is an ideal specimen of feminine beauty, "perfectly proportioned" and "absolutely symmetrical" (40). Though these descriptors make her sound a bit mechanical, they recall the eugenic claims that proportion and symmetry denoted racial superiority.[46] Her physiognomy reflects the balance of nature: "large, wide-spaced eyes like limpid pools under the moonlight on a tropic plain" (40). Dr. Belsidus, the charismatic leader of the Black Internationale, introduces Carl to Pat. Her physical superiority compels Carl's attention; she "out-rank[s]" all others and "seemed more desirable to me than any woman I had ever seen" (41). Her enrapturing beauty, especially as Belsidus's proud accomplice, introduces a sinister note to their meeting. She "reveal[s] two rows of glistening, white, even teeth in an infectious smile," and her eyes are "hypnotic orbs" (40). The mixed-race woman threatens the agency and autonomy of the modern man through her strong effect on his body.

Schuyler echoes "Rappaccini's Daughter" in his characterization of Pat as a potential tool of Belsidus's desired world domination. In Hawthorne's story, Giovanni, Beatrice's would-be lover, marvels at her "expression of simplicity and sweetness" (193); in *The Black Internationale*, Carl calls Pat's "expression . . . one of unbelievable innocence and sweetness" (40). Both women seem otherworldly, Beatrice like "one of those beings of old classic fable, that lives upon sweet odors" ("Rappaccini's Daughter," 193) and Pat "a flimsy pink fairy out of the ages of folk imagination" (*Black Internationale*, 51). Meeting these women in garden settings, the narrators use floral metaphors for their beauty. Beatrice is "another flower, the human sister of these vegetable ones, as beautiful as they, more beautiful than the richest of them" ("Rappaccini's Daughter," 190), and Pat is an "exotic, shimmering flower" (*Black Internationale*, 51). Though they seem timeless, enchanted, and natural, these women turn out to be the tools of power-hungry scientists. Giovanni is disturbed by "strange fantasies in reference to Doctor Rappaccini and the beautiful Beatrice" ("Rappaccini's Daughter,"193), and "the contrast between [Pat] and the sinister physician [Dr. Belsidus] . . . startled [Carl]" (*Black Internationale*, 40). The beautiful woman is merely a screen for the ruthless man.

The artificial environments where Beatrice and Pat flourish reflect the scientists' ambitions for God-like control. Both narratives make the connection between these microcosmic empires and the mixed-race woman explicit.[47] Observing the doctor's garden, Giovanni hears Beatrice's "voice as rich as a tropical sunset . . . which made Giovanni, though he knew not why, think of deep hues of purple or crimson, and of perfumes heavily delectable" ("Rappaccini's Daughter," 190). Surveying the underground farms, "to see better this remarkable sight destined to revolutionize truck gardening," Carl "confronted Pat gorgeously arrayed in flowing pink negligee" (*Black Internationale*, 51). The man's visual command of the terrain is undercut by the allure of the other senses, particularly the sense of smell: "there was a fragrance in the atmosphere around [Beatrice], rich and delightful . . . which the young man . . . scarcely dared to draw into his lungs" ("Rappaccini's Daughter," 199), and "the faint scent of gardenia came from [Pat's] rich robes and luxuriously titillated [Carl's] nostrils" (*Black Internationale*, 51).[48] Where reason might lead Giovanni or Carl to reject the doctors' hubristic schemes, the seductive woman overcomes his defenses and enlists him as a reluctant participant.

In both "Rappaccini's Daughter" and *The Black Internationale*, this iconic woman is crucially untouchable, resisting the entreating suitor's embrace. This imposed separation redoubles the intensity of masculine passion; Giovanni "burn[s]" and "shiver[s]" with "love and horror" ("Rappaccini's Daughter," 195), and Carl is "unable to restrain [himself]" because he "feels it overpoweringly" (*Black Internationale*, 51). At the same time that the woman's body is most obviously objectified, she achieves a numinous power. In *Second Skin*, Anne Anlin Cheng proposes that "the confusion between the artificial and the organic, between life and death" generates a "figure that stands resistant to" the "history of the black female body" as flesh inscribed through torture.[49] She speculates provocatively, "Could it be that the woman-as-fruit is pleasurable both because she/it can be consumed *and* because she/it cannot be eaten, a strange fruit? . . . commodified, yes, but also strangely unconsumable."[50] This figure of the unconsumable fruit reflects back on the tragic mulatta tradition, which treated desecration and corruption as the inevitable consequences of ripening. This is where Hawthorne and Schuyler part ways. Beatrice cannot be eaten, because she is toxic; indeed, she must opt for her own self-annihilation in the name of a healthful future. By contrast, Schuyler imbues Pat with the vitality of the red fruits, strawberries and tomatoes, grown in the hydroponic gardens. The shifting surface of her skin both evidences the flow of her passion and seals it off: "the flush deepened in her cheeks" (51); "her cheeks turned a dull red. It made my pulse leap" (52); "a dark flush [rose] under her clear skin" (55). For once, the mulatta's color reflects her present pleasure rather than guarantees her future pain. Here the association between the mixed-race woman and the juice-filled fruit underscores not her pornotropic availability but her "*sealedness*," to borrow Cheng's apt neologism.[51]

As the plot unfolds, this erotic immanence gives way to ideological sublimation in the mode of *Iola Leroy* and *Herland*. Pat restrains her desires in order to pursue her cause: "she wrapped her negligee closer around her. 'I'm so sorry, Carl,' she murmured, suppressing her emotion with difficulty. 'We mustn't speak of such things. There's too much to be done'" (51–52). Carl must also learn to redirect his hunger and passion to their mission. After carrying out Dr. Belsidus's plans, the two finally embrace and become engaged, and Carl admits, "Busy as I've been in this tremendous undertaking, I've been terribly lonely for you. Just starved" (116). Pat has harnessed his individual appetites to the larger goal of racial advancement, and marriage cements this agenda.

In *The Black Internationale*, the mulatta is *both* a sign of nature and a sign of culture. She is both the gardenia and the perfume of the gardenia, both succulent strawberry and hydroponic farmer. And, notably, she is also eater and eaten; Patricia's "strong white teeth" uncannily anticipate the narrator's later brush with cannibals, yet Slater also "feast[s]" upon her loveliness (51). This ambivalence about the mulatta's relative agency (is she emblem or actor?), modernity (is she archetype or prototype?), and consumability (is she the fruit or the teeth?) characterizes the representation of women and technology in the modern period more broadly, as Rita Felski argues in *The Gender of Modernity*.[52] Industrialization and technology could at once de-essentialize gender categories and simultaneously reassert a patriarchal fantasy of reproductive control and feminine obedience. Racialization heightens this ambiguity between agency and objecthood, sexuality and breeding. The mixed-race woman serves as the eugenic pinnacle of aspirational hybridity at the same time that she threatens the coherence of racial categorization through her own liminality. This tension animates the biotechnological fantasies of *Black Internationale* and its botanical eroticism. Its sequel, *The Black Empire*, by contrast, does all it can to dismiss this paradox and domesticate the woman who serves as its embodiment. In so doing, it shifts the center of gravity from the hydroponic farm to the model kitchen.

Betty Crocker and the Cannibal Woman: Domesticating the Modern Mulatta

Black Empire plays out a gendered romance common in popular nutrition: masculine strength supported by feminine purity.[53] This patriarchal dynamic requires the restoration of man's primitive vigor and the preservation of woman's all too fragile purity. These gendered prescriptions appear in the dietary tracts of Bernarr Macfadden, the muscled proponent of what he called "physical culture," an exercise and dietary regimen designed to ward off modern degeneration.[54] Macfadden claimed that "the body should be looked upon as a machine" and that fasting could "purify the blood" to reset the system for good health.[55] Poisons stealthily infiltrate most people's bodies: "As a rule there are foreign elements or poisons which are seeking an outlet, lurking in the circulation" (273). To illustrate this phenomenon, Macfadden offers the telling examples of one woman who tries to cover up a pimple, not realizing that the defect comes from deep within, and another who "could not rise from her bed" because she has succumbed to "over-feeding" (274). As an antidote to these feminine pathologies and impurities, Macfadden proposes raw food: "I am a great believer in what I would term natural foods—foods used just as they come from nature. Foods that have not changed by contact with fire supply more vitality; they possess a greater proportion of health-building qualities" (275). Implicitly, the kitchen fire, associated with women, saps the vitality of overcivilized men.

At the same time, women could not be cast out of the nutritional project altogether, because this renovation of modern diet is also a recuperation of racial strength. In *Womanhood and Marriage* (1918), Macfadden declares that woman is "the mother of the race, and in this function we shall find embodied her supreme power."[56] The vital and virtuous woman "nourishes and sustains" not merely "the body of her offspring" but "all with whom she comes into contact" (360). In cultivating this strength and purity, "the matter of diet is of the greatest importance." Macfadden recommends that women shun the stimulation of red meat, alcohol, tea, coffee, hot sauces, and condiments and stick to "fruits, green salads, nuts and so forth" (261).[57] *Beauty and Health*, the physical culture magazine for women, depicted this feminine ideal in an article called "Race Suicide": "As cheerful and wholesome a little woman as ever was . . . had gone through the dinner eating nothing but olives and radishes and lettuce and nuts and fruits. Raw food only!"[58] This diet counters the titular threat of "race suicide" by guaranteeing the health of "her children [who] would inevitably partake of her improved health" (229). Given fewer and more vital children, the woman would no longer be a "slave" to multiple births, now "absolute mistress of her own body" (229). In a surprising turn of logic, women's dietary restraint allows for her sexual self-governance; birth control among the elites, the traditional target of predictions of race suicide, could be perfectly acceptable if women would only eat raw foods and make stronger babies.

Macfadden's nutritional ideals were surprisingly portable across the color line, given their implicit and explicit valorization of whiteness.[59] The Schuylers adapted his precepts to support black and mixed-race vigor, and this achievement of racial health depended upon strong, traditional gender roles. In the 1930s, popular eugenics viewed science as the vehicle for the recuperation "of a more perfect past . . . [a] golden age or paradise . . . [when] men were strong and virile, while women breast-fed babies and raised manly sons."[60] As we will see in Schuyler's science fiction, this technological return to a paradisiacal primitivism was perhaps even more appealing to black readers because it could undo the injuries of slavery. As Ytasha Womack explains in her work on Afrofuturism, "Slavery is neither the utopian future nor an ancient far-removed past."[61] Even the gender subordination that characterizes the Schuylers' dietary views and the African utopia in Black Empire seems a radical rejoinder to the institution of slavery, which denied legal standing to slave marriages and stripped gender from reproductive bodies.[62]

Like Macfadden, George S. Schuyler offered himself as a model of healthful masculinity.[63] In one 1930 Pittsburgh Courier column, he proclaimed that "given an absolutely healthy body and a varied and uncooked diet, one can wave the gentleman of the medical fraternity a fond farewell . . . It happens that I haven't had a physician since 1913."[64] To counter the ill effects of occasional indulgences, Schuyler recommends "periodical fastings of 24 or 36 hours," one of Macfadden's favored remedies.[65] The association between natural men and raw foods exalts masculine ideals of hardness and wholeness. Schuyler laments the permeability of the human body: "Most people's diet, in so far as they have any, is actually injurious to the body in that it sets up poisons that break down the resistance of the organism to the onslaughts of the myriad of animal and vegetable organisms (germs, microbes, or what have you) that infest our food, our water, and the very air we breathe."[66] The language that Schuyler uses to describe this inundated body recalls contemporaneous debates about immigration and racial combinations, "the onslaughts of the myriad." Though Schuyler has often been heralded for his rejection of racial biologism, it might be more accurate to say that he saw the body as mutable and manipulable. This lability, in his view, strained the coherence of racial category but could nonetheless be engineered to achieve new pinnacles of health and vitality.[67] Planned breeding and scientific eating could guarantee such progress.[68]

Josephine Schuyler took these racial goals to heart, and she cast them as the special purview of wives and mothers. She published articles in black press magazines like the Messenger and the Crisis exhorting women to improve their culinary and nutritional practices. In an article called "Death and Diet," which she signed with her pseudonym, "Heba Jannath," perhaps to disguise her race, Schuyler warned women about the effects of cooked food on their beauty and health: "if you want to feel and look well, if you dislike being a walking corpse; if you wish to prevent your vital organs from literally rotting away inside you, dispense as much as possible with your cookstove."[69] Not only could the wrong diet turn the modern woman into the walking dead, it could doom her children. In a 1934 Crisis article entitled "The Slaughter of the Innocents," Schuyler called upon "the cooks of Aframerica, the women, to start this revolution in diet which will keep their children from incurring an even worse fate than chattel slavery."[70] In both cases, dietary choice distinguishes subject from object, human being from corpse or slave. The dutiful woman must constantly defend her family against degeneration and death. The emancipatory project of racial uplift is threatened by nutritional ignorance.

The gender politics of the Schuylers' dietary advice shapes the didactic narrative in *Black Empire*. Where Pat is mysterious, even auratic in *The Black Internationale*, in *Black Empire* she is a married woman, a future mother of the race who must unlearn bad habits to renovate Africanism. Dr. Andrew Matson, the surgeon general of the new Black Internationale settlement in Liberia, admonishes Pat for her enthusiasm for "pork chops" (153): "The marvelous physique of the Africans where they have not come into contact with white people is due largely to their superior nutrition. Even where and when they cooked their food, it was fresh food, not preserved food" (156). Here, Patricia's light skin seems an emblem of her regrettable "contact with white people." Industrially refined foods—"flour, rice, hominy and white sugar"—are "outlawed" (152), and white people have set a deleterious dietary model: "We in the Western world have been reared on dead food, embalmed food." By contrast, before colonialism, Africans ate "fresh food, not preserved food" (156). Matson's monologue implies that the white race is "dead" and "embalmed," while Africans are "fresh" and vital.[71] By returning to Africa, Patricia can relearn the salubrious cuisine that is her birthright.

In spite of this purported rejection of Western food, the model diet kitchen that Pat and Carl visit in Liberia resembles the test kitchens sponsored by major US food corporations, including General Mills, General Electric, Campbell's Soup, and Heinz. Home economists tested recipes in these highly publicized, state-of-the-art kitchens, and some offered tours.[72] These kitchens featured gas ranges and mechanical refrigeration, and their appliances, and often their appointments, were glossy white.[73] The white kitchen—hygienic, modernist, futuristic—became a "vogue" in the 1920s and 1930s, culminating in the laboratory-like "Kitchen of Tomorrow" at the 1939 World's Fair.[74] Each of the dominating aesthetic notes of the model kitchen—white, bright, electrical, and cold—fetishizes cleanliness, light, and clinicism, eschewing dirt, darkness, waste, and pathogens.[75] Schuyler retains this aesthetic in his "model diet kitchen," which features "a number of electrical appliances," including "glass cases with coils of frost pipes inside, keeping the great pans of prepared food chilled." Though their skin is dark, unlike the white home economists featured in food companies' publicity photos, the "dietitians" wear "spotless white" (153). Schuyler underscores the hygiene and technology of the model kitchen, not its exoticism or primitivism.

The labor division in the model kitchen reinforces traditional gender roles. Men work with the raw meat, as none of the food is cooked, while women marinate fish and decorate layer cakes made from nuts, raisins, and whole wheat flour. With these cakes, Schuyler recuperates Betty Crocker–style domesticity in spite of his rejection of white flour. As the food historian Laura Shapiro observes, "Few products emerging from the American kitchen have the sentimental heft of the classic frosted layer cake, universally recognized as a triumph of love as much as skill."[76] The dietitian takes pride in her decorative work: "Then whipped cream was spread on top and the girl deftly placed halves of large sliced strawberries in an attractive design. She bore the cake away proudly to the pantry in the rear" (155). Those giant strawberries from *The Black Internationale* have been reduced to the tame decorations on a layer cake, reflecting Patricia's trajectory from glamour girl to housewife.

Accordingly, Patricia's dialogue now sounds as though she is the housewife in an advertisement for a home refrigerator: "'But, Doctor,' said my wife, 'how are you going to keep food without canning it or something?'" (156). Dr. Matson takes Pat and Carl to a basement warehouse where "a profusion of . . . fruits, vegetables, and meats" are "kept fresh indefinitely" by "quickly freezing food seventy-five or one hundred degrees below zero." Home refrigeration and quick-freezing technologies, newly available in the 1930s, supported dreams of purity and futurity.[77] Surveying the freezer room, Dr. Matson connects their food stores with racial futures: "We're building for centuries here, Slater" (156). The serial's radical vision of black nationalism is supported by domestic subordination and heteronormative futurism.

In *The Black Internationale*, hydroponic produce, multicourse meals, and fine wines tantalize the senses. "A dark red, fiery liquor" intoxicates Carl and Pat and "looses primeval urges born in the Mesozoic ooze" (62). In *Black Empire*, this "ooze" is replaced—or perhaps merely covered up—by "figured linoleum" and "white enamel," the shining surfaces of hard modernity (153–54). Though Schuyler seems to endorse the model diet kitchen, reproducing his wife's recipes in some of the descriptions, he troubles this gleaming fantasy with its dark double. Patricia and Carl crash their airplane in a remote village, and in an allegorical collision of the modern and the primitive, their plane "demolishe[s] the front" of "the palaver kitchen, a large, thatched, bandstand-like structure, the pride of the village" (230). They are surrounded by cannibals, "angry brown men, naked except for breech cloths . . . their teeth filed to sharp points" (232). Carl fears that they will be "rended limb from limb with those horrible teeth" (232). Though this encounter is nightmarish, it also restores the fury, fire, and carnal intimacy stripped away by the cold rationalism of the science kitchen.

In the model kitchen, Pat is the genteel practitioner of culinary arts and nutritional sciences. In the tribal one, outside the safety of civilization, her body is raw meat, the object of desire. This passivity may be overdetermined, however.

In her discussion of women and cannibalism, Maggie Kilgour observes that "the category of the other has to be denied autonomy lest it turn into a cannibal, and so it must be represented as secondary, dependent—and ultimately food."[78] This translation of the overwhelming female body into a manageable meal exposes the submerged threat of feminine appetite. When Dr. Belsidus, the head of the Black Internationale, explains to Carl why he will not marry—though "[Pat]'s the sort of girl I'd like to marry if I was the marrying sort"—he describes women as devouring spiders: "'A woman,' he proceeded, warming to the subject, 'invariably tries to devour her mate as does the female spider'" (134–35). This threat takes on racial as well as gendered overtones: "in the process the man loses much of his individuality and takes on some of the color and characteristics of his wife" (135). By erecting his global empire, Belsidus restores dominant masculinity and black authenticity, overthrowing the genteel femininity and pale imitativeness of the mulatta.

In the cannibal village, however, the devouring woman returns. When the ceremonial pyre is prepared and "palm oil had been poured over the faggots," "a native woman . . . run[s] up with a blazing torch" (234). Moments later, the Black Internationale's air force drops tear gas on the assembled natives and parachutes in "with uncanny accuracy that attested to long training" (236). It is significant, given Pat's role as the head of the air force, that all of the soldiers who arrive are men. Masculine discipline and expertise quell the cannibal woman and her "blazing torch." Though she makes only a brief appearance, I read this "native woman" as a representation of Patricia's repressed rapacity, a doppelgänger that resists the Betty Crocker-ization of the modern mulatta. The science kitchen and the conquering air force both evidence the black race's imperial dominance— the title of the serial is *Black Empire*, after all—but the native woman threatens, like Bertha Rochester, to set that edifice afire. Though she fails, she vexes the bland superiority of modernity.

In the transition from *The Black Internationale* to *Black Empire*, Schuyler effectively strips Patricia of her many appetites—for violence and adventure, for meat, even for Carl.[79] As Ann duCille argues in *The Coupling Convention*, "Sexual desire is not *displaced* by social purpose but *encoded* in it—regulated, submerged, and insinuated into the much safer realm of political zeal and the valorized venue of holy wedlock."[80] The same could be said of literary dietetics; the pleasures of eating are sublimated into the satisfactions of eating correctly, at least for women, and that is supposed to be enough. In the concluding installments of the serial, Patricia convalesces, while Carl becomes a trusted adviser in Belsidus's new government.[81] They adopt conventional gender roles, Patricia preparing breakfast and Carl rushing to work: "I hurriedly performed my morning ablutions, threw on my uniform, swallowed a glass of orange juice, and, kissing Pat goodbye, dashed out of the house, and over to the capitol building" (247). The thrill of hydroponic innovation is now replaced by the routine glass of orange juice.[82]

At the same time, perhaps this minor detail signals the achievement of Dr. Matson's nutritional ambitions for the new empire. In "Death and Diet," Josephine Schuyler cited orange juice as a sign of the popularization of raw foods: "The world is coming around to it gradually. Orange juice can be bought on the street corners where five years ago only soda pop was sold."[83] In her view, daily habits renovate racial health, which in turn enhances masculine power. Suggestively, when Carl arrives at the capitol building, he spies Dr. Belsidus, the black übermensch, "a deadly calm and assurance about him . . . He sipped a tall glass of chilled orange juice" (247). In this conclusion, gender hierarchy consolidates racial identity, as black masculinity trumps the indeterminacy of mulatta glamour. Schuyler makes the modern mulatta over into the New Negro helpmeet, her dietary knowledge critical for the maintenance of masculine strength and the reproduction of racial futures.

As Nearly Perfect as Science Can Make Her: Philippa Schuyler the Child Prodigy

Black Empire does not follow Carl and Pat into parenthood, but the Schuyler family papers, maintained scrupulously by Josephine to document their daughter's accomplishments, reveal a good deal about the manipulation of the physical body in the pursuit of a utopian ideal. For example, Macfadden championed milk as an ideal food: "Milk is the greatest of all diet cures. It is already scientifically combined. When you are furnished with this delectable fluid you need not bother about other nourishment."[84] Modern milk harbored contradictory associations: mother's milk and baby's bottle, pastoral cow and hygienic factory.[85] Josephine Schuyler embraced the cult of dairy, but she feared the diminishment of milk's nutritional value through industrial processing. In a 1937 letter, the Walker-Gordon dairy company apologizes to Schuyler, evidently in response to a complaint, for the "discontinuance of their 20% cream." The PR person compliments Mrs. Schuyler on her "remarkable daughter" and makes an odd and revealing comment: "we are indeed grateful to have an opportunity to share in the development of this child."[86] Philippa sounds like a clinical experiment, built by the company's milk. In closing, he invites the mother and daughter for a factory tour.

A good deal of nutritional advice, then and now, blamed industrialization for modern society's ills. The dentist Weston Price influentially argued that refined flours and sugars contributed to tooth decay and declining health. His book, *Nutrition and Physical Degeneration* (1939), featured photo galleries of tribal peoples from all over the world, their white teeth attesting to health and vigor: "tooth decay is not only unnecessary, but an indication of our divergence from Nature's fundamental laws of life and health."[87] Price insisted that degeneration came from nutrition, not racial intermixture as many claimed: "certain preconceived ideas may have to be modified, as for example, that based on the belief that what we see is due to heredity or that deformity is due to mixing of the races."[88] Tellingly, Price endorsed Philippa Schuyler's raw foods diet, calling it "as nearly perfect as science can make it these days."[89]

Scientism and primitivism further the same goal in Schuyler's science fiction serials and Philippa's childhood celebrity: preserving purity against incursions from the outside world, a quest entangled with feminine ideals. For Patricia to stay pure in *The Black Internationale*, she must remain virginal, fruit on the vine; for her to maintain this purity in *Black Empire*, she must be domesticated, cake in the kitchen. As a child celebrity, Philippa performs both childhood innocence and feminine domesticity, as her magazine coverage on both sides of the color line demonstrates. Celebrity emerges at the intersection of cultural narrative and embodied performance. Both Sherrard-Johnson and Spillers emphasize that the "mulatta" is a trope rather than a person, a convention rather than a lived experience.[90] This convention, I suggest, shapes how Philippa Schuyler was understood and represented, as did the role of the child prodigy.

Both roles reflect an exceptionalism often used to support biological racism: the child prodigy shows up the general incapacity of her race; the mulatto demonstrates the superiority of Anglo-Saxon blood.[91] By the same token, the beautiful and bright child could be conscripted to demonstrate the falsehood of racial stereotype and degeneration narratives. The *Crisis* children's issue, for example, featured photographs of cherubic children with a range of skin colors. Though many doubtless viewed this photo spread as a testament to racial health in terms of heredity, Josephine Schuyler penned an article entitled "The Slaughter of the Innocents" for one children's issue that insisted upon the preeminence of nutrition: "racial differences are now generally believed to be largely due to food differences" (295). In support of this contention, she cites the "vigor" of "the Masai people in Africa who live chiefly on a diet of meat and milk" and the Japanese, who are "notoriously small and slender, [because they] live on a diet containing no milk and little meat" (295). Furthermore, she suggests that, as their bodies are particularly susceptible to dietary change, children can be the vehicle for immediate racial transformation: "With slightly more Vitamin A in their diet [Japanese American children] are both taller and heavier ... Even the characteristically small, slant eyes are altered" (295). In Schuyler's view, children are remarkable for their anatomical elasticity, which allows them to achieve utopian embodiment with the right nourishment.

Following this logic, Schuyler describes her daughter as a form of technology. In a 1940 letter to the skeptical editor of the *Sunday School Informer*, defending her choice to take her prodigious daughter on concert tours, Josephine put it bluntly: "we've always contended that we built Philippa to be superior."[92] Nutrition makes the superior child: "That is the way we built Philippa's mentality. I dieted for three years before, all during pregnancy and then I nursed her for thirteen months during which time my food was scientifically prepared" (8). Schuyler concludes that "children could all be superior if they had the proper nutrition before birth and after" (8). This endorsement of nutrition flies in the face of contemporaneous accounts of the gifted child as the static outcome of immutable heredity. Racial superiority is readily available to all black people, Schuyler contends, who can "with knowledge, and no more money . . . increase [their] health and beauty and brains" (8). The nutritional future of Josephine's imaginings sounds a good bit like the utopian science fiction that her husband had published so recently.

Philippa's background clearly deviates from the tragic mulatta convention, which typically describes the offspring of an enslaved mother and a white father. Schuyler emphasizes her deliberation in choosing a "healthy" mate, dieting, breastfeeding, and planning a scientific menu (8). Philippa is the intended and well-tended fruit of racial intermixture: "she had a wonderful physical start" (8). "To build a superior race of humans," Schuyler allies herself with "the Negro," who in spite of his past and present mistreatment, has "had a better start here physically than the European" because of "the natural selection which during slavery times, weeded out all the weaklings among Negroes" (8). Recasting slavery as an evolutionary asset, Schuyler nominates herself to further the black racial future by preaching "proper nutrition," which would make the black man "markedly superior" (8). The mixed-race child is the exemplar of the superiority that this collaboration makes possible, "not a prodigy in the popular sense of the word, but . . . a genius according to her I.Q., E.Q., and all the other 'Q's they record by" (7). Schuyler describes Philippa in terms of her component parts and efficiency: "her cells are all built by vitalized food so that they are stronger, and she functions more rapidly than average children" (8). Philippa's carefully constructed and protected vitality points the way to a stronger future.

In each of these fantasies of a mixed-race future—*The Black Internationale*, *Black Empire*, and Josephine's nutritional advice—the dark-skinned woman is either overlooked or Gothicized, as in the case of the cannibal woman who charges Carl and Pat. Black femininity, a category that betrays "the surplus corporeality of racialized and gendered subjects" in Lauren Berlant's words, is consistently displaced by light-skinned or mixed-race icons. Berlant argues that the mulatta is "the paradigmatic problem citizen . . . imprisoned in the surplus embodiment of a culture that values abstraction." She trenchantly observes, "Sometimes a person doesn't want to seek the dignity of an always already violated body and wants to cast hers off, either for nothingness or in a trade for some other, better model."[93] Nutrition science provided a fantasy of this better model, dietary restriction curbing corporeal excess.

Not all readers were convinced by the Schuylers' claims that diet made genius and transmuted race. Lena Morrow Lewis, a socialist activist and journalist, sent an indignant letter to the *New Yorker* after it ran a profile of Philippa that emphasized her parents' nutritional theories:

> Dear Sir; There is no question that food plays an important part in the life of Philippa Duke Schuyler, whose activities and accomplishments Joseph Mitchell so vividly portrayed in your issue of August 31st. However, we hardly think uncooked green peas and raw meat would have made a genius of "Topsy, who jest growed up."[94]

Lewis refuses to believe that refined Philippa could have become a prodigy with only the help of a scientific diet. The body and mind of a black Topsy could not be improved, in Lewis's view, by forces as feeble as "uncooked green peas and raw meat." Lewis sets up a divide between the mixed-race child who can be cultivated and the black child who remains impervious to training. She means to give credit to Philippa's parents, with whom she may have been personally acquainted.[95] The thrust of her letter is that their tutelage mattered more than mere roughage: "if the facts were all known it would probably be found that Jody and George had very much to do in the planning and directing of Philippa's life from long before her birth and through her eventful nine years." Nonetheless, her allusion to Topsy betrays racial condescension and, indeed, white anxiety that these hereditary categories might not hold. The rigor of training affirms a Eurocentric worldview in a way that the vigor of raw foods does not.

This tension between nature and nurture exposes the vexed status of the black or mixed-race child prodigy.[96] In 1939, Philippa was featured in a photo in the *New York Amsterdam News* dressed as Mozart, perhaps the prototypical child prodigy.[97] Eighteenth-century child prodigies like the poet Phillis Wheatley and the musician George Bridgetower "generated more interest for [their] assumed exceptionality from [their] race than for [their] actual exceptionality from [their] age group."[98] Resisting this imputation of exceptionalism, Josephine Schuyler insisted that "Philippa is not a genius . . . Or a prodigy or anything like that. It's just taking pains and keeping her well. We feed her on a protective diet."[99] At the same time, she collected clippings about child prodigies, clearly numbering her child among this elite.[100] Schuyler thought her child's remarkable abilities pointed the way to producing superior bodies and minds, a method that she propounded to African American readers. The child prodigy could thus be imagined as the generational goal rather than the individual exception.

Nonetheless, the press took up Philippa's example in ways that reflected their ideological and racial tenor. A 1936 *Time* magazine article entitled "Harlem Prodigy" reports that Philippa can play Mozart with "facility" but plays "best" when the subject matter is "Nigerian."[101] The profile emphasizes Philippa's black associations as the "*Harlem-born* daughter of a white mother and *coal-black* father" (emphasis mine) and George Schuyler's working-class origins, "a day laborer and a dishwasher before he became a novelist." The accomplishments of both father and daughter seem to exceed *Time*'s racial expectations. The profile makes perfunctory and skeptical mention of Philippa's diet: "all three Schuylers subsist on raw vegetables, raw meat, a diet which Mrs. Schuyler claims is largely responsible for her daughter's precocity." The Schuylers seem oddities both in their exception from the racial norms of their day and because they are able to "subsist" on such unlikely fare. In this article, the label "prodigy" isolates Philippa's accomplishments, making them an apparent fluke. In a 1939 profile in the *New Amsterdam News*, by contrast, Philippa's achievements are crucially applicable to the problem of race relations: "Interracial Marriage in America Is Workable—Here's Positive Proof: Harlem Family Radical in Views on Races and Food."[102] In the black press, the Schuyler family seems an example to emulate. In her *New Amsterdam News* column for women, a recurring feature called "In the Woman's World," Thelma Berlack-Boozer even gives a rundown of Philippa's daily diet, perhaps as a menu for solicitous African American mothers.[103]

The word "prodigy" is something of a paradox, meaning both "an anomaly; something abnormal and unnatural" and also "a wonderful or outstanding example."[104] This tension between the aberrant and the exemplary also characterizes the reception of Philippa's diet. In "Harlem's Child Prodigy," a profile of Philippa that ran in *Silhouette*, a black press photo magazine, diet numbers among the girl's accomplishments: "she also has the added distinction of never having eaten cooked food."[105] Even the black press, however, registers some uneasiness with the child's regimen. Berlack-Boozer praises the family's diet of "fresh fruits, fresh vegetables [and] . . . fresh nuts" but "hasten[s] to explain" to her black press readers that in spite of the apparent barbarism of raw meat, "by the time that raw beef is seasoned with peppers, onions, and oils, it looks 'civilized' on its bed of lettuce leaves."[106] If even the *New Amsterdam News* wondered how "civilized" the Schuylers were as they devoured raw meat, it seems little wonder that *Time* magazine, which imagined its readership as primarily white, stressed this sanguinary habit in its 1940 follow-up on Philippa: "the Schuylers now broil their meat lightly, instead of eating the raw, bloody, buttered beef and liver they used to."[107] One suspects that this orgy of adjectives—"raw, bloody, buttered"—left readers more queasy than comforted.

As these examples evidence, Philippa's dietary regimen became entangled with racial imaginaries in her periodical coverage. Claude Lévi-Strauss famously defines the symbolic divide between wildness and civilization as the "raw" and the "cooked."[108] Roland Barthes further proposed that rawness ("crudité") both promised purity and betrayed barbarism.[109] These French theories of the raw participate in the colonial tradition that subtly (and not so subtly) shapes Philippa's reception. At the same time, by decoupling these terms from white and black, Lévi-Strauss and Barthes demonstrate the dynamism of this binary, its shifting relationship to racial categories, cultural aspirations, and the cult of nature. Black press periodicals and mainstream magazines (with presumptively white if not actually white readers and majority-white reporters and editors) telegraph their understanding of race, embodiment, and achievement through their representation of Philippa and food. Sometimes, particularly in the white press, they conflate the two. *Newsweek* quipped that hers was "Genius in the Raw."[110]

Periodicals on both sides of the color line associated young Philippa with nature. The black press photo magazine *Flash!* printed a shot of naked Philippa, framed by underbrush, wearing a turban and clutching a bundle of stalks. The caption calls her a "wonder child."[111] A *New York Herald Tribune* profile features a similar image, perhaps from the same photo shoot, of the nude toddler wearing flowers on her head, surrounded by branches.[112] Josephine tells the interviewer, Joseph Alsop, that Philippa eats "all raw foods. She gets her starches from bananas and all the fruit she wants." Between the photograph and this diet, three-year-old Philippa seems like an island native, Alsop the explorer or anthropologist who stumbles upon this virgin land and its denizens.[113] Alsop concludes his piece with a telling tableau, a still life with fruit featuring Philippa:

> Philippa... strolled across to the huge tray of fruit on the table. It seemed almost the largest thing in the tiny sitting room. Philippa chose a ripe fig, and took a healthy bite. "Say good by [sic], Philippa dear heart," said her mother. "Good by. Come again," said Philippa, and returned to her health-giving and protective fig.[114]

Even within this contained and civilized space, "the tiny sitting room," Alsop views the racialized child as a representative of cornucopic abundance and primitive purity. When Philippa bids him farewell and turns back to her fig, she seems to be dismissing modernity and its corrupting influences in favor of paradisiacal fruit.

There is some evidence that the Schuylers welcomed and even encouraged this association between their daughter and fresh fruit. A series of personal photographs from August 1938 in the family scrapbook features Philippa rolling a giant watermelon, sitting on it to play piano, and then eating it with friends. The melon was a birthday present from "Miss Georgia Crosthwaite of

Weatherford, Texas."[115] Crosthwaite, a white high school teacher, may have become one of Philippa's fans thanks to her coverage in the black press. In 1935, Crosthwaite called the magazine "my most reliable aid in my personal attempt to keep informed of the accomplishments of your race" in a letter to the editor of *Opportunity*.[116] *Opportunity* later profiled Philippa, noting that "child prodigies are rare ... and they are exceedingly rare when they are golden brown in color."[117] In spite of this rarity, the article insists that Philippa is "normal ... in every respect" and describes her raw foods regimen dispassionately: "uncooked foods, fruits, nuts, milk—these have been the mainstays of her diet." When Crosthwaite sent the child a giant watermelon, it is likely that she intended the gesture as an endorsement of the diet rather than an allusion to racial stereotype. At the same time, the goofy playfulness of the scrapbook's photo spread seems to poke fun of that well-known racist iconography. Clearly, the Schuylers were aware that their daughter played many roles in the public eye—some of them scripted by her parents and others imposed by the spectator.

Two major magazine features on Philippa from the early 1940s demonstrate the friction between the various racial and gender roles the child was conscripted to embody. The first, "Evening with a Gifted Child," appeared in an August 1940 issue of the *New Yorker*, a "Reporter at Large" installment written by Joseph Mitchell, who was lauded for his vivid portraits of quirky urbanites.[118] The article includes no photographs, though Mitchell offers detailed visual descriptions in his account of visiting the Schuylers and meeting Philippa. The second is not actually an article about Philippa. "Nutrition and Racial Superiority," Josephine Schuyler's manifesto about the value of raw foods for black families, appeared in the *Crisis* magazine in 1942. Though Philippa's name does not appear in the text, which offers impersonal prescription and nutritional authority rather than intimate memoir, it is illustrated with multiple photographs of Schuyler's famous daughter. Mitchell's dramatization of the mixed-race child prodigy as an insulated and isolated figure contrasts sharply with the tone of the *Crisis* spread, which uncritically presents Philippa's image as evidence of the essential soundness of Josephine's theories. Nonetheless, both articles, particularly in their representation of raw foods, intimate the double binds that Philippa finds herself in, at once iconic ideal and racialized body.

Unlike many articles pitched to white readers, which tended to use "Harlem" or "Negro" to refer to Philippa, the title of Mitchell's profile, "Evening with a Gifted Child," makes no allusion to her race. Nonetheless, like the term "child prodigy," the "gifted child" carries a fraught history of racial hierarchy. In *Hereditary Genius* (1870), Sir Francis Galton claimed that the child of "a parent exceptionally gifted in a high degree ... has an enormously greater chance of turning out to be gifted in a high degree."[119] With careful, planned breeding, such children could be the avatars of "a new race."[120] The term became a standard of educational theory in the 1920s, when eugenicist thinkers counted on the gifted child to bear out their theories of immutable and superior heredity.[121] In *The Measurement of Intelligence* (1916), Lewis Madison Terman, an early proponent of gifted classification, "predicts that when this is done there will be discovered enormously significant racial differences in general intelligence, differences which cannot be wiped out by any scheme of mental culture."[122] In *Mental and Physical Traits of a Thousand Gifted Children* (1926), Terman confirms his own prediction and concludes that most gifted children come from English, German, and Scotch stock.[123] He even measured the proportions of their heads because that method was "frequently used by anthropologists for determining race classifications."[124] The only two gifted "Negroes" identified by his study, Terman hastens to explain, "are both part white (exact proportion of white blood is not known)."[125] In Terman's view, the mixed-race child derives her intelligence from her white ancestry.

When the Schuylers insist to the *New Yorker* reporter that Philippa's ability "is explained not by genius but by diet," they may intend to refute such eugenic explanations for giftedness.[126] Nonetheless, when Mitchell mentions George Schuyler's "jet black skin" and identifies Josephine Schuyler as "white . . . a golden-haired blonde," he raises the question of heredity and interracialism that played such a major role in the era's studies of gifted children. Mitchell describes Philippa as if she were an anthropological specimen: "She is a graceful child, slender, erect, and exquisitely boned. Her face is oval, and she has serious black eyes, black curls, and perfect teeth" (30). This catalog of physical traits—grace, slenderness, good posture, fine bone structure, facial symmetry, and perfect teeth—recalls Terman's contention that the gifted child was both mentally and physically superior. At the same time, however, Mitchell associates this perfection with primitivism rather than whiteness. The Schuylers tell him about the numerous gifts their daughter receives from Africa and her pride in "her Negro blood" (30). This collection of artifacts, including a "female fetish," "sable skins and a black pearl," and "a doll from the Virgin Islands," reinforces the impression of Philippa as a kind of primitive artifact herself; when the child enters the room, Mitchell is examining "an ebony elephant" (30). He reinforces this impression of untouched premodernity by mentioning that Philippa's parents have deliberately shielded her from her press clippings, for fear "it might make her self-conscious" (28). Perhaps by emphasizing her isolation from the world, Mitchell reinforces Terman's argument that giftedness is an inherent rather than an acquired trait, but he also implies that this graceful girl derives some if not all of her gifts from her African origins.

Though his characterization shows a pristine and protected Philippa, Mitchell also turns her into a comic naïf at certain points in the article. He observes that "she particularly likes raw green peas, raw corn on the cob, raw yams, and raw sirloin steaks," repeating that telltale adjective "raw" and betraying her uncultivated tastes (28). The other children at her all-white Catholic school "used to stare at her," not because of her brown skin, but rather "because she always fills her pockets with green peas" (34). The very unselfconsciousness that the Schuylers prize becomes racialized in this profile, Philippa as innocent hence comic black child, munching away at her raw yam. She "eat[s] with gusto" (32). Philippa does not recognize that these uncooked foods are bizarre and unpalatable; as in minstrel stereotype, enthusiasm and ignorance go hand in hand.[127]

Mrs. Schuyler is clearly proud of her daughter's innocence and purity.[128] She tells Mitchell, "In this house we use almost no sugar. In her entire life, Philippa has never eaten a piece of candy. Her taste hasn't been perverted by sweets" (32).[129] Philippa's natural "passions" are salubrious: "She has a passion for lemons. She eats them the way most people eat oranges, pulp and all" (32). Mrs. Schuyler brags, "Her teeth... are absolutely perfect. She's never had even a tiny cavity" (34). Like the noble savage, Philippa is as whole and healthy as the lemons and oranges she eats. At the same time, the raw foods diet still carries the imputation of barbarism or animalism, which Mrs. Schuyler attempts to fend off with her own amusement at others' reactions to their regimen. She tells Mitchell, "When we're traveling, Philippa and I amaze waiters. You have to argue with most waiters before they'll bring you raw meat. Then they stare at you while you eat. I guess it is rather unusual to see a little girl eating a raw steak" (32). In "eating a raw steak," Philippa crosses boundaries of age, sex, and even perhaps species.[130]

This scene of the waiters "star[ing] at you while you eat" also carries ambiguous racial implications. At the very moment that Mrs. Schuyler hopes to dismiss the significance of racial difference and to subsume it into her dietary agenda, the geography of segregation intrudes on her reminiscence. Like Toomer recalling his teenage years working at the soda fountain, Mrs. Schuyler does not comment upon the racial hierarchies of food service.[131] The racial indeterminacy of this anecdote multiplies rather than diminishes the possible sources of spectatorial shock.[132] This embodied performance ruptures myths of feminine gentility and white restraint, as blond Josephine and light-skinned Philippa devour raw steak. If they do so in front of black waiters, the girl's carnivorous zeal—not to mention her mother's—violates hierarchies of color and class, even though, as Mitchell notes, Philippa's father was "the son of a dining-car chef on the New York Central" (28). If the waiters are white, this spectacle only takes on a stronger tone of transgression, as the servers are helpless to stop these apparently white women from eating like animals.

This anecdote is not the only reflection on the mixed-race child as a representative of the relationship between the races.[133] The *New Yorker* profile depicts the growing rapport between the worldly white reporter and the spirited but sheltered mixed-race child. When Mrs. Schuyler serves Mitchell dessert, she acknowledges his worldliness by contrast: "It isn't really ice cream, and you might not like it... It's just fresh peaches and cream sweetened with honey and chilled" (32). Perhaps coincidentally but nonetheless suggestively, "peaches and cream" is a common idiom for light complexions. Philippa is kept fresh in the metaphorical icebox of her parents' apartment. More aware of racial and gender protocols than she, Mitchell feels "ill at ease" when "left alone with her": "I didn't know how to go about making small talk with a gifted child" (30). He is reassured when Philippa reveals her boyish literary tastes for Sherlock Holmes, Mark Twain, and the funnies. Though he attributes his discomfort to "the difference in our ages," the silent factors governing their interactions are the differences in gender and race. Philippa tells the reporter how much she loves her "unexpurgated edition" of *The Arabian Nights* and apologizes for becoming so "impassioned" (31). Her innocence is established through the implicit contrast with Mitchell's awareness of a world outside where a mixed-race child might not confide such a taste to an adult, white stranger.

If the mulatta is inevitably tinged with exoticism and sensuousness, Josephine Schuyler manages this implication by ignoring her in the text of "Nutrition and Racial Superiority" (1942). The article consists largely of second-person instruction: "if you can only get one orange, learn to eat the whole fruit, skin and all" (397), but in this advice, Schuyler embeds the heteronormative romance of black racial futurity that subtends so much of her writing. Like "black molasses . . . rich with vitamins and minerals," the African man "carried in his dark skin a reservoir of strength and vitality."[134] Schuyler encourages him to take up "biochemistry" like the Germans and Japanese. If he does, he will tap into primordial power: "Plankton is said to be the original food of the monsters that once inhabited the sea. It is now the food of whales and Nazis" (381). In order to attain this Leviathan-like stature, the black man must depend upon the devoted black woman: "the glory and honor of changing the present downward trend of health in Aframerica and making the Negro again the splendid physical specimen he was on arrival in America, belongs to the mothers of the group" (398). The wife of a black man and the mother of a mixed-race child, Schuyler may slyly intend to include herself in "the mothers of the group" without drawing attention to her own interracial family. However, she distances herself from this racial romance in the concluding line: "I feel sure, if sufficiently aroused, they will enthusiastically embrace this opportunity" (398). In this context, Schuyler is the rational expert rather than the sentimental mother.

The well-fed child still emblematizes the utopian racial future that Schuyler envisions, and she unsexes that figure in her declaration that "every child in the world could be beautiful and bright if, from conception, it had been correctly fed" (298). Schuyler's evasive pronoun use ("it") draws attention to the problem of gender, that troublesome "a" at the end of "tragic mulatta." Though Schuyler does not discuss her daughter in the text of her article, the *Crisis* introduces Philippa as evidence of her theories:

Firm believer in the direct relationship of proper nutrition to superior physique and mentality, Mrs. Schuyler has written widely for the past fifteen years on better diets. Carrying her views into practice, she has reared her daughter, Philippa, on a strict natural diet, with the result that she is physically perfect as to teeth, tonsils, heart action, eyesight and otherwise, and has been cited by leading psychologists as an outstanding example of superior intelligence. (380)

This caption makes Philippa sound like a robot. Her physiology is exemplary and standardized. Though her gender is mentioned, it is hardly emphasized, and no mention is made of her skin color, that overdetermined racial marker. Nutrition science aspires to define a transcendent and "physically perfect" human being, shedding racial stigma and feminine abjection.

Once we move from the text into the photographs of Philippa that illustrate the article, the tone changes dramatically, perhaps because it is impossible to maintain such a detached tone and perfection paradigm in the face of a face. Figure 2.1, the photograph that appears on the first page of the article, presents an apparently domestic scene, Philippa in a school uniform and Anna Wiggins

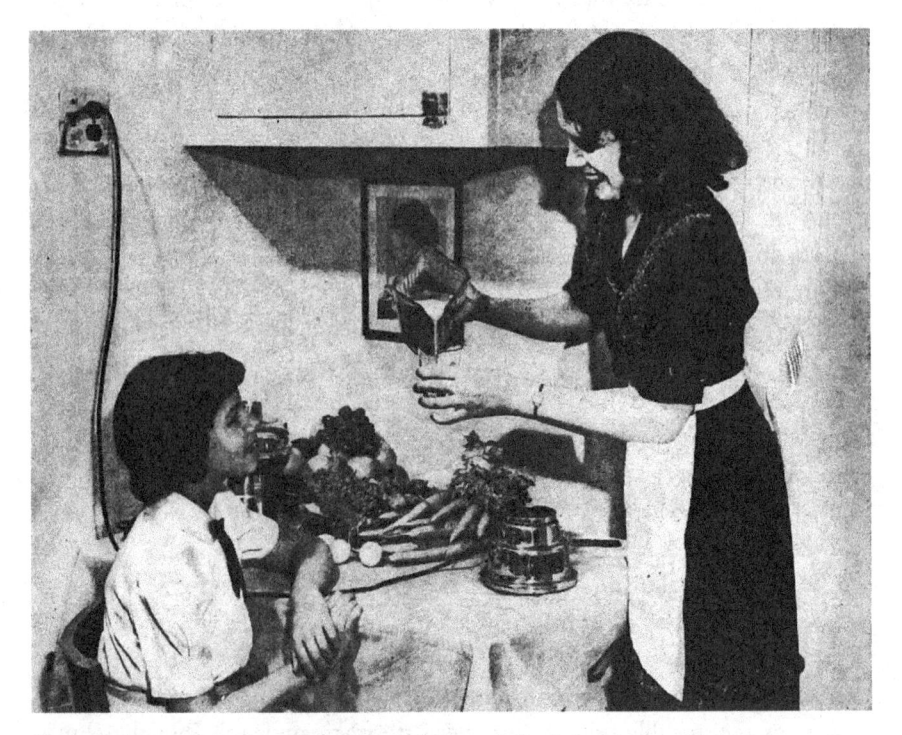

Figure 2.1 Anna Wiggins Brown pours Philippa Schuyler an energy drink in a photograph accompanying Josephine Schuyler's nutrition advice.
Source: *Crisis* magazine, December 1942.

Brown, "noted concert singer and late star of 'Porgy and Bess,'" smiling and wearing an apron. For a reader who did not know the Schuylers, it would be easy to assume that Josephine Schuyler appeared in the photograph, pouring an "energy drink" from a blender into a cup (380). The scandal of interracialism does not touch this wholesome uplift iconography.

Behind the women, a cornucopia of fruits and vegetables spills onto the table, and Philippa, seated in front of it, becomes a part of that still life.[135] A picture of a curly-haired child peeks out from above the tilted blender. This juxtaposition turns the apparently white "energy drink," composed of "liquified fruits and vegetables," into a visual metaphor for the vital mixed-race child. While the pile of fruit suggests natural abundance, the blender inserts cutting-edge technology into the scene.[136] The prominent black plug and wire, snaking beneath Philippa's folded arms, creates the illusion that the girl is plugged into the wall, the child of the future. No wonder the New York World's Fair declared a Philippa Schuyler Day.

This photograph uses the domestic triad of innocent tot, schoolgirl, and motherly woman to suggest a teleology of New Negro womanhood, supported by nutrition science and its health benefits. In this homosocial tableau, the impression of sexuality diffuses into a general aura of feminine beauty and fruitful plenty. In the second photograph accompanying the article, Figure 2.2, Philippa is about to cut into her birthday cakes—"fashioned as a tank, an airplane carrier, and an armored truck"—and to share them with the uniformed men who

Figure 2.2 Philippa Schuyler poses with black servicemen, about to serve them her raw cashew cakes.
Source: *Crisis* magazine, December 1942.

stand beside and behind her (391). The caption reads: "Philippa Schuyler shar[es] her 'vitality' cakes with service men at the Harlem USO club on her eleventh birthday" (281). Though the photograph could be seen as evidence of Josephine Schuyler's theory, expressed in the article, that "Negro women" need to support black men, its awkwardness tells another story about the relationship between the mixed-race girl, this genteel uplift icon, the "physically perfect" child prodigy, and the phenotypically black adult men behind her. The men's hands are decorously folded or held stiffly at their sides; many of them avoid looking at Philippa or even at the camera. In spite of her physical proximity to the soldiers, Philippa seems separated from them by a gulf of age, color, and class. She may represent the ideal for which they are fighting, but she is not for their consumption. The cakes, like Philippa, are "tasty and attractive" and still "uncooked" (381).

"Evening with a Gifted Child" implies that Philippa has appetites that her parents' prescriptions have not accounted for and that these appetites will force a collision with the color line that the Schuylers' protectiveness scrupulously avoided.[137] "Nutrition and Racial Superiority," by contrast, uses feminine respectability, coded as near-whiteness, as a representative of racial uplift, even as the text celebrates a virile black manhood that its illustrations either omit or contain. Both accounts of Philippa's childhood celebrity show that raw foods are a medium for preserving her purity, whether understood as childhood innocence or what Robin Bernstein calls "racial innocence," "not a literal state of being unraced but . . . rather, the performance of not-noticing, a performed claim of slipping beyond social categories."[138] The modern mulatta and the child prodigy both strain after such a slip, yet the conflicts between these visual and rhetorical codes, even within a single article, reveal the persistence of the double binds of race and gender.

What evidence we have of Philippa's childhood attitudes—and that evidence is surprisingly extensive thanks to Josephine Schuyler's archival scrupulousness and faithful scrapbooking—suggests that she embraced pleasure, color, and sensuousness in spite of her parents' purity regime. When she was four years old, Philippa composed a piece called "The Dance of the Vegetables," and she illustrated the sheet music with cartoon vegetables.[139] Her notes explain that "normal, gay folk"—namely, the sweet pea, the carrot, and the watermelon— dance happily, while bland or malodorous white vegetables eschew the fun and stick to their own kind: "the potato is probably a wall flower until she finds the ONION."[140] Josephine Schuyler shared the view that white bodies were unappetizing; before Philippa's birth, she published an anonymous essay, "Fall of the Fair Confederate," in which she compares white skin to "moldy cheese."[141] It is hard to avoid the racialized subtext of Philippa's composition, though she might not have been aware of it herself: her dancing, multi-hued fruits and vegetables evoke people of color, while the raw onions and potatoes suggest awkward and anhedonic white people.

Philippa's 1938 essay "Dates," possibly a school assignment, collected in a family scrapbook, also associates fruit with pleasure, this time in an exotic setting under "the shade of a palm tree" near a "long line of camels."[142] This Orientalist sketch depicts the challenge and gratification of plucking a newly ripe fruit:

> Dates grow in great clusters high up in the tree. They are ripe and ready for picking in November and December. Date picking is a very busy time on the oases. The boys or men climb the rough, straight trunks of the trees until they reach the sweet golden-brown dates . . . Dates are easily bruised so the boys must handle the fruit very carefully.[143]

Though Philippa was only seven when she wrote this, her Mediterranean idyll suggests nascent sexuality. The color of the dates suggests both the erotic allure of Middle Eastern skin and Philippa's own skin tone; coincidentally, the *Silhouette* profile published a year later would refer to Philippa as the "sweet, golden-brown daughter of Mr. and Mrs. George Schuyler."[144] Though this scene could be construed—and was apparently intended—as a factual account of foreign agricultural practices, in the "oases," an imaginative ground she explored in her readings of *The Arabian Nights*, Philippa found a safe space for metaphorical sexuality that made picking and handling as much a part of the natural order of things as growing, each in its own time.

In *Jokes and Their Relation to the Unconscious*, Sigmund Freud proposes that jokes compress aggression and desire, making them socially acceptable and also allowing a cathartic burst of expressive emotion through laughter.[145] Throughout the *New Yorker* profile, Philippa keeps bringing up a riddle: "what's smaller than a flea's mouth?" (34). At the end of the article, Mitchell asks Mrs. Schuyler to give him the answer, and she replies, "What goes in it" (36). The riddle's proposition boggles the mind (what could fit inside a flea's mouth?) because the flea is almost unimaginably small. Similarly, Philippa Schuyler's diminution renders her accomplishments amazing; the little girl dazzles her interlocutors with the amount of information, talent, and experience that she can contain. By controlling what goes into their flea's mouth, both literally and figuratively, Josephine and George exert their power over her, trying to control what she might become when she grows up. While their choice to modify her diet seems like the smallest part of their grand project of racial (re)invention, it is with these intimate details that they try to build the hybrid child, who is supposed to reproduce their vision rather than needle them like a biting flea.

Given the hypercharged relationship between ingestion and exemplarity, renunciation and refinement, perhaps it is no wonder that Philippa's favorite of her childhood compositions tells the triumphant story of hungry cockroaches.

Philippa recounts the tale to Mitchell: "Some cockroaches are feasting on a kitchen floor. A human comes in and kills one of them. He thinks he has killed them all. But after he leaves, one little cockroach peeps out, then another, and another" (32). The moral of the story, according to Philippa, is that "cockroaches will go on forever and ever" (32). While she qualifies this conclusion by saying that their endurance is unfortunate, the cockroaches provide a strong image of childhood's unruliness and generativity. George and Josephine want to script the future through Philippa's child body, but by definition, the next generation exceeds their control. In her "Cockroach Ballet," Philippa parodies (perhaps unwittingly) the utopian futurity imposed on her, whether in the form of modern mulatta or child prodigy. She also perhaps mocks the idealized whiteness that both were imagined to emulate. "I've never seen an angel," she quips irreverently, but "I've seen many cockroaches" (32).

As an adult, Philippa struggled with her biracial identity, fretting about the race of potential sexual and marital partners, passing for "Iberian" under the name Felipa de Monterro, shedding "that dreadful name," Philippa Schuyler.[146] In a sex scandal, her body became all too available and consumable, as a former lover mailed pornographic postcards of Philippa to her parents and other acquaintances.[147] She died young, drowning in Vietnam in 1967 while evacuating orphans. It was all too easy, alas, for Philippa's life story to flesh out the contours of a tragic mulatta trope. Turning to her Mediterranean ideal, she fled the imputation of blackness, which she now understood as contaminating. "I look like any other of the Sicilians, Greeks, Spaniards, or Portuguese here in Rome," she wrote her mother in a letter: "I am not a Negro, and won't stand for being called one in a book that will circulate in countries where that taint has not been applied to me."[148] Though her harsh words, conservative politics, and eugenic theories test the sympathies of contemporary readers, her sense that her mixed race made her a "strange curiosity" is confirmed in the periodical coverage of the child prodigy and her unusual diet.[149]

In the modern imagination, raw foods retained an aura of primitive purity that the Schuylers hoped was recuperable through scientific means. This eugenic ideal blended a dream of the past with a vision of the future, and in *Black Empire*, Liberia provided the imaginative terrain for this once and future Africa. In Chapter 3, we turn to white writers nostalgic for premodern foodways identified with the regions of Europe and their ancient races.

3

Eating Like a Local

Ernest Hemingway, Gertrude Stein, and the Stakes of Terroir

Gertrude Stein and Ernest Hemingway had a notoriously fraught friendship, no less so because of the unmistakable influence that Stein's telegraphic and repetitive prose had on Hemingway's style.[1] One thing that they did agree upon from the very beginning was food and drink. In *A Moveable Feast* (1964), Hemingway admires the menu at 27 rue de Fleurus, particularly the *eaux de vies*:

> They gave you good things to eat and tea and natural distilled liqueurs made from purple plums, yellow plums, or wild raspberries. These were fragrant, colorless alcohols served from cut-glass carafes in small glasses and whether they were *quetsche, mirabelle* or *framboise* they all tasted like the fruits they came from, converted into a controlled fire on your tongue that warmed you and loosened your tongue.[2]

Liqueur that preserves the essence of local fruit, its fragrance and flavor, seems an apt metaphor for the style that Stein and Hemingway innovated. Stein and Hemingway boil language down to workaday words and rediscover the intoxicating strangeness of that distillation. Modernist form is "colorless" and transparent, a geometric and clear "cut-glass carafe."[3] Its very colorlessness, the lack of inflection for which Stein and Hemingway were both famous, flaunts the absence of the actual "purple plums," "yellow plums," or "wild raspberries." But this distillation does nature one better by granting the taster access to a foreign linguistic experience—"*quetsche, mirabelle,* or *framboise*"—irreducible to its translation.[4] Even as modernist form highlights its artifice, its oral pleasures connect the taster to a fantasy of place and cross-cultural belonging.

In this description of Stein's hospitality, Hemingway celebrates her ethnic authenticity: "she had beautiful eyes and a strong German-Jewish face that could also have been Friulano and she reminded me of a northern Italian peasant woman."[5] Hemingway sees vivacity and intensity in Stein's every feature, "her mobile face, and her lovely, thick, alive immigrant hair."[6] Like the liqueurs, she reconnects Hemingway to peasant traditions and ambrosial fruits. By racializing and romanticizing Stein, Hemingway effectively dodges his intellectual debt to her; Stein the peasant woman hands over the "controlled fire" of modernism without recognizing her own Promethean teat.

Though Hemingway identified Stein with the romanticized and racialized peasantry, both expatriate intellectuals were in fact preoccupied with the authenticity of the provinces, their denizens, and their cuisines. Indeed, the interwar years saw a surge of interest in French regional foods due to the rise of automobile tourism.[7] As the gastronome Curnonsky (Maurice Edmond Sailland) and his collaborator, Marcel Rouff, wrote in the English-language *Yellow Guides for Epicures* (1926), "Thanks to the automobile, thanks to the ever-increasing progress of touring, thanks also to the efforts and perfect organization of the Touring Club and the Automobile Club—enterprises which we wish to further to the best of our ability—French cooking has to-day regained its place, which is first in the world."[8] In the 1920s, Rouff and Curnonsky published a popular series of guides, *La France Gastronomique*, on the cuisines of regional France.[9] Hemingway recommended them to Stein and Toklas, and they in turn fell in love with the Bugey region, featured in one of the booklets, and ultimately bought their country home at Bilignin.[10]

Kyla Wazana Tompkins contends that the ideal of local foods either exalts "romanticized" origins that "suspiciously echo nativist ideological formations" or spurs on "food tourism, in which cosmopolitanism at times subtends nativism as an elite practice, as the inheritance of that alliance between consumption and white bourgeois culture."[11] In other words, local foods either keep the (racial) other out or invite the (elite) other in. Hemingway and Stein complicate this dichotomy. They idealize and racialize European regional identities. They also racialize cosmopolitan identities, often with hostility or ambivalence, as Jewish. When we look to the history of the regional foods movement in France, Spain, and Italy during and between the two world wars, we see interlacing, overlying, and competing racial fantasies and fears. While Walter Benn Michaels argues that American expatriates brought their nativist ideologies abroad, it might be fairer to say that Hemingway and Stein had a bird's-eye view of transatlantic nativisms.[12]

The French concept of terroir, that the soil imparts identifiable flavors to the wines and foods of a region, could justify nativism or trouble its investment in origins. In his illuminating work on terroir in early modern France, Thomas Parker demonstrates that this desire to "trace a product to its provenance" reflected a broader cultural project that "attempted to conceptualize nations, classify languages, and make laws using the earth's influence as a gauge for normalcy and authenticity."[13] The French, Parker explains, "posited that terroir affects not only the cheese *but also* the cheese-maker, not only the produce but also the farmer," and thus the agricultural concept extended to racial questions of climatological determinism.[14] The association of terroir with national belonging could reinforce nativist views—only those raised on French soil could possess this signature quality—or it could facilitate cosmopolitan ones, transplantation that allows the expatriate to become a local.[15]

In French culture, the association between terroir and race was explicit.[16] In the wake of the Dreyfus Affair, Maurice Barrès published a novel about his beloved Lorraine region of France entitled *Les Déracinés* (1897), in which he claimed that a Frenchman should be rooted "in his soil and among his dead."[17] Barrès denigrates the Jew, who has no connection to the land and will "poison" the pure Frenchman.[18] For Barrès, Christy Wampole explains, "uprooted people—namely, Jews, foreigners, and cosmopolitan intellectuals were enemies of regional, cultural embeddedness."[19] In a debate in print that came to be known as *La Querrelle du peuplier*, André Gide retorted that travel was educative, transplantation strengthening. He expressed incredulity that one might discern with any certainty the place or people to whom one belongs.[20]

Barrès's anti-Semitic rhetoric and celebration of the land would find new life in the 1930s in Fascist movements in Italy, Spain, and Germany. In spite of this disturbing political genealogy, the metaphor of the soil and its products is a multivalent one. Though terroir often fetishizes origins, Parker points out that it doesn't necessarily do so: "a person or plant can be *transplanted* after birth and the power of a new terroir will take hold."[21] Both Hemingway and Stein were fascinated by the power of terroir to inspire new affiliations.[22] Both writers use Jewishness as a racialized symbol of exile, but they also explore the idea that to be white and American is to be similarly deracinated. As D. H. Lawrence opines in *Studies in Classic American Literature* (1923), "Americans have never loved the soil of America as Europeans have loved the soil of Europe. America has never been a blood-home-land. Only an ideal home-land. The home-land of the ideal, or the *spirit*. And of the pocket. Not of the blood."[23] Building a "home-land of the ideal," though not the one that Lawrence has in mind, Hemingway and Stein create an expatriate identity based upon sensuous immersion in food. As Parker notes, terroir "allow[s] tasters to experience and *live* the land indirectly through its fruits."[24] For Hemingway, terroir connects his white American protagonists with the brown Latin cultures they idolize, frequently leading to a tragic denouement in which they let down the cultural standards they have trained themselves to uphold. For Stein, traditional foraging practices like gleaning and mushroom gathering allow the poet to perform local belonging and ecological enmeshment.

For Hemingway and Stein, the sensuous immediacy of rural Spain, France, and Italy compensates for American rootlessness. The purveyors of these foods belong—in both regional and racial terms—to the places where they live. The fruits of terroir—wine, mushrooms and truffles, fruit, cured meats, cheese—convey the flavor of place to the tourist who wishes to belong.[25] For two writers known for what they leave out, their fulsome descriptions of land and food are telling. In these modernist fictions, the regions of Europe, territories that cut across the dominant paradigm of nation, become utopian spaces where the body recuperates its connection to the soil. The impression of timelessness in the hills of Basque country or the wheat fields of Normandy supports a primitivist fiction about the peasantry and their pure racial antecedents. In the identification between peasant body, sustaining soil, and local food, Hemingway and Stein effectively mourn their own deracination.

Wineskins and Hare Tracks: Hemingway and the Vanishing World of Regional Races

According to modern travel guides, the Basque people represented a last bastion of racial purity in an all too modern world. *Carpenter's Geographical Reader: Europe* (1912) complains that the Spanish are "made up of several race elements" and determines that the Basques are "the best of the Spaniards, being descended from the earliest inhabitants."[26] *A Guide to the Gay World of France* (1929) calls the Basques "a separate and homogeneous race of people."[27] This purported purity only made the Basques more vulnerable to barbarian hordes according to this popular narrative. In *Rambles in Europe* (1934), a guide for schoolchildren, the geographer Roderick Peattie explains that though the Basques were "the first people to live in Spain . . . they were pushed into the corner where they now live by invading armies of the past."[28] He laments that this dynamic of brute force rules history, as "people to whom a country belongs must fly before their enemies to wilder and less desirable places, while the invading people take over the country for themselves."[29] For Peattie, the Basques' very defeat evidences their superiority.

In these travel guides, Basque country preserves a pocket of timeless pastoralism inside modern Europe. The tourist can regain this lost simplicity by sampling the local foods: "You will think you never ate such excellent ham and eggs in your life as this Bayonne ham and the eggs from Basque chickens—and the wine and the home-made bread. It's all very simple, but an Escoffier could not do it better."[30] Cured meats, fermented wine, and dried peppers concentrate the taste of place and the impression of culture thanks to premodern techniques of food preservation passed down through the generations. In *The Basque Country*

(1921), Katharine Waldo Douglas sets the scene of local hospitality, "the wine shop, where hang the acrid goat-skin wine bottles, ready to be filled from the great casks of Spanish wine; [and] strings of red-peppers sway by the door of the house."[31] To complement these culinary offerings comes the voice of the Basque maiden, singing the "songs of her people, full of melancholy."[32] These Basque ballads add a bittersweet note to the enchanting bouquet.

The Sun Also Rises features the Basque region both as a scene of abundance and then, in its second appearance in the text, as a scene of alienation. One of the issues at stake in the novel is whether an outsider can become an insider, whether an expatriate can ever have aficion.[33] It seems possible that whiteness itself is a sign of alienation; as Stein later writes in *Everybody's Biography* (1937), "It is queer the use of that word, native always means people who belong somewhere else, because they had once belonged somewhere. That shows that the white race does not really think they belong anywhere because they think of everybody else as native."[34] In *The Sun Also Rises*, the locals are "Basques," their region "Basque country."[35] This ancestral belonging antedates nation and shows up Jake's rootlessness. Jake is misidentified as an "Englishman" by the Italians he serves with in the war (39), and the one time he is called an "American," it is to express astonishment that he could appreciate bullfighting: "Somehow it was taken for granted that an American could not have aficion" (137). Brett and Mike buy "Basque beret[s]" as souvenirs (138), but these purchases underscore their separation from the locals. For American and English expatriates, regional culture and traditional attire represent something unusual, enchanting, or even pleasantly corny about life in Spain.

Unsurprisingly, given the gourmandism of the Lost Generation, Jake tries to eat and drink his way into local belonging. He admits that "the first meal in Spain was always a shock with the hors d'oeuvres, an egg course, two meat courses, vegetables, salad, and dessert and fruit" (100).[36] Nonetheless, Jake opts for immersive excess—"You have to drink plenty of wine to get it all down"—rather than dietary restraint (100). Robert Cohn's failure to eat in the Spanish way betrays his gaucherie: "Robert Cohn tried to say he did not want any of the second meat course, but we would not interpret for him, and so the waitress brought him something else as a replacement, a plate of cold meats, I think" (100). This clash about how to approach Spanish food reveals Jake's aspirations for acculturation and his scapegoating of Robert Cohn. As an American expatriate, Jake Barnes is also globetrotting and homeless, but Robert Cohn's wanderings are caricatured and racialized. Jake may also be a stranger in a strange land, but because he can adopt aficion and eat and drink like the locals, he seems capable of transplantation in a way that Jewish Cohn is not.[37]

Tourism grants expatriates an intimate view of terroir and its balance of regional culture, animal husbandry, and agriculture. When Jake and Bill begin their fishing trip in Basque country, they cross the border from France into Spain. Basque country appears like a paradise:

> We passed some lovely gardens and had a good look back at the town, and then we were out in the country green and rolling, and the road climbing all the time. We passed lots of Basques with oxen, or cattle, hauling carts along the road, and nice farmhouses, low roofs, and all white-plastered. In the Basque country the land all looks very rich and green and the houses and villages look well-off and clean. (97)

The Basques seem a part of the countryside, while the soldiers hired by Spain and France to guard the border, "Spanish carabineers, with patent-leather Bonaparte hats, and short guns on their backs" and "fat Frenchmen in kepis and mustaches," appear ludicrous and out-of-place (98). When Jake asks the carabineer if he fishes in the stream, "he said no, that he didn't care for it" (98). Meanwhile the Basque people pursue their premodern ways: "Just then an old man with long, sunburned hair and beard, and clothes that looked as though they were made of gunny-sacking, came striding up to the bridge. He was carrying a long staff, and he had a kid slung on his back, tied by the four legs, the head hanging down" (98). Though the soldier waves the goatherd back over the border, he acknowledges to Jake that the old man will "'just wade across the stream'" (98). The locals ignore the incursions of nationalism on their regional culture.[38]

In a famous scene, Bill and Jake ride the bus to Burguete with Basque men, who teach them how to drink wine the local way. Observing his companion, Jake conflates the brown Basque skin with the proffered wine bag: "The Basque lying against my legs was tanned the color of saddle-leather" (110). Like the wine bag, the "tanned neck" and "wrinkle[d]" skin of Hemingway's Basque peasant seems a solid container for his cultural and racial identity, intractable epidermalism. By contrast, Robert Cohn's racial marker, the Jewish nose, is disguisable; it was "permanently flattened" in a boxing match at Princeton (11).[39] For the Basque peasant, skin coincides with self; culture is a satisfying uniform: "He wore a black smock like all the rest" (110). From the novel's anti-Semitic perspective, Cohn's unsheddable inferiority is signaled by the very mutability of his appearance. In the bodies of Basque peasants, race is real, and it offers heady communion to the onlooker thirsty for authentic experience.[40]

Both Jake and Bill make fools of themselves as they try to drink from the unfamiliar wineskin. A young Basque man executes the move masterfully: "raised it high up, squeezing the leather bag with his hand so the stream of wine hissed into his mouth" (111). This description aligns queer pleasure and masculine potency. Nostalgia for a homosocial world and patriarchal order reinforces primitivist fantasies of ethnic purity, and the pastoral ideal creates a sanctioned space for homoeroticism.[41] These encounters are pedagogical; Jake may be easily shocked into spilling by the Basque who imitates the klaxon horn, and Bill may dribble wine "down his chin" (110), but they can be corrected by the good-humored locals. The "farm country" with its "rich grain-fields" leads to a town where "fields of grapes touched the houses" (111). Hemingway catalogs the "hams and slabs of bacon and white garlics and long sausages hanging from the roof" at the local posada (112), and they drink aguardiente with their companions (112). Food and spirits narrow the gap between the Americans and the Basques.

Another old man with "brown" skin approaches the travelers, telling them about his travels in the United States (113). He returned to Basque country to get married; the continuity of his cultural identity—and, Hemingway implies, his family bloodlines —withstand globalization and mobility.[42] The Basque interlude comes closest to exemplifying the epigraph from Ecclesiastes: "One generation passeth away, and another generation cometh; but the earth abideth forever." Counterposed with Jake and Bill's lost generation are the Basque generations and their connection to the earth that abides.[43] "You're an expatriate," Bill tells Jake, mocking the commentators of their day; "you've lost touch with the soil" (120). In the inn at Burguete, Jake and Bill eat a hearty meal that highlights the region's natural abundance: "We had fried trout afterward and some sort of a stew and a big bowl full of wild strawberries" (116). The next day, they head into the woods to fish in the Irati River, and Bill declares, "This is country" (122). They even spot "wild strawberries growing on the sunny side of the ridge in a little clearing in the trees" (122). The dinner at the inn forecasts the simple pleasures to come when they immerse themselves in the local landscape and its rhythms.

When Jake drinks the local wine and fishes for trout, he flirts with becoming a part of this countryside, a part of this people. By contrast, global capital obscures origins and tantalizes the senses with the decadence of decontextualized food. Hemingway associates these two effects in the figure of Count Mippopopolous, whose antecedents are unclear, though his name suggests Greek origins. Lady Brett allows him to squire her about town, as she does later with Robert Cohn, and considers him "one of us" (40). As Forter observes, Brett's potential (and actual) liaisons with racial others draw fire in the novel.[44] The count "owns a chain of sweetshops in the States," and Brett "think[s] he called it a chain. Something like that. Linked them all up. Told me a little about it" (40). When Jake meets the count, Mippopopolous proffers "a basket of champagne" (63). This wine is big business rather than local viticulture like the "fields of grapes touching the houses" in Basque country. Mippopopolous brags:

> "I know we don't get much of a chance to judge good wine in the States now, but I got this from a friend of mine that's in the business." "Oh, you

always have some one in the trade," Brett said. "This fellow raises the grapes. He's got thousands of acres of them." "What's his name?" asked Brett. "Veuve Cliquot?" "No," said the count. "Mumms. He's a baron." "Isn't it wonderful," said Brett. "We all have titles. Why haven't you a title, Jake?" (63)

The count serves as the ethnic embodiment of global capital's dislocations.[45] Unlike the awkward Robert Cohn, the count is seductive, his taste subtle rather than gauche. "It was amazing champagne," Jake admits (66). The count's connoisseurship, however, only makes his capitalist translation of values more insidious: "Food had an excellent place in the count's values. So did wine" (68). The trio visit a jazz club together, where they see a "nigger drummer ... all teeth and lips" (69).[46] Though the count has a seemingly perfect palate and can pass as "one of us," this minstrel stereotype underscores the ethnic menace of the almost-white Greek.[47]

A foil for the count's uncertain origins and suspicious ethnicity, Pedro Romero is indisputably a local boy, "born in Ronda" and trained at the bullfighting school in Malaga (177). The bullfighting critic teases Romero about his rusticity and "the number of *Malagueño* expressions that he used" (178). Romero's local roots evoke historical and geographical continuity. Hemingway named this character after "one of the first and greatest professional bullfighters," whose statue stood in Ronda, a nearly inaccessible mountain town with an ancient bullfighting ring.[48] The altitude of his hometown also connects Romero to the Basques, mountain natives themselves.

Twentieth-century raciologists considered mountains a natural defense of racial purity. Though William Z. Ripley divided the races of Europe between the northern (Teutonic) and the southern (Mediterranean), his third category, Alpine, was, as its name implied, more allied with altitude than region, "pre-eminently a mountain type, whether in France, Spain, Italy, Germany or Albania."[49] The Alpine race's attachment to terroir is their definitive characteristic, "more primitive, deeper seated in the land."[50] By the time Hemingway wrote *The Sun Also Rises*, Ripley's schema was considered outdated; other raciologists, like Joseph Deniker, had expanded the racial lexicon without fundamentally altering the prejudices shaping the earlier model.[51] Nonetheless, Hemingway's recurring association of the mountains with simpler life and pure-blooded peoples recalls this popular tripartite division and its simultaneous condescension to and nostalgia for this connection to the soil.

Hemingway articulates his romantic view of Ronda and its people in *Death in the Afternoon* (1932). Ronda provides a picturesque escape for the expatriate: "That is where you should go if you ever go to Spain on a honeymoon or if you ever bolt with any one. The entire town and as far as you can see in any direction is romantic background."[52] He takes care to point out that the locals are descended from northern Spaniards, not Moors: "The people who settled it when the Moors were driven away, came from Cordoba and the north of Andalucia."[53] Pedro's appearance reflects this romanticized and pure ethnicity: "I noticed his skin. It was clear and smooth and very brown" (189). Robert Cohn assaults this perfect skin, but in spite of the damage done, Pedro carries off the bullfight and the girl.

We might understand both the Basques and Pedro through the lens of "homophile pastoralism," which features rural landscapes, handsome shepherds (or, in this case, bullfighters), and homoerotic bonds.[54] As David Shuttleton observes, "In figuring a return to a lost primitivism, or a reversion to a polymorphously perverse, pre-oedipal imaginary, queer pastoral can be read as personally ennobling and culturally restorative."[55] By contrast, Anglo-American "young men" with "white hands, wavy hair, white faces" are symbols of inversion and decadence in *The Sun Also Rises* (28), as Forter persuasively argues: "This emphasis on the gay man's *whiteness* is striking. It's as if the passage were linking excessive cleanliness, smirking superiority, and the civilized excess of sexual 'perversion' to skin color."[56] This racial proposition—that white homosexuality was perverse—was echoed in sexological studies of the period. In *Sexual Inversion* (1901), for example, Havelock Ellis proposed that homosexuality might be natural in the Mediterranean, but that in England or America, a man who acted on homosexual desire in spite of social prohibition must be "organically abnormal."[57] From Jake's point of view, these white gay men are out of place—both in their sexual behaviors and in their disturbing mobility—while racial rootedness supports pastoral homoeroticism as a sign of belonging. When Brett seduces Pedro and runs away with him, she robs Jake of the object of his aficion and the sense of place that goes along with him.

Jake expresses this unutterable loss through newfound disgust, directed at the formerly cherished other. When Jake returns to Basque country, this time on the French side of the border, he dines at a restaurant where he is served "a Basque liqueur called Izarra" (236). This liqueur is distilled from "the flowers of the Pyrenees." Like those *eaux de vies* Stein and Toklas served, this liqueur offers the essence of the local countryside, what the waiter calls "the veritable flowers of the Pyrenees" (236).[58] Now, Jake does not romanticize the fruits (or, in this case, flowers) of the soil; he is revolted: "It looked like hair-oil and smelled like Italian *strega*. I told him to take the flowers of the Pyrenees away and bring me a *vieux marc*" (236–37). The liqueur assaults Jake's senses: unappetizing, viscous, and smelly. Furthermore, like hair oil, it might stain. Jake does not describe the *marc*, though he orders and consumes two glasses of it in short succession. Its unmarked quality may be part of its appeal.[59] Envious of Pedro's authenticity, his sensuous localism, Jake doubles down on his own consumer rootlessness.

When Brett returns, rejecting Pedro in order to preserve him, she blames the threat that she poses to his masculinity and innocence. She refuses to grow her hair long and be more "womanly," and she is "not going to be one of these bitches that ruins children" (246–47). In an early draft of the novel, Brett (then called "Duff" after Duff Twydsen, the model for the character) also tells Jake that Pedro "was a waiter in a hotel in Gibraltar when he was ~~sixteen~~ fifteen. He came down from Ronda. That's what made him ~~rather overvalue the title at the start~~ put so much value in titles."[60] Anglo-American empires consume local delicacies—people and cuisines—and destroy their purity in their wake. Furthermore, Pedro seems to conflate title and aristocratic bloodline, while Brett recognizes that "We all have titles" now (63). By letting Pedro go, Brett refuses to act out the role assigned her by Robert Cohn when he called her Circe for turning men into swine (148). In *Comus*, Milton tells us that men were undone by the contents of Circe's "charmed cup": "Whoever tasted, lost his upright shape, / And downward fell into a groveling swine" (lines 52–53).[61] By forswearing Pedro, Brett takes this cup of poison away from him.

The fear of contamination by a woman's body reveals a submerged racial dynamic. Defending her renunciation of her young lover, Brett mentions her age: "I'm thirty-four, you know" (246). Contemporaneous eugenicists warning of imminent race suicide urged women to reproduce while young: "Nature evidently intended that the duties of maternity should be assumed between the twenty and twenty-fourth year."[62] Early in the novel, another expatriate offers a bitter diatribe about the loss of her reproductive potential: "I don't want to think I'll never have [children]. I always thought I'd have them" (54). Brett's concern that she might "ruin" Pedro seems reproductive as well as moral. In refraining from acting like a "bitch" (246), a female dog who might produce mongrel pups, and in refusing to turn Pedro into a swine, Brett prevents the potential degeneration of his line.

In light of Brett's unexpected abstinence, Jake's unrestrained gluttony suggests that he has chosen degeneration: "We lunched up-stairs at Botin's. It is one of the best restaurants in the world. We had roast suckling pig and drank *rioja alta* . . . I ate a very big meal and drank three bottles of *rioja alta*" (249).[63] In the nation's capital, the American tourist can compare Botin's to restaurants all over the world; he can eat *cochinello asado*, the specialty of nearby Segovia; and he can drink to excess the regional wines of distant Rioja. Rather than aspire to racial authenticity or adopted localism, Jake has allowed himself to become a pig. The fantasy of transnational belonging and homosocial bonds collapses in the face of sexual competition. It is as troubling for Brett to belong to the virile Spaniard as it is for her to belong to the comically phallic Jew, since Jake's insubstantial whiteness can compete with neither. Even her renunciation exalts Pedro Romero's primitive purity over Jake's decadent appetites.

White men can never regain the connection to the earth or to racial generations that they have lost.

Hemingway's white men are bedeviled by choices between abstinence and excess, rural virtue and urban vice, pure localism and adulterated cosmopolitanism. Because they keep opting for the latter while admiring the former, they seem destined for deracination and decadence. In the opening chapters of *A Farewell to Arms* (1929), Frederic is faced with a choice. He can tour the major cities of Italy and sleep with the women or he can visit Abruzzo, where a young priest invites him to stay with his family: "I would like you to see Abruzzi and visit my family at Capracotta."[64] Frederic's fellow soldiers rib the priest: "Listen to him talk about the Abruzzi. There's more snow there than here. He doesn't want to see peasants. Let him go to centres of culture and civilization" (8). The soldiers' teasing and ribaldry notwithstanding, the priest repeats his request: "I would like you to go to Abruzzi . . . There is good hunting. You would like the people and though it is cold it is clear and dry. You could stay with my family. My father is a famous hunter" (9). Frederic, of course, fails to go to Abruzzo, instead going "everywhere" (11), and this failure is both a breach of good manners (the priest had arranged for his stay) and a moral failure.

Capracotta, the destination Frederic never reaches, serves as a chimeric ideal: "I had wanted to go to Abruzzi. I had gone to no place where the roads were frozen and hard as iron, where it was clear cold and dry and the snow was dry and powdery and hare-tracks in the snow and the peasants took off their hats and called you Lord and there was good hunting" (13).[65] The qualities of the climate, "clear cold and dry," demand corresponding virtues from Capracotta's inhabitants, and in his fantasy Frederic casts himself as a lord among them. With the odd negation "I had gone to no place," Hemingway turns Abruzzo into a utopia, a term that Thomas More invested with "deliberate ambiguity," punning on "eu-topia" (good place) and "ou-topia" (no place).[66] In this imagined space, hardness and clarity reign. The mountain village encapsulates the very qualities that Hemingway strove for in his pared-down style, its crystalline coldness anticipating the iceberg principle of writing that he would articulate a few years later in *Death in the Afternoon*.[67] Frederic's syntax becomes loopily sinuous when he describes the boozy urban adventures that he indulged in instead. A drunk man cannot follow delicate "hare-tracks" in the snow; modern distractions and intoxications sap him of alpine virtues.[68]

While Frederic's wartime experiences are deranged and disordered, life in Capracotta flows steadily, following social hierarchies and seasonal rhythms:

> At Capracotta, he had told me, there were trout in the stream below the town . . . His father hunted every day and stopped to eat at the houses of peasants. They were always honored. It was cool in the summer at night

and the spring in Abruzzi was the most beautiful in Italy. But what was lovely was the fall to go hunting through the chestnut woods. The birds were all good because they fed on grapes and you never took a lunch because the peasants were always honored if you would eat with them at their houses. (73)

Fishing, hunting, and foraging—the three activities celebrated in this passage—each require intimacy with the environment, even more so than agriculture, which attempts to master and change the landscape. Here, even the viticulture supports (and flavors) the local birds. Capracotta seems in perfect harmony with its forest surroundings. The only potential disturbances come from girls (the peasant boys must refrain from nocturnal serenades "because it was bad for the girls to hear the flute at night") and foreigners: "For a foreigner to hunt he must present a certificate that he had never been arrested" (73). These two threats seem telling in a novel about an American who comes to Italy and his love affair with Catherine Barclay, a beautiful nurse who does not need a flute serenade to convince her to slip into his hospital bed at night. The combined forces of expatriation and desire bar Frederic from the Abruzzian paradise of local belonging.

By contrast, the "small" and "brown-faced" priest embodies racial authenticity and regional belonging (68). He dreams of "return[ing] to the Abruzzi," a thought that makes "his brown face . . . suddenly very happy" (71). The priest properly belongs "in his own country" (73). While Fredric belongs everywhere and nowhere, the priest suffers from homesickness, a vestige of rootedness in an increasingly itinerant civilization. One American travel writer, describing the chestnut groves of Italy, insisted that the locals would forever feel the tug of their home and cuisine: "Many an Italian mountaineer who leaves his home becomes homesick for his chestnut groves and fare, and longs for some of the *necci* or *balotte* that was supplied to him so liberally in his boyhood days."[69] Modern war redirects the deeply felt attachment to region ("his own country") to the presiding, though for Italy rather belated, abstraction of nation.[70] Frederic sees this enforced dislocation as the downfall of premodern cultures: "[The soldiers] were beaten when they took them from their farms and put them in the army. That is why the peasant has wisdom, because he is defeated from the start" (179). In this view, the priest's homesickness is a form of mourning for the agricultural social order.

Hemingway may frame the peasant culture of Abruzzo as a pocket of pristine premodernity threatened by the war, but this primitivist view of Italian regional life could cut both ways. Some popular thinkers attributed the survival of peasant culture into the twentieth century to inferior racial strains and cultural degeneration. Italian anthropologists like Giuseppe Sergi and Alfredo Niceforo argued that northern Italians were Aryan and southern Italians derived from inferior African stock.[71] They saw backwardness where Frederic envisions timelessness. According to Niceforo, the peasants in the *Mezzogiorno*, including Abruzzo, were stuck in "primitive and even quasibarbarian times."[72] American nativists cited these theories to rationalize immigration quotas. Frederic's cynical friend, the surgeon Rinaldi, echoes this line of thinking: "We are born with all we have and we never learn. We never get anything new. We all start complete. You should be glad not to be Latin" (171). Frederic dismisses this idea: "There's no such thing as a Latin" (171), but his skepticism cannot foreclose lingering questions about the relationship between racial heredity, Italian nationalism, and global modernity. For the purposes of war, the three should ideally act in concert, but in fact these discursive frames were often at odds.

These disjunctures became particularly clear on the ground. *A Farewell to Arms* focuses on contested terrain, the Isonzo, a site of notorious bloodshed during the war, that makes these conflicts evident, not merely conceptually but affectively and geographically.[73] One British writer visiting the Italian front observed, "You cannot make a kingdom by calling it one: and Italy is still really a bundle of different principalities, different interests, different races almost, still in process of growing together into a whole, but with the fusion not by any means complete as yet."[74] In *A Farewell to Arms*, the Italian soldier Gino confesses that it is hard for him to summon up "love" for the Bainsizza Plateau (184). Trying to rouse patriotic feeling, Gino proclaims, "The soil is sacred," but he admits that he "wish[es] it grew more potatoes" (184). The Austrians cultivated "fields of potatoes" when they occupied the same territory, and the Italians now glean what they left behind: "all the Austrians' potatoes and chestnuts from the woods" (184). These foraging practices give the lie to the stark national and racial differences that are supposed to underwrite the enmity of these two empires.

In one of the novel's most oft-cited passages, Frederic rejects patriotism and propaganda in favor of a strong sense of place:

> I had seen nothing sacred, and the things that were glorious had no glory and the sacrifices were like the stockyards at Chicago if nothing was done with the meat except to bury it. There were many words you could not stand to hear and finally only the names of places had dignity. Certain numbers were the same way and certain dates and these with the names of the places were all you could say and have them mean anything. Abstract words such as glory, honor, courage, or hallow were obscene beside the concrete names of villages, the numbers of roads, the names of rivers, the numbers of regiments and dates. (184–85)

Frederic compares the military to an industrial slaughterhouse, "the stockyards at Chicago." Worse still, this dead meat rots without being eaten; the "sacrifices" of war do not ultimately serve a greater purpose.[75] To counter these deadly abstractions, the "names of villages," "the number of roads," and "the names of rivers" create a regional map. Attention to terroir becomes a failsafe against the distorting vision of conquest.[76]

Hemingway underscores this antiwar message when Frederic and the Italian soldiers retreat from the front. As Frederic and his comrades—Aymo, Bonello, and Piani—search abandoned farmhouses for food, they revive a spirit of commensality and conviviality. They also familiarize themselves with Friuli and its foods.[77] The first night of the retreat, Frederic fears they will have to eat "monkey meat," French corned beef sourced from Argentina or Madagascar (191).[78] Instead, Aymo cooks "*pasta asciutta*" (190), and they salvage "red barbera" and "half a cheese" from the villa's cellar (192–93). As they travel away from the front, they recover surprising abundance—cheese, apples, wine, and sausages—from the cellars of local farmhouses (201, 217).[79] Though Hemingway seems to mourn pastoral life—the peasants too are abandoning the countryside (197–98)—Frederic savors local flavors: "I drank another cup of red wine. It tasted very good after the cheese and apple" (201). He and his companions also extend hospitality to the vulnerable, sharing cheese and apples with two young sisters traveling by themselves (196, 202). Aymo, Bonella, and Piani tell him of their hometown, Imola, and invite him to visit them there after the war (208).[80] Frederic seems to be going local; when they encounter a pair of Italian sergeants on the road, they refuse to believe that Frederic is not Italian (195).

Hemingway makes it clear that these meals carry ethical import when the soldiers' haven is shattered. While the four friends enjoy cheese and wine together, admiring the countryside and protecting the girls in their charge, the two sergeants pillage each farmhouse without taking the time to cook or to share their provisions. "I believe the bastards have eaten already," Piani observes after inviting the sergeants to the repast (201). The failure to dine together is a lapse of fellow feeling: "The sergeants looked at him. They hated the lot of us" (201). This each-man-for-himself attitude is inimical to Frederic and his companions, who are so committed to an ethic of hospitality that they leave a jug of wine inside the door of the farmhouse so that even their enemies can partake: "The Austrians can find it without breaking the door down" (202). In a notorious and ambiguous turn in the novel, Frederic shoots one of the sergeants for refusing to obey an order, and Piani takes great pleasure in killing the wounded man. The other runs away. In the sergeants' failure to respect the countryside they pass through, to show restraint in the food they requisition, and to share their feast with others, Hemingway indicates their moral turpitude. At the front, Gino explained that "dogfish" sell Italian military rations on the black market (184).[81] The sergeants are similarly opportunistic and self-serving.

Although the summary execution of the sergeant is an attempt to protect the camaraderie they have cultivated, the party soon encounters tragedy, as Aymo is shot, likely by friendly fire. It is Aymo who cooked their first meal and who insisted on creating an atmosphere of abundance and fellowship through food. Aymo's death bodes ill for the fate of this ethics of hospitality in the modern world. After Aymo dies, Bonello deserts, and the company is down to two men. Piani and Frederic find their last farmhouse and drink wine that has "gone to pieces and lost its quality and color" (218). These regional traditions and pleasures—and the ethics of interdependence that they foster—will not survive the war because everything "go[es] to pieces."

The sergeants were harbingers of the mechanized cruelty that Hemingway depicts as the military-industrial ethos. Frederic and Piani run into the carabinieri, who speak with "efficiency" and "coldness" (223). These officers champion terroir, not as a source of pleasure or local knowledge, but as a symbol of nation: "It is you and such as you that have let the barbarians into the sacred soil of the fatherland" (223). When the "sacred soil" shifts from region to "fatherland," a xenophobic narrative takes hold, justifying racism to defend Italian civilization against Germanic hordes. In this light, even Frederic seems unfamiliar and alien. When the carabinieri look at him, they see "a German in an Italian uniform" (224). These officers view the world with "beautiful detachment" and see themselves as heroes "saving their country"—now not the local countryside but the concept of the patria (224). Hemingway dramatizes the dangers of such a view as Frederic plunges into the river to escape their deadly interrogation. Terroir lays the groundwork for Italian Fascism, a movement Hemingway despised and that controlled the country by the time he published *A Farewell to Arms* in 1929.[82]

In spite of this genealogy connecting terroir to Fascism, Hemingway insists upon sensation and immediacy as a remedy for impersonality and abstraction. When Frederic flees to save his life, his hunger helps him survive: "it was not your body any more. The head was mine, and the inside of the belly. It was very hungry in there ... I was not made to think. I was made to eat. My God, yes. Eat and drink and sleep with Catherine" (231, 233). Through his hunger, Frederic reclaims his body. He and Catherine reunite and row into Switzerland illegally. There they achieve a brief window of alpine paradise, a bit like the one the priest described in Abruzzo. Like Basque country blurring the lines between Spain and France, the Alps expose the artifice of national boundaries. Here Catherine and Frederic sip the mulled wine that the local woodcutters enjoy: "we sat inside warmed by the stove and drank hot red wine with spices and lemon in it. They called it glühwein and it was a good thing to warm you and to celebrate with" (302). In this snowy interlude, the local is a haven, even when it is served in another language.

Terroir serves another, more disturbing function in this section of the novel, however. The war threatened to turn Frederic into meat. When he was wounded, the doctors' arms were "red as butchers" (57), and another doctor had a reputation as a "hog-butcher" (64). In a rueful aside, Frederic asks Catherine if "the stockyards" are one of the sights she would like to see in America (295). The repeated references to the meat industry—from Hemingway's allusion to the Chicago stockyards to Frederic's joke that dead officers are "white meat" (174)—critique, as I have suggested, the dehumanization of soldiers in the interest of military power. They also, however, bring up another valence of the word "stock," another significance of the descriptor "white." Part of the tragedy of war in this novel is that it kills white men.[83] In *The Passing of the Great Race* (1916), Madison Grant lamented that "the tall Nordic strain was killed off in greater proportions than the little brunet."[84] Though Frederic dismisses race as an explanation for Italian decline, and Hemingway indicts the xenophobia of the carabinieri, the "Anglo-Saxon" body seems particularly fragile and valuable in this novel.[85]

From this vantage point, Hemingway's celebration of the cuisine of northern Italy and Frederic's subsequent escape to Switzerland fall into regional and climatological patterns made all too familiar by raciologists and eugenicists of the period. In these mountainous Norths, terroir becomes a way of protecting alpine purity. The "grand country" and "splendid country" in the Alps grants Frederic and Catherine temporary elevation over the "bloody place" of the Italian front (278). Meals arrest time and merge taste and place in a utopian suspension: "Sitting up in bed eating breakfast we could see the lake and the mountains across the lake on the French side" (290). These gastronomic pleasures keep the pain of war at a distance: "I sat back in the corner with a heavy mug of dark beer and an opened glazed-paper package of pretzels and ate the pretzels for the salty flavor and the good way they made the beer taste and read about disaster" (292). Through cold and salt, Frederic preserves himself from the violence all around him.

This alpine haven, however, stands for extinction as much as purity. In *The Races of Europe*, Ripley claimed that the Swiss Alps "offer us superb illustrations of the effect of geographical isolation upon man . . . [preserving] almost absolute purity of type."[86] However, he also contended that the extreme climate and geography made it difficult for people to thrive in the mountains, even suggesting that these Swiss mountain folk might be whiter due to "the pigmental processes of the mountainous and infertile territory of these high alps."[87] Beginning with a dream of Abruzzo and ending in the Alps, *A Farewell to Arms* is an elegy for the Alpine and perhaps also for the Anglo-Saxon. Unexpectedly, given his early identification with the forces of globalization and corruption in the novel, Frederic becomes another representative, like his friend the Capracottan priest, of nonreproductive racial purity.[88] At the end of the novel, Catherine dies giving birth to their stillborn son. The title bids farewell not only to Catherine's embrace and to warfare but also to the coat of arms, the family crest. When Frederic compares his dead son to a "skinned rabbit" (326), the book thus circles back to the Abruzzo that Frederic never reaches, the "hare-tracks in the snow" that he never follows. Now, Frederic's heir is Frederic's hare—the fading sign of an irretrievable, racially pure past. The fact that this idyllic time and location exist only in fantasy may indicate the novel's deeper skepticism about racial purity and its achievability in lived temporalities and geographies. Nevertheless, the conclusion of the novel implies that its loss is a tragic one.

The Taste of Place: Gleaning and Mushroom Hunting with Gertrude Stein

Both *The Sun Also Rises* and *A Farewell to Arms* turn out to be elegies for white masculine belonging and reproduction, the alienation from terroir a sign of other forms of barrenness. Hemingway's fleeting allusions to goatherding, trout fishing, and hare hunting imply that it would be possible to build a more productive and symbiotic relationship to local spaces, but these fragile utopias are bracketed by the incursions of war and capital. The narrative momentum of these tales drives against the pastoral interludes, implying that these temporary reprieves and preserved spaces will fall to the relentless process of modern development and global dislocation. By contrast, Stein's poetics hold out against forward momentum, offering a recursive investigation of the immediate locale. In other words, while Hemingway mourns the pastoralism that he associates with regional life and racial authenticity, Stein explores the present possibility of local belonging. By connecting her poetic practice with foraging traditions, Stein simultaneously allies her artistry with French peasant culture and models rural cosmopolitanism, a process of transnational affiliation inflected with the cultural legacy of Jewish diaspora.

In *Geography and Plays* (1922), Stein takes up the figure of gleaning, foraging in the field after a harvest, work traditionally performed by women.[89] The food they recovered could provide sustenance for the family, and surplus could be sold in the marketplace.[90] These rights, developed in the premodern commons, were all but eliminated by agricultural enclosure and the rise of capitalism. Theresa Kelley points out that "the moral rhetoric of enclosure and regular wage earning" consigned gleaners to the "widening category of abjected persons," often in explicitly racialized terms.[91] Gleaners, depending upon a livelihood that had once defined collective belonging, now seemed "recalcitrant wanderers . . . who refuse[d] to embrace the new hegemony of wage-earning poverty and alienated labor."[92] The ideal of the commons casts the gleaner as an insider, a member of the village sustained by a shared harvest, while the competitive logic of capital views the gleaner as an outsider, a stranger on the margins who lives on the discarded wealth of the community. Regardless of this characterization, gleaning trains attention on local ground, whether the field is collectively shared or enclosed by a property owner. When Stein takes up this figure in the avant-garde terms of her catalog poetry, she retains this productive ambiguity.

This ambiguity also inheres in the biblical representation of gleaning. In the Old Testament, the Moabite Ruth marries an Israelite who came to her country seeking food during famine. After her husband's death, Ruth reaffirms her dedication to her new family and faith by following her mother-in-law, Naomi, to Bethlehem. There Ruth supports them both by gleaning after the barley harvest. The owner of the field where she gleans, Boaz, observes Ruth's dedication, marries her, and makes a land deal on Naomi's behalf. The practice of gleaning helps the outsider to become an insider, as Ruth sustains her mother-in-law and weds the property owner. Feminist critics and scholars of cosmopolitanism have reclaimed this tale as one of intimacy between women and expatriate belonging, which makes it seem an obvious touchstone for Stein.[93] At the same time, Ruth's foreignness exposes tensions between affiliation and exile, recognition and difference, shared fields and contested property. As Bonnie Honig observes, Ruth's story shows the fault lines in "a kinship-style national identity," which requires the figure of the outsider to consolidate myths of essential belonging.[94]

This biblical story also bore a particular cultural connection to the French countryside thanks to the painter Jean-François Millet, whom Stein admired as a child. The son of peasant farmers in Normandy, Millet dedicated his work to illustrating the lives of rural people in a time of industrialization, and he took a particular interest in French gleaners, holdouts against the new social order. Figure 3.1 reproduces Millet's painting *Harvesters Resting (Ruth and Boaz)*

Figure 3.1 In this painting by Jean-François Millet, Ruth is a gleaner in the French countryside. Jean-François Millet (French, 1814–75), *Harvesters Resting (Ruth and Boaz)*, 1850–53; oil on canvas; 67.3 × 119.7 cm (26½ × 47⅛ in.). Museum of Fine Arts, Boston, bequest of Mrs. Martin Brimmer.
Source: Photograph © 2018 Museum of Fine Arts, Boston.

(1853), which transposes the Ruth story to rural France.[95] Though Ruth appears reluctant as Boaz ushers her toward the rest of the workers, she already appears to belong, her brown skin, broad nose, and blue attire resembling theirs. Millet takes a tale about consent—the Moabite casting her lot with the Israelites—and turns it into one of implied relation, and he identifies the exigencies of peasant life with the sufferings of the chosen people. This association was critical because, as the art historian Alexandra Murphy explains, many "middle-class Parisians" thought that peasants were " 'brute[s],' hardly distinguishable from an animal and often compared unfavorably to the 'savage.' "[96] Millet both reinforces this racializing sensibility through the phenotypic similarity of his figures and rejects its dehumanizing logic with his emphasis on kinship and compassion. Through the biblical allusion, he hoped to make French spectators feel a renewed sense of responsibility to the rural poor.[97]

These three backgrounds—gleaning as the residue of the premodern commons, as a symbol of expatriate affiliation, and as a unifying practice for subaltern peoples—make gleaning a paradoxical yet potentially utopian figure. It is at once historically French and symbolically Jewish.[98] It envisions an unreachable past and an urgent present—the eyes scanning the ground for valuable castoffs. It is a sign both of abundance, the surplus that a society shares with its most destitute, and of vulnerability, the threat of starvation and exile. The *glaneur* or *glaneuse* is both romanticized citizen and reviled alien. In "Scenes. Actions and Disposition of Relations and Positions," a poem that in its very title posits a dynamic relationship between places and persons, Stein plumbs these contradictions as a matter of perspective.[99] Material conditions raise the stakes of judgments about belonging or marginality: "If the precious sand is rich and there is union then there is something. If the precious sand is poor then there is poverty."[100] The "precious sand" of the soil can be a source of collectivity or a spur to xenophobia—the latter an even greater temptation in times of limited resources.

In the poem, Stein offers a vatic, gerund-laden definition of gleaning that riffs on biblical language: "Lightning has no meaning, gleaning has choosing descending, bread has origin, a taste is spreading."[101] By declaring that "Lightning has no meaning," Stein rejects the patriarchal model of epiphany as the source of law. In the book of Exodus, God cows the Israelites and enjoins them to serve Moses: "And all the people saw the thunderings, and the lightnings, and the noise of the trumpet, and the mountain smoking: and when the people saw *it*, they removed, and stood afar off."[102] Instead of this monolithic authority, based on sublimity and fear, Stein chooses the pleasure of "bread," like the manna that God provides for the Israelites: "Then said the LORD unto Moses, Behold, I will rain bread from heaven for you; and the people shall go out and gather a certain rate every day, that I may prove them, whether they will walk in my law, or no."[103] This model of divinity inheres in miraculous generosity, bringing people together not through fear but through food.[104] God instructs the Israelites to gather this bread, and their gleaning creates collectivity and sufficiency: "he that gathered much had nothing over, and he that gathered little had no lack; they gathered every man according to his eating."[105] In turn, the provision of extra wheat and crops for the poor becomes a sacred covenant for the children of Israel: "And when ye reap the harvest of your land, thou shalt not wholly reap the corners of thy field, neither shalt thou gather the gleanings of thy harvest. And thou shalt not glean thy vineyard, neither shalt thou gather *every* grape of the vineyard; thou shalt leave them for the poor and stranger: I *am* the LORD your God."[106] Though "bread" may have an "origin," as Stein declares, "gleaning" invites the stranger into the community, creating an embodied politics of shared need and communicable pleasure: "a taste is spreading."

Significantly for this construction of community through shared resources rather than common blood, Stein grants "descending," that overcharged Darwinian term, and "choosing" equal weight, clustering them in the same clause with nary a comma to divide them.[107] She chooses not to choose between nativism and diaspora, between "origin" and "spreading." Both the child of Israel and the stranger can partake in the plenitude of the local harvest, and presumably both the French peasant and the Jewish cosmopolitan can enjoy the abundance of the countryside as well. In her prose poem, Stein demarcates the field where gleaning takes place: "It is no challenge. It is not more a church. It is not most a circle. It is not a vestibule. It is a single place of growing grass. Grass is not deserving. It has all that to show. It shows a marked meadow. It is not by the baker" (117). Stein's definitions are notoriously elliptical, but this one seems surprisingly straightforward. The field is not a martial challenge or a religious sanctuary; it is not defined by its boundedness, nor is it merely an anteroom to somewhere else. Stein puns on "grace," and especially the French pronunciation "la grâce," when she declares, "Grass is not deserving." Stein recalls agriculture's roots in wild growth; the farmer's field is merely a "marked meadow." The growing wheat represents more than raw material for processing and profit: "It is not by the baker," and local resources exceed human control: "Fishing is sudden" (117). In this shared place, people can harvest and dine together.

This version of localism is open to those who wish to belong there rather than merely those who find themselves there all along.[108] Stein imagines a rural cosmopolitanism that invents rather than inherits family: "A page of no addresses does not mean a mistake it means that there are places where the whole family is glad to eat together. This is not a sign of anger it is the necessary sunshine of the country" (117).[109] But this "necessary sunshine of the country" smacks of tourism, not labor. The speaker even observes picturesque agricultural work, albeit with a conflation of the seasons impossible for an actual farmer: "See

Figure 3.2 Millet's *Man with a Hoe* was an early favorite of Stein's and evidence, according to the eugenicist David Starr Jordan, of the inferiority of Norman peasant stock. Jean-François Millet (French, 1814–75), *Man with a Hoe*, 1860–62; oil on canvas; 81.9 × 100.3 cm (32¼ × 39½ in.).
Source: The J. Paul Getty Museum, Los Angeles.

Thomas bring the grain, see the grain have the color that grain has when grain is growing in any winter which is any summer" (108). Stein's language here sounds like a primer ("See Thomas bring the grain"), as though the peasant and his work teach the tourist how to read the landscape according to a pastoral alphabet.

This view of the native as an element of scene-setting recalls Millet's brown-skinned peasant who seemed almost made of the earth that he tilled. In *Paris France* (1940), Stein describes how moved she was as a child by Millet's controversial painting, *Man with a Hoe* (1863), reproduced in Figure 3.2: "I did have some feeling about what french country was like but The Man With the Hoe made it different, it made it ground not country, and France has been that to me ever since. France is made of ground, of earth... that is the way french country is, it is ground like that and they work at it just that way with just that kind of hoe."[110] From this perspective, French peasants are the ground that throws unraced expatriate subjectivity into relief. Stein's tourism in adult life bears out the "feeling" that art gave her about these authentic, toiling bodies. In "Scenes," Thomas both "turns the shadow darker" and "has the color brighter," a combination of implacable racial difference and enviable primitive intensity (108).

Stein was not alone in racializing the French peasantry. The eugenicist David Starr Jordan cited Millet's *Man with a Hoe* to demonstrate his thesis about racial degeneration and what he called "the survival of the unfit."[111] Rejecting the common interpretation of the painting as an indictment of class exploitation, Jordan insists that the "Man with a Hoe" is a racial type: "This is the Norman peasant, low-browed, heavy-jawed, 'the brother of the ox,' gazing with lack-lustre eye on the things about him ... Millet's 'Man of the Hoe' is not the product of oppression. He is primitive, aboriginal. His lineage has always been that of the clown and the swineherd."[112] As Robert Herbert points out, much nineteenth-century art treated peasants as the "Others ... found within national borders," and "many of the assumptions about non-European primitivism were already in the minds of Parisians whenever they pondered the world of the peasant."[113] This racialization of the peasant connected the laboring body with premodern agriculture and indeed with the land itself, which could bear out backwardness or pastoralism depending on the perspective of the viewer. In *The Races of Europe*, Ripley pinpointed Normandy and Brittany as picturesque regions that could be studied to derive the history of racial isolation and intermixture in France and Europe more generally.[114]

While Millet's Norman peasants were brown-skinned and sunburned, Bretons were often depicted as ethereal and white, their translucent bodies like panes to let in "necessary sunshine." For example, in Figure 3.3, an 1898 advertisement for the Brittany seaside uses pastoral iconography (cow, meadow, flowers) and the Breton maid's traditional attire to promise the train traveler a rural idyll away from the rigors of modern life. The lightness and brightness of the image communicate picturesque beauty, local belonging, and racial purity. This is a distinct version of primitivism, which emphasized not earthy labor but transcendent spirituality.[115] A few decades later, this view of regional peoples as pure, ancient, and superior would be exploited by the Nazis, as Mark Kurlansky observes: "The Nazis had experienced some success in appealing to Flemish and Breton nationalism, claiming that by standing up for European racial purity, Nazism was defending the rights of these ancient peoples."[116] They also courted Hemingway's beloved Basques, "who believed they were the original European race."[117] From this perspective, regional ethnicities ratify nativism based on racial superiority. While nations could be melting pots, no one could be a Breton without the right blood.

Obviously, this iconography and rhetoric complicate Jewish expatriate Stein's insistence on her full belonging in regional France. In "Advertisements," collected with "Scenes" in *Geography and Plays*, Stein describes a Breton woman, perhaps a household servant: "White and be a Briton. This means a woman

Figure 3.3. This advertisement for seaside vacations in Brittany captures the ideal of the pure and pastoral Breton woman.

Source: Andre Wilder, *Chemins de Fer de L'Ouest*, 1898.

from the North of France. They are very religious. They say blue is not a water color ... She washes her hair very often" (343).[118] The Breton maid is "white," pious, and clean.[119] Identified with the olive harvest, she relies on the pastoral poet to tell her story for her: "She likes the poet to mutter. He does. The olive" (343).[120] As an expatriate, Stein opts for shifting "Relations and Positions," to quote the subtitle of "Scenes," but the Breton's body, like the olive tree, is rooted. Stein hints at her discomfort with Brittany's claims to timeless regional identity and racial hygiene. Like a gastronomic map of the region, Stein declares, "Butter comes from Brittany" (343). Yet instead of bearing out the purity and richness of the local culture, it stinks: "In the summer it smells rancid. We do not like it. We have ceased use of it. We find that oil does as well" (343). Stein rejects the local specialty before the local rejects her.

These allusions to olive harvest and dairy culture make it clear why the gleaning paradigm was so important to Stein. Where agriculture and even shepherding assume a home base, foraging shifts sites easily. At the same time, it is a source of knowledge about and intimacy with a new location. Stein's allusions to mushrooming, a passionate pastime of hers, demonstrate this traversal of bounded spaces and creation of ground-level affinity. To unearth mushrooms requires absorbing attention, tramping through underbrush, poking and prodding, peering beneath and uncovering what is not immediately evident.

By the time she wrote about collecting mushrooms, Stein was increasingly invested in rural France as the place where she lived and belonged, rather than as a tourist spot. In 1929, Stein and Toklas leased a house in Bilignin, and as the Stein scholar Ulla Dydo observes, "Though the women did not own it, everything about it, including the landscape in which it stood, comes to sound in her words as if it was theirs."[121] Mushroom hunting allows Stein to take imaginative possession of the land around her, or, perhaps more accurately, to let the land possess her. In "Unruly Edges: Mushrooms as Companion Species," Anna Lowenhaupt Tsing writes evocatively of the intimacies that mushroom hunting occasions: "You visit the spot enough, and you know its seasonal flowers and its animal disturbances; you have made a familiar place in the landscape."[122] This place-making requires a repeated process of wandering and return, a temporality and sense of space evoked by Stein's famed repetitive syntax.[123]

Reading Stein's thicket of poetic excrescences for patterns and tropes is also suggestively parallel to scanning the ground for mushrooms, unearthing their shapes and signs. Freud, also an avid mycophile, characterized the unconscious as a mycelium and the analyst as a mushroom hunter: "The dream-thoughts which we encounter during the interpretation commonly have no termination, but run in all directions into the net-like entanglement of our intellectual world. It is from some dense part of this fabric that the dream-wish then arises, like the mushroom from its mycelium."[124] Stein's experimental poetry offers a similar view of patterned density. Joshua Schuster argues compellingly that Stein's work demands "reading for the feel of the environs" and "things are only revealed or noticeable at varying levels of scale."[125] Stein's repetitions, Schuster opines, trigger "a level of automaticity in our reading, of reading without what is commonly called consciousness, which is usually associated with the crisply attentive, focused, critical side of our thinking."[126] This syntactic inundation produces an "immersive environmental aesthetic."[127] This immersive aesthetic, Stein teaches us in *History or Messages from History* (1930), privileges ground-level observation over the bird's-eye view of historiography: "In history one does not mention dahlias mushrooms or hortensias."[128]

Many modernist writers had an understandable affinity for mycology, spotting overlooked fungal forms in the mulch of the supposed wasteland.[129] In *La Fanfarlo* (1847), Baudelaire writes of "the truffle, that secret and mysterious vegetation of Cybele, that savory sickness that she hides in her entrails."[130] In *Sons and Lovers* (1913), D. H. Lawrence calls mushrooms "the white-skinned, wonderful naked bodies crouched secretly in the green."[131] Alfred Kreymbourg entitled an early poetry collection *Mushrooms: A Book of Free Forms* (1916).[132] In *My Ántonia* (1918), the "penetrating, earthy odour" of dried mushrooms carries the "strange taste" of Bohemian alterity.[133] Combining vegetation myth with interpretive hunt, formalism with eroticism, and nostalgia with exoticism, the mushroom could hardly be a more fitting emblem for modernism's dual infatuation with the quotidian and the mysterious.

In lesbian poetry, the mushroom offered a metaphorical alternative to patriarchal property and heterosexual reproduction. In "After my marriage-night" (1933) by Sylvia Townsend Warner, a new bride surveys her husband's fields:

> I was proud as I went, I scorned the fields that had given increase
> And awaited now like slaves the certain ploughing of winter,
> I turned to those acres I knew unfruitful and forsaken;
> But behold, my bitter pasture was whitened like a fleece
> With mushrooms, and lay at peace. (lines 41–45)[134]

The speaker realizes that she is her husband's property. Her reproductive "increase" belongs to him, like his profit-bearing crops, and the "certain ploughing of winter" does not make that conjugal duty sound like a pleasant one. The mushroom bloom seems to confirm the poem's celebration of fertility; now the field is not "unfruitful," and the speaker "gave thanks and was mild, / Knowing myself with child" (lines 54–55). But the mycological imagery complicates this apparent confirmation of reproductive imperatives. It is not the field that issues "increase"; it is the uncontrollable mushrooms on its margins:

> In a night they had come, whence and how, who could tell?
> Myriads of rounded mushrooms everywhere surrounding me,
> Thrusting out tender from the harsh earth, engendered,
> Frail, with the cleaving grasses broken with their upswell
> That no bondage could quell. (lines 46–50)

This "upswell" of "rounded mushrooms," tender like the buttons in Stein's heralded poetry collection, "engender[s]" rebellion. Resisting the order of patriarchal plowing, mushrooms rise up, and their feminine flesh and pleasing proximity reassure the speaker: "I was at peace with them, seeing them so undefiled, / Knowing the gills so delicate hidden under the chilly flesh, / At a birth so meek and marvelous, so secret and maiden-sleek" (lines 51–53). This virginal imagery, "undefiled" and "maiden-sleek," also contains the erotic trace of hidden folds of feminine flesh. Though the poem's conclusion announces the speaker's pregnancy, Warner evokes a subterranean mycelium of feminine intimacy, a sapphic fairy circle.[135]

Like Warner's poem, Stein's *Lucy Church Amiably* challenges the patriarchal order of agriculture with the marginality of mushrooms.[136] The titular character rents a house in Belley, and she tracks mushrooms through the countryside. Lucy likes mushrooms best when they violate property boundaries, introducing wildness into cultivated spaces: "Mushrooms if they are fresh and very small and wild are always delicious particularly if they grow in fields and not near trees nor woods" (80). This observable phenomenon becomes a social metaphor. In the shadow of cultivated land, these unruly bodies reproduce, modeling queer affiliation through proximity: "Do orange colored mushrooms grow in thickets and were they mother and daughter or only neighbors" (18). Like the mushrooms, both hidden in thickets and in plain view thanks to their bright color, women together flaunt the open secret of cohabitation where others expect consanguinity. Queer mushrooms contest the dominance of patriarchal grains: "if the grass is high do mushrooms grow in the grass" (75). Lucy Church, mushroom hunter, intrepidly presses through the grass to find her prize:

> Lucy Church come to to the best of Timothy the best of Timothy and there find mushrooms there find mushrooms and there have a stick which has been cut around so that the bark having been taken off in such a way it matches matches pleases presses and the best known method of looking is when there is the sun on the head. (76)

Stein capitalizes Timothy, making the type of hay also a masculine character. Sticks were often used in mushroom seeking, and this phallic prosthesis "pleases" and "presses."

Mushroom gathering and the circling that it entails simultaneously refuse two kinds of patriarchal plot, one narrative and the other spatial.[137] Foraging's vigilant present occludes the futurist orientation of narrative completion: "Leave completing completing it to them if they have mushrooms in fields mushrooms in fields" (90). At the same time, this repeated ritual recalls a long history of mushroom collection. As the mycologist Nicholas Money observes, "The field or meadow mushroom, *Agaricus campestris* . . . has been gathered as a wild mushroom in Europe for centuries."[138] This queer continuity hearkens back to alternative pasts, which could in turn model new spatial and social forms. Lucy's mushroom hunts constitute what Elizabeth Freeman calls "erotohistoriography," an embodied encounter with "historical materials" in the present moment.[139] The body, brushing up against such materials, registers the contingency and hybridity of the present, always seeded with the fungal spores of the past.

Indeed, Stein theorizes such an approach to historiography in *History or Messages from History*, published in the same year as *Lucy Church Amiably*. The woman mushroom hunter transforms the terms of history and, in so doing, resists the authority that resides in its telos: "There is no history in gentleness. She gently found mushrooms. She questioned the authority. It might have been many more. There were quite enough. No history is proof against everything. Moonlight in the valley is before and after history" (263). Official history is not "proof against" embodied experience and its reclamation of overlooked forms.

Pleasure is one of the modes of knowing central to erotohistoriography, and Stein repeatedly emphasizes preference and pleasure in describing Lucy's mushroom-hunting forays.[140] Like a Paterian aesthete, Lucy delights in vivid color and flamelike intensity: "She said she preferred the mushrooms that were red and grew like matches so they were called" (95). Eager to sample the world around her, Lucy's tastes are promiscuous: "she would be very much better pleased if all mushrooms were edible" (102–103). Her looping trajectories, though loosely guided by her object, offer their own satisfactions: "There is a great pleasure in wandering underneath trees" (210). The mushrooms themselves demonstrate the marriage of survival and satisfaction, resistance and resilience:

> And mushrooms they have in them every element of beauty and durability of delicacy and determination and resistance and some of them are undoubtedly a great delicacy and have every reason to give every pleasure to those who find them and cultivate them. We will go now and look at them. (212)

Their feminized "beauty" and "delicacy" do not diminish their "durability," "determination," and "resistance." Lucy Church, Gertrude Stein, and the reader are united in a moment of fictive imminence defined by sensory pleasure, a utopian time and place when and where we "will go now and look at them."

Stein adumbrates a queer ecology, which the forager uncovers through observation and participation.[141] As a mushroom collector, Lucy registers her own role in this web of relations:

> Lucy can change mushrooms to daisies and daisies to oxen and oxen to church. Lucy can change oxen to daisies and daisies to mushroom and mushrooms to church. Lucy Church can change oxen to mushrooms and mushrooms to daisies and daisies to daisies and daisies to church. She is to change mushrooms to oxen and oxen to daisies. She is to. (218)

Instead of a hierarchy of being, Stein sketches an ongoing cycle of consumption, digestion, and transformation, which is sacred in its own terms. The smallest (mushrooms and daisies) and the largest (oxen and humans) participate in the same dynamic of rot and regeneration.[142] The weather shapes these ongoing processes, the land's texture and moisture, and the growing things found there: "Inundation in a meadow is different from inundation in a marsh... Lucy Church is indebted to rain for her belief in white and pink" (87). As Money points out, "Rainfall in the days before a [mushroom picking] foray is the most favourable omen for a productive hunt."[143] The colors she spies, pink and white, are the colors of the young growth meadow mushroom.[144]

These revelations about ecology and interdependence in turn support the dissolution of heteronormativity and hierarchy. Stein sinks her reader into a circular sentence, which begins with the announcement of a "wedding wedding" but gradually dissolves "in swimming pleasure in recognizing that they are circling what is circling in a half circle mushrooms are circling in a half circle and they are matches and are so cold pleasing so called pleasing to the palate and pleasing so called half a circle" (115). Like the punning title of *Tender Buttons*, this passage refuses to distinguish between the lesbian and the mycological, merging both in oral pleasure.[145] In observing that "they are matches," Stein generates a suggestive indeterminacy between same-sex couplings and the match-shaped mushrooms that Lucy preferred to harvest. The submerged figure of the "witches' circle," the folk explanation for the surprising uniformity of circular mushroom distribution, connects women's affiliation and the subterranean mycelium.[146]

The witch, variously a symbol of queer sexual appetite, nonreproductive age, and Jewish otherness, is the alter ego of the mushroom hunter, who poses a threat to the social order.[147] In *Civilization: A Play* (1932), Stein includes in her cast of characters "An old woman from the mountains who should sell raspberries but sells mushrooms and her brother."[148] (Though it appears that Stein intends for her brother to be a character, there is also an amusing suggestion in this syntax that she'd happily sell him off too.) Berries blossom but mushrooms bud, sexual reproduction more pastoral than spores. The old woman sticks to her controversial wares, but she does so in the margins: this is the last time Stein mentions her in the text, which focuses instead on "George Couleur," "a tiller, of the soil and owner of very many" (341). The *terre* defined as property takes center stage in civilization, pushing the old woman out.

Perhaps unsurprisingly, the very qualities that made the queer proliferation of mushrooms appealing to Warner and Stein made them ominous for eugenic thinkers. Mushrooms are legion, easy to overlook, and possibly poisonous. Adolph Hitler compared the Jewish people to "poisonous mushrooms" and warned, "The Jew is and remains a parasite, a sponger who, like a pernicious bacillus, spreads over wider and wider areas."[149] A popular German children's book, *The Poisonous Mushroom* (1938) by Julius Streicher, taught children to identify Jewish physiognomies, especially the telltale nose, lest they make the fatal error of taking a poisonous mushroom for an edible one.[150]

If mushrooms are too fecund and potentially fatal, the mushroom hunter is too perverse, poking her nose where it doesn't belong. The expatriate food writer M. F. K. Fisher, a fan of Stein and Toklas, devotes an extended section of *Serve It Forth* (1934) to a virginal French truffle hunter, the last of her kind. Her description evokes the perversity *and* the celibacy (and the celibacy as perversity) associated with this figure:

> And then there are truffles, those mysterious growths which spring seedless and rootless from the oaky soil, which may or may not be as good as they are rare and dear, and which even Brillat-Savarin names aphrodisiac. People tell me that only virgins have the true nose for truffle hunting: virgin sows, virgin bitches. I cannot vouch for this, as I have never hunted truffles—but I do know a man who once saw the last human hunter in all the Périgord country . . . "Yes," he was saying, "I have seen the last virgin woman truffle-hunter in all France! . . . we had gathered secretly because the Church was opposed to woman truffle-hunters. The idea of an old virgin sniffing over the hills, with a pack of men hot at her heels—it is disgusting to the Church, it is—you understand me?—pagan! So this was to be the last hunt, with the only woman left alive who had the truffle nose. She was old, very old, and she was—yes, unquestionably—she was a virgin! And *mon Dieu, mon Dieu*, but what a nose! It was long, most pointed, red at the tip. It quivered." (49)

If the proliferation of mushrooms suggests in other contexts an epidemic of otherness—the trouble with tribbles—in this portrait of a mushroom seeker, the virgin woman will lead her race to extinction, "a pack of men hot at her heels." She simultaneously embodies queer celibacy and phallic potency, with her "long, most pointed, red" nose.[151] This nose anticipates Fisher's portrait of Alice B. Toklas in the introduction to an edition of her cookbook: "her nose was big or even huge, and hooked and at the same time almost fleshy, the kind that artists try not to draw."[152] The phallic nose is too close to the earth, too animalistic, simultaneously a sign of too little sex and too much erotic power. As an anti-Semitic trope, it carries many of the same connotations. In "The Duchess and the Jeweller" (1938), Virginia Woolf compares the nose of a Jewish jeweler to a truffle-hunting snout:

> His nose, which was long and flexible, like an elephant's trunk, [and] seemed to say by its curious quiver at the nostrils (but it seemed as if the whole nose quivered, not only the nostrils) that he was not satisfied yet; still smelt something under the ground a little further off. Imagine a giant hog in a pasture rich with truffles; after unearthing this truffle and that, still it smells a bigger, a blacker truffle under the ground further off.[153]

This description implies that Jews threaten the social order not only because they are not fully human but also because they range over so much ground. Stein's dreams of transnational belonging, gleaning shared pastures, for Woolf become the nightmarish incursion of the oriental elephant on rich British soil, xenophobia rendered all the more distressing given her marriage to a Jewish man.

In light of these misogynistic, homophobic, and anti-Semitic characterizations of the mushroom forager, Stein's reclamation of the figure seems all the more exceptional, though perhaps this very redolence of femininity, queerness, and Jewishness makes the mushroom gatherer a satisfying alter ego for the cosmopolitan modernist. From the margins of the meadow, she envisions an artistic avant-garde united in the pursuit of unexpected beauty and corporeal pleasure. In her personal correspondence, mushroom gathering served as a pretext for invitation, an articulation of hospitality that connected foraging and friendship. In a July 1930 letter, she wrote to Pablo Picasso: "It takes time to get ... the old women ... to search in the mountains for the best mushrooms, all this can't be done so fast so tell us a little in advance, if yes well you'll lunch with us on Sunday August tenth, and we shall be pleased as punch."[154] In 1936, she wrote to Thornton Wilder of her latest mushroom-gathering adventures: "We collect les trompette[s] de la mort a beautiful black tulip of a mushroom and we love you very much and we would like to do something about it, when shall we meet again and so much love."[155] Like the composer John Cage, who took friends on weekly mushroom expeditions, Stein creates imagined community through foraging forays.[156] A transnational and even transatlantic mycelium, as it were, connects these experimental formalists.

But this community was not merely one of fellow modernists. When Stein collected mushrooms, she made necessary connections with rural French women. In her 1954 cookbook, Toklas reminisces about one such incident: "While waiting for lunch to be cooked, we walked in the forest when Gertrude Stein, who had a good nose for mushrooms, found quantities of them. The cook would be able to tell us if they were edible."[157] Though Stein prides herself on her "good nose," the cook is amused by the touristic gusto of this redundant foraging expedition: "She smiled when she saw what Gertrude Stein brought for her inspection and pointed to a large basket of them on the kitchen table" (85). Nonetheless, she rewards her guest's efforts by "us[ing] those Gertrude Stein had found for what she was preparing for our lunch" (85). This collaboration evidences an exchange that Stein doesn't quite achieve in her poetry. "Scenes" and "Advertisements" separate the tourist from the peasant, in spite of Stein's aspirational endorsement of gleaning. In *Lucy Church Amiably*, Stein projects her own foraging sensibility into a protagonist who embodies the countryside, named after the village of Lucey and its church. Neither of these strategies for imagining transnational affiliation involves a two-way exchange; Stein either observes or identifies with the local. But Toklas's cookbook captures this fleeting moment when the cosmopolite turns to the cook and defers to her deeper knowledge of terroir. In this regional romance, putative racial or national differences fade into the background in favor of the culinary and botanical knowledge shared between women: "Once more, a woman was presiding in the kitchen" (85).

"Wine of Wyoming" and the Spirit of Latinity

History or Messages from History and *Lucy Church Amiably* capture a moment of hope for Stein about transnational belonging under the (submerged) sign of Jewishness and the (more overt) sign of queerness. In a grim historical irony, the Fascist movements already consolidating in Germany and Italy at that time would take terroir as their banner and Jews and queers as their enemies. Over the course of the 1930s, it became more difficult to believe in terroir as an imaginative, adopted relation to space and soil that could flourish untroubled by war, empire, or political upheaval. In "Wine of Wyoming" (1930), Hemingway dramatizes the failure of transplantation, and in her late-career works, "The Winner Loses: A Picture of Occupied France" (1940) and *Paris France* (1940), Stein adopts a social conservativism that vindicates her own village life but consigns others to perpetual exile or worse.

"Wine of Wyoming" summons up a transnational ideal through the promise of region.[158] Hemingway describes the wide-open spaces and beautiful prairies of Wyoming, and he places a French couple in the midst of this grassland. His narration superimposes European geography on American landscapes, imbuing the latter with a dignity derived from the former: "the stubble of grain-fields on each side and the mountains off to the right . . . looked like Spain, but it was Wyoming."[159] This vista recalls Hemingway's idyllic depiction of Basque country in *The Sun Also Rises*. This landscape, where "the soil of the hills was red, [and] the sage grew in gray clumps," abuts the mountains, which "looked more like Spain than ever" (353).[160] The American West serves as a sort of secondary Spain, a possible destination for the regional aspirations that have been rooted out of Europe by industry and war.

Hemingway uses two French immigrants to reflect this history and its damaging relationship to regional foodways. Industry seems to have brought them to Wyoming; the husband works at the mines, and both members of the couple came from coal mining regions in France, Madame Fontan "from Lens" (343), and her husband "from "the Centre near Saint-Etienne" (344). Both towns played an active role in World War I, Saint-Étienne thanks to its arsenal, and Lens because of its position on the western front. Indeed, Lens was famously devastated by the war; one postwar commentator remarked that its "ruins" served as "pathetic reminders of the crushing destructiveness of war. The buildings, the homes, the churches are crushed; everything in fact, except the spirit of the people who lived there."[161] The Fontans fail to acknowledge the impact of war on their hometowns or regions, instead emphasizing their ongoing tastes for the foods and wines of home.

Madame Fontan describes these dishes and vintages to the American narrator, and she identifies them with place, even though she and her husband are now uprooted from these regions. Their activities as vintners seem to perpetuate this ideal of the "pays," meaning region rather than nation, in the new context of rural Wyoming. Madam Fontan observes, "Il est crazy pour le vin! Il est comme ça. Son pays est comme ça" (348). The phrase "Il est crazy pour le vin!" was Hemingway's draft title for the story, and it encapsulates the translation that the wine promises to the Fontans and their customers. The passion for wine, translated into American terms, could continue what has been lost with "son pays." Ideally, the vines are transplanted and so is the culture. Nonetheless, Madame Fontan identifies her husband with his region; they are both "comme ça." If a person draws his vitality from his place of origin, as many French thinkers insisted, then it does very little good—and in fact, might do some damage—to bring this wine to Wyoming.

Madame Fontan's perspective seems to bear out the idea that a person's tastes and, indeed, the very body are shaped by place of origin. She describes her own childhood "in the north where they don't drink any wine" (348). As a local, she undergoes a sensory education:

> Everybody drinks beer. By where we lived there was a big brewery right near us. When I was a little girl I didn't like the smell of the hops in the carts. Nor in the fields. Je n'aime pas les houblons. No, my God, not a bit. The man that owns the brewery said to me and my sister to go to the brewery and drink the beer, and then we'd like the hops. That's true. Then we liked them all right. He had them give us the beer. We liked them all right then. (348–49)

Coming of age in beer country is to be immersed in strong smells and then indoctrinated in appealing tastes. Over the course of this anecdote, what "everybody" likes becomes what "We liked." On the one hand, Madame Fontan is describing acquiring a taste, a gradual process of overcoming distaste ("Je n'aime pas les houblons") that one assumes an outsider could undertake. On the other hand, this story is a coming-of-age story. These little girls will take their mature and preordained place in the community—except that Madame Fontan leaves the community, and now she must serve illegal beer to drunken Americans, a step down from the local brewery as a center of town life. This trajectory reinforces the impression that to abandon terroir is to lose something more than the smell of hops.

But the Fontans have not given up. In fact, Madame Fontan emphasizes their efforts to re-create native dishes in their new land. And as in *The Sun Also Rises*, where goatherding and trout fishing allow Jake and Bill to feel momentarily a part of the Basque community, game hunting facilitates cultural and culinary translation. After killing a jackrabbit, Fontan asks his wife "to cook it with a sauce with wine, make a black sauce with wine and butter and mushrooms and onion and everything in it" (349). Fontan recuperates the taste of place with this dish, judging that the sauce itself is better than the jackrabbit. In spite of his denigrating assessment of the local game, this *sauce chausseur* draws a connection between this country and his own. "Dans son pays c'est comme ça," explains Madame Fontan to her American guests. "Il y a beaucoup de gibier et de vin" (349). By making wine in Prohibition-era America, Fontan strives to re-create "son pays" in a new place.

Hemingway hints that this endeavor, however admirable, is bound to fail. The narrator is an American, and though he and his friend speak French, recognize good wines, and appreciate trout fishing, he also seems resigned to the fallen state of taste in his nation: "'How do you like America?' Fontan asked me. 'It's my country, you see. So I like it, because it's my country. Mais on ne mange pas très bien. D'antan, oui. Mais maintenant, no'" (345). Here the narrator lacks a "pays," possessing only a "country" in the abstract terms of nation, which lack the texture of the Fontans' very precise evocation of their regional origins. Furthermore, as he does in both *The Sun Also Rises* and *A Farewell to*

Arms, Hemingway associates another "country," or at least another ideal of what country might mean, with a premodern past. Here, the standards of connoisseurship—"on ne mange pas très bien"—reveal the lapses of modernity. In some ineffable "D'antan," meaning "of yesteryear" or "long ago," eating well was possible. The Fontans' quest to create a space for hospitality in the prairie seems bound to fail because no terrain is safe from the temporal rupture of modernity, the negative space of "maintenant."

American overconsumption becomes sign and symbol of this modernity run amok. Other Americans drive to the Fontans' farm, drunkenly demanding beer and wine; one women vomits on the table and in her shoes (349). In language that recalls Brett's association with Circe, Fontan calls them "cochons" (349). This piggishness threatens to contaminate the Fontan family. Madame Fontan explains that her son has married "une américaine" who is "two hundred twenty-five pounds" and an "Indienne."[162] The continuation of the Fontans' bloodline depends on her, and they have little to look forward to. "Already she can't have another baby," Madame Fontan explains; "she's too fat. There ain't any room" (343). Not only does the American wife fail in her reproductive duties, she also abandons her culinary ones: "She don't cook. She gives him beans en can" (343). "Beans en can" encapsulate American convenience culture, pleasureless accumulation that Hemingway reinforces through the Indian's obesity.

The implication of the daughter-in-law's race is ambiguous. On the one hand, she embodies the stereotype of the fat squaw and represents a miscegenating threat to their virtuous son, who works at a local ranch. On the other hand, she may stand in for *American* indigeneity, regional belonging and forced exile that predated World War I. If the American Indian symbolized the lost past and place-based belonging, then perhaps the "Indienne" mirrors the fate of other natives, like the Fontans, who lose their connection to the land through immigration. Once the member of a people who hunted and fished, the activities most often celebrated in "Wine of Wyoming," now she is only a passive consumer of food, books, and movies.

Ultimately, the sophisticated narrator, in spite of his obvious experiences in Europe and his linguistic and cultural conversance with the French, also embodies the failure of hospitality and the ascent of hollow consumerism in America. His ethical lapse betrays the limits of the transnational ideal of terroir, which can so easily be coopted for tourism and the detached sensibility of visitors who are just passing through. The wine is finally ready, and Fontan invites the narrator and his friend to "a fête" in honor of the occasion. They fail to show up: "We did not want a foreign language" (351). Though these Americans have demonstrated their ability to discern a fine flavor, "light and clear and good," in a "new wine" (344), they still see themselves as customers, not comrades. Connoisseurship need not be world citizenship. Like the Indian bride with her canned beans, the

Americans prioritize convenience, so they ignore their obligation to their hosts. When the narrator and his friend return to say goodbye, Fontan fumbles for a bottle of wine to give them. He drank his supply of wine while waiting for them to show up, and now he struggles to unlock the door of his daughter-in-law's house, where the rest of it is kept.

Though this incident seems minor and even grotesquely comic, Fontan's inability to get to his stores of wine—"My own wine that I made" (352)—suggests a broader alienation associated with the loss of his *pays*. If the vintage that he makes is the taste of the place that he has lost, it adds insult to injury for these bottles to belong to someone else. Furthermore, the fact that he has to depend on his daughter-in-law to give him the wine that he made associates Fontan's bottles with his bloodline. Both the bottles of wine and the paternal line are created with a view to the future. But it seems clear that this transplantation has resulted in loss, not recovery and degeneration, not hybridity. The narrator peers through the window at Fontans' bottles: "Looking through the window I could see where the wine was stored. Close to the window you could smell the inside of the house. It smelled sweet and sickish *like an Indian house*" (352, emphasis mine). Here fermentation signals corruption rather than culture; the wine is now indistinguishable from the stink of racial difference. The narrator observes that Fontan is "ruined," a word that connects economic failure, social humiliation, and rotting grapes (353).

If the "Indienne" and the Fontans are both natives who have lost their homelands, the fate of local cultures is imminent extinction, as the conclusion of the story underscores. The American narrator and his friend contemplate the prairie grouse, which serve as a Wyoming substitute for French game birds, and are struck by their picturesque beauty:

> They flew as we came toward them, their wings beating fast, then sailing in long slants, and lit on the hillside below. "They are so big and lovely. They're bigger than European patridges [sic]." "It's a fine country for la chasse, Fontan says." "And when the chasse is gone? "They'll be dead then." "The boy won't." "There's nothing to prove he won't be," I said. "We ought to have gone last night." "Oh, yes," I said. "We ought to have gone." (354)

This elegiac exchange connects the destruction of the "fine country" and its bird species with the expiration of the social and ecological ritual of "the chasse." In a rather creepy turn, the narrator and his friend protect the Fontans from this inevitable regional decline by predicting their deaths. Many early-twentieth-century conservationists associated the protection of species and the creation of national parks with the eugenicist goal of preserving superior stock.[163] Hemingway seems dubious. The Fontans, his narrator speculates, may all be gone by the time the countryside is developed and the birds are eliminated. Like the peasant soldiers killed in *A Farewell to Arms*, even the boy might be spared the experience of degeneration by virtue of premature death. Hemingway caps off this grim prognostication—this protection of regional identity and racial purity through extinction—with nostalgia. Like the fictive "D'antan" when American eating was "très bien" (345), the narrator and his friend imagine an alternative "last night" when they met the Fontans in the spirit of their hospitality and renewed the possibility of "la chasse" and indeed la cuisine for the future. Instead, they mourn its passing.

In "Wine of Wyoming," Hemingway diagnoses the commodification of terroir as a symptom of the gradual extermination of local places and peoples. Though his divided position as tourist facilitates this critique, it also contributes to the tone of resignation, the implication of inevitability. In Stein's late-career writings, she abandons the nomadic sensibility of *Lucy Church Amiably* in favor of an apparently timeless identification between race and place.[164] Her romanticization of the French countryside and its folk coincided with Fascist propaganda. Schuster speculates that Stein may have agreed to translate Pétain's writing in part because she was sympathetic with his view of *la terre*.[165] Furthermore, her insistence on local attachment abrogated social responsibilities to a wider world. As Joan Retallack observes, "How much Stein and Toklas understood (actually took into their consciousness) about the fate of Jewish deportees is questionable."[166] Janet Flanner marveled at the couple's ability to focus on their immediate environs, as she expressed (perhaps with a hint of exasperation) in a 1939 letter to Stein: "Few ladies in these times have the concentration to ignore the war, and heaven knows it's true that in the end that's all that prevented . . . me from coming down and eating mushrooms with you and Alice."[167] In this context, eating mushrooms seems less a form of resistance than an isolationist expatriate's equivalent of "let them eat cake."

In "The Winner Loses," an article that she published in the *Atlantic Monthly* in 1940, Stein takes up the oversimple pastoral mode that "Scenes" and *Lucy Church Amiably* complicated with gleaning and mushroom gathering. Now, the fertile farmland offers a sanctuary from the deprivations and pressures of war: "the country is a better place in war than a city. They grow the things to eat right where you are, so there is no privation, as taking it away is difficult, particularly in the mountains, so there was plenty of meat and potatoes and bread and honey and we had some sugar and we even had all the oranges and lemons we needed and dates."[168] The diurnal and seasonal rhythms of agriculture make the war seem distant and unreal: "We all dug in our gardens or in the fields all day and every day, and March and April wore away" (572). Threatened by deportation, Stein is digging in and taking root. When Stein and Toklas decide not to flee, Stein's pretext for staying is that "it would be awfully uncomfortable and

I am fussy about my food" (575). In the context of war, Stein sticks to the prewar language of hospitality and tourism. Not only does she want to stay, her French friends and neighbors clamor to keep her: "Everybody knows you here; everybody likes you; we all would help you in every way. Why risk yourself among strangers?" (576). Like Ruth joining the Israelites, Stein is effectively adopted by this new French family: "Here in this little corner we are *en famille*, and if you left, to go where?—*aller, où?*" (576). At the same time, by claiming to be "*en famille*" in Bilignin, Stein denies her own ties to the Jewish people.[169]

Stein's celebration of French character and what she calls the "spirit of Latinity" in *Paris France* (1940) is guilty of similar omissions and projections (49). As Adam Gopnik observes, "It is hard not to wince with pain, at moments, rereading *Paris France*" with its detached meditations on the "threat of war."[170] In this book, Stein treats regional life as evidence of transcendent Frenchness. Suggestively, this mythology takes shape in an anecdote about provincial cuisine after World War I:

> And then slowly it began again. People would begin to talk about some little town far away where a woman cooked, really cooked and everybody would go there no matter how far away it was . . . There was Madame Bourgeois in a little lost town in the center of France . . . And she began to cook, nobody came except a few fisherman and the local tradesmen and every day she cooked her best dinner for them and then one day after two years of this, a man from Lyon came by accident, a lawyer, and he was pleased with his dinner and he asked her if she could undertake to cook for a dozen of them who were going to celebrate the legion of honor of one of them and she said yes, and from then on the place was famous and she always tired as she was cooked with the same perfection. (47–48)

This rumor of real cooking makes "the place . . . famous," and "Paris had to learn from the provinces instead of the provinces learning from Paris" (48). "A little lost town" becomes a metonym for the nation, and the creation of that nation takes place in the kitchen of a woman who "cooked, really cooked." In this fairy tale version of French recovery from the traumas of war, it is hard to imagine the expatriate joining in at this table, Stein bringing a basket of mushrooms for Madame Bourgeois to prepare.[171] The odd phrase that ends this homage to Madame Bourgeois—"she was cooked with the same perfection"—suggests that her own body is devoured by her customers, a symbolic communion that reunifies postwar France.

In this fantasy of "some little town far away" where a woman serves as symbolic, nourishing mother to all of France, Stein moves away from the imaginative affiliation to a genealogical account of national belonging. Now, race is not a shifting categorization or a mulch of intermixture, but rather the transcendent basis for the once and future France.[172] The Stein of *Paris France* considers racial purity the down payment on civilization's survival:

> When you first really get to know the French one of the first things that puzzles you is the insistence upon their latinity. They do not consider Italians or Spaniards latin, but they the french are latin, they insist upon being Gauls but all the same they are latin. Finally I realized that what they meant was that the spirit of latinity was kept purer by them the Gallo-Romans than it was in Italy which lost its latinity when they were overcome by barbarians and never recreated it, they might take on the forms and symbols of Rome but essentially the latin culture went out of Italy and it never existed in Spain so its true home has been France. And there is a good deal of truth in it all. At first I did not know what they were talking about but gradually I did begin to feel what they meant by their latinity. (49–50)

Though Stein plays fast and loose—as did many thinkers in 1940s—with the categories of culture, race, and what we might now call ethnicity, she grants the French the "purity" of "latinity," jettisoning the elasticity and mutability of whiteness. Stein establishes a line of continuity between ancient times and now, thus rejecting the diasporic nature of modernity, even as she is forced to acknowledge invaders (Romans) and natives (Gauls) in this celebration of essential latinity. Cuisine becomes an unchanging symbol of this continuity and civilization: "The French are right when they claim that French cooking is an art and is part of their culture because it is based on latin Roman cooking and has been influenced by Italy and Spain. The crusades only brought them new material, it did not introduce into France the manner of cooking and very little has changed" (42).

In the end, terroir becomes a sign of authenticity and nativism for Stein instead of a site of improvisation and intimacy: "the most striking thing about France is the family, and the terre, the soil of France" (89). The first edition of *Paris France* ends with a portrait of the author by Sir Francis Rose, entitled *Gertrude Stein at Bilignin*. In it, a faceless Stein with pendulous breasts sits in front of her estate, her rocking chair placed on the grooves of a furrowed field. A decorative frame supplies geographical and cultural coordinates: in the upper left corner, a banner announces the department and arrondissement ("BELLEY-AIN"); in the upper right corner, a bottle pours wine into a cup; and below the image, a beribboned globe reads "FRANCE."[173] Tellingly, in this portrait, Stein has no nose. Stein's particularity—and presumably her Jewishness—must be effaced to turn her into an earth mother bearing out the transcendent importance of *la terre*.

4

"A Beaker Full of the Warm South"

The Fitzgeralds and Mediterranean Infusions

In his novel *Banjo* (1929), Claude McKay catalogs the exotic people and tropical goods that pour through the port of Marseilles:

> There any day he might meet with picturesque proletarians from far waters whose names were warm with romance: the Caribbean, the Gulf of Guinea, the Persian Gulf, the Bay of Bengal, the China Seas, and the Indian Archipelago. And oh, the earthy mingled smells of the docks! Grain from Canada, rice from India, rubber from the Congo, tea from China, brown sugar from Cuba, bananas from Guinea, lumber from the Soudan, coffee from Brazil, skins from the Argentine, palm-oil from Nigeria, pimento from Jamaica, wool from Australia, oranges from Spain and oranges from Jerusalem.[1]

While this catalog could appear on an importer's ledger, McKay draws upon the senses—the warmth of "far waters," the "earthly mingled smells of the docks"—to generate an embodied experience of globalization rather than an abstract one. In this novel, black and brown immigrants work on the docks and face discriminatory laws that target them en masse in spite of their divergent nations and faiths: "West Africans, East Africans, South Africans, West Indians, Arabs, and Indians—they were all mixed up together" (312). This form of intermixture comes out of the shared experience of racism, but in response, the dockworkers create a collective culture.

Much as Jean Toomer does in *Cane*, McKay uses liquid figures, particularly sweet wine and sugar syrup, to describe the creation of black community:

> All shades of Negroes came together there. Even the mulattoes took a step down from their perch to mix in. For, as in the British West Indies and South Africa, the mulattoes of the French colonies do not usually intermingle with the blacks. But the magic had brought them all together

to shake that thing and drink red wine, white wine, sweet wine. All the British West African blacks, Portuguese blacks, American blacks, all who had drifted into this port that the world goes through. (46)

These wine-drenched nights in Marseilles recall "the thick, sweaty, syrup-sweet jazzing" in Harlem (284). These transporting solutions recast blackness as pleasure rather than stigma. Dialect itself is sweet: "talking all the time the Martinique dialect in a deep voice of the color and flavor of unrefined cane sugar" (105) and "African dialects . . . tasted like brown unrefined cane sugar—Sousou, Bambara, Woloff, Fula, Dindie" (202).[2] The black community becomes a promised land— "There ain't no Canaan stuff sweeter than this heah wine and honey flowing in this place" (190)—through a sweet "flow" that exalts and unites the seamen.[3]

It is hard to believe that this pan-Africanist reverie describes the same South of France visited by the Fitzgeralds and their circle, yet Fitzgerald met McKay in 1926 while vacationing in Antibes. According to McKay's biographer, Wayne F. Cooper, "McKay had been in the kitchen preparing a meal when Fitzgerald arrived, and much to everyone's merriment he at first thought McKay was a servant."[4] In *Banjo*, immigrants, goods, languages, and wines flow through the Mediterranean in an ecstatic mélange. In *Tender Is the Night*, this warm water both tempts and tints: "a sea . . . mysteriously colored . . . green as green milk, blue as laundry water, wine dark."[5] Each comparison is beautiful and corrupt, brilliant and adulterated. "Green milk" indicated that bacterial growth had escaped the industrial purification process.[6] "Laundry blues" were originally made from indigo, but by the turn of the century, several artificial options overtook the market.[7] While the "wine dark sea" is an ancient poetic phrase, in this company fermented grapes seem like yet another contaminant. This "mysteriously colored" sea begins to resemble the "rising tide of color" feared by eugenicist Lothrop Stoddard.[8] At the same time, these vivid colors appeal to the imagination like the "agates and cornelians" of "childhood" (15). Fitzgerald implies that this subtropical sea is fake, tawdry, even dangerous, and yet he cannot deny its sensuous power.

Fitzgerald tries to stem this warm, colorful tide by imbuing whiteness—or at least pinkness—with equal aesthetic and affective power. He introduces Rosemary, an American teenager who "had magic in her pink palm and her cheeks lit to a lovely flame, like the thrilling flush of children after their cold baths in the evening" (3). Where McKay celebrated "black flesh, warm with the wine of life" (50), Fitzgerald rhapsodizes about white skin after a bracing bath. Rosemary, who shares the name of a native Mediterranean herb, seems as though she may purify the suspiciously exotic and warm Riviera with the "magic in her pink palm." She is a far cry from "Arabian or Persian or Indian" Latnah in *Banjo*, who smokes hashish with her Haitian lover and feeds him the slices of an orange while he dreams of "tropical heat in earth and body glowing" (McKay 10, 284).

Nevertheless, once introduced to southern warmth, Rosemary revels in the erotic touch of the sea: "The water reached up for her, pulled her down tenderly out of the heat, seeped in her hair, and ran into the corners of her body" (5). This tender sea and the polymorphous perversity it inspires will not long preserve "the raw whiteness of [Rosemary's] body" (5). Solidity gives way to seeping.

Though *Banjo* and *Tender Is the Night* diverge tonally in their take on warm seas and racial intermixtures, these narratives respond to the same demographic phenomena. When Fitzgerald's American expatriates go to Paris and Rome, they meet an "Afro-European" (106), "Afro-Americans" (106), "the Senegalese" (108), and "a Bahama Negro" (222). Indeed, they encounter so many immigrants from the African diaspora that the white protagonist, Dick Diver, complains of "an atmosphere of unfamiliar Negro faces bobbing up in unexpected places and around unexpected corners, and insistent Negro voices on the phone" (106).[9] Worse still, white girls like this "atmosphere." While Dick and Rosemary wait for their train, a white girl from Tennessee begins a minstrel pantomime—complete with "tropical eye-rollings and pawings"—when she hears the band play the popular song "Yes, We Have No Bananas" (59).[10] A veritable census of white people also succumbs, as "Wurtemburgers, Prussian Guards, Chasseurs Alpins, Manchester mill hands and old Etonians ... pursue their eternal dissolution under the warm rain" (59).

Mediterranean Europe was an important crucible for white anxieties about racial fluidity. From the climatological perspective of geographers and eugenicists, this region was ambiguous and suspect. On the one hand, they claimed the Mediterranean as a temperate zone and cast it as the Western cradle of civilization. On the other, Mediterranean Europe seemed suspiciously tropical and was connected to Africa and Asia.[11] These atmospheric observations became racial speculations. William Ripley's *The Races of Europe* (1899) divided the population of that continent into three races—Teutonic, Alpine, and Mediterranean—in an influential schema.[12] The Mediterranean race, Ripley declared, "prevails everywhere south of the Pyrenees, along the southern coast of France and in southern Italy, including Sicily and Sardinia."[13] The prominent geographer Ellen Churchill Semple tutted, "The southerners of the sub-tropical Mediterranean basin are easygoing, improvident except under pressing necessity, gay, emotional, imaginative, all qualities which among the negroes of the equatorial belt degenerate into grave racial faults."[14] The so-called Mediterranean race was all too close—climatologically, geographically, and temperamentally—to Africa. They were also, according to eugenicist accounts, thriving in the subpar conditions of industrial modernity.[15]

If the proliferation of Mediterranean brunets was not bad enough, eugenicists also feared that the South would have a sapping effect on properly white bodies. In *The Passing of the Great Race* (1916), Madison Grant warned that "the actinic rays of the sun at the same latitude are uniform in strength the world over and continuous sunlight affects adversely the delicate nervous organization of the Nordics" (38). Nordics would degenerate in places "where the environment is too soft and luxurious and no strife is required for survival" (38–39). He would "grow fat mentally and physically, like overfed Indians on reservations" (39). This metaphorical and literal obesity is effectively sterilizing: "In the south they [Nordics] grow listless and cease to breed" (39). By contrast, the Mediterranean race, "clearly a southern type with eastern affinities," would acclimate quickly: "It is adjusted to subtropical and tropical countries better than any other European type, and will flourish in our Southern States and around the coasts of the Spanish Main" (40). While Nordic men lost their virility, Mediterranean men spread their vitality across the Global South.

In an infamous 1921 letter to Edmund Wilson, Fitzgerald espoused these theories about Mediterranean inferiority and excoriated its spreading influence:

> God damn the continent of Europe. It is of merely antiquarian interest. Rome is only a few years behind Tyre + Babylon. The negroid streak creeps northward to defile the Nordic race. Already the Italians have the souls of blackamoors. Raise the bars of immigration and permit only Scandinavians, Teutons, Anglo Saxons + Celts to enter. France made me sick . . . We are as far above the modern frenchman as he is above the negro.[16]

His description of "Latin" Tommy Barban in *Tender Is the Night* reveals a similar sense of racial hierarchy and interrelation (18). The narrator sees Tommy's brown coloring as the marks of a worn and degraded race: "His handsome face was so dark as to have lost the pleasantness of deep tan, without attaining the blue beauty of Negroes—it was just worn leather" (269). The Mediterranean is here not even redeemed by the primitive purity of the "Negroes." In spite of this negative characterization of Tommy's handsome appearance, Nicole Diver is "fascinated and rested" by the "foreignness of his depigmentation by unknown suns" and "his nourishment by strange soils" (269). The vitality and exoticism of the brown man lure the white woman, and through her the "negroid streak creeps northward."[17]

As these discussions of the Mediterranean race reveal, a climatological and racial imaginary connected the regional Souths of France, Italy, and Spain with the East and Africa. Geographers and eugenicists mapped these connections in an attempt to cordon them off. In so doing, however, they traced regional and global flows—some speculative and spurious, others verifiable—that troubled the solidity of the Nordic iceberg. These racist thinkers thus contributed signally if unintentionally to the invention of what we might now call the Global South.[18] For McKay and other pan-Africanist thinkers, the flows between "far waters" opened up an opportunity to rewrite the Eurocentric history of civilization. In *The Souls of White Folk* (1920), W. E. B. Du Bois wrote: "Why, then, is Europe great? Because of the foundations which the mighty past have furnished her to build upon: the iron trade of ancient, black Africa, the religion and empire-building of yellow Asia, the art and science of the 'dago' Mediterranean shore, east, south, and west, as well as north."[19] For eugenicists like Grant and Stoddard, the welcoming shores of sunny Souths made the possibility of racial contamination a pressing threat. In *The Rising Tide of Color Against White World-Supremacy* (1920), Stoddard enjoined white men to defend their tropical strongholds, or the "Asiatic" would "permeat[e]" and "inundat[e]" these regions.[20]

The expansion of the global industrial food system in the years following the World War I only piqued these racist anxieties about the traffic in bodies and goods between South and North. In *Mankind at the Crossroads* (1923), the eugenicist Edward East describes the contents of the modern American breakfast table:

> In the olden days a people raised its own food, manufactured its own utensils—or went without. Today one sits down to breakfast, spreads out a napkin of Irish linen, opens the meal with a banana from Central America, follows with a cereal of Minnesota sweetened with the product of Cuban cane, and ends with a Montana lamb chop and cup of Brazilian coffee. Our daily life is a trip around the world, yet the wonder of it gives us not a single thrill. We are oblivious.[21]

East sets up a textural and, ultimately, qualitative dichotomy between solid northern foods (cereal and lamb chop) and sweet southern infusions (sugar and coffee). Though these fluids tantalize and please the consumer, they are not morally or physically nourishing like the "bread" that the farmer wins through the "sweat of his brow" (345).[22] East connects climate, overpopulation, and degeneration in an idiom of escalating moisture. "Humid temperature" creates "the sluggishness of the tropical races" (118); superior genes are "swamped by bad company" (298); "the tide of new arrivals" threatens "to swamp the older inhabitants" in "catastrophic waves of immigration" (308); the earth would soon be "saturated with people" (345). East fears the influence of the South on the future of the race:

> Looking to the north, the east, the west, the horizon is unclouded. Only in the south appears a little cloud no bigger than a man's hand. It may be a passing mist, but it bears watching. From the Mason and Dixon's line to the Horn, from Gibraltar to the Cape of Good Hope, the southland outpost is the post of danger. This is the direction in which to double the guard. (145)

This miasmic threat echoes climatological theories about the dangerous "southland." It also serves as a metaphor for racial indeterminacy. East means to minimize the cloud by calling it "a passing mist." However, this adjective evokes racial "passing," hereditary intermixtures unseen. "Mist" obstructs the vision and belongs neither to one state (liquid) nor to the other (gas). Unlike a tide, a mist could not be measured.[23] Mist seems to be everywhere and nowhere; it sticks to the skin and yet it cannot be touched. Imagined as a color line, racial divides offer white supremacists a comforting view of solid walls; even the tide metaphor presumes predictable surges and ebbs. When racial difference becomes instead a "mist," there is no guarding against it, no delineating its shape or location.

This very suspension of droplets in the air, however, in another view provides a textural model for multiplicity, interpenetration, and sensuousness. Rather than accept East's phobic account of the encompassing mist, we might instead reclaim such fluid figures to articulate forms of embodiment not characterized by stark borders and epidermal boundaries. As Darieck Scott argues, this shifting amorphousness characterizes blackness as a figure of abjection:

> Blackness *as* one of the go-to figures for referencing the abject, grants us a vantage point for viewing the movement, direction, and inchoate shapes that characterize or arise from the fluid potentialities of subjectivity formation itself—despite and *because* of, the various cultural, economic, and political operations aimed at producing blackness as fixed and objective.[24]

Zelda Fitzgerald's *Save Me the Waltz* (1932) provides a test case for this view of blackness as an "inchoate shape" that opens up the "fluid potentialities of subjectivity formation." As a southern woman "incubated in the mystic pungence of Negro mammies," Alabama Beggs both defines her whiteness against black bodies and experiences her own body as essentially racialized and pathologically fluid.[25] In this abject identification between femininity, racialization, and contamination, Zelda Fitzgerald begins to unpack some of the slippages that enable the fantasy of white purity to endure in spite of its evident artificiality.

In both *Tender Is the Night* and *Save Me the Waltz*, Mediterranean diet and drink betray how difficult it is to produce and protect the white body. Eugenic narratives about climate and contamination—moisture in the air and poison in the blood—confess a permeated and permeable body. Coffee, wine, and sugar syrup speak to the pleasures of infusion and intermixture, the sweetness of southern circulation. Yet these infused fluids and their associated sediment or stickiness also uncover a history of disgust that betrays white anxieties and armature. This disgust is only heightened by the fact that these encounters with the other happen habitually—they are indeed habit-forming.[26] And with that in mind, I turn to wine and coffee.

Coffee and Black Drink: *Tender Is the Night* and Dark Infusions

In Keats's "Ode to a Nightingale," from which Fitzgerald drew his novel's title, the poet-speaker dreams of "a beaker full of the warm South" (line 15), which would make him "Fade far away, dissolve, and quite forget" (line 21).[27] Echoing this language, Fitzgerald describes the Divers' dinner party on the French Riviera: "the diffused magic of the hot sweet South had withdrawn into them—the soft-pawed night and the ghostly wash of the Mediterranean far below—the magic left these things and melted into the two Divers and became part of them" (35). Under the influence of the climate and the wine, "the two Divers . . . warm and glow and expand" (34); they also become more animalistic, perhaps even predatory like "the soft-pawed night." Nicole takes on the qualities of the champagne they are drinking, "her chow's hair foaming and frothing in the candlelight" (32). Though this dinner is seductive, "giving the people around [the table] a sense of being alone with each other in the dark universe, nourished by its only food, warmed by its only lights," its very appeals—isolation, "darkness," and "warmth"—seem primitive (34).

In this scene, contrasts between darkness and light, warmth and coolness, intoxication and purity trouble the category of whiteness. While Rosemary is "dewy with belief" (34), Nicole is flushed with wine. The girl inspects the older woman's features: "Her face, the face of a saint, a viking Madonna, shone through the faint motes that snowed across the candlelight, drew down its flush from the wine-colored lanterns" (33). Nicole epitomizes the feminine ideal of whiteness as lightness developed in modern photography. In his classic study, *White*, Richard Dyer explains that "idealised white women are bathed in and permeated by light. It streams through them and falls on them from above."[28] Not only does Nicole's saintlike face shine, candlelight illuminates the room, catching even the dust motes in its glow. At the same time, as the passage moves away from the cinematic idiom of black and white into shades of red, the communicability of color brings the stain back into stained glass. Nicole's flush blurs exterior and interior, mirroring the lamps and betraying the intoxicants in her bloodstream.[29] The South infiltrates from outside and in, and the white woman seems like its perfect medium.

While this scene emphasizes the nocturnal pleasures of wine, Nicole gets a morning dose of the "hot sweet South" from Brazilian coffee plantations. When she and Rosemary go on a shopping trip together, the narrator describes the unseen energy expenditures that fuel Nicole's day:

> Nicole was the product of much ingenuity and toil. For her sake trains began their run at Chicago and traversed the round belly of the

continent to California; chicle factories fumed and link belts grew link by link in factories; men mixed toothpaste in vats and drew mouthwash out of copper hogsheads; girls canned tomatoes quickly in August or worked rudely at the Five-and-Tens on Christmas Eve; half breed Indians toiled in Brazilian coffee plantations and dreamers were muscled out of patent rights in new tractors—these were some of the people who gave a tithe to Nicole, and as the whole system swayed and thundered onward it lent a feverish bloom to such processes of hers as wholesale buying, like the flush of a fireman's face holding his post before a spreading blaze. (55)

Like Edward East bemoaning the "globe-girdling" food system (64), Fitzgerald treats the "round belly of the continent" as a symptom of modern excess. The formerly autonomous body of the white consumer becomes a "product" of a "whole system." Indeed, Nicole is doubly snared in the web of the global industrial food system because her father owns a Chicago meatpacking company (127). Not only is she inescapably enmeshed, consumerism itself is febrile, betraying a social body that cannot burn off the intoxicant of materialism.

Though Fitzgerald attributes Nicole's pyrrhic exhilaration to excessive shopping, these circulatory and nervous symptoms echo contemporaneous warnings about caffeine, especially for women.[30] In "The Use and Abuse of Coffee" (1911), Dr. Robert Coughlin cautions readers that, though "coffee has a powerful exhilarant action upon the mental processes," this high comes "at the expense of tissue if the consumer is intemperate."[31] The symptoms of "poisoning by coffee" include "great nervous excitement" and "flushing of face."[32] He concludes that "it should not be allowed to patients who are known to be nervous, especially women."[33] Nicole is a famously "nervous" woman, Dick's former psychiatric patient and now his wife. The food faddist John Harvey Kellogg insisted that "the widespread use of tea and coffee in England and America and in other civilized countries is unquestionably a prolific cause of neurasthenia, especially in women who, on the whole, seem to be more susceptible to these drugs than are men, and who are more addicted to their use."[34] Kellogg's choice of the word "civilized" implies that a racial dynamic contributes to this "neurasthenia," a claim that his niece's husband, the eugenicist William Sadler, made explicit when he listed "chronic poisoning" by coffee and alcohol as a cause of racial degeneracy in his 1922 book on that topic.[35] White women ingest exotic stimulants and threaten the reproductive future of the race. In the passage from *Tender Is the Night* describing the "system" that feeds Nicole, the calamitous pace of the hemispheric food chain echoes caffeine's acceleration of Nicole's pulse, and her compulsive consumption both resembles and enables addiction, a symptom of racial degeneration.[36]

Fitzgerald treats this tropical stimulation of the white woman's body as a form of symbolic miscegenation by blurring consumption and reproduction in this passage. The narrator observes that Nicole "contain[s] in herself her own doom" (55). This ambiguous phrase simultaneously suggests elective poisons (the coffee she sips, the gum she chews), inherited addictions, and reproductive capacities. From a eugenic perspective, both ingestion and reproduction could introduce contaminating matter into the white body. The "round belly of the continent" is an ambiguous personification, indicating fat or pregnancy. In either case, this New World food system relies upon the labor of "half-breed Indians," and arguably, it produces their racial intermixture.[37] Later in the novel, we learn that white Nicole gives birth to a daughter, whom she names Topsy.[38]

Nicole's vitality increases over the course of the book in inverse relation to Dick's inebriation, weight gain, and energy loss. Though I would not want to overstate the role of coffee in Nicole's reinvigoration (after all, Dick orders coffee more often in the novel than his wife does, and it seems to do him little good), her resilience *is* associated with a dose of Latin "nourishment" in the form of her affair with Tommy Barban, whose last name suggests barbarian antecedents (269). Barban is "less civilized" than the other men she knows (19). She gains from him the animation that she has apparently sapped from Dick, "dry suckling at his lean chest" (279). Her "nervous energy" (289), her desire to be "stimulated" (291), her willingness to be "changed in the very chemistry of blood and muscle" (279) all prove to be assets in modern life. This mutability sharpens her "quick guile against his wine-ing and dine-ing slowness, her health and beauty against his physical deterioration" (301). Nicole's literal and metaphorical recourse to stimulants guarantees her survival, while Dick's alcoholism, associated with the "passing of the great race," as I will discuss at greater length later in the chapter, precipitates his decline.

Coffee marketers promised that Brazil would deliver tropical energy to the worn-out French consumer. For example, in Figure 4.1, a 1930 French advertisement pictures a white, Art Deco couple silhouetted against a hilly golf course, presumably not in Brazil. The ad copy promises that such sun-drenched afternoons ("lumineuses journées") inspire "la joie de vivre" and charming, spontaneous adventures ("Adorables ébats pleins de charme et d'imprévu"). However, joy, charm, and spontaneity can be sustained only through chemical mediation, "gràce au délicieux Café du Brésil." This coffee provides incomparable animation and a powerful stimulant for physical and intellectual activity ("cet animateur incomparable, ce stimulant puissant de l'activité physique et intellectuelle"). The advertisement concludes, "Les meilleurs cafés viennent du Brésil" (The best coffee comes from Brazil). In this articulation of the colonial relation, the glamour and leisure of the Global North depend upon infusions of energy and affect from the Global South.

> **LUMINEUSES** journées qui donnent la joie de vivre!...
> Adorables ébats pleins de charme et d'imprévu, dont
> il ne subsistera nulle fatigue grâce au délicieux Café du Brésil,
> cet animateur incomparable, ce stimulant puissant de l'acti-
> vité physique et intellectuelle.
>
> **Les meilleurs cafés viennent du Brésil**

Figure 4.1 This swank Art Deco couple in the South of France drinks Brazilian coffee.
Source: Havas Agency, 1930.

In Fitzgerald's figuration too, the white, expatriate ideal requires constant replenishment. If wine allows them to appear expansive, coffee bestows the perpetual energy that the Divers both strive for: "It was a tradition between them that they should never be too tired for anything" (95). This unsustainable version of consumerism and leisure, imparted by white privilege and financial means, requires constant expenditure, physical as well as economic. The Divers resemble the Art Deco figures in the Havas ad, her features "hard" and "almost stern" (25), his "hard" and "neat" (31). Nonetheless, her "color" and his "brightness" depend upon the tropical goods that they consume (25, 31). In the Havas advertisement, too, a shadow falls across the man's face, a blush colors the woman's cheek. Whiteness is always constructed in relief. Indeed, Fitzgerald reminds his readers twice that Nicole's "once fair hair" has "darkened" and is now "lovelier" (25), and the second time, he recalls her race: "She had been white-Saxon-blonde but she was more beautiful now that her hair had darkened than when it had been like a cloud and more beautiful than she" (67). Nicole's beauty is more successful as a study in contrasts; at the same time, this process of darkening implies a trajectory from "white-Saxon-blonde" to a body quite other.

In *Tender Is the Night*, women are too comfortable with dark infusions, since their bodies are fluid and penetrable, their whiteness none too stable to begin with. Though young Rosemary "embod[ies] all the immaturity of the race" (69), she is notably fluid in her affections: "She felt wildly happy, felt the warm sap of emotion being pumped through her body" (68). Like Nicole, Rosemary is comfortable changing herself through chemistry. When she tries champagne for the first time, she considers it "a part of the equipment for what she had to do," namely seduce Dick (61). Rosemary's willingness to transform her behavior and body with drugs does not bode well for the bucolic pastoralism evoked by her herbal name. Indeed, Dick dreams of "the incorruptible Mediterranean with sweet old dirt caked in the olive trees, the peasant girl near Savona with a face as green and rose as the color of an illuminated missal" (195–96). This "green and rose" peasant girl, straight out of a religious illustration, would ideally be constant as the "sweet old dirt" and the "olive trees."

But Rosemary is an American girl, a changeable consumer rather than a picturesque peasant. She attends a decadent party that foreshadows her eventual transformation in tellingly intoxicating terms: "The outer shell [of the building], the masonry, seemed rather to enclose the future so that it was an electric-like shock, a definite nervous experience, perverted as a breakfast of oatmeal and hashish to cross that threshold" (71). This figure of "oatmeal and hashish" threatens Rosemary's innocence and her whiteness—a child's breakfast hiding a narcotic pleasure, a wholesome grain carrying an exotic intoxicant. Crossing this "threshold" into the "future," Rosemary feels that she and Dick have been consumed by a "Frankenstein ... at a gulp" (72). In this uncanny conflation of ingesting something and being ingested by it, Rosemary experiences "an electric-like shock, a definite nervous experience." In this liminal state, Rosemary can no longer separate herself from her surroundings. She even experiences the intense affects of her fellow partygoers, the "wild beating of wings in the room" (72).[39] Though Rosemary does not literally consume hashish in this scene, her intense sensations and disorientation create an aura of intoxication. She falls into conversation with "a neat, slick girl with a lovely boy's face" and sees women with "heads... like cobras' hoods," who might turn on her as their new prey (72). In this scene, Fitzgerald associates sapphic degeneracy and oriental decadence with ingestion.[40] Whether intoxicating like hashish or hypnotizing like the cobra's gaze, women's consuming bodies threaten rationality. Appropriately, when Dick decides that he will succumb to Rosemary's advances, he hears "Two for Tea," a ditty that associates his desire with the colonial stimulant par excellence (170).

The hints in the first third of the novel that Rosemary may be more like flushed, infused Nicole than she at first appears are borne out in its last third when she affects Dick "as if a drink were acting on him, warming the lining of his stomach, throwing a flush up into his brain" (206). All grown up, Rosemary appears "like a young horse dosed with Black-seed oil," a dietary trick to make equine coats look glossier (207). Black-seed oil is derived from black cumin, a tropical spice grown in the Mediterranean, North Africa, and Asia and associated with Muslim medicine (the Prophet Muhammad recommended its use).[41] This simile exoticizes and animalizes Rosemary.[42] With the help of such "dose[s]," Rosemary seduces and intoxicates: "In a hundred hours, she had come to possess *all the world's dark magic*; the blinding belladonna, *the caffein* [sic] *converting physical into nervous energy*, the mandragora that imposes harmony" (164, emphasis mine). When she receives Dick in her hotel room, clad in black pajamas and sipping coffee, the transformation is complete. Perceiving his flagging powers, Rosemary offers him a dose: "Do you want coffee, youngster? ... You don't look well—you all right now? Want coffee?" (209).

Fitzgerald was particularly sensitive about caffeine consumption because of his alcoholism. In an early interview, he denied claims that he wrote *This Side of Paradise* while drinking whiskey: "For me, narcotics are deadening to work. I can understand any one drinking coffee to get a stimulating effect, but whiskey—oh, no." Fitzgerald admitted that his novel "was written on Coca Cola. Coca Cola bubbles up and fizzes inside enough to keep me awake."[43] Though Coca-Cola's most controversial ingredient, cocaine, was removed in 1901, "rumors about Coca-Cola's drug content" continued and may have "helped more than hindered sales," Mark Pendergast speculates in his history of the brand: "People were intrigued by the stigma associated with the drink and felt a sinful thrill when imbibing it."[44] The formula retained the decocainized coca leaf, and in a 1901 brochure, Coca-Cola promised that it "makes one active, brilliant, vigorous, and able to accomplish great tasks easily."[45] It also claimed that kola nuts were a "specific for inebriation."[46] This reputation for alleviating the symptoms of drunkenness may have contributed to Coca-Cola's popularity as a replacement drink for alcohol.[47] When he went on the wagon, Fitzgerald drank cases of Coca-Cola, and in his Hollywood years, the volume of his soda consumption was legendary.[48] In 1939 (well after the publication of *Tender Is the Night*), he argued with Max Perkins over a cartoon that the editor drew of the author with a drink of Coca-Cola in his hand, which Fitzgerald took as an offensive hint to lay off of the booze.[49]

Like Fitzgerald's beloved Coca-Cola, coffee and caffeine were understood as "the symbolic opposite of or antidote for alcohol."[50] Rosemary's coffee drinking thus draws attention to Dick's escalating alcoholism in the last third of the novel. As the women around him become more stimulated and self-assured, Dick becomes more inebriated and incoherent. He travels to Rome to reunite with Rosemary and winds up in a drunken brawl with the carabinieri, ultimately confessing to a rape that he didn't commit.[51] When he returns to the Swiss sanatorium that he helps run, a patient's father complains that his alcoholic son "has smelt liquor on your breath" (253). Exposing his dependency, Dick parries that "some people are not going to give up *what they regard as food* because of your son" (253, emphasis mine). Encouraged by his partner to take a "leave of abstinence" (256), Dick quits his position at the clinic and returns to the Riviera, where his increased drinking results in extended vituperations—"he would suddenly unroll a long scroll of contempt for some person, race, class, way of life, way of thinking" (267)—and racial slurs (260). One evening on the docks, Tommy Barban gives Dick and Nicole a drive home because Dick is so "vague and sleepy" (274). Tommy's success at wooing Nicole away from her husband seems intimately connected to Dick's self-confessed "deterioration" (285).

Fitzgerald may have intended this degenerative dynamic to underscore Dick's noble whiteness. Though alcoholism and addiction were sometimes cited as evidence of degenerate racial stock, in other eugenic accounts they were construed as the deleterious effects of impure influences on superior bodies. Grant proposed that alcoholism was a "peculiarly Nordic vice" that "attack[ed] those members of the race that are otherwise most desirable" (55). Though he calls this process a form of natural "selection," the destruction of Nordics through alcohol consumption does not serve the advancement of the race but rather its eventual extinction (55). Rather than weeding out the puny or unfit, alcoholism, Grant opines, has "cost the race many of its most brilliant and attractive members" (55). Though inebriation had long been viewed as an Irish racial vice, now it became a sign of fragile whiteness.[52] Dick's susceptibility to drink may signal that he is of racially superior stock that cannot flourish in this debased world as easily as the "brunet Mediterranean" (Grant 45). Both Nicole and Rosemary abandon the racially superior man for his erotic and vital lessers, Tommy Barban and Nicotera, "one of many hopeful Valentinos" (Fitzgerald 212). Dick calls Nicotera a "spic" but also recognizes that "youth calls to youth" (218). Vitality, however racially compromised, wins out over dissipation.

These cases of feminine defection are thematically crucial to the novel's ingestive imaginary. Nicole and Rosemary derive pleasure and energy from their Latin lovers, much as they do from wine and coffee. They take in substances and races without any visible deterioration, resilience that marks women as fundamentally corrupt in Fitzgerald's view. Moreover, women's desirable bodies introduce this contamination into Dick's originally self-contained frame. As a white man, Dick used to be a coherent representative of science, rationality, and agency. In the mid-novel flashback, detailing how Dick met Nicole as a patient at his clinic, Fitzgerald attributes the downfall of Dick's rationality and autonomy not merely to Nicole's madness or to her erotic allure but more specifically to her tendency to dissolve categories, to embody intermixture. In a sequence that recalls the passage from *Gatsby* when Gatsby "wed his unutterable visions to [Daisy's] perishable breath," Dick kisses Nicole and is irrevocably changed: "There were no more plans than if Dick had arbitrarily *made some indissoluble mixture*, with atoms joined and inseparable; you could throw it all out but never again could they fit back into atomic scale . . . he held her and *tasted her*" (155, emphasis mine).[53] With this simile riffing on "indissoluble matrimony," Fitzgerald indicates not only that Dick's fate has been irretrievably wedded to Nicole's but indeed that his relationship to matter itself has changed. Where masculinity used to be elemental, Dick is now a feminized compound. The kiss betrays his incompletion and his openness.

The novel construes femininity as fundamentally impure and contaminating thanks to the all too open body of woman. This very process of contamination and intoxication, however, ultimately exposes the fictitiousness of masculine mastery and self-containment. Substances and systems *also* penetrate the masculine body, and after this kiss, Dick is never again able to recuperate his sense of himself as an autonomous, hermetic unit. At the same time, unlike women, who deliberately use these chemicals to extend their capacities or mobilize particular affects, men preserve their innocence and their impossible belief in purity by staging their substance use as passive. In other words, Dick does not use alcohol, alcohol uses him, which in turn upholds the tragic Nordic narrative.

In his figurative language, Fitzgerald repeatedly emphasizes Nicole's ratiocination and selectivity, even when it comes to alcohol. After their first kiss, Nicole waxes sentimental "as deliberately as a man getting drunk after battle" (155), and when she decides to make a play for Tommy, the narrator observes that "a woman of twenty-nine . . . chooses her apéritifs wisely" (291). The consuming woman and her chemicals are coextensive. In Fitzgerald's admittedly paranoiac formulation, she is both the purveyor of poison and the poison itself. Nicole mourns that Dick has been affected by "my contamination" (301), while Dick admits only limited agency in the interests of exalting his martyrdom: "he had made his choice, chosen Ophelia, chosen the sweet poison and drunk it" (302). Here desirable women and "sweet poison" are one and the same.

I have little doubt that this gendered narrative of contamination, so closely connected to the themes of alcoholism, degeneration, and racial competition in the novel, served as some self-justification for Fitzgerald as his alcoholism became an unavoidable problem in his private life and career.[54] However, this sleight of hand, blaming white women for global capitalism, chemical opportunism, and racial treachery, cannot altogether obscure the fact that Fitzgerald has undercut masculinity and whiteness as transcendent categories. Dick Diver's mouth and stomach betray his vulnerability and permeability, and Nicole is "afraid of what the stricken man . . . would feed on" (279). His stomach also weighs him down. Trying to show off by lifting another man on his shoulders while riding on a board pulled by a motor-boat, Dick is "belly-down" and "could not rise" (284). As gravity defeats erection and belly trumps phallus, Dick's masculine performances collapse.[55]

Dick calls the compulsive beer drinker a "gastropath" (155), and I would like to recuperate this suggestive term. In nineteenth-century medical science, "gastropathia" meant stomach disease, isolating disorder in a particular organ that could be treated.[56] However, by locating in the stomach the capacity for "feeling" and "suffering," this term reveals that ingestion, a constant process of incorporation as well as physiological and affective transformation, gives the lie to a hermetic vision of the human.[57] Dick struggles to control his consumption and metabolism: "He was averaging a half-pint of alcohol a day, too much for his system to burn up. Dismissing a tendency to justify himself, he sat down at his desk and wrote out, like a prescription, a régime that would cut his liquor in half" (254). This managerial, mechanistic, and medical language cannot dispel the distressing animation of the alcohol itself. He is not in control of his feeling stomach—or his circulatory system for that matter.

Alcohol racializes him because it reveals his subjection, his figurative enslavement to desires not fully his own. His patient's father warns him about "Drink—black drink. Do you know what color black is? It's black!" (253). Through this intoxicant, blackness, understood as embodied abjection, enters Dick's system. However, this blurring of body boundaries is not restricted to an ingested poison. Indeed, Fitzgerald seems to associate the vaporous mental state of inebriation with the climatological humidity and racial degeneracy of the Mediterranean: "There was a dirty water in the gutters and between the rough cobblestones; a marshy vapor from the Campagna, a sweat of exhausted cultures tainted the morning air" (224). This lubricious language only underscores the impossibility of Dick's ever separating himself from intermixture and atmosphere. He is a part of, and not the author of, the physical world, and while he may try to explain this descent into the flesh as a racial failure, this imagery betrays that material forms seep into one another.

Ingestion figures forth this consuming relation with particular potency. In an apparent non sequitur, drunken Dick begins a rambling monologue in the back of a cab: "'A charming representative of the—' he stumbled momentarily, 'a firm of—bring me Brains addled a l'Anglaise.' Then he went into an appeased sleep, belching now and then contentedly into the soft warm darkness" (275). Dick begins with the social forms of introduction, niceties that affirm the abstractions of identity and profession, projecting a person as a "charming representative" of "a firm." Midway through, Dick shifts the context of his conventional speech. Instead of introducing someone, he seems to be ordering a dish at a restaurant, but the dish he orders—"Brains addled a l'Anglaise"—reflects his inebriated state. Furthermore, it erodes the purported gap between humans and domesticated animals, as French cuisine regularly served up sheep's, lamb's, and calf's brains.[58] As Dick's surreal speech conveys auto-cannibalistic implications, eating his own addled brains, he settles into the "soft warm darkness" that he has resisted so strenuously for the bulk of the novel.

These tropes of cannibalism and encompassing darkness could still ratify the imperialist vision of white masculinity, Dick swamped by malignant external influences. But Dick's liquidation exposes other deliquescence in the novel. Gossiping women call alcoholic Abe North "entirely liquid" (73), and he introduces black immigrants to the Divers' circle through his befuddled intervention in their affairs. After Abe's death, his wife moves on to a man of the "Kyble-Berber-Sabaean-Hindu strain" (259), and her stepchildren leach dirt and germs into the Diver children's bathwater (261–62).[59] Significantly, both Dick and Abe belong to ethnic groups (Irish and Jewish respectively) that had only recently or provisionally been incorporated into the category of whiteness.[60] Their dissolution signals the fluctuating contours of that racial ideal and the body's failure to reflect it properly.

As Michael Nowlin astutely observes, "Fitzgerald always recognized something fraudulent . . . about the premium he placed upon whiteness."[61] If "soft warm darkness" threatens to envelop and digest white masculinity, then perhaps oleaginous whiteness is even worse, a symptom of the artificiality of the category, its insufficient solidity, and the unctuous texture it shares with abject and sticky categories like femininity and blackness. This oily threat is embodied in the middlebrow writer Alfred McKisco, who joins the Divers' circle but parodies their values—struggling to look like a natural at drinking, talking, and even making art. Nicole jokes that McKisco's name "sounds like a substitute for gasoline or butter" (20), likely an allusion to Crisco, an industrial substitute for lard derived from cottonseed oil.[62] McKisco possesses none of the nobility with which the white male body is classically endowed: "He seemed very puny and cross and white" (45). McKisco "soften[s] and debas[es]" the materials that he works with (205), transposing James Joyce's

Ulysses to aristocratic France and turning its single day into "a hundred years" (10). McKisco is a flavorless shape-shifter, adapting modernism for the masses. The illusive "non-particularity" of whiteness allows him to pursue this pretense.[63] Indeed, the contrast between *Ulysses* and McKisco's imitation implies that Joyce's national identity and working-class affiliations—to say nothing of particular racial derivation or religious investments—save him from damning mediocrity as much as his stylistic innovations do. Though Fitzgerald obviously uses McKisco as a punching bag for his own fears about the degrading implications of commercial popularity, less obviously, the texture of "gasoline or butter," and indeed the concept of the "substitute" itself, expose the artificiality and mutability of the very white masculinity in which he placed such tragic significance.

Zelda Fitzgerald and the Sticky South

In *Tender Is the Night*, Fitzgerald depicts the regional and global South as a contaminating, intoxicating other. He only reluctantly and indirectly acknowledges that these atmospheric and alimentary influences expose the permeability and mutability of the Nordic man's body. Emphasizing Dick's tawny coloring and Celtic features, Fitzgerald echoes the tragic degeneration narrative espoused by Grant and Stoddard.[64] The South may sap Dick Diver of his will, but it is not an inherent part of his makeup; in fact, his deterioration in the Mediterranean demonstrates his hereditary superiority in Grant's terms. In the novel's conclusion, Dick Diver flees to New York State, and the reader is left to speculate whether the colder climate will remedy his physical and psychological ills.

Zelda Fitzgerald came from the US South, a region that, according to Grant, demonstrated "the deleterious effects of residence outside the natural habitat of the Nordic race."[65] Scott Fitzgerald also depicted his wife's southern origins as racially exotic. In *The Cruise of the Rolling Junk* (1923), an account of an impromptu road trip from Connecticut to Alabama, he parodies imperial adventure fiction: "We journey to the equator in quest of strange foods and would sleep once more beneath an Aryan roof before consorting with strange races of men such as the cotton-tailed Tasmanians and the pygmies."[66] Though Fitzgerald's allusion to the equator is tongue-in-cheek, his correlation of the US South with Australia and Africa is a telling one. The climate creates a Global South of "strange races." As the serial goes on, his tone about southern difference becomes more earnest and evocative, desirous as well as exoticizing: "[We went] down, into the warmth, into the dusky mellow softness, into the green heart of the South to the Alabama town where Zelda was born."[67] The South seems the warm, soft womb of the world, and its green heart recalls Joseph Conrad's *Heart of Darkness*. Zelda is its seductive offspring.

The Fitzgeralds' correspondence makes it clear that both writers were preoccupied with the climatological influence of the South. In a 1935 letter to Scott, Zelda recalls their courtship: "The wall was damp and mossy when we crossed the street and said we loved the south. I thought of the south and a happy past I'd never had and I thought I was part of the south. You said you loved this lovely land."[68] In this anecdote, the Fitzgeralds' shared love of the region divides into Zelda's feminine identification with the South and Scott's masculine objectification of "this lovely land." In another suggestive letter, this time from Scott to Zelda, he recounts *her* climatological theories about expatriate trajectories: "You remember your old idea that people ought to be born on the shores of the North Sea and only in later life drift south toward the Mediterranean in softness?"[69] The Fitzgeralds concur that the South softens its inhabitants. By contrast, Scott insists that he'd like their daughter, Scottie, to be "hardy and keen."[70] This shared premise—that superior races and characters come from and thrive in cold climates—highlights Zelda's ambiguous positioning as a white woman from the South.

In her fiction, Zelda Fitzgerald melds moist foods and atmospheric exhalations in a southern sensory onslaught. In "Southern Girl" (1929), northern visitors must be "initiated into . . . the beveled fruit rotting beneath; into the sweet tartness of Coca-Cola cooling in wooden tubs beside a country store; into the savory vapors of Mexican hot dog stands."[71] Between Coca-Cola and Mexican hot dogs, the US South blurs into Latin America.[72] These smells and tastes envelop the bodies that enter this humid atmosphere. The setting swallows up and vomits out the people who live there: "the lacy blackness under the trees disgorges young girls in white and pink" (299). White girls emerge from the belly of southern "blackness." In *Save Me the Waltz*, the "sweet sickly heat" ripens crops and carries black voices through the dense air: "Humming Negroid intonations circulated plaintively through the lull. 'H'ye ho' tomatoes, nice ripe tomatoes. Greens, colla'd greens" (15).[73] In the South, Fitzgerald implies, white girls are soaked by the permeating influence of the "Negroid" and the humid. Alabama's "Anglo-Saxon eyes" have been "liquidated" (20).

The association of black bodies with sensory intensity echoes white supremacist thinkers of the antebellum South. As the historian Mark Smith explains, "The apologists for slavery attempted to expand the definition of blackness beyond the eye. Blackness was not just seen—it could be smelled, heard, and felt."[74] While blackness emanated beyond the body, assailing the senses, whiteness became "normative" through its very lack of "sensory dimensions."[75] Though designed to provoke disgust, this hypersensory construction of blackness also imbued it with an affective charge: "encouraging an emotional, visceral, and febrile understanding of racial identity."[76] The very attempts to articulate the stark difference between whiteness and blackness succeeded in making blackness sticky in the sense that Sara Ahmed adumbrates in *The Cultural Politics of Emotion*:

> Economies of disgust also involve the shaping of bodies. When the body of another becomes an object of disgust, then the body *becomes* sticky. Such bodies become "blockages" in the economy of disgust: they slow down or "clog up" the movement between objects, as other objects and signs stick to them. This is how bodies become fetish objects: as we shall see, feelings of disgust stick more to some bodies than others, such that they become disgusting, as if their presence if what makes "us sick."[77]

In Fitzgerald's fiction, both the erotic, white, feminine body *and* the black or brown body are physically and figuratively sticky. Indeed, when Alabama observes her older sister in a clinch with a beau, she compares them to "moist stamps in a pocketbook" (26). Some of this feminine stickiness emerges from the possibility of miscegenation that F. Scott Fitzgerald follows so doggedly in *Tender Is the Night*; racial difference could thus stick to white women through copulation and reproduction. Because of the history of disgust associated with white supremacy, Alabama struggles to symbolically clean herself of the residue of southern racialization carried in her own feminized flesh.

Stickiness is crucial to Zelda Fitzgerald's view of the South in general and race in particular, and it is this texture that both links her work to *Tender Is the Night* and differentiates it from that novel. For F. Scott Fitzgerald, the solutions of the South are infusing and addictive. They can dye or intoxicate the body; they can even bloat it, as one alcoholic character's "gigantic obscenity" evidences (83). They can burn in the blood and fail to metabolize. What they can't—or at any rate don't—do is stick to you. Dick Diver's exterior, no matter how black the black drink inside him, remains phenotypically white. While Nicole's hair darkens and her cheeks flush, she also appears to be an Anglo-Saxon woman. Their bodies are vessels for these intermixed, transformational substances. In *Save Me the Waltz*, however, these substances that seem so seductive in *Tender Is the Night* reveal their ambiguous cultural, material, and racial status in their very texture. Where F. Scott Fitzgerald emphasizes intoxication, Zelda Fitzgerald explores stickiness.

This difference is significant, I would suggest, because stickiness betrays the transformation of the subject that encounters the substance or atmosphere. As Ahmed persuasively argues, "Stickiness becomes disgusting *only when the skin surface is at stake such that what is sticky threatens to stick to us*."[78] Stickiness emerges, then, "*as an effect of the histories of contact between bodies, objects, and signs*."[79] In *Save Me the Waltz*, the US South is stuck to the French Mediterranean, which in turn adheres to the South of Italy. There is no extricating these climes or regions of the globe from one another—nor, as it turns out, from racial difference. When Alabama circulates through these southern regions, she reveals her own racialization and abjection—but it is important that she does so through pleasure. Unlike her Nordic husband and vulnerable child, she enjoys the sweet wines and saturating colors of the humid South. When she feels herself becoming more diffuse, she attempts to discipline and solidify her flesh, but invariably these attempts fail. Elizabeth Grosz speculates that the construction of stickiness as horrifying is an effect of stigmatizing and marginalizing feminine sexuality.[80] Alabama experiences her sexual abjection as a failure of whiteness, construed as solidity and purity. But while Alabama's fear of her own seeping body internalizes racism and misogyny, the sweet stickiness of subalternity provides an epistemological and affiliative opportunity. The residue of race requires that she think the body differently.

A good example of this philosophical reorientation comes in the first section of the novel when Alabama comes of age in the South and meets her future husband, David Knight. Fitzgerald begins with a conventionally panicked reading of the sexual fecundity of southern white girls. World War I brings "men to town like swarms of benevolent locusts eating away the blight of unmarried women" (37). Anticipating this pestological simile, Fitzgerald describes the ripening fruit on the local fig trees just a few pages earlier: "June bugs covered the moist fruit in the fig trees with the motionless activity of clustering flies upon an open sore" (34). Rather than paint a still life of a tempting yet untouched fig, Zelda implies that female sexuality is always already rotting, even in virginal girls. The paired images of the "moist fruit" and the "open sore" metaphorize the vagina as both temptation and wound. Like oozing figs, girls are destined to be passively consumed. Significantly, "clustering flies" are both predatory and contaminating; not only will men consume these girls—they will symbolically sully them.

Just as the moist fruits of white femininity seem to fester—a convention of the southern Gothic—this stickiness that seems like corporeal doom becomes the source of erotic reverie and even cosmic epiphany.[81] Alabama meets David, and they enjoy a southern summer together:

> summer flooded the South with sweat and heat waves . . . they pressed their bodies against the cosmos, the gibberish of jazz, the black heat from the greens in the hollow like people making an imprint for the cast of humanity. They swam in the moonlight that varnished the land *like a honey-coating*. (41, emphasis mine)

The initial imagery of inundation and perspiration—the "flood[s]" of "sweat" and "heat"—recall imperial narratives of tropical collapse. But rather than pathologize this immersion, Fitzgerald makes it ecstatic and revelatory. At first glance, this passage seems to derive solid and normative whiteness—"an imprint for the cast of humanity"—from a diffuse backdrop of primitive and indistinguishable, even incomprehensible blackness ("the gibberish of jazz, the black heat"). Such a mythos would do little to destabilize the implicit humanist bias toward white subjectivity. However, Fitzgerald's figure emphasizes not the hard "cast" but rather the quality of impressibility. David and Alabama "press[] their bodies against the cosmos" and try to "make an imprint." This figure makes the cosmos itself soft, the stuff of the universe waxen and receptive. Furthermore, David and Alabama can register their own bodies only through soft stuff of this responsive, material universe. The implied form of "humanity"—imagined as a solid statue that could be cast in one particular mold—recedes in this passage in favor of the gleaming, fluid, and sticky surfaces of the world: "the moonlight that varnished the land like a honey-coating." In this view, the intersubjectivity of erotic communion reveals the corporeal interpenetration of the material world, the susceptibility of each body—human or nonhuman —to the other, the transitive contact of stickiness, here not panic-inducing but deliciously sweet.

In this pairing of the festering fig with the luminous honey-coating, Fitzgerald demonstrates the cultural ambivalence crouching inside stickiness. While he reveled in the romantic South, "varnished" with a "honey-coating," David writes to Alabama from New York that "humanity clings to the streets like flies upon a treacle stream" (41). Urban crowds bring back the disgusting implications of bodily proximity and humid textures. But it is also important that this observation comes in one of David's letters; as Grosz would anticipate, it is critical to the construction of white male mastery that other bodies be kept at bay, that stickiness not adhere to the smooth surface of the patriarchy. Once David is away from Alabama and their romance, he is no longer happily lost in an erotic reverie of a soft universe; he'd like to defend the contours of his body against other, inferior bodies that could stick to him and potentially stain.

Indeed, David embodies the sensory impoverishment that characterizes whiteness and, however counterintuitively, consolidates its claim to superiority. If mind rules over body and spirit over flesh, the very absence of sensory qualities bears out the successful rejection of bodiliness as a primary category for identity. David "smell[s] like new goods," and Alabama is "jealous of his pale aloofness" (39). At the same time, neither of these descriptions is terribly alluring or specific (what manner of goods does David smell like?). Odorlessness, pallor, and disengagement sacrifice more pleasure than they afford. Fitzgerald endorses color at the same time that she seems to be exalting David's purity. Unlike her pale lover, Alabama "glowed in the firelight like a confectioner's brewing, an advertisement of a pretty girl drinking a strawberry sundae in June" (39).[82] This multilayered metaphor emphasizes communicability, solubility, and intermixture, each cast as a positive quality. The fire flushes Alabama with its light and heat; a confectioner's brewing turns sugar into liquid and then back again into new, delightful shapes and flavors; a strawberry sundae infuses cream with fruity syrup. Alabama may not be as white as her fiancé, but her rosy glow betokens pleasures undreamt of in his philosophy.

The simmering metaphorics of infusion comes to a boiling point when David and Alabama move to the South of France.[83] Fitzgerald's own racism consigns the blackness of the US South to a womb metaphor where a generalized mammy gives metaphorical birth to white girls. The South of France is slightly different, however, and in a sense, more threatening because the "Negroid" influence that F. Scott Fitzgerald excoriated in that 1921 letter travels "northward" through brown, Mediterranean bodies. These Mediterranean bodies, as Scott Fitzgerald's depiction of Tommy Barban makes clear, were vital and seductive. Eugenicists like Grant and Stoddard feared that it was the in-between races, the Asiatics and the Mediterraneans, that would seduce and corrupt white woman, leading to the "passing of the great race" and the "rising tide of color" respectively. In other words, if David's appeal is characterized by his complete absence of appeal, then he could be threatened by a southern man who shares Alabama's roseate capacity to channel the atmosphere around her. As she sets the scene for southern romance in France, Zelda Fitzgerald elaborates a barely submerged racial allegory:

> It was as if the sun had absorbed the coloring of the countryside to brew its sunset mixtures, boiling and bubbling the tones blindingly in the skies while the land lay white and devitalized awaiting the lavish mixture that would be spread to cool through the vines and stones in the late afternoon. (82)

Once again, we have the fluid language of liminal states: "brew[ing]," "boiling and bubbling," and Fitzgerald repeats the word "mixture." Indeed, she echoes the word "brew" from her earlier simile alluding to the confectioner. This metaphor, which imagines the "lavish mixture" of sunset's colors "spread to cool," also implies that this molten color will become sweet candy.

This metaphorical celebration of intermixture has racial connotations—not least because eugenicists prognosticated that the sun was setting on white masculinity. If read as a comment not merely on the local terrain but on the local people, who personify the "coloring of the countryside," this passage implies that these southerners will reinvigorate the "white and devitalized" through "lavish mixture." In spite of eugenicists' belief in the superiority of the Nordic, they also conceded that modernity had drained him.[84] By contrast, primitive races—like that of the Mediterranean—retained their vitality.[85] Not only were they more willing to intermingle with other peoples, having none of the Nordic's justified purism, but they also posed a temptation for white women craving such vitality.

Unsurprisingly, this is the plot twist that succeeds this romantic vision of the South of France. Alabama has an affair with the Frenchman Jacques, and her husband describes their intimacy with an image that condenses animalism and pleasure, atmosphere and stickiness: "They were as wet and smooth as two cats who had been licking themselves" (89). Jacques ultimately ends the affair and goes to China, but this brief romance leaves the lingering impression that Alabama might be seduced by exotic climes and circulating seas. She tears up his last letter and "scatter[s] it over the black water of the harbor beneath the masts of many fishing boats from Shanghai and Madrid, Colombia and Portugal" (94).

Wine serves as the objective correlative for Alabama's sensual yearning to go native. She jokes that she will "luxuriate in this voluptuous air and grow fat on bananas and Chablis while David Knight grows clever," and he answers, "Sure. A woman's place is with the wine" (78). When her daughter's British governess demands her attention, Alabama gives it reluctantly: "She wanted to think about how brown her legs were going to be and how the wine would have tasted if it had been cold" (84). Heliophilia and oenophilia, both encouraged by southern climes, woo Alabama away from her duties as a mother of the race. At the same time, this longing is charged with ambivalence. In order to "luxuriate in this voluptuous air," Alabama has to "grow fat." Her wine, though a source of pleasure, is also ever so slightly off-putting. It would have been better if it were cold. Ahmed theorizes that the expression of disgust sticks not only to the object of disgust but also to its enunciator.[86] The same may also be true of sticky pleasures that lie on the edge of disgust. Though Alabama tries to lose herself in wine, her thoughts go to the fly in the ointment, the disgust inside the desire. That disgust, I suggest, is connected with the specter of race, the brown-skinned, banana-eating body that Alabama both longs for and fears becoming.

Disciplining the Body: Diet and Whiteness

This interlude in the South of France establishes the seductiveness of what Iain Chambers has evocatively called "Mediterranean crossings," which Fitzgerald represents as sensuous, even intoxicating fluidity.[87] In the middle section of the novel, however, Fitzgerald shifts her focus from percolating intermixtures to managing the all too solid flesh that adheres to the white body. In this sense, Alabama's fantasy of "growing fat on bananas and Chablis" exposes the anorexic logic that will organize the northern section of the novel—northern both in location (Paris) and in the cast of characters, expatriates from England and New England and ballerinas from Poland and Russia.[88] This section of the novel betrays the stickiness of the white body that tries so hard to be either marble or air, as we shall see.

Diet strains to produce and manage the white body. At a party, expatriates compare reducing tips. A young man "as sleek and brown as pulled molasses candy" confides that he has been living on "nothing but spinach" (109, 101). White women also try to reshape their bodies: "'There's a scheme,' said Miss Axton; 'you put six encyclopaedias on your stomach and recite the multiplication table. After a few weeks your stomach is so flat that it comes out at the back, and you begin life again hind part before'" (109). Miss Axton's account of the body makes it sound like moldable clay, but the stomach and butt insist upon extruding, no matter what pedagogical paces the woman puts them through.[89] The discussion turns scatological:

> "Of course," contributed Miss Douglas, punching herself where a shade of flesh rose above her girdle like fresh rolls from a pan, "the only sure thing is"—leaning across she sputtered something in Miss Axton's ear. The two women roared. "Excuse me," finished Dickie hilariously, "and in England they take it in a highball." (100)[90]

The women share uproarious laughter over the unspeakable solution to gaining weight, a modern laxative.[91] These solutions to fat—flattening it or chemically purging it—are externalized; neither bespeaks the self-control promoted by dietary discourse of the period.[92] Furthermore, the women's excremental humor, which "sputtered" and "roared," reflects not modesty but the bawdiness at the center of supposedly civilized life: "in England they take it in a highball." The efforts to control and contain whiteness give way to shit.

In this party scene, Fitzgerald uses two poles to describe white femininity, the first insubstantial and the second sculptural. Miss Douglas embodies the former: "Miss Douglas opened her translucent eyes; she was so much the essence of black chic that she was nothing but a dark aroma. Pale and transparent, she anchored herself to the earth solely by the tenets of her dreamy self-control" (100). Like Chanel No. 5, Miss Douglas is "translucent," "pale," and "transparent."[93] Though she alludes to "self-control," the traditional source of whiteness's claim to superiority, Fitzgerald evacuates the contents of whiteness ("she was nothing"). Furthermore, the glamorous effect of whiteness is contingent upon blackness: "the essence of black chic," "nothing but a dark aroma." Like the atomized liquid of a perfume, this essence can never be grasped or tasted, only scented on the breeze. On the other end of the textural spectrum, the ballerina Gabrielle Gibbs appears strikingly solid, "like white marble'" (102). She is also cold. One guest compares her to "Blue ice cream!" and speculates that her "frozen New England blood [has been] extracted from the world by the pressure of modern civilization on inherited concepts and acquired traditions" (104). Both figures, dark perfume and blue ice cream, emphasize essences and extracts, the chemical palette of the flavor and fragrance industry. Whether diffuse or solid, aromatic or edible, whiteness appeals to the senses through its artificiality.

Ideally, neither element is sticky. Only an excess of perfume creates a slick on the skin; only melted ice cream becomes adhesive on the hands. If whiteness carries off its cultural work, it leaves no mark; its impressions are exquisite and ephemeral. Of course, this untouchable quality is difficult to maintain. Though the ballerina imitates the white marble of classical statuary, men gossip about her beauty, and their eroticizing view softens her skin: "'And,' said David's voice excitedly, 'he said that your breasts were like marble dessert—a sort of blancmange, I presume'" (104). Stone, which might break the teeth, gives way to the custardy surface of "marble dessert." Her icy aura does not repel the touch. On the contrary, one sign of the successfully executed blancmange is that it trembles.

It is worth pausing over David's culinary figures for Gabrielle's tantalizing body. Recipes for "marble dessert" in *Physical Culture* magazine included several shredded and chopped ingredients: dates, figs, bananas, apples, and coconut.[94] While the dominant visual impression could be a cream color, its nutritional value stemmed from unseen combinations. Blancmange also contained multitudes. The critical ingredients were milk and gelatin—or some other jellifying agent—which would keep other flavors and ingredients in suspension. Though its name, often translated as "white food," combines the adjective for "white" with the verb "to eat," its gelatinous texture and molded shape were the dish's more consistent attributes.[95] It came in variety of flavors and colors.[96] The trope of blancmange, bland and beautiful, reveals much about whiteness as a social form. Like blancmange, whiteness as a racial designator declares that color is its key attribute, but in fact it is effectively monumental, taking the shape of whatever imperial spectacle it is called upon to materialize. Its surface tension may project a sleek, untouchable skin, but within its supposedly uniform substance reposes an array of textures and flavors—perhaps even chocolate.

Liminal states permeate the elemental ideal of uniform whiteness. Its impossible purity is too hard to achieve either conceptually or physically.[97] It continually reveals the percolation, infusion, and emulsion at its core. Fitzgerald associates this process of intermixture with the incorporation of the Global South into Europe. The hostess of the party "served up the slithered frontiers of Europe in a *céleri-rave*—Spaniards, Cubans, South Americans, even an occasional black floating through the social mayonnaise like bits of truffle" (96). Though Fitzgerald objectifies exotic, racialized bodies, this buoyant image recuperates emulsion as a feature of the miraculous mundane—an unlikely yet common suspension. Even the light-colored parts of the "social mayonnaise" are made with the vigorous intermixture of eggs and oil.[98] "You needn't be so highhat," Alabama tells David: "All the people [at the party] will be white—or were once" (96). A rumor circulates that their hostess has "slept with a Negro" (100), and Miss Douglas confesses that she now "draw[s] the color line at the Chinese" (107). As in *Tender Is the Night*, white women's sexuality is the mechanism that shakes up that "social mayonnaise."

Though Fitzgerald sets up these feminine ideals of whiteness in order to debunk them, Alabama's intimations of contamination make her feel overwhelmed and ailing. Her failure to embody pure whiteness—a quality that she ascribes to idealized figures like Miss Douglas and Gabrielle Gibbs—feels septic.[99] She cannot contain herself. She imagines that her fellow party guests are surgeons, "mov[ing] about like officials under masks in an operating room" (105). In an oddly depersonalized statement, Alabama registers that a "visceral femininity suffused the umber glow" (105). Like a hernia, "visceral femininity" escapes the interior of the body. It "suffuse[s]" and "glow[s]," its affects communicable, even contagious. Her association of this "visceral femininity" with earth-colored "umber" implies that femininity itself is racialized and pathologized. Alabama internalizes this negative valuation of color and fluidity, calling herself "bilious" (111). Classical and medieval humoral theory commonly concluded that women suffered from an excess of black bile, an imbalance evidenced by menstrual bleeding, breast cancer, and melancholic tendencies.[100] A bilious body is permeated by blackness. Just as the "umber glow" pours out of her, Alabama fears that poison circulates within her. She would like to concentrate this toxicity in one organ so it could be removed like "a poisoned appendix" (111). Modernity and its rational arts of anesthesia and surgery purport to perfect the pure female body.[101] By contrast, Alabama's glowing, seeping body seems like an embarrassing spectacle; everywhere she goes, people can see and feel her "visceral femininity." She cannot escape her own disgust.

Faced with this syrupy, brown body, Alabama turns to the ballet to achieve the self-contained whiteness that she admired in Gabrielle Gibbs. Ironically, this process makes her more aware of her animal embodiment: "her toes pick[ed] the floor like the beaks of many feeding hens" (120). She achieves solidity, all right, but the solidity of meat rather than marble: "her legs felt like dangling hams" (120). Physical exertion does not make her feel weightless and controlled; instead, it makes her more keenly aware of how interior spills into exterior: "She worked till she felt like a gored horse in the bullring, dragging its entrails" (144). The guts and gore of balletic training belie its effortless elegance, much as the sensing and suffering body ruptures the white ideal. Alabama's abjection dogs her even—or perhaps especially—when she tries to achieve that transcendence.

Part of the problem is the incipient eroticization of feminine flesh. Like David coveting the blancmange of Gabrielle's breasts, the male gaze appropriates the female form by imagining its edibility. Alabama arrives in Naples to perform in a ballet there, and an Italian man stares hungrily and openly at her: "As she gave the man his money his brown eyes swung on hers like cups set on a tree to catch a precious sap. She thought he would never quit looking" (156). Though on one level, this is a scene of sexual aggression—the stranger who sees her as sap to be consumed—it is also one of uneasy recognition tied to a sense of shared origins. Like this "brown eye[d]" stranger, Alabama comes from the sunny, syrupy South, just a different one. The Italian South brings Alabama face to face once more with the racialized stickiness she has tried so hard to shed: "The syrupy drippings of the fly-specked south seeped up on the breeze that blew the vast aquamarine translucence into emotional extinction" (156). This description of the horizon echoes the earlier scene in the South of France when Fitzgerald imagines the sunset as miscegenating confectionary, an allegory for Mediterranean sensuality and its revitalizing capacity. But here in the South of Italy, which was more often associated with racial degeneration than with touristic recuperation, the allegory seems straightforwardly negative. "Syrupy drippings" and "fly-speck[s]" are both excremental, contaminating images, and they seem inescapable as they "seep" into the very air. Furthermore, if we read the sky and its "vast aquamarine translucence" as a trope for racial whiteness, it faces imminent "extinction" at the hands of that corrupting South. Even as Fitzgerald successfully undermined—and arguably mocked—the vision of pure white femininity in the Parisian scenes, this return to the South is a return of the repressed, the stickiness and disgust that make it impossible for Alabama—and maybe for Fitzgerald herself—to accept infusion as an opportunity rather than an invasion. In other words, Alabama accepts white supremacy as her horizon and perceives her own physicality and sensuality as a sign of her perversion and corruption.

This implication becomes abundantly clear in the overwhelming series of sticky substances that adhere, not to Alabama, but to her innocent daughter, Bonnie, who comes to visit her in Naples. In a sequence of almost luxuriously paranoid encounters, Bonnie confronts the encompassing alimentary universe of southern savageness and is simultaneously ecstatic and sickened. She gobbles "candy and sweets," which make her "chok[e]" and "sputter[]" as they "plaster[] her mouth" (137). The "melted chocolate" stains her hands and paints her face (137). Later, Bonnie attends a birthday party where "honey and warm pink lemonade" are the refreshments (165), and a little boy's pet monkey bites her. Her mother dismisses the assault with a cannibalistic quip: "Monkeys have to have *something* to eat" (166). While there, Bonnie requests "the compote" and then "drip[s] the purple stain down the knife pleats of her best dress" (166). These sticky, staining substances reveal Bonnie's racial corruptibility. If her whiteness is to be preserved, she must get out of the South: "'I feel sick, a little,' confessed Bonnie. She was ghastly pale. The doctor said he thought it was the climate" (167). For her protected pallor to endure, the white girl must flee to the cooling influence of Switzerland and her father.

The fact that Bonnie can escape—at least temporarily—and Alabama stays implies that mature femininity is inherently sticky. While Bonnie is not yet an oozing fig or a shivering blancmange, to draw upon Fitzgerald's own images for the erotic feminine body, she need not steep in those substances that seem to convey the uncanny moisture—the bile, as it were—of postpubescent women.[102] Femininity and race converge in this fluid imagery. The "purple" stain of the compote, after all, anticipates both menstruation and deflowering. Its juxtaposition with that melted, plastering chocolate and the ravening monkey connects racial and sexual abjection. This equation casts new light on the novel's narrative resolution, as Alabama is prevented from making her balletic debut because she contracts blood poisoning as the result of a toe injury.[103] No part of her body—no matter how small—is effectively closed from the contaminating world. The world in turn is too sticky: "the infection [came] *from the glue* in the box of the toe shoe—it had seeped into a blister" (178, emphasis mine).

Blood poisoning, which toxifies the symbolic vehicle of racial inheritance, is a pathologized form of infusion. Alabama now vomits up the contents of her syrupy interior, exposing her brown, smelly, sticky abjection: "David will bring me some chocolate ice cream and I will throw it up; it smells like a soda fountain, thrown-up, she thought" (179). Rather than demonstrating the white woman's management of her body through careful and planned purgation, excrement reveals her passive and horrifying openness: "The bottom fell out of her stomach. She could feel the things dropping through" (181). Associating this abjection with the moisture of the South, Alabama dreams that she is floating in "the curious chemical growths of stagnant waters" (180). Fitzgerald's language to describe this surreal swamp reveals her ambivalence. "Stagnant" waters are a source of disease; there is not enough circulation to keep this imaginary South from decaying. At the same time, they produce "curious chemical growths"; this moisture makes new forms possible. Pathology and possibility are proximate.

I have glossed this depiction of Alabama's sickness as essentially ambivalent. Fitzgerald, unable to purge her own sense that a pure body was preferable, sets her heroine afloat in a climate that materializes the moisture of femininity, southernness, and racial abjection. Perhaps, however, I am not giving enough credit to Fitzgerald's capacity for critique. The surreal orthographic turn that the dream takes next makes it clear that Fitzgerald was aware of how categorizations like woman and man, black and white, sick and well were used to control and even to harm bodies. In the midst of her swamp dream, Alabama sees the word "'sick'... halted on the white road that ran straight through the middle" of an island (180). The label "'Sick' turned and twisted about the narrow ribbon of the highway like a roasting pig on a spit, and woke Alabama gouging at her eyeballs with the prongs of its letters" (180). Anticipating the contemporary insights of disability studies about pathologized bodies and the way that the label of sickness consolidates the wellness of a select few, Fitzgerald reveals the animality and penetrability of the female body. The idea of gouging out one's own eyes is, of course, a foundational masculine myth—the construction of subjectivity through guilt. But Alabama doesn't feel guilty because of incestuous desire—far from it. Her guilt has no origin story besides the labeling of her body as "sick." Like the inescapable attribution of southernness, which follows her across the globe, the diagnostic elasticity of sickness outpaces Alabama's ability to prove that she is well. The patriarchal culture of white supremacy can cannibalize her at will because it claims that clinical authority.

Fitzgerald gives her reader some hope that this dream could transform Alabama's view of her own body and its relationship to the world. Returning to the US South, Alabama demands that her dying father defend the hopeless double bind of mind–body dualism:

> why when our bodies ought to bring surcease from our tortured minds, they fail and collapse; and why, when we are tormented in our bodies, does our soul desert us as a refuge? . . . Why do we spend years using up our bodies to nurture our minds with experience and find out minds turning then to our exhausted bodies for solace? (185)

Sick himself now, he cannot provide a satisfactory reply: "'Ask me something easy,' the old man answered, very weak and far away" (185). Refusing philosophy, he requests some "breakfast bacon" (185). Even in the form of an old white man, the human body hungers, revealing its necessary and inevitable incompletion.

Coda

At the end of *Save Me the Waltz*, Fitzgerald returns to the trope of wine that earlier evidenced Alabama's thirst for the South. She introduces it in a comic register, as an unidentified voice at a party offers fellow guests "homemade wine . . . strained . . . through an old pair of underwear" (193). With underwear as a filter, "homemade wine" seems at once excremental and intimate, but Fitzgerald treats it with a light touch. The do-it-yourself vintner admits without embarrassment that there might still be a "little sediment" (193). In response to this awkward yet somehow heartwarming offering, Alabama reminisces about a wine that she had while vacationing on the Mediterranean: "In St-Raphaël, she was thinking, the wine was sweet and warm. It clung like syrup to the roof of my mouth and glued the world together against the pressure of the heat and dissolution of the sea" (194). This beautiful reminiscence is, for once, not preoccupied with the perils of stickiness. By contrast, this clinging texture manages to "glue" the fractured world together.

This erotic and oral interlude unites interior and exterior. The inside of her mouth is as wet and warm as the humidity and the ocean. Dissolution here seems like sweetest consummation. The potential of disgust embedded in a stranger's old underwear, in wine clogged with sediment, becomes the very source of interconnection and pleasure. Her reminiscence embraces the intermingling sensibility of what Stacy Alaimo might call the "transcorporeal," a "time-space where human corporeality, in all its material fleshiness, is inseparable from 'nature' or 'environment.'"[104] The wine both facilitates and affirms the flow between body and world, mouth and south.

At the end of her life, Zelda Fitzgerald lived on a strict diet prescribed by the psychiatrist at Highland Hospital in Asheville, North Carolina. In March 1940, she wrote to her husband that "it is impossible to exist under this severest of regimentation for as long as I have and not take a few liberties . . . If you knew how dreary and miserable it is to be held accountable for the least of ones [sic] ice-cream sodas I know that you would forgive the social indiscretion."[105] It seems a grim irony indeed that a woman who wrote so keenly and insightfully about the destructive fantasy of bodily purity was killed in a fire that began in the hospital's experimental kitchen.

Fitzgerald's abject identification with racial difference was, of course, an adopted one that she could cast off at will and articulates a deep-seated association of color and contamination, blackness and pathology. As promising as I find Zelda Fitzgerald's surreal aesthetics and corporeal politics, this narrative about the southern white woman and her degenerating body echoed a familiar eugenicist refrain and was in some ways not that far from Scott Fitzgerald's tragic take on racial infusion. In the last chapter of *Artificial Color*, I turn to two black women writers who deliberately dismantle patriarchal and racial hierarchies in their stories of southern circulation and tropical fruits.

5

The Monstropolous Beast

Animacy and Industry in Zora Neale Hurston and Dorothy West

In the 1930s, both Zora Neale Hurston and Dorothy West were employed by the America Eats Project of the Works Progress Administration (WPA). The Florida branch hoped that Hurston would produce a piece about "a Negro picnic" or "Negro foods."[1] The New York office sent West to interview black Harlemites from the South.[2] In their WPA writings, both Hurston and West summon up visions of plenty. Hurston's "Diddy-Wah-Diddy" describes a magical land where "the food is... already cooked" and calls out to be eaten: "If a traveler gets hungry all he needs do is to sit on a curbstone and wait and soon he will hear something hollering 'Eat me!' 'Eat me!' 'Eat me!'"[3] In November 1938, West interviewed a black woman named Mrs. Ayer, who had grown up in South Carolina and reminisces about blackberrying expeditions:

> Everybody would pick, the women and the children. You didn't put the berries in any special basket. You figured out how much everybody would get after you got back to the house. And everybody always got the same share. When you filled one big pan, you'd start filling another one, and you kept on 'till you'd picked as much as you could. 'Course the children ate more than they picked, and sometimes they'd run off and play.[4]

This description of blackberry picking emphasizes leisure, pleasure, and community. The children can play as they work, and everyone shares equally in the sweet results: "'Course if there was a little left over, you'd eat as much of it as you could that night for supper and the rest you left to the woman whose house you were in."[5] Hospitality rules the day.

Hurston and West articulate the contradictions of black life, caught between the richness of their culinary culture and the poverty of the Great

Depression. In "Diddy Wah Diddy," a land of abundance greets the reader, but "the baked chicken [that] comes along with a knife and fork stuck in its sides" recalls violated brown flesh.[6] In "The Gilded Six-Bits" (1933), soul food brings bliss to the marital table, but the molasses kisses that Joe buys for his philandering wife and probable son are eerily fungible figures for black reproduction.[7] In "Blackberrying" and "Quilting," West's WPA interviews with southern black women, collective endeavor provides an occasion for feasting and fun. In her 1938 story, "Pluto," however, a mother and her little boy visit West's Harlem apartment, begging for food, and West reflects that "it is not right to take a child's joy away and give him hunger."[8] In an even grimmer tale, "Jack in the Pot" (1940), a wife wins the jackpot at a beano game and buys steak for dinner: "the good blood of the meat had filtered through her skin."[9] However, she fails to share her remaining money with the impoverished janitor in her building, who must donate his baby girl's corpse to a medical school because he cannot afford a funeral. The child's cut-up cadaver is an uncanny echo of the meat feast.[10]

In these stories, racialized bodies blur the boundaries between human and nonhuman, living and inanimate. In Hurston's "Gilded Six-Bits," Missie Mae's breasts, "like broad-based cones with tips lacquered in black," resemble the ice-cream cones that she and her husband consume at the new ice-cream parlor in town.[11] This image betrays the commodification and objectification of black women's bodies, but it also imbues Missie Mae with auratic and nourishing power. In West's "Pluto," the little boy cannot perceive "the collapsible wooden image" of Disney's animated dog as comic and alive until he himself has eaten.[12] After the boy leaves her apartment, West is consumed by the dog's persistent melancholy: "The sad-eyed hound looked up at me, and his tail drooped wistfully. He did not look funny, and I did not want to laugh at him, and he is supposed to make you laugh."[13] The cuteness of the black boy, like the pathetic appeal of the "sad-eyed hound," is overdetermined in a culture that treats black pain in a minor, even comic register, but Pluto's animated visage conveys an affect that exceeds Disney's intent to entertain.

These animate figures postulate forms of resistance or resilience even in the absence of obvious agency. As Anne Anlin Cheng observes in *Second Skin*:

> Our culture is quick to assign personhood and agency to those long deprived of both, but this gift is often granted at the expense of recognizing or even allowing those inevitable moments when the exceptionalism of subjectivity fails . . . The premium we place on subjectivity as an antidote against discrimination is understandable, but, as I am trying to suggest here, subjectivity gets invoked too often precisely at those very moments when its condition for being is most at risk.[14]

If racism obstructs or vitiates the achievement of subjectivity based upon "received concepts of individualism," as Cheng puts it, then perhaps the racialized body as object manifests forms of imminent or immanent resistance.[15]

In these explorations of the borderlands between human and animal, animate and inanimate, Hurston and West anticipate the insights of recent work in critical race studies that explores how race "discipline[s] full humans, not-quite humans, and non-humans."[16] In their novels about the modern food system, *Their Eyes Were Watching God* (1937) and *The Living Is Easy* (1948), Hurston and West dramatize the failure of the black man's attempts to inhabit the transcendent category of Man.[17] They taxonomize the dangers of this humanist fiction—its hostility to the vulnerable and permeated body, its abjection of femininity and disability, its elevation of ownership over empathy, its treatment of nature as raw material for exploitation, and its ineluctable whiteness, which can suddenly and without remedy deny its categorical protections to black men.[18] While they debunk the category of Man, Hurston and West also document how animals and fruits have been racialized, black people bestialized, and exotic women botanized in a justification of the colonial world order and its pursuit of disposable labor and novel pleasures. In her play with what Mel Y. Chen calls "animacy hierarchies"—the elevation of the human over other forms of life and inanimate objects—Hurston demonstrates that black people have been consigned to animality and death but that this abject position opens up new possibilities of embodiment, humanity, and ecological and social enmeshment.[19] As Darieck Scott speculates, "Blackness-as-abjection [can] be understood or experienced as an aspect of historical experience—a resource for the political present—that broadens and even enriches the expanse of what is human being rather than setting its limit or marking its terror-bound underside."[20] By exploiting a common metaphor that naturalizes the rapine practices of colonialism, the woman of color as tropical fruit, West both diagnoses the heterosexualism that structures the global market and reclaims this erotic language for queer affiliation.[21]

Both novels follow a loosely naturalistic trajectory, as black men who hope to master the food system—grocers, migrant workers, fruit importers—turn out to be mastered by it, their bodies deteriorating and their fortunes dissipating. *Their Eyes Were Watching God* pioneers a folklore-influenced modernism, a lyrical realism that emphasizes the developing interior life of Hurston's heroine, Janie, while *The Living Is Easy* combines the class and family concerns of domestic realism with the ironic sensibility of a comedy of manners to expose the snobbery and bloodlessness of the black bourgeoisie in Boston, a sacred precinct entered by the ruthless social climber Cleo Judson. In some ways, these novels seem an odd choice to conclude a study so invested in genres that propose the transformation of the world through the word, like experimental modernism and science fiction.

But even as both novels contain elements of the documentary realism associated with the period and their naturalist plots move relentlessly toward their heroes' downfall, their imagery resists that motion. Both books take common figures for racialized flesh—the black man as an animal, the exotic woman as a tropical fruit—and explore their uncanny resonances. As Chen might predict, the vehicle that is supposed to be less alive than the tenor—a mule no match for a man, a peach less pressing than a person—turns out to have unexpected vitality.[22] Furthermore, the edibility that these tropes have in common—the dog-eat-dog world of *Their Eyes Were Watching God*, the ripening bananas of *The Living Is Easy*—reveals the materiality of the flesh that undercuts the premise of the human being as a higher and separate life form. Even as the trope of the edible person indicts a capitalist system that preys on racialized flesh, it also embodies the potential for social, physical, and ecological enmeshment.

In many ways, Hurston and West are an obvious pair to consider together as sources of black feminism during the modern period.[23] Hurston and West were friends; West sublet Hurston's apartment, and she complained of Hurston stealing her fur coat.[24] They both participated in the Harlem Renaissance, sharing second place in the 1926 *Opportunity* magazine writing contest, but they produced their most famous work well after its end, *Their Eyes Were Watching God* in 1937 and *The Living Is Easy* in 1948. Their belatedness infuses their novels' tones and politics. Written and published after the Great Depression, both novels communicate a sense that the game is rigged, that global markets benefit white-owned corporations and destroy black laborers. At the same time, they raise the rich possibilities of interracial and diasporic identification facilitated by—though not defined by—global trade. Both writers knew the industries they documented intimately; Hurston did anthropological fieldwork with migrant workers in the US South, and West was the daughter of Isaac West, the so-called Black Banana King of Boston, and she kept the gold banana and pineapple charms from his watch chain all of her life.[25]

Until the advent of chain stores in the 1930s, grocery stores represented an avenue to prosperity for black men. The historian Susan Spellman observes that "grocery stores were among the most popular black enterprises in the 1920s, undoubtedly for what at the time were its low entry barriers."[26] In an 1899 talk, "The Negro Grocer," W. O. Murphy, a black business owner, insisted that commerce was the distinguishing characteristic of Man:

> Well has it been said that "Man is the only animal that buys and sells or exchanges commodities with his fellows. Other animals make an attempt at least, to do every other thing that men can do except trade; and among them are types of every profession except the merchant. The beaver, the bee, and the bird, can build as well as some of our mechanics;

the fox surpasses some lawyers in cunning; musicians are content to be called nightingales of song; the tiger is an uneducated warrior; lions are the lords of the forest; but the merchant who buys from one people to sell to another has no representative in the animal creation."[27]

This catalog of animals implies that business ownership demonstrates that the black man ought to be included in the category of Man. Murphy ignores the glaring detail that merchants once bought *people* and turned them into objects of trade.

In spite of such encomiums to entrepreneurship, black-owned grocery stores were a target of racist violence, legislative opposition, and monopolist exclusion.[28] By the late 1920s, black grocers struggled to obtain loans, and white-owned chain stores pushed them out of the market.[29] One response to the collapse of this individualist model was intraracial cooperation and profit sharing; some African American grocers established merchant cooperatives.[30] Indeed, George Schuyler cofounded the Young Negroes' Co-Operative League in 1930, a group that opened a "cooperative grocery store and meat market" in Buffalo, New York.[31]

In *Their Eyes Were Watching God* and *The Living Is Easy*, the black grocers Jody Starks and Bart Judson embrace an individualist and masculinist business ethic. Hurston and West cast a critical eye on Jody's ruthless opportunism and Bart's unfounded optimism respectively. When they internalize these philosophies of Man, these characters view black women as fungible commodities, status symbols, and reproductive vehicles, an equivalence they express with metaphors that move women's bodies down the animacy chain (women as chickens, women as flowers or fruit, etc.). When confronted with their own vulnerability and corporeality, whether through illness or animal bite, barrenness or bankruptcy, they either blame women (*Their Eyes Were Watching God*) or abandon them (*The Living Is Easy*). This misogyny exposes the myopia of humanist thought, especially as it ratifies and is ratified by global capitalism. In both novels, black feminist critique provides the grounds for "thinking humanity creatively" and "designing novel assemblages of relation."[32] The fates of Jody and Bart reflect the dire costs of the failure to do so.

Predation and Poison in *Their Eyes Were Watching God*

It is important to remember, in light of Jody's vilification in *Their Eyes Were Watching God*, how central the store owner was to visions of black success in a postbellum world. "With no business experience at the beginning of our freedom," Booker T. Washington exulted in his address at the unveiling of the Harriet Tubman Memorial in June 1914, "we now own and operate about ten thousand grocery stores, drygoods stores, shoe stores."[33] In his sociological study "The Negroes of Farmville, Virginia," W. E. B. Du Bois praised the "proprietors of [grocery] stores" for their "good common-school training" and "good business judgment."[34] In *I Know Why the Caged Bird Sings* (1969), Maya Angelou recalls the prominence of her grandmother's Arkansas store: "it was always spoken of with a capital *s*."[35] Though a woman owned and ran the store, its sign played up the ideal of masculine proprietorship, as "the formal name of the Store was the Wm. Johnson General Merchandise Store."[36]

Though the black grocer was an uplift icon, the town merchant was a symbol of postbellum debt peonage that kept black southerners in poverty and de facto indenture. In *The Souls of Black Folk* (1903), Du Bois describes the perfidy of the white merchant who thrives on the perpetual debt of black laborers and concludes, "Once in debt, it is no easy matter for a whole race to emerge."[37] Historically, Florida represented an escape from the Black Belt and cotton; Hurston's father, John, had been a tenant farmer in Alabama and then moved to Eatonville, where he became mayor.[38] Nonetheless, when Jody sets up his store, he keeps close tabs on his customers' accounts, and they in turn spend what they don't have.[39] When one of his tenants tries to make off "with a wagon load of his ribbon cane," Jody "took the cane away from Pitts and made him leave town" (48). The townspeople debate this punishment: "Colored folks oughtn't tuh be so hard on one 'nother," one opines, while another objects: "Let colored folks learn to work for what dey git lak everybody else. Nobody ain't stopped Pitts from plantin' de cane he wanted tuh. Starks give him uh job. What mo' do he want?" (48). The politics of racial uplift are incommensurate with the economics of tenant farming and debt peonage.

These two forms of incorporation are thus incompatible. When Jody proposes that the town "incorporate" and name him mayor, he implies an interdependent relationship between the parts and the head: he volunteers to act as the people's representative, to embody their ambitions and plans. The townspeople greet him on those terms, calling him "Brother Starks" and accepting his bid for leadership (43). In fact, Jody means to incorporate the town by cannibalizing their labor. The townspeople quickly realize that Jody lives "offa de rest of us" (49). Unconstrained by racial affiliation in his cupidity, Jody is willing to devour his symbolic kin: "It was bad enough for white people, but when one of your own color could be so different it put you on a wonder. It was like seeing your sister turn into a 'gator. A familiar strangeness. You keep seeing your sister in the 'gator and the 'gator in your sister" (48). Racial kinship renders capitalist carnivory uncanny, making it visible where it might otherwise operate unnoticed, but it does not change the underlying dynamic.

Jody imagines himself impervious to larger food chains because he is the biggest voice in an all-black town. "I god," he repeats habitually. Through predation, however, Hurston exposes the sliding scale of relative power; there is always a larger animal to prey on a smaller. Sam and Lige contemplate the dinosaur on the Sinclair sign at the gas station: "Look at dat great big ole scoundrel-beast up dere at Hall's fillin' station—uh great big old scoundrel. He eats up all de folks outa de house and den eat de house.... Dey caught him over dere in Egypt. Seem lak he used tuh hang round dere and eat up dem Pharaoh's tombstones" (66). This tall tale comically literalizes the Sinclair dinosaur logo and crucially misreads it as well; the gas industry feeds on dinosaur bones, not vice versa. Nonetheless, the "scoundrel-beast" at the filling station embodies a deeper truth about the operations of capital, which has little respect for the pomp of the pharaohs or the pretensions of black business owners.[40]

This tale of the "big ole scoundrel-beast" demonstrates a central problem with positing masculine agency as a remedy for the history of slavery and subjection: the operations of capital can easily turn the emancipated man back into meat.[41] To explore this problematic, Hurston introduces a folkloric hero, Big John the Conqueror, "a man wid salt in him" (66). Through this figure, she queers this apparent representative of ur-masculinity. The salt that "makes up [a] strong man" also makes him delicious and consumable: "He could give uh flavor to *anything*" (66, emphasis in original). John the Conqueror proves to be a figure not of individualism but of a shared feast. By lending "salt" and "flavor," John the Conqueror acts like pork in soul food, enhancing other ingredients.[42] His example inspires Sam and Lige to dream of being eaten and eating others: "Ah got salt in *me*. If Ah like man flesh, Ah could eat some man every day, some of 'em is so trashy they'd let me eat 'em" (67). This cannibal queerness, even phrased pejoratively, opens up the possibility of intimacy and pleasure.[43] Furthermore, salt connects human and nonhuman creatures in shared meatiness; the men speculate that the "varmint," an allusion to the scoundrel-beast, is also "high" in "salt."[44] At the same time that "salt" is slang here for the boldness of a successful predator, it also confesses our saline composition and evidences our likely tastiness.[45]

For Hurston, the legend of John the Conqueror is centrally a legend about the flesh and meat, particularly pig meat, which plays a prominent role in *Their Eyes Were Watching God*.[46] In her story "High John de Conqueror" (1943), John steals and cooks his master's pig.[47] The slaveholder owns both human and animal bodies. When John appropriates the pig, he symbolically reclaims his own appetites and agency. However, Hurston also reminds the reader of the fleshly vulnerability of the slave; the Old Massa threatens "to have the hide off [John's] back" (928). The word "hide" animalizes John's skin and attempts to reduce it to an emblem of the master's power. In the sequel to John's mortal adventures with pig stealing, he visits hell and "put[s] some of the Devil's hogs to barbecue over the flames" (929). He runs for "High Chief Devil" and wins (929). The emancipatory ethos of taking the Devil's property and unseating him in an election recalls the aspirations of Reconstruction. The image of the hogs barbecuing over the flames, however, underscores the suffering of hell's human inhabitants and resonates with contemporary accounts of lynching. As Orlando Patterson points out in *Rituals of Blood*, lynchers often "explicitly referred to the roasted Afro-Americans as barbecued meat."[48] Even inside this triumphant tale lie reminders of the tortured flesh and the continuing history of racial violence.

In the face of this past and present violence, John the Conqueror chooses to embrace the flesh rather than to abjure it. In "Mama's Baby, Papa's Maybe," Hortense Spillers argues that "the sociopolitical order of the New World" robbed slaves of their bodies and produced "a hieroglyphics of the flesh" through "the tortures and instruments of captivity."[49] In John's prehistory, Hurston encapsulates this narrative of black bodies stolen and turned into flesh:

> [John] had come from Africa. He came walking on the waves of sound. Then he took on flesh after he got here. The sea captains of ships knew that they brought slaves in their ships. They knew about those black bodies huddled down there in the middle passage, being hauled across the waters to helplessness. (924)

By taking on flesh, John the Conqueror both shares in slave suffering and bears witness to violence: "Maybe he was in Texas when the lash fell on a slave in Alabama, but before the blood was dry on the back, he was there" (924). In cooking and relishing the pig, John not only remedies slave hunger but also reclaims the black body for pleasure.[50] As she celebrates John's sensuous rebellion, Hurston categorically condemns white supremacy as a form of cannibalism:

> John knew that it is written where it cannot be erased, that nothing shall live on human flesh and prosper. Old Maker said that before He made any more sayings. Even a man-eating tiger and lion can teach a person that much. His flabby muscles and mangy hide can teach an emperor right from wrong. If the emperor would only listen. (925)

The pretense of power inadvertently confesses the denied fleshiness and indeed disguised vulnerability of the predator's body. In other words, by identifying with rather than repudiating the sufferings of slavery, John perceives a truth about human embodiment, while white supremacy clings to the pretense of sovereignty like a Cowardly Lion.[51]

Imitating the lion, Jody tries to transmute his own flesh into a symbol of affluence. Janie is "proud" of Jody's appearance because he's "kind of portly like rich white folks" (34). Ultimately, however, the body is not under his command: "his back ached and his muscle dissolved into fat and the fat melted off his bones"

(78). Jody has done everything he can to establish his humanity in the model of white masculinity—building a house, marrying and controlling a beautiful wife, owning a store, making speeches. The aching, dissolving, melting body troubles the agency and autonomy to which he aspires; indeed, it gives the lie to Man as a disembodied ideal. In fact, Jody resembles the mule he freed that now lives next to the general store. In his newfound leisure, the animal is well nourished, even overnourished: "Nearly everybody took the habit of fetching along a handful of fodder to throw on the pile. He almost got fat and they took a great pride in him" (58). Like Janie admiring her portly husband, the townspeople take "pride" in the mule's fat; it speaks to the town's prosperity (34). But Hurston reframes this fat as a symptom of disease when the mule dies and buzzards chant around his corpse: "'What killed this man?' The chorus answered, 'Bare, bare fat.' 'What killed this man?' 'Bare, bare fat.' 'What killed this man?' 'Bare, bare fat'" (62). The very emblem of the mule's new freedom and comfort becomes the agent in his premature demise. The mule's edible flesh also recalls a history of racial violence that Jody would rather forget. Devouring buzzards appear in abolitionist literature, slave narratives, and lynching journalism to evoke the indignities visited upon the black body.[52] Tellingly, when Jody begins to die, metaphorical carrion birds come to call: "[Janie] was liable to find a feather from [Death's] wings lying in her yard any day now" (84).

In the parallel between Jody and the mule, Hurston delineates the limits of freedom conceptualized as prosperity and leisure. Jody's vision of success is based upon white power—from the "gloaty, sparkly white" paint on his house to the "spittoon just like his used-to-be bossman used to have in his bank up there in Atlanta" (47). Such success does not require—and indeed avoids—physical exertion: "Didn't have to get up and go to the door every time he had to spit" (47). On the one hand, then, Jody's dissolution into fat reflects his successful ascension into the managerial class and its sedentary lifestyle. On the other hand, as I will expand upon in a moment, Jody's failing kidneys reveal that in spite of his apparent wealth, he still suffers from nutritional deficits unevenly apportioned by structural racism. His status within the town does not extricate him from the racial geographies of the market, just as the mule's emancipation does not alter his species subordination and dependence upon the community's discarded fodder. In other words, both the mule and Jody get the worst of both worlds: the lassitude of the leisure class and the inferior surplus allotted to marginalized populations.

The cultural meaning of fat changed with the advent of industrial farming and the proliferation of grocery stores like Jody's.[53] In the face of consumer indulgence, the control of fat signaled restraint and virtue.[54] The mule's compulsive consumption, and by extension Jody's, undermine the agential ideal of consumer autonomy. The mule eats the excess fodder automatically, because it is there, just as Jody "eat[s] fast... wip[ing] his lips of ham gravy" while rushing to the mule's funeral (59–60). When Jody begins ailing, his stomach "didn't seem to be a part of him anymore" (77). Even as it figured forth prosperity, the fat body betrayed the primacy of the corporeal within an economy of apparent choice.

Though contemporaneous diet regimens suggested that it was up to the individual to control his consumption, broader market structures shaped the menu. Southern monocultures left tenant farmers dependent upon the town store for food. The townspeople largely depend upon the "three 'm's'—meal, meat, and molasses"—that they can buy at the store.[55] Matt Bonner tries to scam small amounts of meat and meal (56), and Mrs. Robbins begs for slices of salt pork, which Jody adds to her husband's bill (73–74). Stores like Jody's stocked cheap and shelf-stable food supplies from industrial mills and Midwestern meatpackers.[56] Janie misplaces the bill of lading for a keg of pigs' feet and slices meat from the "salt pork box" (70, 73). These processed meats were cheap to buy and easy to ship, but their salt content was high, their nutritional value limited. Though malnutrition was associated with the poverty of tenant farmers, Jody's wealth may not shield him from the limits of the local diet.[57] Indeed, Tea Cake, who later brings Janie fresh trout that he caught, may have a more nutritious diet than Jody (103). Skills like fishing and hunting supplement his sporadic income and sustain him through the itinerancy of seasonal work. Jody's fatness, then, betrays his vulnerability to a system that may feed yet still not nourish him. Structural racism contributes to Jody's physical deterioration, in spite of his wealth and status. Because there is no doctor in all-black Eatonville, Janie must send to Orlando for a doctor, and by then, it is too late (83).

Jody fends off intimations of vulnerability by accusing Janie of poisoning him (82). In *The Signifying Monkey*, Henry Louis Gates, Jr., suggests that "Janie kills her husband, rhetorically, by publicly naming his impotence... His image fatally wounded, he soon succumbs to a displaced 'kidney' failure."[58] His kidneys are a suggestive site for wounding, however, since these organs filtrate toxins out of the body. Unable to expel waste, Jody becomes permeated and contaminated. His paranoid fantasy about secret poison operates much as Geoffrey Sanborn argues the cannibal threat does in colonial fictions. The predatory vengeance of the fantasized cannibal exposes the colonizer's "secret lack," his anxieties about whiteness and masculinity as sources of power.[59] In order to restore his shaken belief in the impenetrability of the masculine body, Jody must project a fantasy of toxic femininity.

Elsewhere in her work, Hurston associates poison and predation with disguised weakness. In *Mules and Men* (1935), the snake acquires his poison from God because "everything trods upon me and kills off my generations."[60] When God gives the snake poison, the snake's indiscriminate use of his weapon reflects his insecurity: "All Ah kin see is feets comin' to trample me. Ah can't tell who my enemy is and who is my friend" (97). In another fable, the alligator acquires his gaping maw when a dog plays a practical joke on him: "Brer Dog kept right on cuttin' till he ruint Brer 'Gator's face. Brer 'Gator was a very handsome gent'-man befo' Brer Dog done him that a way, and everytime he look in de lookin' glass he cry like a baby over de disfiggerment of his face" (101). The apparent source of their power, the snake's poison and the dog's bite, proves to be the sign of their weakness. The open mouth of the striking snake or the ravening alligator can, in another light, resemble Jody's "vacant-mouthed terror" facing death (86).

Death is the ultimate testament to the body's coextensiveness with the inanimate world, a collapse of boundaries that Jody experiences as abjection. Illness disassembles and consumes his body:

> she noticed how baggy Joe was getting all over. Like bags hanging from an ironing board. A little sack hung from the corners of his eyes and rested on his cheek-bones; a loose-filled bag of feathers hung from his ears and rested on his neck beneath his chin. A sack of flabby something hung from his loins and rested on his thighs when he sat down. But even these things were running down like candle grease as time moved on. (80)

Jody's skin now resembles an array of domestic items: cloth, a sack, a pillow, a candle. Several of these inanimate objects are made from animal parts; goose feathers stuff pillows and dipped animal fat makes tallow candles. The potential use-value of bodies is uncanny, marking the proximity between the inanimate and the (formerly) agential.[61] Illness marks the return of the repressed, the excremental particularity of the body. By comparing Jody's ailing body to "candle grease," Hurston condenses embodiment, temporality, and abjection in a single image. For Hegel, death is the moment when the "human being truly *becomes a subject*—that is separated from the animal," spirit rather than flesh.[62] In other words, the subject's command of death demonstrates the side of the master–slave dialectic to which he belongs. Hurston eschews this racist fantasy of spiritual transcendence, and she evacuates the phallus in favor of the flesh ("a sack of flabby something hung from his loins").

For Hurston, death reveals the shared edibility of all flesh. The "body of death" is "infinite hunger," and death has "the first and last taste of all things."[63] This predation is an inescapable consequence of embodiment: "*Thing* lies forever in her birthing-bed and glories. But hungry Time squats beside her couch and waits ... his mouth set wide for prey" (247). The would-be master of his town, his wife, and his body, Jody experiences his own death as inescapably, claustrophobically animal, while Janie sees his panic as the direct result of this misplaced bid for control: "Have yo' way all yo' life, trample and mash down and then die" (86). Faced with corporeality that he cannot master, Jody sobs, "It was like beating a bass drum in a hen-house" (86). Death metaphorically decapitates him, like a chicken in the farmyard, depriving him of the voice and reason on which he so prided himself: "A sound of strife in Jody's throat ... The icy sword of the square-toed one had cut off his breath" (87). That overdetermined marker of human agency, the hands, remain "in a pose of agonizing protest" (87). Neither masculinity nor the market could free him from the body as potential meat; he would have done well to recognize the fleshliness that connects him with black women, whom he denigrated as mindless chickens and cows (71).[64]

Zombies and Mad Dogs: Living and Dying on the Muck

Hurston dismantles the body of the black grocer to show his vulnerability in a white supremacist system and the limitations of humanist philosophy. In this section of my chapter, I explore her depiction of Florida agribusiness as a celebration of diasporic invention, the deliberate creation of pan-African racial culture, and as a condemnation of the necropolitics that make these laboring bodies disposable.[65] In this part of the novel, Hurston moves away from the metaphor of the food chain into a suspended space between life and death, predator and prey. Exploring the imagery of animal possession that she played with when the gator looks out of Jody's face, Hurston turns her attention from eating to biting, from fattening to choking, thus interrogating the oral idiom of bodies that seem powerless and are consigned to life-in-death, yet find a way to leave their mark on the world that would sweep them away. In this metaphorics, Hurston both stresses the continuity between the plantation form and the corporate farm and also emphasizes the unruly margins of agribusiness.

Perhaps the most relevant cultural coordinate for Hurston's exploration of life-in-death on the muck is the mythology of the zombie. The first Hollywood zombie movie, *White Zombie* (1932), featured Haitian zombies, enslaved in Bela Lugosi's sugar mill, so mindless that they don't notice when one of their number falls into the mill and is crushed along with the stalks of cane.[66] In *Tell My Horse*, Hurston explains that corpses were reanimated to work on cane and banana plantations. This dark magic takes a "culture[d]," "loved" person and turns that body into a "beast": "working like a beast, unclothed like a beast and like a brute crouching in some foul den in the few hours allowed for rest and food. From an educated, intelligent being to an unthinking unknowing beast."[67] As Mimi Sheller points out, the figure of the zombie links a slave past with new racialized labor regimes.[68] In *Their Eyes Were Watching God*, the migrant workers are "ugly from ignorance and broken from being poor" (131). They "work all day for money, fight all night for love" (131). They continue to labor for hourly wages even when the hurricane is coming. What looks to Tea Cake like perfect agency—nothing but "money and fun and foolishness" (128)—may be compelled movement: "It's hard trying to follow your shoe instead of your shoe following you . . . All night, all day, hurrying in to pick beans . . . herded and hovered on the inside, chugging onto the muck" (131).

In spite of the zombie mythology linking cane production to compelled servitude, Hurston emphasizes the unanticipated effects of gathering people together. Brought to the muck as migrant workers to provide cheap labor for agribusiness, these "wild" people make the Everglades their own and produce pericapitalist economies (128).[69] While living on the muck, Tea Cake and Janie plant seeds, fish, gamble, sell alligator hides and teeth, pick beans, and gather dried beans to sell to planters. Industry sets all this into motion, but the ecologies, intimacies, and economies that emerge in its wake exceed its terms.[70] In this sense, the "wild" people on the muck are the antithesis of zombies. Hurston's gerundial extravaganza—"dancing, fighting, singing, crying, laughing, winning and losing love every hour" (131)—suggests the range of pleasures through which they reclaim their bodies.

At the same time, these promises of freedom, these intimations of wildness, have limits. Agribusiness takes the place of the plantation in the daily lives of the migrant workers. Many people wield power over the migrant workers: "de big men," "mah boss-man" (130), "the man whose land they slept on" (132). Those impressive wages don't make it far off the muck: "They made good money, even the children. So they spent good money. Next month and next year were other times. No need to mix them up with the present" (132). Each week, "Saturday afternoon when the work tickets were turned into cash everybody began to buy coon-dick and get drunk" (149). These Saturday sprees recall Frederick Douglass's account of slave holidays, the drunkenness to the master's advantage—in this case, doubly so because the wage earners spend their money at the jook-joints on the muck.[71] In addition, agribusiness drains the swamplands and places worker camps on flood plains. As Susan Scott Parrish points out, black bodies are often instrumental in carrying out industry's damage while also most vulnerable to its consequences.[72]

Their Eyes Were Watching God fictionalizes the historical hurricane of 1928, which killed more than eighteen hundred people, the majority of whom were black migrant workers. This "natural" disaster was the outcome of years of draining, development, and denial.[73] For big business, ecological crises could present profitable opportunities; after Lake Okechobee flooded in 1922, the Southern Sugar company bought out debt-ridden independent growers.[74] Such companies put pressure on local legislatures and media outlets to play down the potential for catastrophe. As the environmental historian Ted Steinberg puts it, "Private-property-driven economic development helped to sow the seeds of future destruction, while Florida's business community sought to deny the very real risks involved and, where possible, to blame nature or God where disaster did occur."[75] In a stark example of modern necropolitics, agribusiness deemed workers of color disposable, their mass deaths an acceptable byproduct of raising crops on the muck.[76]

In the hurricane, the migrant workers inhabit what Achille Mbembé calls the "status of *living dead.*"[77] Hurston ironizes the workers' faith in their bosses' protection: "If the castles thought themselves secure, the cabins needn't worry. Their decision was already made as always. Chink up your cracks, shiver in your wet beds and wait on the mercy of the Lord. The bossman might have the thing stopped before morning anyway" (158). The white owners living on literal and metaphorical high ground have consigned these workers to death by drowning. Through the environmental forces of "wind and water," unleashed by willful negligence, agribusiness reveals its genealogical and philosophical relation to "topographies of cruelty" like the plantation.[78]

In the wake of catastrophe, however, new possibilities for affiliation and embodiment emerge. The storm suspends the predatory relation between the human and the animal as they recognize their common flesh: "A baby rabbit, terror ridden, squirmed through a hole in the floor and squatted off there in the shadows against the wall, seeming to know that *nobody wanted its flesh at such a time*" (159, emphasis mine).[79] A man shares an above-water perch with a coiled rattlesnake too scared to strike (165). Faced with the flood, predatory relations are suspended, revealing common need. Each creature leaves its accustomed place; there are "stray fish swimming in the yard" (160), and the lake is a "monstropolous beast" that "left his bed. The two hundred miles an hour wind had loosed his chains" (161). These radical displacements are potentially fatal but also potentially revolutionary. In the storm, Hurston measures the conditions of black life in terms of animal vulnerability and elemental power. Both fish and lake seem passive and manipulable, but they adapt to new circumstances ("swimming in the yard") and destroy man-made structures ("loosed his chains"). Through resilience and rebellion, they model forms of resistance irreconcilable with humanist agency.

This animacy that is not identical to agency also inflects Hurston's characterization of Tea Cake, an alternative to Jody and his individualist ethos. Tea Cake's name conflates the human and the inanimate, as he jokingly acknowledges to Janie: "Who ever heard of uh teacake bein' called Mister!" (98). Insofar as Tea Cake resembles food, however, this resemblance imbues him with power rather than strips him of it, much like John the Conqueror and his salt. Tea Cake's element is sugar and spice, and he invites Janie to sample his sweetness: "You better try me and see" (97). His erotic body exudes spicy perfume: "crushing scent out of the world with his footsteps. Crushing aromatic herbs with every step he took. Spices hung about him" (106). His sensuousness affects other bodies and even the environment. When Tea Cake shares Coca-Colas with Janie, the night is suffused with an amber glow: "she sat on the porch and watched the moon rise. Soon its amber fluid was drenching the earth, and quenching the thirst of the day" (99). This imagery draws upon the association between Coca-Cola, colonial ingredients, racialized bodies, and affective replenishment traced in Chapter 1. At the same time, Hurston directs this exotic and refreshing language toward an intraracial love affair, claiming sweetness for black bodies, not white ones.

In the hurricane, Tea Cake is no longer a sweet cookie or a thirst-quenching soda but vulnerable flesh. A mad dog stands on a quaking cow that fears she will be devoured by a gator. The mad dog threatens Janie, and Tea Cake fends him off, only to be bitten "high up on his cheek-bone" (166). The zombie mythology returns in Tea Cake's implacable transformation into "something" rather than someone (181), into a "fiend" that "must kill" rather than a man who defends helpless creatures (184). In a scene of compulsive predation, Tea Cake "closed his teeth in the flesh of her forearm" (184). Tea Cake's hydrophobia seems a reversal of Hurston's position on the potential of nonhuman models of animacy to inspire new ways of being human. The racist myth of the black man as mad dog seems to play out its bloody course.[80]

Tea Cake's life-in-death, however, resonates beyond this brutal script. During the hurricane, white people sought to consolidate their hierarchical power by consigning black bodies to the flood: "White people had preempted that point of elevation and there was no more room" (164). Even after the storm, the Florida authorities force black men to bury bodies in segregated mass graves. Whiteness, then, operates through its claim on life and its identification of blackness with death. In the emergency of the storm, Hurston invests death itself with a utopian, ethical potential: "They passed a dead man in a sitting position on a hummock, entirely surrounded by wild animals and snakes. Common dangers made common friends. Nothing sought a conquest over the other" (164). The corpse sitting in a circle with "wild animals and snakes" acknowledges "common dangers" and shared mortality.[81] Tea Cake, like a communion wafer, recalls the edibility of all flesh.

There is a good deal of evidence in Hurston's biography that interspecies affiliation appealed to her. As a child, she reports, "inanimate things ... commune[d] with me like natural men" (*Dust Tracks*, 78). Subsequently, in her imaginings, "animals took on lives and characteristics which nobody knew anything about except myself" (78). This affinity for the nonhuman began early, according to a family fable. A "sow with her litter of pigs" approached infant Zora, "smell[ing] the cornbread I was messing with," and "began to nuzzle around" (31). Hurston's mother panicked "because hogs have been known to eat human flesh" (31). Hurston reflects, "[The sow] had much less intention of eating Mama's baby, than Mama had of eating hers" (32). Building on that unexpected breakfast bowl intimacy, Hurston sees the pig as compatriot rather than competition. The hogs' movements inspire Zora's; the child walks that day and "never stops thereafter" (32). Indeed, she "wander[s] off in the woods all alone, following some inside urge to go places" (32), an instinctive drive that recalls a pig rooting for food in the forest. This passage of traits between animals and humans becomes explicit in *Mules and Men*, where she describes boiling a black cat alive and sucking on its bones in a voodoo initiation: "the bones of the cat must be passed through my mouth until one tasted bitter" (221). In the book's famous conclusion, she compares herself to a cat: "I'm sitting here like Sis Cat, washing my face and usin' my manners" (246). If animal possession stirs up qualities that the category of the human masked or even curtailed, perhaps Tea Cake too gains access to urgent affects by inhabiting (and being inhabited by) the dog.

Tea Cake's hydrophobia dramatizes the physical toll of the madness of racial regimes. This symptomatic fasting, choking, and disgorging emphasizes the impossibility of nurturance "with an enemy that was at his throat" (174). Like the zombie, whom Hurston describes as making "broken noises in its throat" (*Tell My Horse*, 182), and like Jody "deep-growling" with a "sound of strife in [his] throat" (*Their Eyes Were Watching God*, 85, 87), Tea Cake is unable to speak back to power, to demand redress. He complains that the water has been tainted by dead bodies, a conjecture with symbolic if not literal truth (176). Tea Cake's hydrophobia literalizes the "nausea" that Frantz Fanon identifies in the colonized subject, "responsible not only for my body but for my race and my ancestors" and yet "incapable of confronting the Other, the white man, who had no scruples about imprisoning me."[82] Indeed, Fanon uses the metaphor of the "raging wolf, rabid with hunger" to describe the affective force of the colonial demand for recognition.[83]

This affect reflects the frustration of disenfranchisement, the anger that comes from "coerc[ion] . . . into nonbeing, or . . . demot[ion] on an animacy hierarchy."[84] When Janie is prosecuted for killing Tea Cake, black men huddle in the back of the courtroom, silenced and wracked with rage. They are "packed tight like a case of celery only much darker than that" (185). Figure 5.1 shows celery "packed tight" in wooden cases, their leaves spilling out at the top. This simile invokes overcrowding and unwilling stillness. Celery farming was a major Florida industry that employed migrant workers. In Figure 5.2, a photograph taken in the same year that *Their Eyes Were Watching God* was published, a black man stacks bundles of celery in Sanborn, Florida. When she compares the men from the muck to the products they package, Hurston indicates that both

Figure 5.1 This 1941 photograph shows celery crammed into its crate. John Vachon, photographer, *Celery at Produce Market, Chicago, Illinois*, July 1941.
Source: US Farm Security Administration / Office of War Information Black-and-White Negatives, Library of Congress Prints and Photographs Division.

Figure 5.2 This photograph of a black migrant worker packing celery crates in Sanford, Florida, was taken in the same year that *Their Eyes Were Watching God* was published. Arthur Rothstein, photographer, *Packing Celery at Sanford, Florida. Many of these workers here are migrants*, 1937, US Resettlement Administration, Sanford, Florida.
Source: US Farm Security Administration / Office of War Information Black-and-White Negatives, Library of Congress Prints and Photographs Division.

agribusiness and law cage and constrain these racialized workers. Their violent hatred of Janie reflects the powerlessness of this living entombment.

In the face of such enervating industries, Hurston recuperates the peripheral space and perennial hope of a personal garden:[85]

> She had given away everything in their little house except a package of garden seed that Tea Cake had brought to plant. The planting never got done because he had been waiting for the right time of the moon when his sickness overtook him. The seeds reminded Janie of Tea Cake more than anything else because he was always planting things. (191)

Tea Cake the sower—spreading seed like diasporic peoples—replaces Tea Cake the mad dog. Transplantation from the muck to Eatonville contains a slim promise that some of the collective ethics Janie learned there might take root here. At the same time, Hurston is no blithe optimist; the thirst that plagued Tea Cake in his final days also afflicts the people in Eatonville: "dey's parched up from not knowin' things" (192). Their failure to extend empathy or create kin turns them into "meatskins [that] is *got* to rattle tuh make out they's alive" (192, emphasis in original), an uncomfortable evocation of the zombie. Hurston ends her novel not with agribusiness and its determination to drain profit from every ounce of swamp but with fishing, casting a net wide and delighting in the sea's grace: "She pulled in her horizon like a great fish-net. Pulled it from around the waist of the world and draped it over her shoulder. So much of life in its meshes! She called in her soul to come and see" (193). Here is the nourishment that endures catastrophe and acknowledges interdependence, "meshes" rather than hierarchies, as the nature of the human condition—indeed, the condition of life, whatever its form.

Banana Breasts, Passionate Peaches, and Fruitful Women

Like *Their Eyes Were Watching God*, *The Living Is Easy* explores the racialization of edible flesh within the modern food industry, this time through the trope of women as tropical fruit. First, the plot of *The Living Is Easy* merits a quick summary. A lively young black girl from South Carolina, Cleo, comes north with a chaperone and meets prosperous, middle-aged Bart Judson, the "Black Banana King of Boston." Cleo and Bart wed, but the marriage is an unhappy one. Through her machinations, Cleo collects her sisters and their children together under one roof, ultimately convincing each one to abandon her husband and stay in this new household instead. For a time, the extended family lives happily and lavishly, but the World War I and the rise of white-owned chain stores destroy Bart's business. At the end of the novel, he decides to leave the family.

The banana industry supported US corporate imperialism in Latin America.[86] Since bananas were an unfamiliar fruit, the advertising industry had to create a US consumer appetite for bananas, and create it they did, often through the appetizing bodies of women of color.[87] Josephine Baker wore her famous banana skirt in 1926; the United Fruit Company introduced "Chiquita Banana" in 1944.[88] This iconography both racialized and feminized the banana. Its yellow skin seemed a token of exotic difference. At the same time, its peel promised a tropical strip tease, a seductive reveal of the soft, edible flesh underneath. When Bart first peels a banana, he "watch[es] the petals fall away" and observes "the delicate filament of their undersides" (62). An androgynous, vaguely tribal shape emerges, a "slender, golden-white spear" (62). Like the tomboy wife whom Bart will eventually court, the banana is "small and uncultivated, but firm-fleshed" (62). Though the banana seems slight and delicate, it gives off a "heavy exotic odor," which "struck some dormant stream of atavistic longing for the breast of jungle earth" (62). This sensuous aroma acts upon the consumer's body; the figure of the "dormant stream" evokes salivation. When Bart finally eats the banana, the nursing metaphor, "the breast of jungle earth," comes to full fruition: "the taste ran down his throat like milk and melted butter and honey" (62). This taste creates an imaginative attachment to racial identity envisioned as maternal love, the milk and honey of a black Canaan. Because he has internalized market values, however, Bart's revelation is reduced to an imperial wet dream: "All night he dreamed on his narrow bed of bananas and Boston and ships setting sail from Jamaica" (62). Here, the parallel between the firm, golden flesh of the banana and the body of Bart's wife becomes significant. He wants to control female flesh and amass his fortune—economic and reproductive—through it.

West sets up a tension between sensation and mastery, description and plot. The intense sensuousness of feminine fruit temporarily suspends time and creates a space for Bart to revel in his own susceptibility. Later he experiences similar tenderness toward the fruit in his storeroom: "he loved his fruit almost as much as he loved his wife. There was rich satisfaction in seeing it ripen, the downiness on it, the blush on it, feeling the firmness of its flesh" (35). There is erotic tactility in the shared "downiness," "blush," and firm "flesh" of peach and woman. But all too soon these amorphous qualities give way to the teleological; Bart must make this fruit ripen in order to bring it to market. Furthermore, peaches shipped from the South had to be picked unripe or they would spoil.[89] Cleo's prolongation of her virginity suggests that she too has been circulated prematurely in the service of Bart's profits rather than her pleasure. She turns to "ice" in Bart's arms (35).

When Cleo expresses her wish to "preserve" her "maidenhood," her choice of verb recalls the suspension of fruit bodies between ripeness and rot (35). As "a man of vigor," Bart is confident that he can "wait without wasting for Cleo's awakening" (35). In this rationalization, Bart confirms his own capacity to endure unwonted abstinence and perhaps also to refrain from masturbation often understood as a form of reproductive waste. However, waiting and wasting also threatened the solvency of the fruit business, which frequently sacrificed whole shipments to the vagaries of transport and time. In this sense, Cleo's refusal to ripen threatens his stocks. As Kathryn Stockton points out, "There are kinds of figures of speech that carry (truly, hand over) the girl to conventional plots: metaphors culturally shared and repeated in a kind of fixed chain."[90] The ripening peach would seem to be one of those metaphors. Bart clearly expects time to move forward, from unripe to ripe, from girlhood to womanhood to motherhood.

The sign of feminine fruit, however, restores the erotic past to Cleo rather than delivers her maturing body to the future. As a child, Cleo "watched the dimples going in and out of Mama's round arms . . . A flush lay just under the surface, giving them a look of tender warmth" (16). Like Bart's banana as jungle breast, Mama's body resembles a flushed and dimpled peach. Cleo envies that "all the loving in Mama's arms" goes to Pa "at night" (17). Her beautiful sisters also embody "softness and roundness, the flush just under the thin skin . . . liquid and vulnerable" (21); one has a "cherry-red mouth" and "dimpled cheeks" (21). The softness and juiciness of the female body inspire Cleo's desirous gaze: "her face had to smile a bit as she watched," "You could almost touch their softness with your eyes," "Looking at her sisters . . . she saw in each some likeness of Mama" (21). The intensity of Cleo's longing, her "immeasurable frustration," comes from "despair at knowing that nothing lasts—that sisters turn into wives, that men take their women and ride away" (22). Childhood, "no longer than a summer day," is the suspended season when Cleo can indulge lesbian desire (22). Bananas are not the only fruit.

Dorothy West's sexuality is a matter of some biographical speculation. In interviews, she never acknowledged same-sex relationships.[91] As a teenager, she went on tour in Europe with bisexual Edith Lewis Thomas in *Porgy and Bess*, the musical that gives *The Living Is Easy* its title.[92] As a young woman in the Harlem Renaissance, she spent much of her time with a gay male coterie, including Countee Cullen and Thurman Wallace. While visiting Russia, West had an affair with Mildred Jones, all the while writing letters proposing marriage to Langston Hughes.[93] She lived with Marian Minus for "over a decade."[94] In one of Minus's short stories, "The Fine Line," a white mill girl steals figs from the garden of a neighboring black family. The fruits are "firm and full inside their rich, dark skins" and leave "thick white fluid where it smeared her fingertips."[95] Though this short story fictionalizes the interracial marriage of Minus's grandmother, it may also translate the erotic transgression of lesbianism into interracialism.[96] Though

Mitchell and Davis opine that West did not have the "language" for a same-sex relationship, it seems clear in *The Living Is Easy* that she did have a language for it, only that language was metaphorical.[97]

While her mother and sisters inspire Cleo's desire, her vitality in turn titillates others. Though it would be possible to read this sensuousness as a product of the colonizing gaze, West implies that Cleo's queer eroticism suffuses daily life and creates transitive affects. Cleo's effulgent embodiment anticipates Audre Lorde's definition of the erotic as that which "flows through and colors my life with a kind of energy that heightens and sensitizes and strengthens all my experience."[98] Cleo's "aliveness" and "vitality" convey an almost pheromonal quality: "The wild horse smelled her wildness" (14). In childhood, Cleo and her white best friend, Josie, flourish like plants, "their bare feet drinking in the dew, their faces lifted to feel the morning" (12). Their haptic pleasures transcend language: "They did not talk. They had no words to express their aliveness. They wanted none. Their bodies were their eloquence . . . The wildness was in her, the unrestrained joy, the desire to run to the edge of the world and fling her arms around the sun, and rise with it, through time and space, to the center of everywhere" (13). Cleo and Josie absorb light and heat, and Cleo in turn projects it, even as an adult: "She looked herself now, gay and earth-rooted and intensely alive" (38). Like fruit, Cleo takes in energy and gives out pleasure.

White viewers find Cleo particularly seductive. An "elderly spinster . . . seeking sun for her sciatica . . . was entranced by Cleo's beauty as she returned from work, her hair flying free, the color still staining her cheeks from the heat of the cookstove" (24). Cleo's communicable affects extend the promise of passion to the "spinster," even as she claims to protect Cleo's chastity: "Miss Peterson, hating to see *this sultry loveliness ripen* in the amoral atmosphere of the South, urged Mama to let her take Cleo North" (24, emphasis mine). Her next white chaperone, this time in Boston, expressly associates the girl's allure with her race: "Cleo seemed a light in the gathering gloom. She was southern, she was colored" (27). The chaperone's nephew is affected even more forcefully by Cleo, as her body represents forbidden fruit: "he saw her with all her aliveness, her dark hair streaming, her eyes sparkling green stars, the blood in her cheeks with the tear streaks and dust streaks, and her apple breasts betraying the pulse of her angry heart" (32). The white male spectator construes this "aliveness" and these "apple breasts" within the paradoxical frame of primitivism, which names her as both essentially sexual and timelessly untouched. These Edenic figures naturalize white rapacity.

Furthermore, this pomological palette reinforces colorism. The "blood in her cheeks" reveals the pallor of her skin; her "apple breasts" are presumably pink and gold rather than dark brown or black. As I explored in Chapter 2, the trope of the woman of color as fruit often exalts hybridity and light skin. In a literalization of this metaphor, the eighteenth-century scientist Dr. Benjamin Rush prognosticated that "the juice of unripe peaches" might contribute to a "cure for blackness."[99] Once Cleo moves to New England, the class pretensions of colorism dominate the black community. One woman whose illustrious family has fallen into genteel poverty maintains her status in part through her "peaches and cream" color: "[She] could have married any man short of a Zulu, and still have had children who passed the test of hair and color" (94). This eugenic vision of light-skinned beauty also inspires masculine lust and dreams of reproductive mastery. At a party the Judsons host, the caterer, Mr. Davies, stares at Cleo, "stirred" by her "glowing skin ... engaging mouth and lively eyes" (254).[100] To him, Cleo's indefinable exoticism "seemed infinitely preferable to the marble dignity of the blond Duchess or the unapproachable apartness of chestnut-haired Thea" (254). By contrast, Mr. Davies reads Cleo's body as erotic and available: "There was something about this golden-skinned Southerner suggestive of excitement" (254). He scoffs that Bart Judson is "spending the night with his bananas," another "golden-skinned" fruit, and he longs to take the dark-skinned man's reproductive place: "In that magnificent body were golden sons. In that heart beneath those lovely lifting breasts was unrequited passion" (254). Davies's daydream entwines the incipient eroticism of Cleo's flesh with eugenic, hybrid futures. The beauty of "breasts" signifies in both directions, a seductive secondary sex characteristic and a sign that she can nourish children.

West thus develops opposed resonances of golden fruit—as lesbian eroticism on the one hand and heteronormative colorism on the other. In her conflicted adulthood, Cleo conflates the two, using colorist snobbery as a pretext for creating a woman-centered household. Cleo contemplates the failure of dark-skinned Bart's paternal designs with satisfaction: "Mr. Judson was going to have more babies than he'd bargained for, but none of them would bear him the slightest resemblance" (76). The fruit metaphor, after all, in some ways privileges the sororal; multiple flowers on a branch blossom, bud, and bear fruit together, while the bee flies away. (Tellingly, Bart's place of business, Faneuil Hall, is described as a "droning hive" [68].)

West's cousin, the poet Helene Johnson, with whom she grew up and then shared a small New York apartment, agreed with West that men could provide children and then leave.[101] This queering of maternity also took shape in West's fiction. In "Prologue to a Life" (1929), light-skinned Lily Bemis feels the "mother instinct" but imagines reproduction as a narcissistic extension of herself: "In her supreme egoism she believed the male seed would only generate it. She would not conceive of its becoming blood of her child's blood, and flesh of her child's flesh."[102] Achieving her dream, Lily bears twins with "soft yellow skin," "two golden babies" (73). The twins die, and Lily becomes pregnant again, but this time the baby's dark skin reflects her paternity, and Lily denies her. This short story demonstrates the entanglement of race and gender—only "golden skin" figures forth femininity. In this figuration, black skin seems both abject and inherently masculine, placing the black daughter outside the preserve of beauty.

The Living Is Easy bears out this connection between abject blackness and masculinity. Cleo's brother-in-law laments that "his little honey-colored daughter" will learn disgust from her mother and aunt, recoiling "from her own daddy because he was dark" (182). West traces this disgust to Cleo's childhood when "Pa spit tobacco juice" in the "fireplace ashes" (16). Cleo knew that Mama "bleached her corn in lye water" made from those ashes and "hated" eating it. Mama, by contrast, overlooks this dirt: "Mama thought everything about Pa was wonderful, even his spit" (16).[103] Expectoration figures ejaculation as Cleo contemplates with horror the fact that Pa's black juice goes into her mother's yellow concoctions, whether hominy grits or light-skinned daughters. Cleo's erotic envy, her desire for her mother's tender skin and her resentment of her father's power over Mama, ends up reinforcing her colorism, her disdain for masculine bodies that sweat, smell, and stain.

In Cleo's view, men confer the stigma of blackness. Like Lily in "Prologue to a Life," Cleo resents her daughter, Judy, for having "Papa's cocoa-brown skin" (39). As this adjective reveals, Cleo assesses blackness in terms of edibility—not the luminous gold of tropical fruit but the sticky brown of melting candy. The former emits a tempting glow, the latter smears everything it touches. Traveling through Boston to meet a prospective landlord in a desirable neighborhood, Cleo threatens Judy: "If you get yourself dirty before we get to Brookline, I'll give you to a Chinaman to eat" (38). When they meet with the white landlord, he dubs Judy the "Candy Kid" and feeds her chocolate, warning her not to "stick up yourself or the furniture" (43). The resulting "ring of chocolate around her mouth made her look comical," and it leaves "a smudge ... on one of her gloves" (48). The chocolate paints her smile into a minstrel mouth and tarnishes the impression of genteel femininity.

From Cleo's perspective, Judy and her father are too close to stereotyped sweetness, sticky and messy like her father's spurned kisses. Cleo complains when her nieces and nephews clamber all over her husband: "Anyone would think you were molasses" (237). Given the choice between southern, lower-class, black pleasure and northern, upper-class, light-skinned restraint, Cleo would rather have her daughter be a cold fish: "She herself would not want to look like a fish, but she would like to own someone who did" (40). Whiteness embodies either active anhedonia or closely controlled repression: "There were white people everywhere with sallow-skinned, thin, austere Yankee faces. They had the look that Cleo coveted for her dimpled daughter" (39). Cleo does not see the irony that the "dimpled" flesh of her mother and sisters inspired so much joy; she avers that "a Bostonian, black or white, should consider himself a special species of fish" (5). Judy, her daughter and descendent, should be a status symbol, slick and cold like fish scales.

Cleo's wish that her daughter resemble a fish alludes to a local industry. Later in the novel, a white attorney disparages the banana business by insisting that New Englanders had "better stick to fishing" because "Everybody eats fish" (61). Rejecting the imputation of exoticism and strangeness, Cleo wants to transform her daughter from a product of southern food chains (fruit or chocolate) into a northern native (fish). This transformation would be whitening, certainly, but it would also be deadening; when one of the upper-crust men in their circle dies suddenly, Cleo calls him "dead as a haddock" (147). The modern food industry habitually framed the exotic body as livelier, juicier, chocolatier, and sweeter than the unmarked white body. West adapts that sensory imaginary to her own ends, exposing whiteness as a form of lack. In this way, West embeds a queer of color critique within the very terms of the global food industry.[104]

Banana Boats and Stockrooms: Imperial Masculinity, Diasporic Identification, and Racial Abjection

Cleo's identification with fruit refracts feminine ideals and reproductive pressures. Bart's desire for fruit is equally fraught, shaped by masculine enterprise and economic ambition. As a boy, Bart receives his first banana from a white sea captain, who "indulg[es]" the boy by giving him the fruit. Bart plays up his ignorance: "You eats it, Cap'n, suh?" (60). While he is "bowing and scraping," Bart secretly hopes that this "marketable edible" will allow him to make his fortune. In spite of his canny ability to manipulate the captain's view of him, Bart does not recognize the irony that he plays a dehumanizing role in an attempt to achieve capitalist agency. In his ode to Latin American abundance, the captain denigrates the Honduran pickers: "Bananas grow there on trees. And trees grow in the jungles. And nigger natives climb them trees like monkeys" (60). His words imply that the natives scamper up the trees for sustenance, not profit, just like the monkeys he takes them to resemble. Ironically, many of those Honduran banana farmers were entrepreneurs, whose businesses would be bankrupted by the monopolistic operations of the United Fruit Company, much as Bart's business is eventually bankrupted by white-owned chain stores.[105] Bart denies the evidence that racism organizes hemispheric capitalism, insisting that money makes men equal: "In the North they respected money whether it was white or black. You could look a man in the eye and keep your hat on your head if you had as much cash on the line as he did" (62). His business ethic reinforces a fantasy of masculinity that could supersede racial difference. In spite of his ideal of individualism, Bart and the Hondurans are in the same boat, though he fails to recognize it.

There are some indications that the global shipping business does create connections that could short-circuit the racial imaginary invested in binaries and nativism. West's catalog of fruit in Boston's Faneuil Hall Market recalls Claude McKay's catalog of abundance on the docks of Marseilles in *Banjo* (1929):

> The scent of fruit and vegetables struck the morning freshness from the air and substituted the headiness of summer produce. Color overwhelmed the eye, glowing apples, golden apricots, oranges, lemons, green avocados, cream-yellow cantaloupes, purple plums, buttery pears, prickletop pineapples, wine-red cherries, blush peaches, sweet Georgia melons, dust-brown figs, the dark oblong of dates, and the last of the season's strawberries. Out of crates and barrels and bags and boxes poured summer squash, asparagus, broccoli, beets, artichokes, onions, lettuce, peas, cucumbers, peppers, potatoes, corn, string beans, spinach, tomatoes and limas in the more modest livery of vegetables. (*The Living Is Easy*, 68)

This catalog of "color" that "overwhelmed the eye" turns the docks and the market into the utopian diasporic space that the muck is in *Their Eyes Were Watching God*. Many of these fruit colors evoke human skin tones: "golden," "cream-yellow," "buttery," "dust-brown," and "dark"; the peaches "blush" like Cleo's mother and sisters. West follows this cornucopic catalog with a list of the ethnicities in the crowd: "Italian faces, Greek faces, Jewish faces, and Yankee faces swirled past Bart as he ducked a box of apples and slid around a slice of beef" (68). Each of these groups—Italian, Greek, and Jewish—was targeted by anti-immigrant legislation in the 1910s and 1920s, yet here "Yankee faces" do not get pride of place, and indeed, Bart's black face is not objectified. He is the assessing spectator, not the object of the racializing gaze.

Bart's own store models interracial cooperation. His white secretary, Miss Muldoon, considers him a "hard-working, sober-minded man" (74), and his white assistant, Chris, "loved him" and learns everything he knows about fruit from Bart (325). The workers in his storeroom are Greek, which could easily create racial tensions; Greek immigrants in turn-of-the-century Chicago, for example, fought Italians for control of the fruit business.[106] Instead, they work harmoniously with Bart because he is as skilled as they are: "They respected the black man who was their exacting boss because he could do any one of their tasks, from making a crate to sizing fruit for the count, with more speed and efficiency than any one of them" (82). Racial difference becomes a uniting rather than a dividing idea: "[The workers] lifted their peasant faces. They had the same look of earth and toil as Bart" (82). By championing physical labor, these descriptions bridge the gulf between supposedly disparate classes and races.

This harmonious heterotopia exposes the ethnic tensions that dominate larger Boston. Cleo expects the prospective landlord in Brookline to be reluctant to rent to a black family when in truth he is moving to flee the Irish (47). Judy thinks the Irish children in her school have "monkey faces" (207), and the children yell racial slurs at one another (209). The black bourgeoisie "did not consider themselves a minority group," unlike "the Irish ... the Jews, the Italians, the Greeks, who were barred from belonging by old country memories, accents, and mores" (105). In order to establish their own status, they have internalized nativist hierarchies. They also unconsciously accept the rule of white supremacy, making "a daily desperate effort to ignore their racial heritage" and priding themselves on passing for "Jews" or "Latins," even though they think those groups are beneath them (105). This backdrop makes Bart's cooperation with his Greek employees even more remarkable. Affiliation and identification between many disparate groups of working-class, immigrant, and dark-skinned peoples would be politically and socially preferable to the stratification and anxiety that rules the day.

At the same time, Bart's affiliative philosophy stops short of dismantling patriarchal hierarchy. He and the Greek men share physical power understood as masculine prowess. When he shows off the store to his wife and daughter, he cherishes the opportunity to demonstrate his own mastery: "He ruled a store and all the people in it" (70–71). Furthermore, when Cleo enters the store, the white employees assess her physical form and pigeonhole her racial type: Chris appreciates "a beautiful Negro woman," and Miss Muldoon "prefer[s] to picture Negro women as fat, black, and plain-faced" (73–74). While Bart's masculinity and property ownership allow him, at least temporarily, to rise above such stereotypic categorizations, the black woman is doubly and inescapably embodied. Indeed, Bart's own perspective on Cleo reveals that this is the case; he is quick to embrace a misunderstanding that she is pregnant again, as he "wanted a son to follow him in business" (75). For Bart, Cleo is primarily a reproductive asset. As he takes his wife and child through his storerooms, "stock" takes on the double connotation of investment and offspring (80). He imagines that Cleo is a mere vessel for the unborn son, inspecting his future property: "In a way he was going to show his store to his son" (80). The subordination of women is a central part of Bart's achievement of proprietorship and subjectivity.

Cleo topples this illusive hierarchy through her own ironic awareness and corporeal excess. While Miss Muldoon and Chris both "star[e] ... at her stomach," thinking that she is "in a special way" (75), "her whole Rabelaisian soul shook with silent laughter" (76). Cleo, for all of her snobbery, embraces the comic, excessive body, especially ass and belly.[107] Though Bart sees his basement storeroom as the symbol of his success, Cleo cringes at "the sunless rooms below" (72). This "flight of unswept stairs" bears a "slippery trail of peels and pulps," the excremental mark of rotting fruit (71). It "made you sick of the sight of it" and presumably of the smell too (72). From Cleo's perspective, the storeroom is like a rectum, the repository of Bart's hoarded waste. Freud famously associates money with excrement, associating stockpiling (like Bart's) with anal retention.[108] Furthermore, Bart continues the association of paternity and racial stain established through Cleo's father. Bart leaves a mark on everything he touches: "He stretched out his hand to smooth [his daughter]'s mussed frock. He saw his grimy palm" (72). Even his handkerchief is "fruit-stained" (73). On the one hand, West plays out this abjection to generate sympathy for Bart, who can never embody Cleo's racial ideal. On the other hand, she uses this inversion of the Midas touch to indicate the benightedness of his wealthy, white ideal. Bart cannot transcend the corporeal contamination associated with blackness, even in this cultural moment when he thinks that the possession of capital renders all men equal.[109]

The contrast between imperial vision and abject stink bears out the contradictions in Bart's role as a black businessman. Waiting for a merchant ship to return from Jamaica, Bart "stares over the shimmering sea, his eyes screwed up against the sun," and the seagulls embody his dreamed-of ascent into white power: "In their upward flight toward the sun, their breasts had the beauty of alabaster" (56). By contrast, "Greek stevedores . . . descended like dirty gods into the holds of ships at anchor" (56). Imperial vision is ascendant, while racialized embodiment is dirty, dark, and down below. However, the other senses compromise Bart's soaring aspirations: "His weekly bath could not wash away the odor of tropical fruit" (57). This "tropical" smell recalls the racist attribution of recognizable stink to racial blackness.[110] Furthermore, the smell connects "ripening" and rotting, just as the stevedores' descent into the holds below suggests a visit to the underworld. Blackness figures forth the mortality that imperialism and its fantasy of endless expansion rejects. Bart's moniker, the "Black Banana King," generates a suggestive adjectival ambiguity. He is the black king of the banana business, but he is haunted by the threat of "black bananas," rotting waste and premature death. From the vantage point of his competitors, he is expendable, particularly so because of his racial difference. Bart has ignored his own vulnerability.

West dramatizes this process of capitalist disidentification early in the novel when Bart has a prophetic vision that a banana boat has gone down. Like the hurricane in *Their Eyes Were Watching God*, this crisis disrupts the usual order of business. In fact, because of the unexpected banana shortage, Bart becomes a very rich man. Much like the white agribusiness owners on the muck, Bart capitalizes on others' suffering. The bananas are "washed out of the hold" like waste and "plunged heavily to the bottom of the sea" (63). So too are the human bodies: "He had waked in a cold sweat, with the cries of drowning men in his ears" (63). This sweat links Bart's body to those of the drowning men, but instead of mourning, he "corner[s] the market and make[s] a killing" (69). West's murderous pun insists on the corpses that Bart willfully forgets.

Rotting bananas and drowned bodies both threaten Bart's ego with the specter of decay and nonentity.[111] This could be grounds for empathy and compassion, even self-sacrifice in the interests of the collective. When Bart was born again as a child, he had a vision of Jesus, "the water and blood in a sad stream down his side" (66). He saw himself wrestling with the Devil and perceived the vulnerability of his own flesh: "the red flames leaped like horrible licking tongues" (66). This Christian vision recalls Hurston's use of John the Conqueror to redeem black embodiment through collective suffering and redress. However, once Bart becomes an adult and takes his place as a business owner, he comes to believe in his own ego as an untouchable brand: "when you buy a stem of bananas from Bart Judson, you know you're buying the best the market offers" (149). Relegated to the life of the body and barred from business concerns, Cleo recognizes the threat to his fortune posed by the white chain stores before he does and warns him that "Nothing is certain in life except death" (149). Bart overlooks the fact that his name, which stands in "fancy gold lettering over his store," is in fact the patronym of the plantation master who owned him and his mother. The "cries of drowning men" on the banana ship echo the history of the Middle Passage and the Zong Massacre. Black bodies were once traded across the seas that Bart scans with a proprietor's eyes, their corpses considered unavoidable waste or profitable commodity.

Rotting bananas, stinking shit, drowning corpses—the repressed abjection of colonialism swamps Bart, who thought that he could rise. After he learns of his bankruptcy and his store's closure, Bart is "bent under his load, and his head was down" (343). Cleo suddenly registers his mortality: "fear of his dying oppressed her heart" (343). She longs to help him with this new weight—"today she wanted him to know they pulled in harness together" (343)—but her recognition of their shared vulnerability comes too late. Bart is leaving Boston and taking up the itinerant life of working-class black men during the Great Migration. The two tools, masculine vigor and monetary power, that were supposed to withstand and even erase racism have failed him. A white monopoly has pushed him out of business. This naturalist ending despoils Bart's hopeful beginnings as a businessman. "Ships at a distance have every man's wish on board," as Hurston opens *Their Eyes Were Watching God* (1). Bart now sees that his ship has gone down too.

In the final scene of the novel, West uses food to materialize Bart's abjection rather than his golden dream of banana fortunes. In his last act as a "provider," Bart turns his paycheck into a "pyramid" of groceries: "A ham took shape in her hands, a great thick steak, a leg of lamb, a roast by the feel of it, a slab of bacon, boxes of sausages and frankfurters. The pyramid's base was a small crate filled with choice fruits and vegetables" (344). The "pyramid" recalls the tombs of pharaohs and erects an ironic monument to the fallen Banana King (344). West's careful catalog of meats in various forms draws attention to their animal antecedents and to Bart's body, reduced to a "pack horse" (342). White capital has cannibalized the black man, and West implies that he may not survive very long: "He wanted to die with her beside him. He did not know now if he would" (346). His desire to climb the pyramid of imperial power has given way to his burial in its dehumanizing wake. Throughout the novel, Cleo mocks Bart for his blackness, his stink, and his dirt—calling him "Mr. Nigger" (150). Now, for the first time, she recognizes his fleshly vulnerability as a source of pathos and registers the ruthless operations of the market as the proper site of disgust: "She let the money fall from her hands. It scattered over the mounds of meat, and she looked at everything with revulsion" (345). Money and meat, emblems of prosperity and masculinity, are now defiled and disgusting, filthy lucre and dead flesh in shapeless mounds.

Conclusion

Both Hurston and West are skeptical of views of racial agency that do not take into account the deep structures that support white supremacy in this country. Their naturalist plots remind readers that racial imaginaries have material histories and consequences. Tea Cake's death, Bart's bankruptcy and defection—these plots take an irrevocable toll. The narrative projections of the future are also ambivalent, even pessimistic. While Janie's horizon gathering is lyrical, the reader is left to wonder whether she will be infected by Tea Cake's bite. While Cleo seems chastened by Bart's failure, she responds to his departure with narcissism, wondering who will love her and choosing her young nephew to be the new man of the house, the object of her obsessive affections. Neither prospect seems particularly salubrious for the women at the center of these texts, who have worked so hard to dream their own designs for their lives, in spite of many constraints. At the same time that these narratives tell the story of the fated, the inescapable, the broken, Hurston and West both embrace the potential of form, the epistemological revelations of figure and metaphor working against ideological trajectory and toward new possibilities of relation. In this sense, they continue the project that Toomer began with simmering cane and purple bubbles and Schuyler attempted with hydroponic farms and deep freezers. Like Zelda Fitzgerald, they recognize that the operations of disgust discipline women's bodies and that the racialization and abjection of that flesh can actually provide an opportunity to imagine embodied existence from an enmeshed, ecological point of view rather than through the illusion of self-containment and sterility. Like Gertrude Stein, they emphasize the quotidian endeavors that cultivate intimate knowledge and knowledge of intimacy, whether by hunting gators on the muck or tending fruit in a storeroom.

Weheliye, arguing for blackness as "an integral structuring assemblage of the modern human," a relational form that shapes the very concept of subjectivity, insists, "Once we take this into account, we can practice a politics, which, rather than succumbing to the brutal facticity of blackness, introduces invention into existence."[112] Hurston and West do not look away from the "brutal facticity" of blackness—the continuing necropolitics of colonialism and corporatism, the white supremacist structures of capitalism undoing the market's false promises of emancipation.[113] They do, however, insist upon its "invention." Diaspora is not a discovery of shared African origins on the muck; it is an experience of shared precarity and cultural expressivity—created around dance, food, and song. Cleo may be nostalgic for the South Carolina of her youth, but she mitigates this fantasy with her attempts to create a woman-centric family around other rules, sharing the fruits of her husband's labor with her beloved nieces and nephew. In the face of contemporary politics, the urgency of Black Lives Matter, to advocate an aesthetics of artificial color might seem benighted at best, dangerously complacent at worst. Hurston and West remind us that we can do both, that we can memorialize lives lost and protest white supremacy, while seeing in poesis the nourishing possibility of a different world.

NOTES

Introduction

1. F. Scott Fitzgerald, *The Great Gatsby* (New York: Scribner, 2004), 68. Further citations appear parenthetically in the text.
2. Lisa Lowe argues that "literary representation, by foregrounding *metaphor* as a process that both evokes through equivalence and occludes through exchange ... may offer us instruction on how to read for the presence of colonial goods and the absence of colonial labor and imperial trade in the history, politics, and economics of the modern world." Lowe, *The Intimacies of Four Continents* (Durham, NC: Duke University Press, 2015), 97.
3. Nella Larsen, *Quicksand* (New York: Penguin Books, 2002), 33.
4. On Delmonico's and US popularization of French cuisine, see Andrew F. Smith, *Eating History: 30 Turning Points in the Making of American Cuisine* (New York: Columbia University Press, 2011), 21–23.
5. On subtleties, see Sidney W. Mintz, *Sweetness and Power: The Place of Sugar in Modern History* (New York: Penguin, 1985), 90–92.
6. Richard Dyer traces the paradox of whiteness as a spectacle and an empty set: "with its emphasis on purity, cleanliness, virginity, in short, absence, inflects whiteness once again towards non-particularity, only this time in the sense of non-existence." Dyer, *White* (New York: Routledge, 1997), 70. Judith Brown's delineation of "blankness" is also apposite here, both for Fitzgerald's intimations about wealth and industry and for the production of whiteness: "blankness during the modern period signified absence (in the form of things lost or cast off) *and* presence in the form of the overwhelming recognition of technological power." Brown, *Glamour in Six Dimensions: Modernism and the Radiance of Form* (Ithaca, NY: Cornell University Press, 2009), 161.
7. On New York's role in the sugar industry, see Andrew F. Smith, *New York City: A Food Biography* (Lanham, MD: Rowman & Littlefield, 2013), 19, and "Sugar Refining," in *Savoring Gotham: A Food Lover's Companion to New York City*, ed. Andrew F. Smith (New York: Oxford University Press, 2015), 575–77. Deborah Jean Warner observes, "Immigrants filled most of the unskilled refinery jobs: Irishmen and Germans predominated in the nineteenth century and Poles and Lithuanians in the early twentieth." Warner, *Sweet Stuff: An American History of Sweeteners from Sugar to Sucralose* (Washington, DC: Smithsonian Institution Scholarly Press; Lanham, MD: Rowman & Littlefield, 2011), 17. An 1896 *Brooklyn Eagle* article admitted that "few 'Americans' sought work in the local sugar refineries, 'perhaps' because the wages were not high and the work was hot, exhausting, and dangerous. Steam boilers and sugar dust tended to explode ... vats of boiling sugar were hazardous" (qtd. in Warner, *Sweet Stuff*, 17). The sugar industry consumed racialized bodies that were more distant as well. César J. Ayala argues that "sugar refining was responsible for the epochal transformation

in corporate law" and cemented the "economic structure of U.S. colonial enterprise in the Caribbean." Ayala, *American Sugar Kingdom: The Plantation Economy of the Spanish Caribbean, 1898–1934* (Chapel Hill: University of North Carolina Press, 1999), 24. For a discussion of black labor in Louisiana and Caribbean cane fields, see Andrew F. Smith, *Sugar: A Global History* (Chicago: University of Chicago Press, 2015), 32.
8. Charles Baudelaire, *The Prose Poems and "La Fanfarlo,"* trans. Rosemary Lloyd (New York: Oxford World's Classics, 2001), 24.
9. See Larsen, *Quicksand*, 141n1.
10. Allison Carruth uses "literature of food" to widen generic boundaries and include texts like cookbooks often left out of considerations of the literary. She writes: "The literature of food is . . . a social field where writers employ different modes to comprehend complex systems of production and consumption, while also shaping food and agriculture practices." Carruth, *Global Appetites: American Power and the Literature of Food* (New York: Cambridge University Press, 2013), 166.
11. Ibid., 5.
12. Parama Roy, *Alimentary Tracts: Appetites, Aversions, and the Postcolonial* (Durham, NC: Duke University Press, 2010), 25.
13. On critical eating studies, see Kyla Wazana Tompkins, *Racial Indigestion: Eating Bodies in the 19th Century* (New York: New York University Press, 2012), 2.
14. Toni Morrison, *Playing in the Dark: Whiteness and the Literary Imagination* (New York: Vintage, 1993), 65–66.
15. See Andrew Warnes, *Hunger Overcome? Food and Resistance in Twentieth Century African-American Literature* (Athens: University of Georgia Press, 2004); Psyche A. Williams-Forson, *Building Houses Out of Chicken Legs: Black Women, Food, and Power* (Chapel Hill: University of North Carolina Press, 2006); and Doris Witt, *Black Hunger: Soul Food and America* (Minneapolis: University of Minnesota Press, 2004).
16. Michael North, *The Dialect of Modernism: Race, Language, and Twentieth-Century Literature* (New York: Oxford University Press, 1994); Walter Benn Michaels, *Our America: Nativism, Modernism, and Pluralism* (Durham, NC: Duke University Press, 1995).
17. hooks writes: "In the cultural marketplace the Other is coded as having the capacity to be more alive, as holding the secret that will allow those who venture and dare to break with the cultural anhedonia . . . and experience sensual and spiritual renewal." hooks, *Black Looks: Race and Representation* (New York: Routledge, 1992), 26. hooks argues that in consumer culture, this interracial encounter does nothing to inhibit or compromise white supremacy; I would argue that in literature, it has a more transformative effect.
18. Gauguin saw these peasants as "savage," "almost Asiatic," repressing "a Southern verve." Henri Dorra, *The Symbolism of Paul Gauguin: Erotica, Exotica, and the Great Dilemmas of Humanity* (Berkeley: University of California Press, 2007), 57, 59; Paul Gauguin, *Seaweed Gatherers* (1889) and *Kelp Gatherers* (1890); T. S. Eliot, "The Love Song of J. Alfred Prufrock," in *The New Anthology of American Poetry: Modernisms, 1900–1950*, ed. Steven Gould Axelrod, Camille Roman, and Thomas J. Travisano (New Brunswick, NJ: Rutgers University Press, 2011), 398.
19. Wallace Stevens, "The Emperor of Ice-Cream," in *The New Anthology of American Poetry*, 162–63. On the racial makeup of Key West, see George Monteiro, ed., *Conversations with Elizabeth Bishop* (Jackson: University Press of Mississippi, 1996), 146.
20. Zora Neale Hurston, "Story in Harlem Slang," in *The Complete Stories* (New York: Harper Perennial, 1995), 132.
21. Ibid., 133.
22. Upton Sinclair, *The Jungle* (New York: Oxford University Press, 2010), 75, 260.
23. Ibid, 274.
24. See David R. Roediger, *Working toward Whiteness: How America's Immigrants Became White* (New York: Basic Books, 2006), 82–87.
25. Mary Douglas argues that "ideas of impurity . . . are sensitive to change. The same impulse to impose order which brings them into existence can be supposed to be continually modifying or enriching them." Douglas, *Purity and Danger: An Analysis of Concepts of Pollution and Taboo* (New York: Routledge, 2002), 5.

26. I share Caroline Levine's sense that narrative is a particularly productive vehicle for investigating the production and circulation of social forms like race and for speculating about possible alternatives: "Narratives are valuable heuristic forms . . . because they can set in motion multiple social forms and track them as they cooperate, come into conflict, and overlap, without positing an ultimate cause . . . fictional narratives [are] productive thought experiments that allow us to imagine the subtle unfolding activity of multiple social forms." Levine, *Forms: Whole, Rhythm, Hierarchy, Network* (Princeton, NJ: Princeton University Press, 2015), 19.
27. Anita Mannur, *Culinary Fictions: Food in South Asian Diasporic Culture* (Philadelphia: Temple University Press, 2010), 7.
28. Morrison, *Playing in the Dark*, 66.
29. As Morrison eloquently observes of white-authored American literature's "encounters with Africanism," "images of blackness can be evil *and* protective, rebellious *and* forgiving, fearful *and* desirable—all of the self-contradictory features of the self. Whiteness, alone, is mute, meaningless, unfathomable, pointless, frozen, veiled, curtained, dreaded, senseless, implacable" (ibid., 59; emphasis in original).
30. See Karen Brodkin, *How Jews Became White Folks and What That Says about Race in America* (New Brunswick, NJ: Rutgers University Press, 1998); Eric L. Goldstein, *The Price of Whiteness: Jews, Race, and American Identity* (Princeton, NJ: Princeton University Press, 2006); Matthew Pratt Guterl, *The Color of Race in America, 1900–1940* (Cambridge, MA: Harvard University Press, 2001); Noel Ignatiev, *How the Irish Became White* (New York: Routledge, 1995); Matthew Frye Jacobson, *Whiteness of a Different Color: European Immigrants and the Alchemy of Race* (Cambridge, MA: Harvard University Press, 1998); Nell Irvin Painter, *The History of White People* (New York: W. W. Norton, 2009); David R. Roediger, *The Wages of Whiteness: Race and the Making of the American Working Class* (New York: Verso, 1991); and Roediger, *Working toward Whiteness*.
31. See Floyd Cheung and Keith Lawrence, *Recovered Legacies: Authority and Identity in Early Asian American Literature* (Philadelphia: Temple University Press, 2005); Michael Denning, "*Grapes of Wrath*: 'The Art and Science of Migratin,'" in *The Cultural Front: The Laboring of American Culture in the Twentieth Century* (New York: Verso, 1997), 259–82; George L. Henderson, *California and the Fictions of Capital* (New York: Oxford University Press, 1999); Colleen Lye, *America's Asia: Racial Form and American Literature, 1893–1945* (Princeton, NJ: Princeton University Press, 2005); Sarah D. Wald, *The Nature of California: Race, Citizenship, and Farming since the Dust Bowl* (Seattle: University of Washington Press, 2016); and Sau-Ling Cynthia Wong, *Reading Asian American Literature: From Necessity to Extravagance* (Princeton, NJ: Princeton University Press, 1993), 18–76.
32. On humoral theory and New World colonization, see Rebecca Earle, *The Body of the Conquistador: Food, Race and the Colonial Experience in Spanish America, 1492–1700* (Cambridge: Cambridge University Press, 2012).
33. Catherine Cocks, *Tropical Whites: The Rise of the Tourist South in the Americas* (Philadelphia: University of Pennsylvania Press, 2013); April Merleaux, *Sugar and Civilization: American Empire and the Cultural Politics of Sweetness* (Chapel Hill: University of North Carolina Press, 2013); Gary Y. Okihiro, *Pineapple Culture: A History of the Tropical and Temperate Zones* (Berkeley: University of California Press, 2009); and Mimi Sheller, *Consuming the Caribbean: From Arawaks to Zombies* (New York: Routledge, 2003).
34. Helen Zoe Veit, *Modern Food, Moral Food: Self-Control, Science, and the Rise of Modern American Eating in the Early Twentieth Century* (Chapel Hill: University of North Carolina Press, 2013), 106.
35. On Tompkins's philosophy of "deformalism," see "Crude Matter, Queer Form," *ASAP Journal* 2, no. 2 (May 2017): 264–68. On the historical racialization of particular foods and ingredients, see Tompkins, "'Hearty and Happy and with a Lively, Yeasty Soul': Feeling Right in Louisa May Alcott's *Candy Country*," *Women and Performance: A Journal of Feminist Theory* 24, nos. 2–3 (2014): 153–66. Chen theorizes the racialization of matter in *Animacies: Biopolitics, Racial Mattering, and Queer Affect* (Durham, NC: Duke University Press, 2012).
36. Alexander Weheliye, *Habeas Viscus: Racializing Assemblages, Biopolitics, and Black Feminist Theories of the Human* (Durham, NC: Duke University Press, 2014), 4.

37. See Tim Armstrong, *Modernism, Technology, and the Body: A Cultural Study* (Cambridge: Cambridge University Press, 1998); Sara Danius, *The Senses of Modernism: Technology, Perception, and Aesthetics* (Ithaca, NY: Cornell University Press, 2002); Mark Goble, *Beautiful Circuits: Modernism and the Mediated Life* (New York: Columbia University Press, 2010); and Cecelia Tichi, *Shifting Gears: Technology, Literature, Culture in Modernist America* (Chapel Hill: University of North Carolina Press, 1987).
38. Colleen Lye, "Racial Form," *Representations* 104, no. 1 (2008): 96.
39. Ibid.
40. Levine writes that the "collision" is "the strange encounter between two or more forms that sometimes reroutes intention and ideology" (*Forms*, 18).
41. Ibid., 14. Levine writes specifically of the usefulness of this kind of multivalent formalism for critical race studies: "Racism, for example, operates most often as a stark binary, a blunt political instrument rather than a complex formation in itself. But what literary formalists know well is that any simple order gets complicated fast once we start attending to the dense intertwining and overlapping of multiple forms ... political forms *try* to contain and control us, while often in fact overlapping and colliding with other forms, and sometimes getting in one another's way" (xi).
42. Drawing on Raymond Williams, Colleen Lye helpfully proposes that "race construed as form rather than as formation may help us keep in focus how race is an active social relation rather than a transhistorical abstraction" ("Racial Form," 99).
43. Carruth, *Global Appetites*, 46, and Martin Bruegel, "How the French Learned to Eat Canned Food, 1809–1930s," in *Food Nations: Selling Taste in Consumer Societies*, ed. Warren Belasco and Philip Scranton (New York: Routledge, 2002), 113–30.
44. See Marcelo Bucheli, *Bananas and Business: The United Fruit Company in Colombia, 1899–2000* (New York: New York University Press, 2005); Peter Chapman, *Bananas: How the United Fruit Company Shaped the World* (New York: Publishers Group West, 2007); Jason M. Colby, *The Business of Empire: United Fruit, Race, and U.S. Expansion in Central America* (Ithaca, NY: Cornell University Press, 2013); Lester D. Langley, *The Banana Wars: United States Intervention in the Caribbean, 1898–1934* (Lexington: University Press of Kentucky, 1985); Ivan Musicant, *The Banana Wars: A History of United States Military Intervention in Latin America from the Spanish-American War to the Invasion of Panama* (New York: Macmillan, 1991); Ana Patricia Rodríguez, *Dividing the Isthmus: Central American Transnational Histories, Literatures, and Cultures* (Austin: University of Texas Press, 2009); Steve Striffler and Mark Moberg, *Banana Wars: Power, Production, and History in the Americas* (Durham, NC: Duke University Press, 2003); Steve Striffler, *In the Shadows of State and Capital: The United Fruit Company, Popular Struggle, and Agrarian Restructuring in Ecuador, 1900–1995* (Durham, NC: Duke University Press, 2002); and James Wiley, *The Banana: Empires, Trade Wars, and Globalization* (Lincoln: University of Nebraska Press, 2010).
45. See Carruth, *Global Appetites*, 13–14; Ron Kroese, "Industrial Agriculture's War Against Nature," in *The Fatal Harvest Reader: The Tragedy of Industrial Agriculture*, ed. Andrew Kimball (Washington, DC: Island Press, 2002), 92–105; Harvey A. Levenstein, *Revolution at the Table: The Transformation of the American Diet* (Berkeley: University of California Press, 2003), 101–18; and Eric Schlosser, *Fast Food Nation: The Dark Side of the All-American Meal* (Boston: Houghton Mifflin, 2001), 113–24.
46. For more on the role of the kitchen in the postwar racial imaginary, see Kate A. Baldwin, *The Racial Imaginary of the Cold War Kitchen: From Sokol'niki Park to Chicago's South Side* (Hanover, NH: Dartmouth College Press, 2016).
47. See Howard Winant, *The World Is a Ghetto: Race and Democracy Since World War II* (New York: Basic Books, 2001), 30–31.
48. Of Toomer's physical culture regimen, Mark Whalan observes that "discourses of mass culture can become appropriated into practices which are socially and politically subversive." Whalan, "'Taking Myself in Hand': Jean Toomer and Physical Culture," *Modernism/modernity* 10, no. 4 (2003): 597–615, 612.
49. The "heavy Nordic blond ... needs exercise, meat, and air and cannot live under Ghetto conditions." Madison Grant, *The Passing of the Great Race, or The Racial Basis of European History* (New York: Scribner, 1916), 209.

50. Weston A. Price, *Nutrition and Physical Degeneration: A Comparison of Primitive and Modern Diets and Their Effects* (New York: Hoeber, 1939).
51. Charlotte Biltekoff, *Eating Right in America: The Cultural Politics of Food and Health* (Durham, NC: Duke University Press, 2013); E. Melanie DuPuis, *Dangerous Digestion: The Politics of American Dietary Advice* (Berkeley: University of California Press, 2015); and Veit, *Modern Food, Moral Food*.
52. William Carlos Williams, *In the American Grain* (New York: New Directions, 1956), 177.
53. See Jennifer Schuessler, "The Forgotten Man Behind William Carlos Williams's 'Red Wheelbarrow,'" *New York Times*, July 6, 2015, https://www.nytimes.com/2015/07/07/books/the-secret-of-william-carlos-williamss-the-red-wheelbarrow.html?mcubz=1, and William Logan, "The Red Wheelbarrow," *Parnassus* 34, nos. 1–2 (2015).
54. William Carlos Williams, *Yes, Mrs. Williams: A Personal Record of My Mother* (New York: New Directions, 1959), 102; Williams, "This Is Just to Say," in *The New Anthology of American Poetry*, vol. 2: *Modernisms, 1900–1950*, eds. Steven Gould Axelrod, Camille Roman, and Thomas Travisano (New Brunswick, NJ: Rutgers University Press, 2005), 234.
55. Claude McKay, *Home to Harlem* (Boston: Northeastern University Press, 1987), 161–62. Further citations appear parenthetically in the text.
56. Mary Douglas, *Purity and Danger* (New York: Routledge Classics, 2002), 44.
57. Ibid., 159. Food studies scholars like Roy and Tompkins build upon Douglas's claims, connecting them with biopolitics. Tompkins usefully expands the notion of the biopolitical beyond the "classic Foucauldian sense," namely "the project of state intervention into the well-being of its population," into "a series of uneven, asynchronous, and local campaigns, each of them . . . constru[ing] the ideal citizen as self-policing, temperate, and moral . . . The ideal citizen was to be made and remade via the quotidian practices of correct consumption, self-care, and sexual hygiene" (Tompkins, *Racial Indigestion*, 5–6). Roy and Tompkins implicate dietary prescriptions in the broader cultural projects of nationalism and colonialism, and they show the unexpected effects, the quotidian insurrections that this bodily idiom occasions.
58. Sara Ahmed, *The Cultural Politics of Emotion*, 2nd ed. (New York: Routledge, 2015), 83.
59. Douglas, *Purity and Danger*, 44. Jennifer DeVere Brody points out that "(falsely) conflicting categories, such as race and gender, blackness and femininity, the human and the animal . . . complicates and even violates categories that are supposed to be whole, pure, and inviolate." Brody, *Impossible Purities: Blackness, Femininity, and Victorian Culture* (Durham, NC: Duke University Press, 1998), 10.
60. Alexis Shotwell, *Against Purity: Living Ethically in Compromised Times* (Minneapolis: University of Minnesota Press, 2016), 15. See also María Lugones, *Pilgrimages/Peregrinajes: Theorizing Coalition Against Multiple Oppressions* (Lanham, MD: Rowman & Littlefield, 2003), 121–50.
61. Frantz Fanon, *Black Skin, White Masks* (New York: Grove Press, 2008); Saidiya Hartman, *Scenes of Subjection: Terror, Slavery, and Self-Making in Nineteenth-Century America* (New York: Oxford University Press, 1997); Eric Lott, *Love and Theft: Blackface Minstrelsy and the American Working Class* (New York: Oxford University Press, 1993); and Hortense J. Spillers, *Black, White, and in Color: Essays on American Literature and Culture* (Chicago: University of Chicago Press, 2003).
62. Chen writes: "I reside in this so-called negative zone, one of abjection, racial marking, toxic queerness, and illness, to think about the epistemic riches of possibility within" (*Animacies*, 17). In similar terms, Darieck Scott reclaims corporeal abjection for erotic possibility. Scott, *Extravagant Abjection: Blackness, Power, and Sexuality in the African American Literary Imagination* (New York: New York University Press, 2010), 129.
63. Weheliye, *Habeas Viscus*, 124.
64. Zelda Fitzgerald, *Save Me the Waltz*, in *The Collected Writings of Zelda Fitzgerald*, ed. Matthew J. Bruccoli (Tuscaloosa: University of Alabama Press, 1991), 179.
65. Dorothy West, *The Living Is Easy* (New York: Feminist Press at City University of New York, 1982), 276.
66. Qtd. in Edward L. Gibson, *Boundary Control: Subnational Authoritarianism in Federal Democracies* (Cambridge: Cambridge University Press, 2012), 59. See also J. Morgan Kousser, *The Shaping of Southern Politics: Suffrage Restriction and the Establishment of the One-Party South, 1880–1910* (New Haven, CT: Yale University Press, 1974), 134.

67. Tompkins, *Racial Indigestion*, 5.
68. Denise Ferreira da Silva explains that "the sociohistorical logic of exclusion ... writes blackness and whiteness as the 'raw material' and not as the products of modern strategies of power" (8). Silva, *Toward a Global Idea of Race* (Minneapolis: University of Minnesota Press, 2007).
69. I do not mean, as some commentators have done before me, to dismiss the category of race or to detach it from the body. As Michael Hames-García points out, "An important dimension of what race is and how it functions results from the interaction of racial practices and beliefs about race with visible human difference" (58). In spite of Toomer's fantasies about artificial color as a liberatory trope, therefore, "it certainly helps to be light skinned in order to qualify as white" (61). Hames-García concludes that "bodies do not have inherent meanings. Yet given the physical properties of bodies and the historical sediment of their intra-actions with cultural ideas and political-economic practices, one cannot attach just any meaning to any body" (61). Indeed, the consideration of bodies and the historical frames through which they were understood is central to my project here: "throughout [race's] history as a concept, it has presumed the truth of various biological fictions that have not held up to contemporary scientific scrutiny" (40). Many such fictions figure in this book. But the writers in my study also offer a view of how we might accomplish the goal that Hames-García so eloquently articulates: "what is needed now is creative experimentation with racial identities rather than their abandonment" (40). Much of this literature offers a model of "racial identity projects that do not simply reaffirm what race is and has been, but rather seek a transformation of race into something new" (66). Hames-García, *Identity Complex: Making the Case for Multiplicity* (Minneapolis: University of Minnesota Press, 2011).

Chapter 1

1. Jean Toomer to Waldo Frank, January 1923, in *The Letters of Jean Toomer, 1919–1924*, ed. Mark Whalan (Knoxville: University of Tennessee Press, 2006), 115.
2. Ibid., 116.
3. Tristan Donovan, *Fizz: How Soda Shook Up the World* (Chicago: Chicago Review Press, 2014), 7–9.
4. Toomer to Frank, January 1923, in *The Letters of Jean Toomer*, 115.
5. Tristan Donovan explains: "Henry's law, one of the physical laws explaining the nature and behavior of gases ... stated that the amount of gas absorbed in water is in proportion to the pressure of the gas. This explained why carbonated water would keep its fizz when bottled under pressure but go flat when the pressure is reduced by opening the bottle." Donovan, *Fizz*, 16. Two of the major breakthroughs in the soda industry in the last two decades of the nineteenth century, cylinders of compressed liquid CO_2 and crown caps, effectively maintained this pressure. See John J. Riley, *A History of the American Soft Drink Industry: Bottled Carbonated Beverages (1807–1957)* (Washington, DC: American Bottlers of Carbonated Beverages, 1958), 91–93, 101–102.
6. Jean Toomer, *Cane*, ed. Darwin T. Turner (New York: Norton Critical Editions, 1988), 7. Further citations appear parenthetically in the text.
7. Charles Scruggs and Barbara Foley see the cultivated apoliticism of Toomer's late-career positions as a repression of history, placing Toomer in bad faith as he tried to invent a new race. By contrast, George Hutchinson and Matthew Pratt Guterl insist that Toomer's work, imaginative and polemical, responds to the legislative erasure of mulatto identities from the US legal system in the 1920s. Barbara Foley, *Jean Toomer: Race, Repression and Revolution* (Urbana: University of Illinois Press, 2014); Charles Scruggs and Lee VanDemarr, *Jean Toomer and the Terrors of American History* (Philadelphia: University of Pennsylvania Press, 1998); Matthew Pratt Guterl, *The Color of Race in America, 1900–1940* (Cambridge, MA: Harvard University Press, 2001), 154–83; George Hutchinson, "Jean Toomer and American Racial Discourse," in *Interracialism: Black–White Intermarriage in American History, Literature, and Law*, ed. Werner Sollors (New York: Oxford University Press, 2000), 369–90.
8. Jean Toomer, "On Being an American," in *The Wayward and the Seeking: A Collection of Writings by Jean Toomer*, ed. Darwin T. Turner (Washington, DC: Howard University Press, 1980), 92.

9. See Guterl, *The Color of Race in America*, 176, and Mark Whalan, "'Taking Myself in Hand': Jean Toomer and Physical Culture," *Modernism/modernity* 10, no. 4 (November 2003): 603–604.
10. Jean Toomer, "Book X: First Draft," February 1935, box 11, folder 350, Jean Toomer Papers, Beinecke Rare Book and Manuscript Library, Yale University. Hereafter cited as Jean Toomer Papers.
11. Ibid.
12. Ibid.
13. Sophia Wellbeloved, *Gurdjieff: The Key Concepts* (New York: Routledge, 2003), 80–81. For more on Toomer and Gurdjieff, see Cynthia Earl Kerman and Richard Eldridge, *The Lives of Jean Toomer: A Hunger for Wholeness* (Baton Rouge: Louisiana State University Press, 1987), 119–210, and Jon Woodson, *To Make a New Race: Gurdjieff, Toomer, and the Harlem Renaissance* (Jackson: University Press of Mississippi, 1999).
14. Jean Toomer, "The Americans," in *A Jean Toomer Reader: Selected Unpublished Writings*, ed. Frederick L. Rusch (New York: Oxford University Press, 1993), 106–107.
15. Kyla Wazana Tompkins, *Racial Indigestion: Eating Bodies in the 19th Century* (New York: New York University Press, 2012), 4, 70–73, 117.
16. Toomer, "The Americans," 107.
17. Jean Toomer, "Book X: Second Draft," February 1935, box 11, folder 351, Jean Toomer Papers.
18. Mark Whalan, "Jean Toomer, Technology, and Race," *Journal of American Studies* 36, no. 3 (2002): 471.
19. Toomer, "Book X: Second Draft."
20. Dennis Brindell Fradin and Judith Bloom Fradin, *Fight On! Mary Church Terrell's Battle for Integration* (New York: Clarion, 2003), 126–28.
21. "It is evident at once that none of the standard color labels can do anything but misrepresent me." Jean Toomer, "Synthesis: Internationalism: Interracialism," n.d., box 28, folder 635, Jean Toomer Papers.
22. Toomer's fascination with machine culture also set him apart from other Harlem Renaissance writers, as Whalan notes. Whalan, "Jean Toomer, Technology, and Race," 463.
23. James Weldon Johnson, "Why Should a Negro Fight?," in *The Selected Writings of James Weldon Johnson*, vol. 1: *The New York Age Editorials (1914–1923)*, ed. Sondra Kathryn (New York: Oxford University Press, 1995), 33.
24. George S. Schuyler, *Black No More* (New York: Dover, 2011), 37.
25. Langston Hughes, *The Big Sea*, ed. Arnold Rampersand (New York: Hill & Wang, 1993), 51.
26. Henry Kane, "Duke Ellington," in *How to Write a Song as Told to Henry Kane* (New York: Macmillan, 1962), 8.
27. Ibid., 5.
28. Ibid., 9.
29. Anne Cooper Funderburg, *Sundae Best: A History of Soda Fountains* (Bowling Green, OH: Bowling Green State University Popular Press, 2002), 21, 77.
30. See Frederick Allen, *Secret Formula: How Brilliant Marketing and Relentless Salesmanship Made Coca-Cola the Best-Known Product in the World* (New York: HarperCollins, 1994), 46–47; Grace Elizabeth Hale, "When Jim Crow Drank Coke," *New York Times*, January 28, 2013; Mark Pendergrast, *For God, Country and Coca-Cola: The Unauthorized History of the Great American Soft Drink and the Company That Makes It* (New York: Scribner's, 1993), 89–91.
31. Anne Anlin Cheng, *Second Skin: Josephine Baker and the Modern Surface* (New York: Oxford University Press, 2011), 6. See also Sianne Ngai, "Animatedness," in *Ugly Feelings* (Cambridge, MA: Harvard University Press, 2005), 89–125.
32. See Tim Armstrong, *Modernism, Technology, and the Body: A Cultural Study* (Cambridge: Cambridge University Press, 1998), and Sara Danius, *The Senses of Modernism: Technology, Perception, and Aesthetics* (Ithaca, NY: Cornell University Press, 2002). On race science and modern literature, see Daylanne K. English, *Unnatural Selections: Eugenics in American Modernism and the Harlem Renaissance* (Chapel Hill: University of North Carolina Press, 2004), and Werner Sollors, *Interracialism: Black–White Intermarriage in American History, Literature, and Law* (New York: Oxford University Press, 2000).

33. Ezra Pound to William Carlos Williams, November 10, 1917, in *The Selected Letters of Ezra Pound*, ed. D. D. Paige (New York: New Directions, 1971), 124.
34. Ezra Pound, "Pastiche. The Regional," *New Age*, August 21, 1919, 284. The Modernist Journals Project (searchable database); Brown and Tulsa Universities, ongoing. http://www.modjourn.org.
35. John Dos Passos, *Manhattan Transfer* (Boston: Houghton Mifflin, 2000), 171. Further citations appear parenthetically in the text.
36. E. H. S. Bailey and Herbert S. Bailey, *Food Products from Afar: A Popular Account of Fruits and Other Foodstuffs from Foreign Lands* (New York: Century Company, 1922), 161.
37. Hart Crane, "America's Plutonic Ecstasies," in *The Complete Poems of Hart Crane*, ed. Marc Simon (New York: Liveright, 1986), 157.
38. Ibid.
39. See *The Letters of Jean Toomer*, 36, 41, 44, 89, 111.
40. Waldo Frank, "Candy Cigar and Stationary," *Broom*, January 1923, 253. http://library.princeton.edu/projects/bluemountain/broom-international-magazine-arts-0. Further citations appear parenthetically in the text.
41. Tompkins, *Racial Indigestion*, 3.
42. Parama Roy, *Alimentary Tracts: Appetites, Aversions, and the Postcolonial* (Durham, NC: Duke University Press, 2010), 7.
43. Tinsley insists on both the historicity and queer (re)configurations of the material: "My point is never that we should strip theory of watery metaphors but that we should return to the materiality of water to make its metaphors mean more complexly, shaking off settling into frozen figures." Toomer accomplishes this through his attunement to the racialized histories of sorghum syrup, sweet gum resin, and Coca-Cola. Omise'eke Natasha Tinsley, "Black Atlantic, Queer Atlantic: Queer Imaginings of the Middle Passage," *GLQ: A Journal of Lesbian and Gay Studies* 14, nos. 2–3 (2008): 212.
44. Riley, *A History of the American Soft Drink Industry*, 127.
45. Robert Cumming Wilson, *Drugs and Pharmacy in the Life of Georgia, 1733–1959* (Athens: University of Georgia Press, 2010), 228. Another source suggests that there were "three 'first-class' soda fountains in Sparta." Kent Anderson Leslie, *Woman of Color, Daughter of Privilege: Amanda America Dickson, 1849–1893* (Athens: University of Georgia Press, 1995), 82.
46. See *Seventh Annual Report of the Commissioner of Commerce and Labor of the State of Georgia for the Fiscal Year Ending December 31st, 1918* (Atlanta: Byrd Printing Company, 1918), 62.
47. "Million in Nine Years: Original Capital Stock of $75,000 in 1912 Increased to $1,000,000 by Chero-Cola Bottling Co.: Industry Gains Place in Van of the South," *American Bottler*, August 1921, 38, 43–44.
48. Toomer to Waldo Frank, 116.
49. Toomer, "A First Ride," qtd. in Robert B. Jones, *Jean Toomer and the Prison-House of Thought* (Amherst: University of Massachusetts Press, 1993), 70.
50. Jean Toomer, *The Sacred Factory*, in *The Wayward and the Seeking*, 368. Further citations appear parenthetically in the text.
51. On *The Sacred Factory*, see Jones, *Jean Toomer and the Prison-House of Thought*, 109–110.
52. Sidney Mintz, *Sweetness and Power: The Place of Sugar in Modern History* (New York: Penguin Books, 1985), 50.
53. Ibid., 50–51.
54. In more critical readings of Toomer's fascination with sugar, Barbara Foley cites Toomer's nostalgic treatment of the cane boil as a sign of his detachment from the real economic circumstances of southern black laborers, and Donald Shaffer reads the cane fields as "emblematic of the declining system of agriculture in the South of the 1920s." Foley, "'In the Land of Cotton': Economics and Violence in Jean Toomer's *Cane*," *African American Review* 32, no. 2 (Summer 1998): 186; Donald M. Shaffer, Jr., "'When the Sun Goes Down': The Ghetto Pastoral Mode in Jean Toomer's *Cane*," *African American Review* 32, no. 2 (Summer 1998): 117.
55. As the historian April Merleaux points out, "African American laborers produced cane and sorghum syrup and molasses as a way to assert autonomy in a labor system that worked to their

Notes to pages 25–33

disadvantage in most other respects." Merleaux, *Sugar and Civilization: American Empire and the Cultural Politics of Sweetness* (Chapel Hill: University of North Carolina Press, 2015), 19.
56. Jean Toomer, "Withered Skin of Berries," in *The Wayward and the Seeking*, 139. Further citations appear parenthetically in the text.
57. In "Withered Skin of Berries," Vera dates her white co-worker Carl at the same time that she spends time with Art.
58. On homoeroticism and diaspora in literature of this period, see Michelle Ann Stephens, *Black Empire: The Masculine Global Imaginary of Caribbean Intellectuals in the United States, 1914–1962* (Durham, NC: Duke University Press, 2005), 168–69, 288n35. On the theoretical and political possibilities of queer diaspora, see David L. Eng, "Transnational Adoption and Queer Diasporas," *Social Text* 21, no. 3 (Fall 2003): 4.
59. See Siobhan Somerville on the connection between the mulatta and "sexual mobility." Somerville, *Queering the Color-Line: Race and the Invention of Homosexuality in American Culture* (Durham, NC: Duke University Press, 2000), 80.
60. For more on Toomer's fascination with intermediate states and their racial significance, see Charles-Yves Grandjeat, "The Poetics of Passing in Jean Toomer's *Cane*," in *Jean Toomer and the Harlem Renaissance*, ed. Geneviève Fabre and Michel Feith (New Brunswick, NJ: Rutgers University Press, 2001), 57–67.
61. Stefan Hutzler and Denis Weaire, *The Physics of Foams* (New York: Oxford University Press, 1999), 3, 114.
62. A 1911 soda fountain guide explains that "foam" is one of the "principal ingredients... added to syrups" and that "syrups served with cream will foam sufficiently through the use of that agent." William S. Adkins, *Practical Soda Fountain Guide* (St. Louis, MO: National Druggist, 1911), 155.
63. "Chero-Cola: There's None So Good," *Charlotte News*, August 2, 1914.
64. Julia Ellen Rogers, *The Tree Book: A Popular Guide to a Knowledge of the Trees of North America and to Their Uses and Cultivation* (New York: Doubleday, Page, & Company, 1914), 275.
65. Laura Doyle observes that for the women in *Cane* "this intercorporeal connection to the phenomenal world is a burden as much as a kind of freedom." Doyle, *Bordering on the Body: The Racial Matrix of Modern Fiction and Culture* (New York: Oxford University Press, 1994), 86.
66. Rogers, *The Tree Book*, 276.
67. "Gathering Storax from the Sweet Gum Tree: An American Substitute for the Imported Drug," *Scientific American Supplement No. 2084*, December 11, 1915, 377.
68. Francis Peyre Porcher, *Resources of the Southern Fields and Forests, Medical, Economical, and Agricultural: Being Also a Medical Botany of the Confederate States: with Practical Information on the Useful Properties of the Trees, Plants, and Shrubs* (n.p.: Steam-Power Press of Evans & Cogswell, 1863), 61.
69. See Charles T. Hart, "Liquidum Liquidambar Styracifluae in the Treatment of Spasmodic Asthma," *Eclectic Medical Journal*, June 1853, 258; J. W. Pruitt, "For Bronchitis," *Eclectic Medical and College Journal*, March 1860, 190; and Rogers, *The Tree Book*, 277.
70. For more on Du Bois's gendering of double consciousness, see Hazel Carby, *Race Men* (Cambridge, MA: Harvard University Press, 2009).
71. Paul Stasi shares my view that Fern ruptures the narrator's nostalgic, confining frame. In his compelling reading, Stasi points out the importance of Fern's song: "Fern's interiority is not adequately represented by her external appearance. Aurality here escapes the visual logic of racial classification—the imagined homology between exterior and interior—allowing for the construction of an identity that is multiple, we might even say miscegenated." Stasi, "A 'Synchronous but More Subtle Migration': Passing and Primitivism in Toomer's *Cane*," *Twentieth Century Literature* 55, no. 2 (Summer 2009): 160.
72. Eric Lott, *Love and Theft: Blackface Minstrelsy and the American Working Class* (New York: Oxford University Press, 1993), 90.
73. Walter Benn Michaels, *Our America: Nativism, Modernism, and Pluralism* (Durham, NC: Duke University Press, 1995), 63.
74. It is suggestive that Art shares a name with the southern black man from Toomer's earlier story, "Withered Skin of Berries," who describes the mystical rendering of the sugarcane. "Art" on either side of the color line seems to require a transmutation of the material and the epiphanic blurring of the body as a coherent unit.

75. Michaels, *Our America*, 63.
76. Michaels argues that "the story insists not only that the color of Paul's skin be racialized... but also that Paul experience this racialization as the truth about himself" (ibid.).
77. Richard Dyer, *White* (New York: Routledge, 1997), 47.
78. On "art and literature," see Toomer to James Weldon Johnson, July 11, 1930, in *A Jean Toomer Reader,,* 106. On "artificial color," see "The Question of Colors in Standard Soda," *American Bottler,* May 1920, 45.
79. See, for example, Leaders Concord Grape Extract and Orange Concrete advertisement, *American Bottler,* August 1921, 19.
80. "The Question of Colors in Standard Soda," *American Bottler,* May 1920, 45.
81. Ibid.
82. Ibid.
83. Ibid.
84. "U.S. Sues over Coloring," *American Bottler,* September 1921, 59–60.
85. Donovan, *Fizz,* 54–55.
86. Ngai, "Animatedness," 94, 91.
87. Maas Carbonator advertisement, *American Druggist and Pharmaceutical Record,* May 1919, 34. For other allusions to the "snappiness" of carbonation, see Joseph Fox, "Thirst Quenchers," *National Druggist,* July 1921, 326, and *Soda Fountain,* July 1922, 28.
88. "Soda Quips," *Meyer Brothers Druggists,* May 1921, 7.
89. In an unpublished essay, Toomer debunked the trope of blood as a communicator of race: "Moreover it is a mistake to speak of blood as it had various colors in the various races. All human blood is the same. When we use color adjectives what we really are referring to are skin pigmentations. This is one of our main troubles. We see a surface and assume it is a center. We see a color or a label or a picture and assume it is a person" ("The Americans," 109).
90. Barbara Foley, "Jean Toomer's Washington and the Politics of Class: From 'Blue Veins' to Seventh-Street Rebels," *Modern Fiction Studies* 42, no. 2 (Summer 1996): 308.
91. Danius, *The Senses of Modernism,* 12. Armstrong, *Modernism, Technology, and the Body,* 6; emphasis in original.
92. Frantz Fanon, *Black Skin, White Masks,* trans. Richard Philcox (New York: Grove Press, 2008), 92.
93. Jean Toomer, "Man's Home Companion," in *A Jean Toomer Reader,* 167. Further citations appear parenthetically in the text.
94. Byrd and Gates are vigorous in expounding this point: "In the course of the twenty-five years between his 1917 and 1942 army registrations, Toomer was endlessly deconstructing his Negro ancestry." Rudolph P. Byrd and Henry Louis Gates, Jr., "'Song of the Son': The Emergence and Passing of Jean Toomer," in *Cane: Authoritative Texts, Contexts, Criticism,* second edition (New York: Norton Critical Editions, 2011), lxviii.
95. Jean Toomer, "Thus May It Be Said," n.d., box 51, folder 112, Jean Toomer Papers.
96. Toomer praises the complexity and flavor of "those New Orleans dishes—gumbo, calves head, gumbalaia"—and champions local produce: "The Maryland growth is fullbodied and full-flavored; the California, comparatively tasteless—and, I might add, odorless. I know, the California products ship better; but I am not eating the shipping I am eating the fruit. Some time someone will write the tragic life of a fruit, telling us what happens to a peach or an orange between the time when it is taken prematurely from the tree and the time when, in the guise of a sunripened fully-matured edible, it makes a bid to be consumed" ("Book X: First Draft," chaps. 10–12).
97. Jean Toomer, "'The Flavor of Man': Outline of a Talk," 27 April 1947, box 53, folder 1174, Jean Toomer Papers.
98. Jean Toomer, "The Flavor of Man," in *Jean Toomer: Selected Essays and Literary Criticism,* ed. Robert B. Jones (Knoxville: University of Tennessee Press, 1996), 118–19. Further citations appear parenthetically in the text.
99. Dyer, *White,* 91, 212.
100. Ironically and perhaps predictably, the Crystal Apple cucumber is now considered an heirloom fruit. See Jennifer Jordan, *Edible Memory: The Lure of Heirloom Tomatoes and Other Forgotten Foods* (Chicago: University of Chicago, 2015), 126.

101. Byrd and Gates introduce their proclamation about Toomer passing with a rhetorical drumroll, evoking in their very vehemence the continuing cultural scandal associated with such boundary crossing: "It is our carefully considered judgment, based upon analysis of archival evidence previously overlooked by other scholars, that Jean Toomer—for all of his pioneering theorizing about what today we might call a multicultural or mixed-race ancestry—was a Negro who decided to pass for white" ("Song of the Son," xx).
102. See Aaron Bobrow-Strain, *White Bread: A Social History of the Store-Bought Loaf* (Boston: Beacon Books, 2012).
103. See Allison Carruth, *Global Appetites: American Power and the Literature of Food* (New York: Cambridge University Press, 2013), 46.
104. Jean Toomer, "Friends of the Future," box 53, folder 1180, Jean Toomer Papers.
105. This section of "The Flavor of Man" is not reprinted in *Jean Toomer: Selected Essays and Literary Criticism* but can be found in the Beinecke Library. Toomer, "William Penn Lecture 1949: The Flavor of Man" (Philadelphia: Young Friends Movement, 1949), box 53, folder 1175, Jean Toomer Papers.
106. Ibid.
107. James Baldwin, *The Fire Next Time* (New York: Vintage, 1993), 42–43.

Chapter 2

1. David G. Croly and George Wakeman, *Miscegenation; the theory of the blending of the races, applied to the American white man and Negro* (New York: H. Dexter, Hamilton & Co., 1864), 36.
2. For the full story of the *Miscegenation* pamphlet, see Elise Lemire, *"Miscegenation": Making Race in America* (Philadelphia: University of Pennsylvania Press, 2002), 115–43.
3. Ibid., 131.
4. See Erica Hannickel, *Empire of Vines: Wine Culture in America* (Philadelphia: University of Pennsylvania Press, 2013), 144–48.
5. Tavia Nyong'o, *The Amalgamation Waltz: Race, Performance, and the Ruses of Memory* (Minneapolis: University of Minnesota Press, 2009), 24–27.
6. George S. Schuyler, *Black No More* (New York: Penguin Books, 2018), 9.
7. Robert A. Hill and R. Kent Rasmussen, "Editorial Statement," in *Black Empire*, by George S. Schuyler (Boston: Northeastern University Press, 1991), xvii.
8. Qtd. in Hill and Rasmussen, "Afterword," in *Black Empire*, 260.
9. Schuyler, *Black Empire*, 49. Further citations appear parenthetically in the text.
10. On the significance of teeth in pop eugenics of the period, see Nicole Rafter, "Apes, Men, and Teeth: Earnest A. Hooten and Eugenic Decay," in *Popular Eugenics: National Efficiency and American Mass Culture in the 1930s*, ed. Susan Currell and Christina Cogdell (Athens: Ohio University Press, 2006), 249–68.
11. Warren Belasco, *Meals to Come: The History of the Future of Food* (Berkeley: University of California, 2006), 187.
12. Heinz 57 Brochure, 1939 New York World's Fair (H. J. Heinz and Company).
13. Belasco, *Meals to Come*, 187. On Schuyler's canny adaptation of white supremacist pulp tropes, see Brooks Hefner, "Signifying Genre: George S. Schuyler and the Vagaries of Black Pulp," *Modernism/modernity*, forthcoming 2019.
14. Nella Larsen, *Quicksand* (New York: Penguin Books, 2002), 42.
15. Joseph W. Alsop, Jr., "Harlem's Youngest Philosopher Parades Talent on 3d [sic] Birthday: Philippa Schuyler Spells, Draws, and Then Rushes for Her Health Ice Cream," *New York Herald Tribune*, August 3, 1934. For an extended and insightful discussion of this article, see Ann Hulbert, *Off the Charts: The Hidden Lives and Lessons of American Child Prodigies* (New York: Penguin Random House, 2018), 127–29.
16. Kathryn Talalay, *Composition in Black and White: The Life of Philippa Schuyler* (New York: Oxford University Press, 1995), 51.
17. Ibid., 52.
18. See Jacqueline Warwick, *Musical Prodigies and Childhood Performance: Child's Play* (New York: Routledge, 2017).
19. "The Shirley Temple of American Negroes," *Look*, November 7, 1939, 4.

20. As the daughter of cattle ranchers in Texas, "Josephine would have heard talk around the dinner table about hybridization." Talalay, *Composition in Black and White*, 13–14.
21. Qtd. in ibid., 75.
22. Jeffrey Ferguson, *The Sage of Sugar Hill: George S. Schuyler and the Harlem Renaissance* (New Haven, CT: Yale University Press, 2005), 151.
23. This romance assigning healthfulness to prehistoric diets conflicts with the evolutionary record. Although some hominins that predated *Homo sapiens* did eat "the raw vegetarian diet that is the norm among primates . . . humans are not equipped to process large amounts of bulky, fiber-rich, energy-poor foods. If our diet had not changed during evolution, a primate of our size would need a colon more than 40 percent larger than ours in order to provide the capacity required to digest raw plant food." Jonathan Silvertown, *Dinner with Darwin: Food, Drink, and Evolution* (Chicago: University of Chicago Press, 2017), 21.
24. Qtd. in Talalay, *Composition in Black and White*, 14.
25. Nicholas Sammond, *Babes in Tomorrowland: Walt Disney and the Making of the American Child* (Durham, NC: Duke University Press, 2005), 123.
26. Ibid., 124.
27. On botany, hybridity, and racial purity in the nineteenth century, see Jennifer DeVere Brody, *Impossible Purities: Blackness, Femininity, and Victorian Culture* (Durham, NC: Duke University Press, 1998), 59–67.
28. Nathaniel Hawthorne, *Nathaniel Hawthorne's Tales*, ed. James McIntosh (New York: W. W. Norton, 1987), 126, 202. Further citations appear parenthetically in the text.
29. Nicholas Bauch, *A Geography of Digestion: Biotechnology and the Kellogg Cereal Enterprise* (Oakland: University of California Press, 2017), 132.
30. Ibid., 73.
31. On "The Birth-Mark" and race, see Robyn Wiegman, *American Anatomies: Theorizing Race and Gender* (Durham, NC: Duke University Press, 1995), 87–88. On "Rappaccini's Daughter" and racial allegory, see Anna Brickhouse, "'I Do Abhor an Indian Story': Hawthorne and the Allegorization of Racial 'Commixture,'" *ESQ* 42, no. 4 (1996): 232–53.
32. Lydia Maria Child, "The Quadroons," in *The Liberty Bell* (Boston: Massachusetts Anti-Slavery Fair, 1842), 133.
33. Harriet Beecher Stowe, *Uncle Tom's Cabin*, second edition, ed. Elizabeth Ammons (New York: Norton Critical Editions, 2010), 331. On the significance of the orange trees, see Kathryn Cornell Dolan, *Beyond the Fruited Plain: Food and Agriculture in U.S. Literature, 1850–1905* (Lincoln: University of Nebraska Press, 2014), 113–14.
34. William Wells Brown, *Clotelle; or, The Colored Heroine: A Tale of the Southern States* (Boston: Lee & Shepard, 1867), 57.
35. Lucia Hodgson observes that the tragic mulatta's "privileged and protected childhood was a crucial element of her whiteness and of the pathos generated by her fall into slavery." Hodgson, "All But White: Mulattas and White Womanhood," presentation, Society for the Study of American Women Writers, Philadelphia, November 4–8, 2015.
36. Frances E. W. Harper, *Iola Leroy* (Boston: Beacon Press, 1987), 200, 214.
37. Charlotte Perkins Gilman, *"The Yellow Wall-Paper," "Herland," and Selected Writings*, ed. Denise D. Knight (New York: Penguin Books, 1999), 17. Further citations appear parenthetically in the text. Though it may seem surprising that I place these characters in the mulatta tradition, especially since the narrator notes that they were "a 'pure stock' of two thousand uninterrupted years" (121), the women in this utopia reflect a range of skin tones and eye colors: "Celis was a blue-and-gold-and-rose person; Alima, black-and-white-and-red . . . Ellador was brown: hair dark and soft, like a seal coat; clear brown skin with a healthy red in it; brown eyes—all the way from topaz to black velvet they seemed to range—splendid girls, all of them" (92). Gilman explicitly compares their marriages to the adventurers to interracial unions: "no combination of alien races, of color, caste, or creed, was ever so basically difficult to establish as that between us, three modern American men, and these three women of Herland," more challenging than "any other imaginable marriage among the peoples of the earth, whether the women were black, red, yellow, or brown" (120). On Gilman's use of the tragic mulatta trope in her polemical writings, see Gail Bederman, *Manliness and Civilization: A Cultural History of Gender and Race in the United States, 1880–1917* (Chicago: University of Chicago Press, 1995), 146–47.

38. Gilman actually describes this abstinence with a food metaphor: "It was as if I had come to some new place and people, with a desire to eat at all hours, and no other interests in particular, and as if my hosts, instead of merely saying, 'You shall not eat,' had presently aroused in me a lively desire for music, for pictures, for games, for exercise, for playing in the water, for running some ingenious machine; and in the multitude of my satisfactions, I forgot the one point which was not satisfied, and got along very well until mealtime" (128).
39. Fannie Hurst, *Imitation of Life*, ed. Daniel Itzkovitz (Durham, NC: Duke University Press, 2004), 99, 241–42. Further citations appear parenthetically in the text.
40. See Lauren Berlant, *The Female Complaint: The Unfinished Business of Sentimentality in American Life* (Durham, NC: Duke University Press, 2008), 120–22, and Doris Witt, *Black Hunger: Soul Food and America* (Minneapolis: University of Minnesota Press, 2004), 35.
41. Or at least into expatriation, as Peola and her white fiancé move to Bolivia. Though Bolivia instated segregation laws in the 1920s that targeted its indigenous population, this new context turns Peola's stylized pallor—whether construed as white or mixed-race—into an asset: "In the Bolivian racial imaginary, q'aras—whites and mestizos who shared a common commitment to a universal modernizing process—were at the top of the social structure." Waskar Ari, *Earth Politics: Religion, Decolonization, and Bolivia's Indigenous Intellectuals* (Durham, NC: Duke University Press, 2014), 81, 91–92.
42. Peola is "a pale-tan infant … with fierce black Indian-looking eyes." Hurst, *Imitation of Life*, 78.
43. When Schuyler describes her as "the color of a pale Indian with the softness of feature of the Negro," he employs a common trope for racial intermixture. Cherene Sherrard-Johnson explains: "Rather than attribute a particular genetic trait like green or blue eyes and straight or wavy hair to a white progenitor, who may have been a sexual aggressor, some oral family histories claim the anomalous features come from an Indian ancestor." Sherrard-Johnson, *Dorothy West's Paradise: A Biography of Class and Color* (New Brunswick, NJ: Rutgers University Press, 2012), 49.
44. Cherene Sherrard-Johnson, *Portraits of the New Negro Woman* (New Brunswick, NJ: Rutgers University Press, 2007), 19.
45. Hill and Rasmussen, "Afterword," 268.
46. On the shared ideal of symmetry in eugenics and design, see Christina Cogdell, *Eugenic Design: Streamlining America in the 1930s* (Philadelphia: University of Pennsylvania Press, 2004), 65–67.
47. Michelle Ann Stephens notes that "in black internationalist narratives, female protagonists often come to represent a multinational and multiracial black world, one that could be seen as mirroring the hybridity of the world of empire, more so than representing separate and separatist racial ideologies." Stephens, *Black Empire: The Masculine Global Imaginary of Caribbean Intellectuals in the United States, 1914–1962* (Durham, NC: Duke University Press, 2005), 57.
48. Chanel Gardenia, the first gardenia perfume, was launched in 1927. Axel Madsen, *Chanel: A Woman of Her Own* (New York: Henry Holt, 1990), 140. Benzyl acetate, the primary ingredient in this fragrance, was also used in artificial strawberry flavor. Right before Pat shows Carl giant strawberries in the underground hydroponic farm, she exudes the artificial aroma of fruit and flowers. On benzyl acetate in gardenia perfume, see "Schimmel Briefs," *Drug and Cosmetic Industry* 35, no. 6 (September 1935): 256. Another article indicates that the central ingredient in "artificial strawberry flavors," ethyl methyl phenylglyceride, was rarely used in perfumes except those "of tuberose and gardenia type." "Perfumers Shelf," *Drug and Cosmetic Industry* 35, no. 2 (August 1934): 411.
49. Anne Anlin Cheng, *Second Skin: Josephine Baker and the Modern Surface* (New York: Oxford University Press, 2011), 118–20.
50. Ibid., 118–19.
51. Ibid., 120.
52. Rita Felski, *The Gender of Modernity* (Cambridge, MA: Harvard University Press, 1995), 20.
53. This dynamic continues in contemporary culture. For example, Laura Wright notes the "sexualization and often-contradictory gender-specific rhetorical construction" of the vegan diet. *The Vegan Studies Project: Food, Animals, and Gender in the Age of Terror* (Athens: University of Georgia Press, 2015), 22.

54. On Bernarr Macfadden and physical culture, see Mark Adams, *Mr. America: How Muscular Millionaire Bernarr Macfadden Transformed the Nation Through Sex, Salad, and the Ultimate Starvation Diet* (New York: Harper, 2009), and Aaron Bobrow-Strain, *White Bread: A Social History of the Store-Bought Loaf* (Boston: Beacon Press, 2013), 91–95.

55. Bernarr Macfadden, "General Rules for Health-Building: Some Further Details of the Fundamental Principles on Which the Science of Physcultopathy is Based: Lecture VI," *Physical Culture* (March 1910): 272–73. Further citations appear parenthetically in the text.

56. Bernarr Macfadden, *Womanhood and Marriage* (New York: Physical Culture Corporation, 1918), 2. Further citations appear parenthetically in the text. On the racial and sexual politics of eugenics and its management of the woman's body, see Wendy Kline, *Building a Better Race: Gender, Sexuality, and Eugenics from the Turn of the Century to the Baby Book* (Berkeley: University of California Press, 2001), 14–17.

57. These dietary prescriptions appear in the "Masturbation" chapter, which suggests a continuity between the sexual politics of nineteenth-century Grahamite dietetics and physical culture. On Sylvester Graham and anti-masturbation discourse, see Kyla Wazana Tompkins, *Racial Indigestion: Eating Bodies in the Nineteenth Century* (New York: New York University Press, 2012), 63–65.

58. Margaret Grant, "Race Suicide," *Beauty and Health*, August 1903, 229.

59. On Macfadden's white supremacist views, see R. Marie Griffith, *Born Again Bodies: Flesh and Spirit in American Christianity* (Berkeley: University of California Press, 2004), 129–30. On the adaptation of physical culture by African American thinkers, see Mark Whalan, "'Taking Myself in Hand': Jean Toomer and Physical Culture," *Modernism/modernity* 10, no. 4 (November 2003): 598–99.

60. Rafter, "Apes, Men, and Teeth," 262.

61. Ytasha Womack, *Afrofuturism: The World of Black Sci-Fi and Fantasy Culture* (Chicago: Lawrence Hill Books, 2013), 157.

62. On slave marriage, see Tera W. Hunter, *Bound in Wedlock: Slave and Free Black Marriage in the Nineteenth Century* (Cambridge, MA: Harvard University Press, 2017). On the ungendering of slave bodies, see Hortense Spillers, *Black, White and in Color: Essays on American Literature and Culture* (Chicago: University of Chicago Press, 2003), 206.

63. Helen Veit notes that euthenics theorists generally took a "self-aggrandizing" tack in their "conjectures about their own racial fitness." Veit, *Modern Food, Moral Food: Self-Control, Science, and the Rise of Modern American Eating in the Early Twentieth Century* (Chapel Hill: University of North Carolina Press, 2013), 104.

64. George S. Schuyler, "Views and Reviews," *Pittsburgh Courier*, April 5, 1930.

65. Ibid.

66. Ibid.

67. Miriam Thaggert, for example, suggests that Schuyler's work "foreshadow[s] poststructuralist concepts of race." Thaggert, *Images of Black Modernism* (Amherst: University of Massachusetts Press, 2010), 90–91. Though *Black No More* seems to attribute racial difference to social distinction and discursive convention, Schuyler's famous essay debunking racial prescriptivism, "The Negro-Art Hokum," stressed the transformative impact of environment on human biology. See George S. Schuyler, "The Negro-Art Hokum," in *Double-Take: A Revisionist Harlem Renaissance Anthology*, ed. Maureen Honey and Venetria K. Patton (New Brunswick, NJ: Rutgers University Press, 2001), 36–39. The step from prioritizing environmental influence over heredity to rejecting race as a biological category altogether may seem small, but it is nonetheless significant. As Veit points out, many euthenists did not reject "the notion of biological race," even as they proposed that "races could ... change more quickly than previously imagined" (*Modern Food, Moral Food*, 106). For a helpful account of the inconsistency of Schuyler's apparent anti-essentialism, see Stacy Morgan, "'The Strange and Wonderful Workings of Science': Race Science and Essentialism in George Schuyler's *Black No More*," *CLA Journal* 42, no. 3 (March 1999): 331–52.

68. In this conclusion, I diverge sharply from Ewa Barbara Luczak, who acknowledges Schuyler's "prodigious knowledge of eugenics" but insists that "Schuyler managed not only to challenge eugenic tenets but to shake them to the core." Luczak, *Breeding and Eugenics in the American Literary Imagination: Heredity Rules in the Twentieth Century*

(New York: Palgrave Macmillan, 2015), 158. Instead, I am inclined to agree with Jeffrey B. Leak and Daylanne K. English, who contend that Schuyler repurposes eugenics for alternative racial ends. As English persuasively argues, eugenics *"in its historical context"* held "a widely shared, utopian aim of improving the national or racial stock by conscious intervention. In fact, eugenicists like Toomer and Schuyler who advocated racial mixture as a source of genetic superiority could, perhaps even more legitimately than could the racial purists, consider their version of eugenics truly progressive and truly Darwinian." English, *Unnatural Selections: Eugenics in American Modernism and the Harlem Renaissance* (Chapel Hill: University of North Carolina Press, 2004), 18 (emphasis in original); see also Leak, *Rac[e]ing to the Right: Selected Essays of George S. Schuyler* (Knoxville: University of Tennessee Press, 2001), xxviii.
69. Heba Jannath [Josephine Schuyler], "Death and Diet," *Messenger*, April 1928, 105.
70. Josephine Schuyler, "The Slaughter of the Innocents," *Crisis*, October 1934, 297. Further citations appear parenthetically in the text.
71. The idea that white civilization had been exhausted and only black bodies could thrive in modern times was a common refrain in eugenic tracts, many of them decrying such a state of affairs. Josephine Schuyler, by contrast, drew upon this narrative to support racial intermixture: "the white race, the Anglo-Saxon especially, is spiritually depleted, and America must mate with the Negro to save herself." Qtd. in Talalay, *Composition in Black and White*, 36.
72. Susan Marks, *Finding Betty Crocker: The Secret Life of America's First Lady of Food* (Minneapolis: University of Minnesota Press, 2007), 183–84.
73. On white kitchen design, see Carroll Ganz, *Refrigeration: A History* (Jefferson, NC: McFarland, 2015), 129–30, and Christopher Innes, *Designing America: Broadway to Main Street* (New Haven, CT: Yale University Press, 2005), 252–55.
74. Belasco, *Meals to Come*, 93, 216.
75. See Ellen Lupton and J. Abbott Miller, *The Bathroom, the Kitchen, and the Aesthetics of Waste* (New York: Princeton Architectural Press, 1992), 1–5.
76. Laura Shapiro, *Something from the Oven: Reinventing Dinner in 1950s America* (New York: Viking, 2004), 68.
77. On refrigeration, see Susanne Freidberg, *Fresh: A Perishable History* (Cambridge, MA: Harvard University Press, 2010); Ganz, *Refrigeration: A History*; and Jonathan Rees, *Refrigeration Nation: A History of Ice, Appliances, and Enterprise in America* (Baltimore: Johns Hopkins University Press, 2013). On quick-freezing, see Freidberg, *Fresh*, 251–52, and Mark Kurlansky, *Birdseye: The Adventures of a Curious Man* (New York: Random House, 2012).
78. Maggie Kilgour, *From Communion to Cannibalism: An Anatomy of Metaphors of Incorporation* (Princeton, NJ: Princeton University Press, 1990), 245.
79. This taming may be endemic to the tragic mulatta convention. Eve Allegra Raimon observes a similar phenomenon in Cassy's characterization in *Uncle Tom's Cabin*. Raimon, *The "Tragic Mulatta" Revisited: Race and Nationalism in Nineteenth-Century Antislavery Fiction* (New Brunswick, NJ: Rutgers University Press, 2004), 117.
80. Ann duCille, *The Coupling Convention* (New York: Oxford University Press, 1993), 45.
81. In the final chapter, Belsidus gives Pat permission to accompany them to watch "this last decisive battle." Now they enjoy "a swallow of orange juice all around" (254).
82. On orange juice and vitamania, see Harvey Levenstein, *Fear of Food: A History of Why We Worry about What We Eat* (Chicago: University of Chicago Press, 2012), 85.
83. Heba Jannath [Josephine Schuyler], "Death and Diet," 106.
84. Bernarr Macfadden, *The Miracle of Milk: How to Use the Milk Diet Scientifically at Home* (New York: Macfadden Book Co., 1923), vii.
85. On the industrialization and purification of milk in the Progressive era and the cultural contradictions that ensued, see Kendra Smith-Howard, *Pure and Modern Milk: An Environmental History* (New York: Oxford University Press, 2014), 12–35.
86. Alfred S. Cook to Mrs. George Schuyler, 21 August 1937, box 25, Schuyler Family Papers, Schomburg Center for Research in Black Culture, New York Public Library. Hereafter cited as Schuyler Family Papers.
87. Weston Price, *Nutrition and Physical Degeneration: A Comparison of Primitive and Modern Diets and Their Effects* (Los Angeles: Citizens Print Shop, 1939), 415.

88. Ibid., 6.
89. Marion Porter, "Child Pianist Gets 'Extra Vitality' from Raw Foods, Mother Says," *Courier-Journal*, May 12, 1941.
90. Sherrard-Johnson, *Portraits of the New Negro Woman*, 17–19, and Spillers, *Black, White and in Color*, 27.
91. See Gillian Brown, *The Consent of the Governed: The Lockean Legacy in Early American Culture* (Cambridge, MA: Harvard University Press, 2001), 55, and Paul Gilmore, *The Genuine Article: Race, Mass Culture, and American Literary Manhood* (Durham, NC: Duke University Press, 2009), 59–60.
92. Josephine Schuyler, "Mrs. George S. Schuyler Answers the Challenge of the Editor Regarding Her Prodigious Daughter," *Sunday School Informer*, October 1940, 8. Further citations appear parenthetically in the text.
93. Berlant, *The Female Complaint*, 111–12.
94. Lena Morrow Lewis to Harold Ross, 7 September 1940, box 48, Schuyler Family Papers.
95. Lena Morrow Lewis is mentioned in a June 1922 article in the *Messenger*, a black press socialist magazine that George Schuyler wrote for and eventually edited. Josephine Schuyler was also a contributor; indeed, the couple met in the magazine's offices. In the article, Lewis introduces the *Messenger*'s editor, Chandler Owens, to the white eugenicist David Starr Jordan, an association that perhaps indicates her racial views. Chandler Owen, "Through the Northwest and up the Pacific Coast," *Messenger*, June 1922, 424.
96. In *My Ántonia* (1918), for example, Willa Cather describes the blind "mulatto" pianist Samson d'Arnault as a "Negro prodigy who played barbarously and wonderfully" (126, 129). "As a very young child he could repeat, after a fashion, any composition that was played for him" (128). Though Cather praises his "vitalized" music, his embodiment and rhythm, his prodigiousness, like her primitivist view of his race, marks his performances as instinctive rather than accomplished. Also, when she mentions his "yellow fingers" on the "black-and-white keys," Cather may mean to underscore that d'Arnault's facility comes from his mixed-race background. Cather, *My Ántonia* (New York: Bantam Classics, 2005), 129.
97. "Philippa as Mozart," *New York Amsterdam News*, 13 May 1939, box 47, Schuyler Family Papers.
98. Brown, *Consent of the Governed*, 55. One reviewer called Phillis a "prodigy in literature" and marveled that she "was, but a few years since, an illiterate barbarian." Tobias George Smollett, *The Critical Review, or, Annals of Literature*, (London: W. Simpkin and R. Marshall, 1773), 36:232–33. A French reviewer of Bridgetower's performance noted: "Son talent, aussi vrai que precoce, est une de meilleures responses que l'on puisse faire aux Philosophes qui veulent priver ceux de sa Nation & de sa couleur, de la faculté de se distinguer dans les Arts." (His talent, as true as it is precocious, is one of the best responses that one could make to philosophers who want to deprive those of his nation and color of the faculty to distinguish themselves in the arts.) Qtd. in F. G. Edwards, "George P. Bridgetower and the Kreutzer Sonata," *Musical Times* 49 (1908): 303; translation mine.
99. Alsop, "Harlem's Youngest Philosopher."
100. Scrapbook 1935, box 3, Philippa Schuyler Collection, Special Collections Research Center, Syracuse University.
101. "Harlem Prodigy," *Time*, June 1936, 40.
102. Thelma Berlack-Boozer, "Interracial Marriage in America Is Workable—Here's Positive Proof: Harlem Family Radical in Views on Races and Food," *New York Amsterdam News*, May 20, 1939.
103. Berlack reports that "a day's supply of food for the child includes cod liver oil every day (summer and winter); two oranges; one lemon; one tomato; one quart of certified milk; two raw eggs beaten and flavored with honey; one small piece of beef-steak (raw or slightly broiled); any raw fruits or vegetables in season that she wishes to eat." Thelma Berlack-Boozer, "How a Genius Celebrates Her Seventh Birthday Anniversary," *New Amsterdam News*, August 13, 1938.
104. *OED* online, June 2017,. Oxford University Press, http://www.oed.com/view/Entry/151956?redirectedFrom=prodigy
105. Beatrice Adair, "Harlem's Child Prodigy," *Silhouette*, April 1939.

106. Berlack-Boozer, "Interracial Marriage in America Is Workable."
107. "Philippa's Day at the Fair," *Time*, July 1940, 48.
108. Claude Lévi-Strauss, *The Raw and the Cooked*, trans. John Weightman and Doreen Weightman (Chicago: University of Chicago Press, 1983).
109. Roland Barthes, *Roland Barthes*, trans. Richard Howard (New York: Hill & Wang, 1977), 62–63.
110. "Music by Philippa," *Newsweek*, August 14, 1944, 84.
111. *Flash! Weekly Newspicture Magazine* clipping, family scrapbook 1937, box 44, Schuyler Family Papers.
112. Alsop, "Harlem's Youngest Philosopher."
113. At the same time, Alsop associates the child with ancient civilizations and exotic empires, noting her "admirable silk turban" and her "attitude of which Cleopatra in her best days would not have been ashamed" (ibid.).
114. Ibid.
115. Josephine Schuyler notes in the scrapbook that "Miss Georgia Crosthwaite sent a huge watermelon from Weatherford, Texas" for Philippa's birthday in August 1938. Family scrapbook 1937–38, box 45, Schuyler Family Papers.
116. Correspondence, *Opportunity*, January 1935, 30.
117. "In the News Columns," *Opportunity*, September 1936, 262.
118. On Mitchell and his style, see Tamar Katz, "Anecdotal History: The *New Yorker*, Joseph Mitchell, and Literary Journalism," *American Literary History* 27, no. 3 (2015): 461–86.
119. Sir Francis Galton, *Hereditary Genius: An Inquiry into its Laws and Consequences* (New York: D. Appleton & Co., 1870), 64.
120. Ibid.
121. On the eugenic history of gifted classification and the racist views of its interwar proponents, see Leslie Margolin, *Goodness Personified: The Emergence of Gifted Children* (New York: Aldine de Gruyter, 1994), 19–34.
122. Lewis M. Terman, *The Measurement of Intelligence: An Explanation of and a Complete Guide for the Use of the Stanford Revision and Extension of the Binet-Simon Intelligence Scale* (New York: Houghton Mifflin, 1916), 92. For more on Terman and race science, see Robert Wald Sussman, *The Myth of Race: The Troubling Persistence of an Unscientific Idea* (Cambridge, MA: Harvard University Press, 2014), 91–94.
123. Lewis M. Terman, *Mental and Physical Traits of a Thousand Gifted Children*, Genetic Studies of Genius, vol. 1 (Stanford, CA: Stanford University Press, 1926), 55.
124. Ibid., 166.
125. Ibid., 56.
126. Joseph Mitchell, "Evening with a Gifted Child," *New Yorker*, August 31, 1940, 28. Further citations appear parenthetically in the text.
127. See Robin Bernstein on the commodity trope of the impervious pickaninny. Bernstein, *Racial Innocence: Performing American Childhood from Slavery to Civil Rights* (New York: New York University Press, 2011), 30–68.
128. I refer to Josephine Schuyler as "Mrs. Schuyler" throughout my discussion of "Evening with a Gifted Child," following Mitchell's nomenclature in order to indicate that she is a character represented in the article. Elsewhere, when I cite her writing, I follow scholarly convention and refer to her by last name.
129. With their typical ironic sensibility, the *New Yorker* editorial staff placed an ad for Louis Sherry Confections next to this declaration.
130. Both Schuylers alluded approvingly to predatory animals in their dietary advice, and Josephine Schuyler lamented that cooked food reduces humans to "carrion-eaters in a class with the buzzard, the jackal, and the fly." Heba Jannath [Josephine Schuyler], "Death and Diet," 107. See also George Schuyler, "Views and Reviews," *Pittsburgh Courier*, July 10, 1937.
131. Though Schuyler does not specify whether these waiters serve Philippa on a train or in a restaurant, biographer Kathryn Talalay recounts that Philippa shocked the steward on her first train trip by eating a raw Porterhouse steak (*Composition in Black and White*, 77–78).
132. The steward mentioned in the anecdote was probably white, as black dining car workers did not get to serve as stewards until the union won them that right in the mid-1940s. See

Larry Tye, *Rising from the Rails: Pullman Porters and the Making of the Black Middle Class* (New York: Henry Holt, 2004), 243. For more on the parlor car, class, and racial difference, see Amy Richter, *Home on the Rails: Women, the Railroad, and the Rise of Public Domesticity* (Chapel Hill: University of North Carolina Press, 2005), 81.

133. Hazel Carby suggests that the mulatta is "a narrative device of mediation" that serves "as a vehicle for an exploration of the relationship between the races and, at the same time, an expression of the relationship between the races." I contend that Philippa's celebrity operates similarly. Carby, *Reconstructing Womanhood: The Emergence of the Afro-American Woman Novelist* (New York: Oxford University Press, 1987), 89.

134. Josephine Schuyler, "Nutrition and Racial Superiority," *Crisis*, December 1942, 380, 398. Further citations appear parenthetically in the text.

135. The association of mixed-race children with fruit and produce has a long history in the iconography of the New World, as in Agostino Brunias's *Two Mulattresses and a Child with a Black Woman Selling Fruit* (painted sometime between 1764 and 1796). The light-skinned woman in the painting stands with a gourd suggestively placed over her uterus, a child clinging to her leg. Through the visual juxtaposition of the gourd and the child, Amanda Michaela Bagneris notes, creolization "is metaphorically connected to the land itself rather than the realities of interracial sex." Bagneris, "Coloring the Caribbean: Agostino Brunias and the Painting of Race in the British West Indies, 1765–1800" (PhD diss., Harvard University, 2009).

136. The blender was invented in 1922 and improved and popularized in 1935. Meryl S. Rosofsky, "Blenders," in *The Oxford Companion to Food and Drink*, ed. Andrew F. Smith (New York: Oxford University Press, 2007), 55.

137. As an adult, Philippa wrote that she "grew up . . . without any consciousness of America's race prejudices, because I lived in a special atmosphere and unusual circumstances." When she "encountered vicious barriers of prejudice . . . it was a ruthless shock to me that, at first, made the walls of my self-confidence crumble. It horrified, humiliated me." Philippa Duke Schuyler, "My Black and White World," *Sepia*, June 1962, 13.

138. Bernstein, *Racial Innocence*, 6.

139. Though the sheet music is undated, a concert program explains that this song was "Composed by Philippa at the age of 4." "Philippa's Program," box 45, Schuyler Family Papers.

140. "Dance of the Vegetables," box 35, folder 3, Schuyler Family Papers.

141. Qtd. in Carla Kaplan, *Miss Anne in Harlem: The White Women of the Black Renaissance* (New York: HarperCollins, 2013), 121; "The Fall of a Fair Confederate," *Modern Quarterly* (Winter 1930–31): 528.

142. Philippa Schuyler, "Dates," 8 November 1938, box 47, Schuyler Family Papers.

143. Ibid.

144. Adair, "Harlem's Child Prodigy."

145. "[Jokes] make possible the satisfaction of an instinct (whether lustful or hostile) in the face of an obstacle that stands in its way. They circumvent these obstacles and in that way draw pleasure from a source which the obstacle had made inaccessible." Sigmund Freud, *Jokes and Their Relation to the Unconscious*, trans. and ed. James Strachey (New York: Norton, 1960), 120–21.

146. Talalay, *Composition in Black and White*, 223, 228.

147. Ibid., 237.

148. Ibid., 224.

149. Ibid.

Chapter 3

1. As Adam Gopnik puts it, "Hemingway's style was the most influential in American prose for more than fifty years, and this makes Stein's style . . . less an eccentricity than a bedrock of modern American writing." Gopnik, introduction to *Paris France*, by Gertrude Stein (New York: Liveright, 2013), iv.

2. Ernest Hemingway, *A Moveable Feast* (New York: Scribner, 1964), 14.

3. See Judith Brown on Stein's aesthetic and the modernist ideals of transparency and blankness. Brown, *Glamour in Six Dimensions: Modernism and the Radiance of Form* (Ithaca, NY: Cornell University Press, 2009), 160–61.
4. Walter Benn Michaels points out that the status of foreign language is crucial to Hemingway's aesthetics and that its "linguistic untranslatability" reinforces the "claim of authenticity." Michaels, *Our America: Nativism, Modernism, and Pluralism* (Durham, NC: Duke University Press, 1995), 73. See also Gayle Rogers on Hemingway and the allure of foreign languages. Rogers, *Incomparable Empires: Modernism and the Translation of Spanish and American Literature* (New York: Columbia University Press, 2016), 203–204.
5. Hemingway, *A Moveable Feast*, 14.
6. Ibid.
7. See Amy Trubek on terroir and interwar tourism in France. Trubek, *The Taste of Place: A Cultural Journey into Terroir* (Berkeley: University of California Press, 2008), 32–38. See also Stephen Harp, *Marketing Michelin: Advertising and Cultural Identity in Twentieth-Century France* (Baltimore: Johns Hopkins University Press, 2001).
8. Curnonsky and Marcel Rouff, *The Yellow Guides for Epicures: Paris, the Environs of Paris, and Normandy* (New York: Harper & Brothers, 1926), 15.
9. On Curnonsky, see Priscilla Parkhurst Ferguson, *Accounting for Taste: The Triumph of French Cuisine* (Chicago: University of Chicago Press, 2004); Stephen Mennell, *All Manners of Food: Eating and Taste in England and France from the Middle Ages to the Present* (New York: B. Blackwell, 1985), 276–77, 128–29, 157–58; Jean-Robert Pitte, *French Gastronomy: The History and Geography of a Passion* (New York: Columbia University Press, 2002); and Trubek, *Taste of Place*, 35–40.
10. Both Stein and Toklas allude to the *guides gastronomiques* in their memoirs. See Gertrude Stein, *The Autobiography of Alice B. Toklas* (New York: Vintage Books, 1990), 223, and Alice B. Toklas, *The Alice B. Toklas Cookbook* (New York: Harper & Row, 1984), 90, 92. Harvard University has digitized the volume of *La France Gastronomique* on "La Bresse, le Bugey, le Pays de Gex" (Paris: F. Rouff, 1921), https://iiif.lib.harvard.edu/manifests/view/drs:47309969$9i.
11. Kyla Wazana Tompkins, *Racial Indigestion: Eating Bodies in the Nineteenth Century* (New York: New York University Press, 2012), 2, 186.
12. Describing *The Sun Also Rises*, Michaels writes, "The attraction of the bullfight, then, is its utility in the construction of a race—not, to be sure, a Spanish race but rather one that is nativist American in structure and international Nordic in personnel" (*Our America*, 164n133).
13. Thomas Parker, *Tasting French Terroir: The History of an Idea* (Oakland: University of California Press, 2015), 2, 3–4.
14. Ibid., 3, emphasis in original.
15. Ibid., 8–9.
16. See Trubek, *Taste of Place*, 23; Parker, *Tasting French Terroir*, 38–40, 133–38.
17. Qtd. in Alan Sheridan, *André Gide: A Life in the Present* (Cambridge, MA: Harvard University Press, 1999), 3.
18. Benjamin H. Isaac, *The Invention of Racism in Classical Antiquity* (Princeton, NJ: Princeton University Press, 2006), 133. See also Sarah Hammerschlag, *The Figural Jew: Politics and Identity in Postwar French Thought* (Chicago: University of Chicago Press, 2010), 31–41.
19. Christy Wampole, *Rootedness: The Ramifications of a Metaphor* (Chicago: University of Chicago Press, 2016), 114. Barrè's arguments about race, culture, and land would later inspire Léopold Sédar Senghor, a prominent figure in the Négritude movement. Jacques Louis Hymans, *Léopold Sédar Senghor: An Intellectual Biography* (Edinburgh: Edinburgh University Press, 1971), 25.
20. Wampole, *Rootedness*, 112–16. Stein met Gide and had "rather a dull evening" (*Autobiography of Alice B. Toklas*, 131). Stein also reports a conversation with her close friend and later Vichy official Bernard Fäy, who said that "the three people of first rate importance that he had met in his life were Picasso, Gertrude Stein and André Gide." Stein's characteristically egoistic and withering response: "Gertrude Stein inquired quite simply, that is quite right but why include Gide" (246).
21. Parker, *Tasting French Terroir*, 9.

22. In *A Moveable Feast*, Hemingway observes that "in one place you could write about it better than in another. That was called transplanting yourself, I thought, and it could be as necessary with people as with other sorts of growing things" (5).
23. D. H. Lawrence, *Studies in Classic American Literature* (New York: Penguin Books, 1977), 119.
24. Parker, *Tasting French Terroir*, 12.
25. It is difficult if not impossible to derive a definitive list of foods imbued with terroir, perhaps because, as Matt Kramer observes, "[Terroir] sanctions what cannot be measured, yet still located and savored." Kramer, "The Notion of *Terroir*," in *Wine & Philosophy: A Symposium on Thinking and Drinking*, ed. Fritz Allhoff (Hoboken, NJ: Wiley-Blackwell, 2008), 223–34, 225. Parker assembles a list of products "marketed, conceived, and appreciated" through the lens of terroir: "wine, cheese, salt, prunes, olive oil, ham, honey, and red pepper" and "also anchovies, oysters, and mussels (whose characteristics are influenced by different areas of the sea or the '*merroir*')" (*Tasting French*, 2). Ken Albala associates terroir particularly with "fermented products." Albala, "Bacterial Fermentation and the Missing *Terroir* Factor in Historic Cookery," in *Cured, Fermented and Smoked Foods: Proceedings of the Oxford Symposium on Food and Cookery, 2010*, ed. Helen Saberi (London: Prospect Books, 2011), 30. Trubek lists "wines," "cheeses," and "charcuterie" as the characteristic regional foods of France (*Taste of Place*, 19), and in a later chapter on American terroir, she includes nuts and truffles (148–50).
26. Frank G. Carpenter, *Carpenter's Geographical Reader: Europe* (New York: American Book Company, 1912), 440–41.
27. Basil Woon, *A Guide to the Gay World of France* (New York: American Book Company, 1929), 138.
28. Roderick Peattie, *Rambles in Europe* (New York: American Book Company, 1934), 69.
29. Ibid.
30. Francis Miltoun, *Castles and Chateaux of Old Navarre and the Basque Provinces* (Boston: L. C. Page & Company, 1907), 389.
31. Katharine Waldo Douglas Fedden, *The Basque Country* (Boston: Houghton Mifflin Company, 1921), 26.
32. Ibid.
33. See Michaels's persuasive discussion of aficion and the similarities between Robert Cohn and Jake Barnes, in *Our America*, 27–28.
34. Gertrude Stein, *Everybody's Autobiography* (London: Virago, 1985), 13.
35. Ernest Hemingway, *The Sun Also Rises* (New York: Scribner's, 1954), 97. Further citations appear parenthetically in the text.
36. Fedden also notes the "astounding lunch of many courses, cooked in the Spanish style with oil and garlic and mysterious sauces" (*Basque Country*, 171).
37. On anti-Semitism in *The Sun Also Rises*, see Greg Forter, *Gender, Race, and Mourning in American Modernism* (New York: Cambridge University Press, 2011), 71–73, and Michaels, *Our America*, 72–73.
38. Raymond Williams observes that "culture in all its early uses was a noun of process: the tending *of* something, basically crops or animals." In the Romantic era, it came to "include the new concept of folk-culture" and to criticize the "'mechanical' (q.v.) character of the new civilization then emerging" (89). Williams, *Keywords: A Vocabulary of Culture and Society* (New York: Oxford University Press, 1985), 87.
39. See Sander L. Gilman on "the Jewish nose," in *The Jew's Body* (New York: Routledge, 1991), 169–93.
40. Basques were so often cited as proof of the continued existence of a pure, ancient race that William Z. Ripley devotes a whole chapter of his influential book, *The Races of Europe*, to debunking this premise. See Ripley, *The Races of Europe: A Sociological Study* (New York: D. Appleton and Company, 1899), 192–93.
41. Hemingway was not alone in his appreciation of Basque masculinity; see Fedden for a fulsome tribute to "men of typical Basque physiognomy" (*Basque Country*, 103).
42. This world-traveling Basque local also resembles the "informant" James Clifford describes in his classic essay, "Traveling Cultures": "A great many of these interlocutors, complex individuals routinely made to speak for 'cultural' knowledge, turn out to have their own 'ethnographic'

proclivities and interesting histories of travel." Clifford, "Traveling Cultures," in *Cultural Studies*, ed. Lawrence Grossberg, Cary Nelson, and Paula A. Treichler (New York: Routledge, 1992), 97.
43. Hemingway does not articulate or even acknowledge the vexed politics of Basque nationalism. This omission is particularly glaring given that the 1926 publication of *The Sun Also Rises* followed so closely on the heels of the 1923 coup in Madrid that led to the suppression of non-Spanish nationalism, including the imprisonment and exile of Basque nationalists. See Gloria Pilar Totoricagüena, *Identity, Culture, and Politics in the Basque Diaspora* (Reno: University of Nevada Press, 2004), 38.
44. See Forter, *Gender, Race, and Mourning*, 77.
45. The count speaks up for another immigrant, whose name is Zizi and whom Brett speculates is Greek, but it's unclear where they are all from or if it even matters (40). The count observes that he has fought in "seven wars and four revolutions" (66), but he doesn't seem particularly passionate about which side he was on or what it was for.
46. See Forter on the primitivism of this stereotype and its relationship to Jake's feelings of racial loss (*Gender, Race, and Mourning*, 67).
47. On anti-Greek racism in the United States, see Ioanna Laliotou, *Transatlantic Subjects: Acts of Migration and Cultures between Greece and America* (Chicago: University of Chicago Press, 2004), 185–86. See also Philip Perlmutter, *Legacy of Hate: A Short History of Ethnic, Religious, and Racial Prejudice in America* (Armonk, NY: M. E. Sharpe, 1999), 154. Nell Irvin Painter points out that "modern Greeks were said not to have descended from beautiful ancient Greeks" (316), and the white supremacist and popular novelist Kenneth Roberts deplored "damned half-negro Italians, half-Mongol Jews, and thoroughly bastardized Greeks and Levantines." Painter, *The History of White People* (New York: W. W. Norton, 2010), 316, 303.
48. Ernest Hemingway, *Death in the Afternoon* (New York: Scribner Classics, 1999), 42. For a description of Hemingway's first visit to Ronda, when he observed the statue, see Kenneth Schuyler Lynn, *Hemingway* (Cambridge, MA: Harvard University Press, 1987), 207. Ronda's mountain perch helped preserve its historical atmosphere; one travel article complained of the "steep and crooked streets—for the most part, all too steep for wheeled vehicles . . . Indeed, our consumptive omnibus was the only wheeled conveyance in town." Clara Crawford Perkins, "How We Found Ronda," *Outlook* 97 (April 22, 1911): 926.
49. Ripley, *The Races of Europe*, 128.
50. Ibid., 147.
51. Richard McMahon explains that "Ripley definitively restated the forty-year orthodoxy of the three race Europe" (134). However, Deniker's "new multi-race system became anthropological convention by the 1920s" (210). "After about 1905," McMahon observes, "few outside of the English-speaking world relied just on Ripley's three races to represent increasingly detailed and complex new regional data" (210). McMahon, *The Races of Europe: Construction of National Identities in the Social Sciences, 1839–1939* (New York: Palgrave Macmillan, 2016).
52. Hemingway, *Death in the Afternoon*, 41.
53. Ibid. This was not the only way to imagine the genealogy of Ronda's inhabitants, as Perkins's description of the "imp[ish] . . . boys of Ronda" demonstrates. She associates them with pagans and Moors: "No need of the Piper's magic flute to keep a train of them at our heels; and before the day was half over we were fully convinced that these were the lineal descendants of the daring Gomeres, who, under the leadership of the intrepid Hamet el Zegri, so long terrorized the borders of Castile and held the Christian advance at bay" ("How We Found Ronda," 926).
54. David Shuttleton, "The Queer Politics of Gay Pastoral," in *De-Centring Sexualities: Politics and Representation beyond the Metropolis*, ed. Richard Phillips, Diane West, and David Shuttleton (London: Routledge, 2000), 131.
55. Ibid., 127.
56. Forter, *Gender, Race, and Mourning*, 66.
57. Havelock Ellis, *Studies in the Psychology of Sex: Sexual Inversion* (Philadelphia: F. A. Davis Company Publishers, 1901), 29.
58. "The veritable flowers of the Pyrenees" presumably translates the server's assurance in French that the ingredients are the real thing; it also echoes the brand's slogan, "veritable liqueur Basque." Izarra, "Over Time," Izarra online, http://www.izarra.fr/en/izarra-house/over-time

59. *Vieux marc* can come from any region of France. See N. M. Penzer, "Marc, Vieux," in *The Book of the Wine-Label* (London: Home & Van Thal, 1947), 118. Picasso featured a bottle of *vieux marc* in an early collage entitled *Bottle of Vieux Marc, Glass, and Newspaper* (1913), and the Spanish painter, from Málaga, where Pedro Romero trained, spoke of bottles as "displaced object[s] that ha[ve] entered a universe for which [they were] not made and where [they] retain[ ], in a measure, [their] strangeness . . . The world was becoming very strange and not exactly reassuring." Qtd. in Katherine Hoffman, ed., *Collage: Critical Views (Studies in the Fine Arts Criticism)* (Ann Arbor, MI: UMI Research Press, 1989), 7. In *The Sun Also Rises*, both the *vieux marc* and Jake's body are displaced objects.
60. Ernest Hemingway, *The Sun Also Rises: The Hemingway Library Edition*, appendix II (New York: Scribner's, 2014), 258.
61. John Milton, *Milton's "Comus,"* ed. William Bell (London: Macmillan and Company, 1907), 8.
62. W. Grant Hague, *The Eugenic Mother and Baby: A Complete Home Guide* (New York City: Hague Publishing Co., 1913), 276.
63. See Nicole Rafter on gluttony and degeneration. Rafter, "The Criminalization of Mental Retardation," in *Perpetual Children*, ed. Steven Noll and James Trend (New York: New York University Press, 2004), 234. Perhaps Jake would do better in a clean, well-lighted place.
64. Ernest Hemingway, *A Farewell to Arms* (New York: Scribner, 1995), 8. Further citations appear parenthetically in the text. This region of Italy is now more commonly known as "Abruzzo" than "the Abruzzi."
65. This idealization of Capracotta seems to reflect Hemingway's own sentiments. He wrote in a 1921 letter that Capracotta was the "most wonderful place you ever heard of." Lynn, *Hemingway*, 136.
66. Ruth Levitas, *The Concept of Utopia* (New York: Peter Lang, 1990), 2–3.
67. In an oft-quoted line, Hemingway contends that "the dignity of movement of an ice-berg is due to only one-eighth of it being above water." His celebration of high-altitude chill elsewhere in his writing suggests that some of its dignity, and its metaphorical applicability to his style, may come from its icy solidity. Hemingway, *Death in the Afternoon*, 154.
68. Contemporaneous geographers promoted this thesis of Abruzzian purity and virtue as well. Ellen Churchill Semple praises the "terrace cultivation" of the Apennines, which "involv[es] an immense expenditure of labor" and has thus "produced in Italy a class of superior gardeners" (128). She derides "the less civilized mountain races, whose tastes or low economic status unfit them for emigration" (130). The Italians and other European mountain folk, Semple opines, "are characterized by habits of industry and frugality" (131). Semple, "A Study in Human Geography: Mountain Peoples in Relation to Their Soil," *Geographical Teacher* 3, no. 3 (1905): 128–31.
69. George E. Walsh, "The Chestnut Farms of Italy," *Interior* 30 (November 2, 1899): 1366.
70. See Emile Gentile, *The Struggle for Modernity: Nationalism, Futurism, and Fascism* (Westport, CT: Praeger, 2003).
71. Thomas A. Guglielmo, *White on Arrival: Italians, Race, Color, and Power in Chicago, 1890–1945* (New York: Oxford University Press), 22.
72. Ibid. On Niceforo's ideas about the Italian South and nation, see John Dickie, *Darkest Italy: The Nation and Stereotypes of the Mezzogiorno, 1860–1900* (New York: St. Martin's Press, 1999), 2–4.
73. On Isonzo, see John Gooch, *The Italian Army and the First World War* (Cambridge: Cambridge University Press, 2014), 99–100.
74. Reginald John Farrer, *The Void of War: Letters from Three Fronts* (Boston: Houghton Mifflin, 1918), 241.
75. This impression of senseless sacrifice was widely held by the Italian soldiers: "For the rural peasantry who provided the army with its largest numerical component, there was no commanding moral cause behind the nation's mobilisation for war" (Gooch, *The Italian Army*, 102).
76. Parker points out that the word "terroir" "derives from the Latin *territorium*, signifying the land round a town, that is, a domain, district or territory" (*Tasting French Terroir*, 5). *Territorium* carries military and imperial connotations. As the classical historian Pat Southern explains, "Roman auxiliary forts and legionary fortresses were surrounded by clearly demarcated lands that were owned and administered by the army, usually designated by the terms *prata* and

territorium." Southern, *The Roman Army: A Social and Institutional History* (New York: Oxford University Press, 2007), 113. The word that now champions local, place-based flavor has a direct etymological relationship to the expansion of territory. Though Hemingway doesn't use either word, he explores the tension between the greed for land that fuels military conflict and the intimacy with the land that can be the soldier's experience.

77. Perhaps the most influential gastronomic writer in Italy, Pellegrino Artusi, featured the foods of the North in his heralded *Scienza in cucina* (1891). Alberto Capatti and Massimo Montanari, *Italian Cuisine: A Cultural History*, trans. Aine O'Healy (New York: Columbia University Press, 2003), 26–27.
78. On "monkey meat," see Susanne Freidberg, *Fresh: A Perishable History* (Cambridge, MA: Harvard University Press, 2010), 81–82, and Lauren Janes, *Colonial Food in Interwar Paris* (New York: Bloomsbury, 2016), 37–40.
79. All of these ingredients are featured in Artusi's guide to Italian cuisine. See Pellegrino Artusi, *Science in the Kitchen and the Art of Eating Well*, trans. Murtha Baca and Stephen Sartarelli (Toronto: University of Toronto Press, 2003).
80. Imola is in Emilia-Romagna, one of the two regions of Italy that provides "the basic axis of [Artusi's] cuisine" (Capatti and Montanari, *Italian Cuisine*, 27).
81. The Italian army experienced notorious problems getting food to the troops. See Gooch, *The Italian Army*, 118, 142.
82. See John Robert Bittner (completed and revised by Joseph M. Flora), "Anti-Fascist Symbols and Subtexts in *A Farewell to Arms*: Hemingway, Mussolini, and Journalism in the 1920s," in *Hemingway's Italy: New Perspectives*, ed. Rena Sanderson (Baton Rouge: Louisiana State University, 2006), 100–102.
83. On war as dysgenic, see Jonathan Peter Spiro, *Defending the Master Race: Conservation, Eugenics, and the Legacy of Madison Grant* (Burlington: University of Vermont Press, 2009), 149, and Michaels, *Our America*, 29.
84. Madison Grant, *The Passing of the Great Race; or, the Racial Basis of European History* (New York: Charles Scribner's Sons, 1916), 197.
85. Rinaldi teases Frederic that his hygiene rituals reflect his racial aspirations: "I will wait till I see the Anglo-Saxon brushing away harlotry with a toothbrush" (168). Though Rinaldi is kidding, his quip reveals the casual association of mundane biopolitics and race.
86. Ripley, *The Races of Europe*, 281.
87. Ibid., 289.
88. On sterility and racial purity in Hemingway's work, including *A Farewell to Arms*, see Michaels, *Our America*, 95–96.
89. Stein would not be the last feminist to take up gleaning as a figure for artistry and a perspective for social critique. See Agnès Varda, *The Gleaners and I* (London: Artificial Eye, 2009).
90. See Raj Patel and Jason W. Moore, *A History of the World in Seven Cheap Things: A Guide to Capitalism, Nature, and the Future of the Planet* (Oakland: University of California Press, 2017), 119.
91. Theresa M. Kelley, *Clandestine Marriage: Botany and Romantic Culture* (Baltimore: Johns Hopkins University Press, 2012), 141–43.
92. Ibid., 143.
93. See Julia Kristeva, *Strangers to Ourselves* (New York: Columbia University Press, 1991), 65–76, and Cynthia Ozick, "Ruth," in *Reading Ruth: Contemporary Women Reclaim a Sacred Story*, ed. Judith A. Kates and Gail Twersky Reimer (New York: Random House, 1994), 211–32.
94. Bonnie Honig, *Democracy and the Foreigner* (Princeton, NJ: Princeton University Press, 2001), 71.
95. Alexandra R. Murphy observes that "Millet had been fascinated by the issue of gleaning. Since arriving at Barbizon, he seems not to have wanted to relinquish the theme until he understood all the social and economic complexities that underlay the plight of the figures he kept drawing so carefully . . . Millet underscored the uneasy relation between large-scale, commercialized farming—seen in the far distance—and the local workers it left unemployed who, marginalized in life, take center stage in Millet's composition." Murphy, *Jean-François Millet: Drawn into the Light* (New Haven, CT: Yale University Press, 1999), 21; Jean-François Millet, *Harvesters Resting (Ruth and Boaz)*, oil on canvas, 1853, Museum of Fine Arts, Boston, http://www.mfa.org/collections/object/harvesters-resting-ruth-and-boaz-31288.

96. Murphy, *Jean-François Millet*, 17.
97. Ibid., 20–21.
98. On gleaning as a bone of contention after the French Revolution, see P. M. Jones, *The Peasantry in the French Revolution* (Cambridge: Cambridge University Press, 1988), 19, 127–33.
99. In her consideration of John Clare's poetry and its view of the commons through botanical figures, Kelley offers a suggestive definition of what she calls "commonability," an issue at stake in Stein's work as well: "As a set of relationships among individuals, particulars, and a collective idea of land use, commonability addresses questions about how to align individuals with states, abstract principles, or whatever larger system is said to supervise or speak for individuals . . . sorting out how being singular also means being plural is the unyielding dilemma at work in thinking about individuals and particulars as part of or outside a community" (*Clandestine Marriage*, 142).
100. Gertrude Stein, *Geography and Plays* (Boston: Four Seas Company, 1922), 117. Further citations appear parenthetically in the text.
101. Obscure definitions are a hallmark of Stein's style, as Brian Glavey observes: "A little more than kin and less than kind, Stein's indeterminacies are frequently grounded in definitions . . . Such definitions invoke a mimetic relationship and empty it out in the same stroke, playing identity and difference off of one another." Glavey, *The Wallflower Avant-Garde: Modernism, Sexuality, and Queer Ekphrasis* (New York: Oxford University Press, 2015), 30. Robert Alter also points out that Stein "exhibited a fondness for chains of parallel utterances linked by 'and' in which the basic sentence-type is the same structurally as that used again and again in biblical prose." *Genesis*, trans. and commentary by Robert Alter (New York: W. W. Norton, 1996), xviii.
102. Exod. 21:18 (AV), emphasis in original.
103. Exod. 16:4 (AV).
104. Honig argues that "Ruth replays the script" of Moses as a foreign leader to the Jewish people: "This is a repetition with a difference: Ruth is seen to model a relation to the law that is one of loving choice, not violent submission" (*Democracy and the Foreigner*, 59).
105. Exod. 16:18 (AV).
106. Lev. 19:9–10 (AV), emphasis in original.
107. The contrast between "choosing" and "descending" anticipates Werner Sollors's argument that the tension between "consent" and "descent" animates the US racial imaginary. See Sollors, *Beyond Ethnicity: Consent and Descent in American Culture* (New York: Oxford University Press, 1986), 4–5.
108. Jessica Berman argues that writers of "the Left Bank who were privileged enough to feel themselves to exist without boundaries" nonetheless often made "an intense effort to specify the location and limitation of that cosmopolitanism." In Stein's model, "the local community colors, shapes, and constrains the ways the world can be imagined." Berman, *Modernist Fiction, Cosmopolitanism, and the Politics of Community* (New York: Cambridge University Press, 2006), 27.
109. Stein's ideal of cosmopolitan ruralism (or rural cosmopolitanism) might seem surprising but reflects a common aspiration of her age. See Sollors on wholesome provincialism; Berman on shifting communities; and Posmentier on rural cosmopolitanism. Sollors, *Beyond Ethnicity*, 174–207; Berman, *Modernist Fiction, Cosmopolitanism*, 197–98; Sonya Posmentier, "The Provision Ground in New York: Claude McKay and the Form of Memory," *American Literature* 84, no. 2 (2012): 274–75.
110. Gertrude Stein, *Paris France* (New York: Liveright, 2013), 7. Further citations appear parenthetically in the text.
111. David Starr Jordan, *The Blood of the Nation: A Study of the Decay of Races Through the Survival of the Unfit* (Boston: American Unitarian Association, 1903), 33.
112. Ibid., 22. Jordan, a famous ichthyologist, was a subject of conversation in Stein's *Autobiography of Alice B. Toklas* (145).
113. Robert L. Herbert, *From Millet to Léger: Essays in Social Art History* (New Haven, CT: Yale University Press, 2002), 50.
114. According to Ripley, their "pleasing landscapes and quaint customs" provide a backdrop for "an ethnic struggle in progress" that "[depends] upon the topography of the country" (*The Races of Europe*, 150).

115. As Sarah Warren observes, "Gauguin may have found 'savagery' in the Breton countryside, but the Breton peasant was 'savage' in her primitive piety and Christianity. The frank sexuality of Gauguin's Tahitians (who were, after all, also Christians) would not have been possible in his representations of women in traditional Breton costume." Warren, *Mikhail Larionov and the Cultural Politics of Late Imperial Russia* (New York: Routledge, 2013), 28. On Breton piety and primitivism, see also Gill Perry, "Primitivism and the 'Modern,'" in *Primitivism, Cubism, Abstraction: The Early Twentieth Century*, ed. Charles Harrison, Francis Frascina, and Gill Perry (New Haven, CT: Yale University Press, 1993), 10–27.
116. Mark Kurlansky, *The Basque History of the World* (New York: Penguin, 2001), 212.
117. Ibid.
118. In their memoirs of the period, both Stein and Toklas mention a Breton servant named Jeanne. Stein, *Autobiography of Alice B. Toklas*, 165–66 and Toklas, *The Alice B. Toklas Cookbook*, 180–83.
119. The French use "Breton" to describe the residents of Brittany. It is not clear why Stein uses "Briton" in "Advertisements"; she uses "Breton" in *The Autobiography of Alice B. Toklas*. "Briton" can refer to Celtic people in France or England, so it is possible that Stein means to underscore the ethnic designation rather than mere regionalism. See "Breton, n. and adj.," *OED* online, December 2016, Oxford University Press, http://www.oed.com/view/Entry/23092?redirectedFrom=Breton See also "Briton, n. and adj.," *OED* online, December 2016, Oxford University Press, http://www.oed.com/view/Entry/23468?redirectedFrom=briton
120. Stein may allude here to the sixteenth-century French poet Du Bellay, whose collection *L'Olive* (1549) celebrates his homeland Anjou, then a part of Brittany. The olive tree serves as a metaphor for his lady love, who in turn embodies the region. See Louisa Mackenzie, *The Poetry of Place: Lyric, Landscape, and Ideology in Renaissance France* (Toronto: University of Toronto Press, 2011), 55–58.
121. Ulla E. Dydo, *Gertrude Stein: The Language That Rises, 1923–1934* (Evanston, IL: Northwestern University Press, 2008), 328–29.
122. Anna Lowenhaupt Tsing, "Unruly Edges: Mushrooms as Companion Species," *Environmental Humanities* 1 (2012): 142. On contemporary mushroom hunting, see Nicholas Money, *Mr. Bloomfield's Orchard: The Mysterious World of Mushrooms, Molds, and Mycologists* (New York: Oxford University Press, 2002); Gary Alan Fine, *Morel Tales: The Culture of Mushrooming* (Cambridge, MA: Harvard University Press, 1998); Langdon Cook, *The Mushroom Hunters: On the Trail of an Underground America* (New York: Ballantine Books, 2013); and Anna Lowenhaupt Tsing, *Mushroom at the End of the World: On the Possibility of Life in Capitalist Ruins* (Princeton, NJ: Princeton University Press, 2015).
123. Tsing writes, "the best way to find mushrooms is always to return to the places you found them before . . . Foraging worked just this way for most of human history. To find a useful plant, animal, or fungus, foragers learned familiar places and returned to them again and again" ("Unruly Edges" 142). Of Stein's claim that she never repeated herself in the famously repetitive *The Making of Americans*, Joshua Miller opines: "Stein's demonstration that no two speech acts can be identical repetitions multiplies meaning within recursive passages that demand attentive reading to perceive slight changes in rhythmically cyclical phrases." Miller, *Accented America: The Cultural Politics of Multilingual Modernism* (New York: Oxford University Press, 2011), 151.
124. Sigmund Freud, *Interpretation of Dreams*, ed. Ritchie Robertson, trans. Joyce Crick (New York: Oxford World's Classics, 2008), 341.
125. Joshua Schuster, *The Ecology of Modernism: American Environments and Avant-Garde Poetics* (Tuscaloosa: University of Alabama Press, 2015), 47–48.
126. Ibid., 48.
127. Ibid., 49.
128. Gertrude Stein, *History or Messages from History*, in *Gertrude Stein: Selections*, ed. Joan Retallack (Berkeley: University of California Press, 2008), 263. Further citations appear parenthetically in the text.

129. Mushroom hunting also figured in immigrant fiction. In Michael Gold's *Jews Without Money* (1930), an otherwise relentless exposé of brutal urban conditions, the one pastoral interlude comes when the Hungarian peasant mother leads her children on a mushrooming expedition through the Bronx Park. Gold, *Jews Without Money* (New York: International Publishers, 1930), 149–55.
130. Charles Baudelaire, *The Prose Poems and "La Fanfarlo,"* trans. Rosemary Lloyd (New York: Oxford World's Classics, 2001), 24.
131. D. H. Lawrence, *Sons and Lovers* (New York: Mitchell Kennerley, 1913), 86.
132. Alfred Kreymborg, *Mushrooms: A Book of Free Forms* (New York: John Marshall Co., Ltd., 1916).
133. Willa Cather, *My Ántonia* (New York: Bantam Classics, 2005), 56.
134. Sylvia Townsend Warner, "After my wedding-night," in *Gender in Modernism: New Geographies, Complex Intersections*, ed. Bonnie Kime Scott (Urbana: University of Illinois Press, 2007), 329. Further citations appear parenthetically in the text.
135. On fairy rings, see Nicholas Money, *Mushrooms: A Natural and Cultural History* (London: Reaktion Books, 2017), 16–17. Whitney Chadwick and Tirza True Latimer point out, "In France, lesbianism, too, had foreign associations. If not universally perceived as a foreigner in the most literal sense of the word, the lesbian as a rhetorical figure often took the form of an outsider, an intruder, an infiltrator, or an invader. In everyday speech, words like *sapphist, lesbian,* and *amazon* (a euphemism for the virile woman) all pointed to origins distant in both time and space, as did the cliché defining feminism as the Trojan horse of lesbianism" (13). They refer to a popular French play, *La Prisonnière* (1926), which laid out the threat of lesbians hiding in plain sight: "Under the cover of friendship, she [the lesbian] wrecks [sic] havoc everywhere ... [through] a secret alliance between two beings who understand each other, who divine each other's needs, because they are alike, because they are of the same sex" (13). Whitney Chadwick and Tirza Latimer, "Becoming Modern: Gender and Sexual Identity after World War I," in *The Modern Woman Revisited: Paris Between the Wars*, ed. Whitney Chadwick and Tirza True Latimer (New Brunswick, NJ: Rutgers University Press, 2003).
136. Gertrude Stein, *Lucy Church Amiably* (McLean, IL: Dalkey Archive Press, 2000). Further citations appear parenthetically in the text. Stein also mentions other foraged foods in *Lucy Church Amiably*, including "honey perfumed by accacia [sic]" and "the blackening of grapes and blackberries" (123, 98).
137. Stein scholars note the correspondence between landscape immersion in *Lucy Church Amiably* and the evacuation of narrative progression. See Dydo, *Gertrude Stein*, 204, and Jennifer Ashton, *From Modernism to Postmodernism: American Poetry and Theory in the Twentieth Century* (Cambridge: Cambridge University Press, 2008), 57–58.
138. Money, *Mushrooms*, 123.
139. Elizabeth Freeman, *Time Binds: Queer Temporalities, Queer Histories* (Durham, NC: Duke University Press, 2010), 95.
140. "Erotohistoriography admits that contact with historical materials can be precipitated by particular bodily dispositions, and that these connections may elicit bodily responses, even pleasurable ones, that are themselves a form of understanding. It sees the body as a method, and historical consciousness as something intimately involved with corporeal sensations" (ibid., 95–96). Freeman singles out eating as a potentially "queer social practice ... involving enjoyable bodily sensations" that can "intervene into the material damage done in the name of development, civilization, and so on" (120).
141. On queer ecologies, see Catriona Mortimer-Sandilands and Bruce Erickson, "Introduction," *Queer Ecologies: Sex, Nature, Politics, Desire* (Bloomington: Indiana University Press, 2010), 5.
142. Money writes evocatively of this process in his work on mushrooms: "The decomposition of human artefacts by fungi highlights the fact of our inescapable participation in the carbon cycle. Everything that we manufacture from natural products ... will be broken down, eventually, into carbon dioxide and water by fungi and other micro-organisms ... A foray in the woods after rainfall to look at the fungi that live by decomposition can, with a little reflection, become a life-affirming experience" (Money, *Mushrooms*, 130).

143. Ibid., 114.
144. The US Department of Agriculture described the meadow mushroom, *Agaricus campestris*, as "fleshy" and "white" upon its first appearance, its "gills . . . a beautiful pink in color. It has an enticing fragrance, and the white flesh is sometimes inclined to turn to pink when broken. It grows in open grassy places, in fields and rich pastures, but never in thick woods." *Report of the Commissioner of Agriculture* (Washington, DC: Government Printing Office, 1885), 104.
145. See Sandra M. Gilbert on tender buttons as mushrooms, nipples, and clitoris. Gilbert, *The Culinary Imagination: From Myth to Modernity* (New York: W. W. Norton, 2014), 133.
146. In *The Story-Book of Science* (1917), a group of children ask their scientist uncle how these "perfect circles" could exist in nature, and their uncle explains that "the mycelium spreads equally on all sides, and so produces circular groups of mushrooms, which the country people sometimes call witches' circles" (315). He reassures the children that there are no witches. Jean-Henri Fabre, *The Story-Book of Science* (New York: Century Co., 1917).
147. See Susan Lanser, *The Sexuality of History: Modernity and the Sapphic, 1565–1830* (Chicago: University of Chicago Press, 2014), 68–69, and Lyndal Roper, *Witch Craze: Terror and Fantasy in Baroque Germany* (New Haven, CT: Yale University Press, 2004), 127–78.
148. Gertrude Stein, *Civilization: A Play in Three Acts*, in *The Gertrude Stein Reader: The Great American Pioneer of Avant-Garde Letters*, ed. Richard Kostelanetz (New York: Cooper Square Press, 2002), 323.
149. Spiro, *Defending the Master Race*, 376.
150. See Claudia Koonz, *The Nazi Conscience* (Cambridge, MA: Harvard University Press, 2003), 150.
151. I draw the idea of "queer celibacy" from Benjamin Kahan's excellent book, *Celibacies: American Modernism & Sexual Life* (Durham, NC: Duke University Press, 2013). On celibacy and race suicide, see 16.
152. M. F. K. Fisher, "Introduction," *Alice B. Toklas Cookbook*, xii.
153. Virginia Woolf, "The Duchess and the Jeweller," in *The Complete Shorter Fiction of Virginia Woolf*, ed. Susan Dick (London: Hogarth Press, 1985), 249.
154. Laurence Madeline, ed., *Correspondence: Pablo Picasso, Gertrude Stein* (New York: Seagull Books, 2005), 331.
155. Stein to Wilder, October 10, 1936, in *The Letters of Gertrude Stein and Thornton Wilder*, ed. Edward Burns and Ulla E. Dydo (New Haven, CT: Yale University Press, 1996), 117.
156. George J. Leonard, *Into the Light of Things: The Art of the Commonplace from Wordsworth to John Cage* (Chicago: University of Chicago Press, 1994), 118.
157. Toklas, *The Alice B. Toklas Cookbook*, 85.
158. See Peter Messent, "Food and Drink," in *Ernest Hemingway in Context*, ed. Debra A. Moddelmog and Suzanne Del Gizzo (New York: Cambridge University Press, 2013), 259–60.
159. Ernest Hemingway, "Wine of Wyoming," in *The Complete Short Stories of Ernest Hemingway: The Finca Vigía Edition* (New York: Scribner, 1987), 353. Further citations appear parenthetically in the text.
160. The Basque country was also well known for its "rusty red soil." Francis Miltoun, *Castles and Chateaux of Old Navarre and the Basque Provinces* (Boston: L. C. Page & Company, 1907), 389.
161. An *American Guide Book to France and Its Battlefields* (1920) observes that the ruins of the city are "pathetic reminders of the crushing destructiveness of war. The buildings, the homes, the churches are crushed; everything in fact, except the spirit of the people who lived there." E. B. Garey, O. O. Ellis, Ralph Van Deman Magoffin, *American Guide Book to France and Its Battlefields* (New York: Macmillan, 1920), 127.
162. On the stereotype of the fat squaw, see Rayna Green, "The Pocahontas Perplex: The Image of Indian Women in American Culture," *Massachusetts Review* 16, no. 4 (Autumn 1975): 711–12. On the denigration of indigenous diets, including beans, see Julia McCrossin, "The Fat of the (Border)land," in *The Fat Studies Reader*, ed. Esther Rothblum and Sondra Solovay (New York: New York University Press, 2009), 243.

163. As Alexandra Stern and Jonathan Spiro point out, early conservationists often also espoused eugenics, both movements "attempts to save as much as possible of the old America," in the words of Madison Grant. Qtd. in Spiro, *Defending the Master Race*, xiii. For more on eugenics and conservation, see *Defending the Master Race*, 67–72, and Alexandra Minna Stern, *Eugenic Nation: Faults and Frontiers of Better Breeding in Modern America* (Berkeley: University of California Press, 2005), 121–25.
164. On Stein's late-career conservatism, see Schuster, *The Ecology of Modernism*, 75–76. On Stein and the Vichy regime, see Janet Malcolm, *Two Lives: Gertrude and Alice* (New Haven, CT: Yale University Press, 2007), and Barbara Will, *Unlikely Collaboration: Gertrude Stein, Bernard Fäy, and the Vichy Dilemma* (New York: Columbia University Press, 2011).
165. Schuster, *Ecology of Modernism*, 75.
166. Retallack, "Introduction," *Gertrude Stein: Selections*, 67.
167. Qtd. in Annalisa Zox-Weaver, *Women Modernists and Fascism* (New York: Cambridge University Press, 2011), 94.
168. Gertrude Stein, "The Winner Loses: A Picture of Occupied France," *Atlantic Monthly*, November 1940, 571. Historian Lizzie Collingham points out that rural France did have more and better food during the war. Collingham, *The Taste of War: World War II and the Battle for Food* (New York: Penguin Press, 2012), 163.
169. On Stein's ambivalence about her Jewishness and the distressing politics of "The Winner Loses," see Will, *Unlikely Collaboration*, 74–75, 103–105.
170. Gopnik, Introduction to *Paris France*, xiii.
171. In fact, Stein and Toklas were friends with Madame Marie Bourgeois. James Mellow, *Charmed Circle: Gertrude Stein and Company* (New York: Henry Holt, 1974), 315.
172. Gopnik observes that "'civilisation' . . . is the key word in her book, the one that appears most often and stands for an idea at once fundamental and diffuse" (introduction to *Paris France*, xiii). Gopnik does not mean "race," though his phrasing is beautifully apposite for the contradictions of this concept that has weighed so heavily on the twentieth and now the twenty-first centuries. As Forter sagely observes: "The category of race is rarely far away when 'civilization' is at stake" (*Gender, Race* 66).
173. Sir Francis Rose, *Gertrude Stein at Bilignin*, in *Paris France*, by Gertrude Stein (London: B. T. Batsford, 1940).

Chapter 4

1. Claude McKay, *Banjo: A Novel* (Fort Washington, PA: Harvest Books, 1979), 67. Further citations appear parenthetically in the text.
2. On the significance of dialect and its relationship to hunger in McKay's work, see Michael North, *The Dialect of Modernism: Race, Language, and Twentieth-Century Literature* (New York: Oxford University Press, 1994), 100–23.
3. On homosociality and the significance of the sea in *Banjo*, see Michelle Ann Stephens, *Black Empire: The Black Global Imaginary of Caribbean Intellectuals in the United States (1914–1962)* (Durham, NC: Duke University Press, 2005), 177–203.
4. See Wayne F. Cooper, *Claude McKay, Rebel Sojourner in the Harlem Renaissance: A Biography* (Baton Rouge: Louisiana State University Press, 1987), 246.
5. F. Scott Fitzgerald, *Tender Is the Night* (New York: Scribner's, 1995), 15. Further citations appear parenthetically in the text.
6. See Kenelm Winslow, *The Production and Handling of Clean Milk* (New York: William R. Jenkins Co., 1907), 18; George M. Kober, "Abnormal Milk and Milk-Borne Diseases," Statement before the Committee on Agriculture, US House of Representatives, Tuesday, January 14, 1902, 135.
7. A. M. Garance, "About Laundry Blues," *American Soap Journal and Perfume Gazette: A Monthly Journal of the Soap, Candle, Perfume, and Fat Industries*, July 1, 1897, 128–30.
8. Lothrop Stoddard, *The Rising Tide of Color Against White World-Supremacy* (New York: Charles Scribner's Sons, 1921).

9. Several critics have addressed the racial paranoia central to *Tender Is the Night*: Mark Goble, *Beautiful Circuits: Modernism and the Mediated Life* (New York: Columbia University Press, 2010), 207–18; Chris Messenger, "'Out upon the Mongolian Plain': Fitzgerald's Racial and Ethnic Cross-Identifying in *Tender Is the Night*," in *Twenty-First-Century Readings of "Tender Is the Night*," ed. William Blazek and Laura Rattray (Liverpool: Liverpool University Press, 2007), 160–76; Michael North, *Camera Works: Photography and the Twentieth-Century Word* (New York: Oxford University Press, 2005), 135–39; Michael Nowlin, *F. Scott Fitzgerald's Racial Angles and the Business of Literary Greatness* (New York: Palgrave Macmillan, 2007), 85–122; and Felipe Smith, "The Figure on the Bed: Difference and American Destiny in *Tender Is the Night*," in *French Connections: Hemingway and Fitzgerald Abroad*, ed. Gerald Kennedy and Jackson R. Bryer (New York: St. Martin's, 1999), 187–213.

10. Goble points out that popular song often communicates racial meaning in Fitzgerald's work (*Beautiful Circuits*, 199).

11. On the geographical concept of climate zones and its racial dimensions, see Gary Y. Okihiro, *Pineapple Culture: A History of the Tropical and Temperate Zones* (Berkeley: University of California Press, 2009), 5–25.

12. William Z. Ripley, *The Races of Europe: A Sociological Study* (New York: D. Appleton and Company, 1899). Madison Grant scoffed at Ripley's climatological explanations but accepted his classifications, following Deniker in substituting Nordic for Teutonic. Nigel Eltringham, "'Nordics' and 'Hamites': Joseph Deniker and the Rise (and Fall) of Scientific Racism," in *Ideas of "Race" in the History of the Humanities*, ed. Amos Morris-Reich and Dirk Rupnow (New York: Palgrave Macmillan, 2017), 264.

13. Ripley, *The Races of Europe*, 128–29.

14. Qtd. in Catherine Cocks, *Tropical Whites: The Rise of the Tourist South in the Americas* (Philadelphia: University of Pennsylvania Press, 2013), 20. Original quotation found in Ellen Churchill Semple, *Influences of Geographic Environment on the Basis of Ratzel's System of Anthropo-Geography* (New York: Henry Holt, 1911), 10.

15. Grant conjectured that "heavy, healthful work in the fields of northern Europe enables the Nordic type to thrive, but the cramped factory and crowded city quickly weeds him out, while the little brunet Mediterranean can work a spindle, set type, sell ribbons, or push a clerk's pen far better than the big, clumsy, and somewhat heavy Nordic blond, who needs exercise, meat, and air, and cannot live under Ghetto conditions." Madison Grant, *The Passing of the Great Race or The Racial Basis of European History* (New York: Charles Scribner's Sons, 1916), 186. Further citations appear parenthetically in the text.

16. F. Scott Fitzgerald to Edmund Wilson, July 1921, in *A Life in Letters: F. Scott Fitzgerald*, ed. Matthew J. Bruccoli (New York: Macmillan, 1994), 46–47.

17. On Fitzgerald's anxiety about Mediterranean men, see Jeffory A. Clymer, "'Mr. Nobody from Nowhere': Rudolph Valentino, Jay Gatsby, and the End of the American Race," *Genre: Forms of Discourse and Culture* 29, nos. 1–2 (1996): 161–92.

18. Recent studies of the US South and the Mediterranean contextualize these regions in a global imaginary of "the South." For an overview of this development in US Southern Studies, see Kathryn McKee and Annette Trefzer, "Preface: Global Contexts, Local Literatures: The New Southern Studies," *American Literature* 78, no. 4 (December 2006): 677–90. On the Mediterranean, see Franco Cassano, *"Southern Thought" and Other Essays on the Mediterranean*, ed. and trans. Norma Bouchard and Valerio Ferme (New York: Fordham University Press, 2012), and Iain Chambers, *Mediterranean Crossings: The Politics of an Interrupted Modernity* (Durham, NC: Duke University Press, 2008).

19. W. E. B. Du Bois, *W. E. B. Du Bois: Selections from His Writings*, ed. Bob Blaisdell (New York: Dover Publications, 2014), 171.

20. Stoddard, *The Rising Tide of Color*, 232.

21. Edward M. East, *Mankind at the Crossroads* (New York: Scribner, 1923), 64. Further citations appear parenthetically in the text. East, Grant, and Fitzgerald shared the same publisher. On East and his Malthusian views, see Warren Belasco, *Meals to Come: A History of the Future of Food* (Berkeley: University of California Press, 2006), 29–32.

22. On the climatological implications of bread advocacy, see Kyla Wazana Tompkins, *Racial Indigestion: Eating Bodies in the Nineteenth Century* (New York: New York University Press, 2012), 60–63.

23. Because the droplets in vapor could not be measured, one book summarizing scientific theory for a popular audience recommended using liquid infusions to demonstrate a parallel relationship: "Take a cupful of some dark-colored liquid, such as coffee or China ink, dissolved in water; warm it, and place it in the sun's rays: if the air be still, the vapor will ascend and soon disappear; if looked at through the glass, it will be seen that globules are rising" (364). It is suggestive, in my view, that the "dark-colored liquid[s]" come from the tropics and the Orient respectively. Color makes the relationship between intermixed substances visible. Mist, on the other hand, evades inspection, as the author ruefully concludes:

> De Saussure and Kratzenstein attempted to measure by aid of microscope the diameter of the vesicles which compose the vapor of water. But it is difficult to arrive at any positive result, for it is the vesicles rising from mist, and not those from hot water, which it is necessary to measure. Fortunately, some of the optical phenomena which occur, when the sun shines through clouds, furnish us with a means of arriving at this result. (364)

Camille Flammarion, *The Atmosphere that which Gives Life to the Earth and by which Everything has its Being an Ethereal Sea that Covers the Whole World*, ed. James Glaisher, trans. C. B. Pitman (New York: Drallop Publishing Company, 1873).

24. Darieck Scott, *Extravagant Abjection: Blackness, Power, and Sexuality in the African American Literary Imagination* (New York: New York University Press, 2010), 12; emphasis in original.

25. Zelda Fitzgerald, *The Collected Writings of Zelda Fitzgerald*, ed. Matthew J. Bruccoli (Tuscaloosa: University of Alabama Press, 1991), 10. Even when she hardens her muscles through balletic training, Alabama views her body as black and compares its form to a tribal fetish: "By springtime, she was gladly, savagely proud of the strength of her Negroid hips, convex as boats in a wood carving" (127). Further citations appear parenthetically in the text.

26. On imperialism and addictive substances, see Wolfgang Schivelbusch, *The Tastes of Paradise: A Social History of Spices, Stimulants, and Intoxicants*, trans. David Jacobson (New York: Vintage Books, 1993).

27. John Keats, "Ode to a Nightingale," in *John Keats: The Complete Poems*, ed. John Barnard (New York: Penguin Classics, 1988), 346.

28. Richard Dyer, *White* (New York: Routledge, 1997), 122.

29. Fitzgerald conflates the flush of lighting and of drinking in his description of another party guest: "A gracious table light, emanating from a bowl of spicy pinks, fell upon Mrs. Abrams' face, cooked to a turn in Veuve Cliquot" (33).

30. In *The Sun Also Rises* (1926), Hemingway jokes about the gendered messages regarding the dangers of caffeine: "Coffee is good for you. It's the caffeine in it. Caffeine, we are here. Caffeine puts a man on her horse and a woman in his grave." Ernest Hemingway, *The Sun Also Rises* (New York: Charles Scribner's Sons, 1954), 120.

31. Robert Coughlin, "The Use and Abuse of Coffee," *New York Medical Journal: Incorporating the Philadelphia Medical Journal and the Medical News, A Weekly Review of Medicine* 94 (New York: A. R. Elliott Publishing Company, 1911), 283.

32. Ibid., 283–84.

33. Ibid., 285.

34. John Harvey Kellogg, *The New Dietetics: What to Eat and How: A Guide to Scientific Feeding in Health and Disease* (Battle Creek, MI: Modern Medicine Publishing Co., 1921), 459.

35. William S. Sadler, *Race Decadence: An Examination of the Causes of Racial Degeneracy in the United States* (Chicago: A. C. McClurg & Company, 1922), 65.

36. The eugenicist William Josephus Robinson claimed that it was a "weakened constitution or degeneracy which is generally responsible for the development of the drug addiction" (226). He also advised readers, particularly pregnant women, against drinking coffee. Robinson, *Woman: Her Sex and Love Life*, 7th ed. (New York: Cosmopolis Press, 1922), 96.

37. Sylvia Wynter locates the invention of race in the colonial encounter and underscores the extension of this logic and hierarchy into the twentieth century:

> The new symbolic construct was that of "race." Its essentially Christian-heretical positioning of the *nonhomogeneity of the human species* was to provide the basis for new metaphysical notions of order. Those notions provided the foundations of the post-1492 polities of the Caribbean and the Americas, which, if in a new variant, continue

to be legitimated by the nineteenth-century colonial systems of Western Europe, as well as the continuing hierarchies of our present global order.

Wynter, "1492: A New World View," in *Race, Discourse, and the Origin of the Americas: A New World View*, ed. Vera Lawrence Hyatt and Rex Nettleford (Washington, DC: Smithsonian Institution Press, 1995), 34 (emphasis in original).

38. On the topsy-turvy doll and the notion of racial reversal, see Robin Bernstein, *Racial Innocence: Performing American Childhood from Slavery to Civil Rights* (New York: New York University Press, 2011), 87–90. There is some textual evidence to support a connection between Topsy the daughter and the topsy-turvy doll. Nicole fends off perhaps hallucinated accusations that her "baby is black" (161), and she describes herself as physically reversible like the doll: "If you want to turn things topsy-turvy, all right, but must your Nicole follow you walking on her hands, darling?" (162). Topsy is fascinated by the Punch puppet at the guignol (188), and Dick observes that Topsy is "very fair and exquisitely made," a phrase that makes her sound almost porcelain (257).

39. See Theresa Brennan on the group transmission of affect, or what she calls "the affect *in the room*" (emphasis in original). Brennan, *The Transmission of Affect* (Ithaca, NY: Cornell University Press, 2004), 68–69.

40. See John William Crowley, *The White Logic: Alcoholism and Gender in American Modernist Fiction* (Amherst: University of Massachusetts Press, 1994), 85.

41. See Lance D. Laird, "Health and Medicine among American Muslims," *Oxford Handbook of American Islam*, ed. Yvonne Y. Haddad and Jane I. Smith (New York: Oxford University Press, 2014), 442, and "fitches," *Cyclopedia of Biblical, Theological, and Ecclesiastical Literature*, ed. Rev. John McClintock and James Strong (New York: Harper & Brothers, 1891), 583.

42. Fitzgerald extends this equine metaphor to suggest that Rosemary is a primarily bodily creature: "Rosemary, for all her delicate surface, was a young mustang, perceptibly by Captain Doctor Hoyt, U.S.A. Cross-sectioned, Rosemary would have displayed an enormous heart, liver, and soul, all crammed close together under the lovely shell" (164–65).

43. Matthew J. Bruccoli with Judith S. Baughman, *F. Scott Fitzgerald on Authorship* (Columbia: University of South Carolina Press, 1996), 68.

44. Mark Pendergast, *For God, Country, and Coca-Cola: The Unauthorized History of the Great American Soft Drink and the Company That Makes It* (New York: Charles Scribner's Sons, 1993), 60.

45. Pamphlet published by the Coca-Cola Corp. titled *What Is It? COCA-COLA What It Is*; U.S. Circuit Court of Appeals, *Coca-Cola Company v. Henry A. Rucker*, 1901, Records of District Courts of the United States, Record Group 21 (online version, https://www.docsteach.org/documents/document/pamphlet-published-by-the-coca-cola-corp-titled-what-is-it-cocacola-what-it-is-us-circuit-court-of-appeals-cocacola-company-versus-henry-a-rucker

46. Ibid.

47. See Mariana Valverde, *Diseases of the Will: Alcohol and the Dilemmas of Freedom* (Cambridge: Cambridge University Press, 1998), 184–86.

48. Scott Donaldson, *Fitzgerald and Hemingway: Works and Days* (New York: Columbia University Press, 2009), 223–24; Francis Kroll King, *Against the Current: As I Remember F. Scott Fitzgerald* (Los Angeles: Figueroa Press, 2005), 41; Arthur Krystal, *Except When I Write: Reflections of a Recovering Critic* (New York: Oxford University Press, 2011), 131.

49. Scott A. Berg, *Max Perkins: Editor of Genius* (New York: Pocket Books, 1979), 386.

50. Valverde, *Diseases of the Will*, 183.

51. This incident was based upon Fitzgerald's own drunken brawl with Italian police. See James Mellow, *Invented Lives: F. Scott and Zelda Fitzgerald* (New York: Ballantine Books, 1986), 227.

52. Grant avowed that the Irish were "as fully Nordic as the English" (59). Fitzgerald treats Dick's racial markers as a sign of his nobility and authenticity; his "reddish Irish coloring" attests to "his more masculine side" and contributes to the impression that "'he was the real thing'" (142, 31). Matthew Pratt Guterl explains that "popular science . . . the wartime thirst for national unity . . . [and] the economic parity achieved by most Irish communities in the 1910s" resulted in the "softening and gradual elimination of racialized representations of the Irish." Guterl, *The Color of Race in America, 1900–1940* (Cambridge, MA: Harvard University Press, 2001), 80.

53. In *The Great Gatsby*, Fitzgerald associates the purity of Gatsby's cosmic vision with breast milk: "once there he could suck on the pap of life, gulp down the incomparable milk of wonder." F. Scott Fitzgerald, *The Great Gatsby* (New York: Scribner, 2004), 110. Although Fitzgerald contrasts Daisy's kiss with this divine manna, Nicole's kiss is more insistently aligned with intermixture and indissoluble compounds. There is no pure milk, even metaphorical, with which to compare her. The evolution of this fluid imagery demonstrates the tonal difference—Michael North calls it "sour shame"—between *The Great Gatsby* and *Tender Is the Night* (*Camera Works*, 129).
54. On Fitzgerald's escalating problems with alcohol in the years leading up to the publication of *Tender Is the Night*, see Scott Donaldson, *Fool for Love: F. Scott Fitzgerald* (Minneapolis: University of Minnesota Press, 2012), 161–70.
55. This display draws attention to phallic rivalry, as Dick "put[s] the back of his neck in the other man's crotch" (283), and, predictably, to racial anxieties, as "the Mexican driving the motor boat" volunteers to serve as Dick's partner (284).
56. *OED* online, January 2018, Oxford University Press, http://www.oed.com/view/Entry/77033?redirectedFrom=gastropathy
57. Ibid. In *Gut Feminism*, Elizabeth A. Wilson elaborates on the metamorphosing, incorporating, and feeling capacities of the stomach:

> The belly takes shape both from what has been ingested (from the world), from its internal neighbors (liver, diaphragm, intestines, kidney), and from bodily posture. This is an organ uniquely positioned, anatomically, to contain what is worldly, what is idiosyncratic, and what is visceral, and to show how such divisions are always being broken down, remade, metabolized, circulated, intensified, and excreted.

Wilson, *Gut Feminism* (Durham, NC: Duke University Press, 2015), 44.
58. Auguste Escoffier, *A Guide to Modern Cookery* (London: William Heinemann, 1907), 428–30.
59. Eugenicists saw Jewish immigrants as harbingers of the "Asiatic menace" in America, as historian Nathaniel Deutsch explains: "Most dangerous of all from a eugenical perspective were those Asiatics whose physical appearance allowed them to pass as white; those who laid claim to a white legal identity for the purpose of naturalization; those who possessed hybrid Asiatic-European ancestry, and those who were racially European but whose behavior was Asiatic. In practical terms, this spectrum included Levantines, Jews, 'Alpines,' [and] Mediterraneans." Deutsch, *Inventing America's "Worst" Family: Eugenics, Islam, and the Rise and Fall of the Tribe of Ishmael* (Berkeley: University of California Press, 2009), 140.
60. See Guterl, *The Color of Race in America*; Matthew Jacobson, *Whiteness of a Different Color: European Immigrants and the Alchemy of Race* (Cambridge, MA: Harvard University Press, 1998); Nell Irvin Painter, *The History of White People* (New York: W. W. Norton, 2010); and David Roediger, *Working toward Whiteness: How America's Immigrants Became White, The Strange Journey from Ellis Island to the Suburbs* (New York: Basic Books, 2006).
61. Michael Nowlin, "F. Scott Fitzgerald's Elite Syncopations," *English Studies in Canada* 26, no. 4 (December 2000): 431.
62. On Crisco, see David Shields, *Southern Provisions: The Creation and Revival of a Cuisine* (Chicago: Chicago University Press, 2015), 302–303.
63. Dyer, *White*, 70.
64. In the first extended physical description of Dick, Fitzgerald mentions his light skin, blue eyes, and sharp nose, all racial markers. He associates them with Irishness and virtue, which he tellingly defines as hard: "[Rosemary] felt the layer of hardness in him, of self-control and self-discipline, her own virtues" (19). This passage implies that Nordics instinctively recognize one another, even when sunburned by the South.
65. Grant, *Passing of the Great Race*, 39.
66. F. Scott Fitzgerald, *The Cruise of the Rolling Junk* (London: Hesperus Press, 2011), 36.
67. Ibid., 44.
68. Zelda Fitzgerald to Scott Fitzgerald, June 1935, in *Dear Scott, Dearest Zelda: The Love Letters of F. Scott and Zelda Fitzgerald*, ed. Jackson R. Bryer and Cathy W. Barks (New York: St. Martin's Griffin, 202), 213.
69. Scott Fitzgerald to Zelda Fitzgerald, June 1940, in ibid., 346.

70. Ibid.
71. Fitzgerald, *The Collected Writings of Zelda Fitzgerald*, 302. Bruccoli reports that though this story was published under a joint byline with Fitzgerald, it was in fact written by Zelda. Further citations appear parenthetically in the text.
72. The only other use of the phrase "Mexican hot dog" from the period that I have found suggests that its etymology describes the frank itself rather than the ethnicity of the vendor: "for mile and mile the cry of the vender of the Mexican hairless or Chihuahua hot dog is heard in the land." Irwin Shrewsbury Cobb, *Some United States: A Series of Stops in Various Parts of this Nation with One Excursion across the Line* (New York: George H. Doran Company, 1926), 290.
73. This nostalgia for "Negroid" voices and cooking may well have reflected Zelda's feelings about her own childhood. In a scrapbook, she preserved two photographs of the Sayre family's black servants standing next to the kitchen building, and she recorded their names as "Malvima, Ella, Estella." Fitzgerald Family Photo Album, 1924–1929, Matthew J. and Arlyn Bruccoli Collection of F. Scott Fitzgerald, Irvin Department of Rare Books and Special Collections, University of South Carolina Libraries, Columbia.
74. Mark Smith, *How Race Is Made: Slavery, Segregation, and the Senses* (Chapel Hill: University of North Carolina Press, 2006), 47.
75. Ibid.
76. Ibid.
77. Sara Ahmed, *The Cultural Politics of Emotion*, 2nd ed. (New York: Routledge, 2015), 92.
78. Ibid., 90; emphasis in original.
79. Ibid.; emphasis in original. In her theorization of disgust and stickiness, Ahmed draws upon the work of Julia Kristeva, Jean-Paul Sartre, Mary Douglas, and Elizabeth Grosz, all of whom posit stickiness and sliminess as a texture that compromises the boundaries of bodies. See Mary Douglas, *Purity and Danger* (New York: Routledge, 2002), 47–48; Elizabeth Grosz, *Volatile Bodies: Toward a Corporeal Feminism* (Bloomington: Indiana University Press, 1994), 192–98; Julia Kristeva, *Powers of Horror* (New York: Columbia University Press, 1982), 1–4; Jean-Paul Sartre, *Being and Nothingness: A Phenomenological Essay on Ontology* (New York: Washington Square Press, 1992), 774–77.
80. Citing Irigaray, Grosz concludes: "It is not that female sexuality is like, resembles, an inherently horrifying viscosity. Rather, it is the production of an order that renders female sexuality and corporeality marginal, indeterminate, and viscous that constitutes the sticky and the viscous with their disgusting, horrifying connotations" (*Volatile Bodies*, 195). See also Luce Irigaray, *This Sex Which Is Not One*, trans. Catherine Porter with Carolyn Burke (Ithaca, NY: Cornell University Press, 1984), 106–18.
81. In "A Rose for Emily" (1930), for example, the titular aging belle is "bloated, like a body long submerged in motionless water" and sticky like "a lump of dough." William Faulkner, "A Rose for Emily," in *Selected Short Stories* (New York: Modern Library, 2012), 49.
82. The iconography of consumer culture shapes Alabama's view of herself. See Simone Weil Davis, *Living Up to the Ads: Gender Fictions of the 1920s* (Durham, NC: Duke University Press, 2000), 155–56.
83. Their friends think that they are crazy to go to such a backwater: "Their friends expected they'd be bitten to death by French mosquitoes and find nothing to eat but goat. They told them they'd find no sewage on the Mediterranean in summer and remembered the impossibility of ice in the highballs; there was some suggestion of packing a trunk with canned goods" (60).
84. Stoddard, for example, claims that Europe is "devitalized and discouraged" and calls it "the white homeland, the heart of the white world." By contrast, "the colored world remains virtually unscathed" (*The Rising Tide of Color*, 196).
85. Stoddard says that the "brown world" has been "gathering headway" thanks to "its own inherent vitality" (ibid., 56). He bemoans the "resurgence of the primitive Mediterranean stock" (167).
86. Ahmed, *Cultural Politics of Emotion*, 94.
87. In *Mediterranean Crossings*, Chambers writes about the fluidity of the Mediterranean:

> The Mediterranean as a sea of migrating cultures, powers, and histories continues to propose a more fluid and unstable archive, a composite formation in the making, neither conclusive nor complete. Today's immigrants from the south of the planet,

however feared, despised, and victimized by racism and social and economic injustice, are the historical reminders that the Mediterranean, firmly considered the origin of Europe and the "West" has always been part of a more extensive elsewhere. (39)

88. On *Save Me the Waltz* and anorexia, see Michelle Payne, "5'4" × 2": Zelda Fitzgerald, Anorexia Nervosa, and *Save Me the Waltz*," *Bucknell Review* 39, no. 1 (1995): 39–56.
89. Mikhail Bakhtin writes about the comic grotesque that "efface[s]" the boundary between "the body and the world . . . [by] accentuat[ing] one grotesque part, stomach, buttocks, or the mouth." Bakhtin, *Rabelais and His World*, trans. Hélène Iswolsky (Bloomington: Indiana University Press, 1984), 354.
90. Highballs were a popular method for administering laxatives. For example, the Pluto Company advertised its mineral water laxative: "A Pluto highball will have you feeling worlds better in one hour." "Pluto Water from Famous French Lick Springs," *Life*, March 11, 1940, 110.
91. See Tim Armstrong on the significance of laxatives in a Taylorizing age. Armstrong, *Modernism, Technology, and the Body* (New York: Cambridge University Press, 1998), 63–66.
92. On modern diets and ideals of self-control, see Amy Erdman Farrell, *Fat Shame: Stigma and the Fat Body in American Culture* (New York: New York University Press, 2011); Hillel Schwartz, *Never Satisfied: A Cultural History of Diets, Fantasies, and Fat* (New York: Doubleday, 1990); and Peter N. Stearns, *Fat History: Bodies and Beauty in the Modern West* (New York: New York University Press, 2002).
93. Judith Brown emphasizes the empty-set, artificial quality of this iconic perfume: "No. 5 offered no visual image, no metaphor, no description of the contents of the bottle. Instead, it announced nothing, save for the perfume's clinical, or industrial, modernity." Brown, *Glamour in Six Dimensions: Modernism and the Radiance of Form* (Ithaca, NY: Cornell University Press), 2.
94. "Menus and Recipes for Three Days: Uncooked Foods," *Physical Culture*, March 1910, 247.
95. The fact that blancmange could be dyed easily and brilliantly was one of its perceived virtues. Priscilla Mary Işin explains, "In fourteenth-century France, blancmange prepared for banquets was sometimes tinted in different colors and arranged in patterns. At a state banquet given during his visit to France in 1377, the Holy Roman Emperor Charles IV was served blancmange with green and white stripes." Işin, "blancmange," in *The Oxford Companion to Sugar and Sweets*, ed. Darra Goldstein (New York: Oxford University Press, 2015), 66.
96. In *A Guide to Modern Cookery*, the renowned French chef Auguste Escoffier expressed his outrage at this development:

> As a matter of fact, in order to justify its name, blanc-mange ought always to be beautifully white; but, for a long time since, the compound word has lost its original meaning. The adjective and noun composing it have fused one with the other to form a simple generic title, which may now be applied with equal propriety to both coloured and white preparations. (759)

97. I borrow this phrase from Jennifer DeVere Brody, who writes about the "convoluted constructions of pure whiteness and pure blackness in Victorian culture," which reveal that both categories are "always already impure, hybrid terms." Brody, *Impossible Purities: Blackness, Femininity, and Victorian Culture* (Durham, NC: Duke University Press, 1998), 11.
98. See María Lugones on mayonnaise as an image of intermixture, impurity, and multiplicity. Lugones, *Pilgrimages/Peregrinajes: Theorizing Coalition Against Multiple Oppressions* (Lanham, MD: Rowman & Littlefield, 2003), 122–23. In a recent interview, Fred Moten observes, "I think mayonnaise has a complex kind of relation to the sublime . . . And I think emulsion does generally. It's something about that intermediary—I don't know—place, between being solid and being a liquid that has a weird relation to the sublime, in the sense that the sublimity of it is in the indefinable nature of it." Fred Moten, "Fred Moten's Radical Critique of the Present," interview by David Wallace, *New Yorker*, April 30, 2018, https://www.newyorker.com/culture/persons-of-interest/fred-motens-radical-critique-of-the-present.
99. On failure as a mode of critique, see Bethany Tisdale, "Unbecoming an Artist: Zelda Fitzgerald's *Save Me the Waltz* and Passive Resistance," in "Creating the Self: Women Artists in Twentieth-Century Fiction" (PhD diss., University of South Carolina, 2015), 74–105. DA 3725401.

100. See Jennifer Radden, ed., *The Nature of Melancholy from Aristotle to Kristeva* (New York: Oxford University Press, 2000), 61–68, and Merry E. Wiesner, *Women and Gender in Early Modern Europe*, 2nd ed. (New York: Cambridge University Press, 2000), 32.
101. Roy Porter explains that "operative surgery entered a 'golden age'" in the early twentieth century, and "appendectomy not for acute but for so-called 'chronic' appendicitis became fashionable in the 1920s and 1930s." Porter, "Hospitals and Surgery," in *The Cambridge Illustrated History of Medicine*, ed. Roy Porter (New York: Cambridge University Press, 2006), 233.
102. See Grosz on bodily fluids, defilement, and puberty for girls (*Volatile Bodies*, 205).
103. On the autobiographical resonance of the end of Alabama's dance career, see Linda Wagner-Martin, *Zelda Sayre Fitzgerald: An American Woman's Life* (New York: Palgrave Macmillan, 2004), 147.
104. Stacy Alaimo, "Trans-corporeal Feminisms and the Ethical Space of Nature," in *Material Feminisms*, ed. Stacy Alaimo and Susan Hekman (Bloomington: Indiana University Press, 2008), 238.
105. Zelda Fitzgerald to F. Scott Fitzgerald, March 1940, in *Dear Scott, Dearest Zelda*, 332.

Chapter 5

1. Mark Kurlansky, *The Food of a Younger Land: A Portrait of American Food* (New York: Riverhead Books, 2010), 142.
2. Camille Bégin, *Taste of the Nation: The New Deal Search for America's Food* (Urbana: University of Illinois Press, 2016), 90–91.
3. Zora Neale Hurston, "Diddy-Wah-Diddy," in Kurlansky, *The Food of a Younger Land*, 142.
4. Dorothy West, "Blackberrying," in *Where the Wild Grape Grows: Selected Writings, 1930–1950*, ed. Verner D. Mitchell and Cynthia Davis (Amherst: University of Massachusetts Press, 2005), 64.
5. Ibid., 65.
6. Marcie Cohen Ferris observes that "Hurston's retelling of an African American folktale remembers a hungry South, the violent history of enslaved blacks in the plantation South denied humane treatment, and the subsistence food rations." Ferris, *The Edible South: The Power of Food and the Making of an American Region* (Chapel Hill: University of North Carolina Press, 2014), 182.
7. Zora Neale Hurston, "The Gilded Six-Bits," in *The Complete Stories* (New York: HarperCollins, 1995), 86–98.
8. Dorothy West, "Pluto," in *Where the Wild Grape Grows*, 104. See also "Quilting," in *Where the Wild Grape Grows*, 67–69.
9. Dorothy West, "Jack in the Pot," in *The Richer, the Poorer: Stories, Sketches, and Reminiscences* (New York: Doubleday, 1995), 31.
10. Ibid., 41.
11. Hurston, "Gilded Six-Bits," 89.
12. West, "Pluto," 102. Once he has eaten, the boy brings Pluto to comic life through his "loving touch[]" and "laugh[ter]" (104).
13. Ibid., 104.
14. Anne Anlin Cheng, *Second Skin: Josephine Baker and the Modern Surface* (New York: Oxford University Press, 2011), 121.
15. Ibid.
16. Alexander Weheliye, *Habeas Viscus: Racializing Assemblages, Biopolitics, and Black Feminist Theories of the Human* (Durham, NC: Duke University Press, 2014), 4.
17. Zora Neale Hurston, *Their Eyes Were Watching God* (New York: HarperPerennial, 2006) and Dorothy West, *The Living Is Easy* (New York: Griot Editions, 1996). Further citations appear parenthetically in the text.
18. Although Hurston and West might be called posthumanist *avant la lettre*, I would instead place them—and, indeed, my own analysis—in a long tradition of critical race studies that registers the exclusivity of the term "human." In this vein, Mel Y. Chen explains that *Animacies* expands upon "posthumanist understandings" of the vibrancy of "object life"

but insists that the various categories of life and non-life are "shaped by race and sexuality." Chen, *Animacies: Biopolitics, Racial Mattering, and Queer Affect* (Durham, NC: Duke University Press, 2012), 5. Similarly, Weheliye counters proponents of posthumanism who see race as another category to be superseded, by arguing that "race ... [is] a constitutive category in thinking about the parameters of humanity" (8) and pointing out that self-professed posthumanists "rarely consider[] cultural and political formations outside the world of Man that might offer alternative versions of humanity" (10). For Weheliye's powerful critique of the identity politics of posthumanism, see *Habeas Viscus*, 9–11. See also Robert F. Reid-Pharr, *Archives of Flesh: African America, Spain, and Post-Humanist Critique* (New York: New York University Press, 2016), 5–11.
19. Chen, *Animacies*, 13.
20. Darieck Scott, *Extravagant Abjection: Blackness, Power, and Sexuality in the African American Literary Imagination* (New York: New York University Press, 2010), 6.
21. See María Lugones, "Heterosexualism and the Colonial/Modern Gender System," *Hypatia* 22, no. 1 (Winter 2007): 186–209. On recasting colonial metaphors to describe lesbian eroticism and further the goals of black feminism, see Omise'eke Natasha Tinsley, *Thiefing Sugar: Eroticism Between Women in Caribbean Literature* (Durham, NC: Duke University Press, 2010), 2.
22. Chen observes that "animacy can work to blur the tenuous hierarchy of human-animal-vegetable-mineral with which it is associated. Recentering on animality (or the animals who face humans) tugs at the ontological cohesion of 'the human,' stretching it out and revealing the contingent striations in its springy taffy; it is then that entities as variant as disability, womanhood, sexuality, emotion, the vegetal, and the inanimate become more salient, more palpable as having been rendered proximate to the human, though they have always subtended the human by propping it up" (*Animacies*, 98).
23. For biographical discussions of their friendship, see Cherene Sherrard-Johnson, *Dorothy West's Paradise: A Biography of Class and Color* (Piscataway, NJ: Rutgers University Press, 2012), 72–76, and Mitchell and Davis, *Where the Wild Grape Grows*, 23–25.
24. Mitchell and Davis, *Where the Wild Grape Grows*, 23; Sherrard-Johnson, *Dorothy West's Paradise*, 76.
25. Mitchell and Davis, *Where the Wild Grape Grows*, 6.
26. Susan Spellman, *Cornering the Market: Independent Grocers and Innovation in American Small Business* (New York: Oxford University Press, 2016), 160.
27. W. O. Murphy, "The Negro Grocer," in *The Negro in Business*, Fourth Conference for the Study of the Negro Problems (Atlanta Atlanta University Publications, 1899), 64. The passage he quotes here comes from Edwin T. Freedley, *Common Sense in Business: or, Practical Answers to Practical Questions on the True Principles and Laws of Success in Farming, Manufactures, Speculation, and Buying and Selling Merchandise: With Some Suggestions on Making Wills and the Causes of Failures in Business* (Philadelphia: Claxton, Remsen, & Haffelfinger, 1879), 182.
28. In March 1892, a black grocer and two of his employees were murdered in Memphis, inspiring the anti-lynching journalism of Ida B. Wells. See Cecelia Tichi, *Civic Passions: Seven Who Launched Progressive America (and What They Taught Us)* (Chapel Hill: University of North Carolina Press, 2009), 263–65. The *Crisis* documented the case of the Goldsmith Brothers, black grocers who bought property on the main street in Greenville, South Carolina: "Immediately the city council passed an ordinance to forbid the ownership of property by Negroes in white districts." "Along the Color Line," *Crisis* 4, no. 3 (1912): 116.
29. Spellman, *Cornering the Market*, 159–60.
30. Jessica Gordon Nembhard, *Collective Courage: A History of African-American Cooperative Economic Thought and Practice* (University Park: Pennsylvania University Press, 2014), 130–32.
31. Ibid., 122.
32. Weheliye, *Habeas Viscus*, 11, 13.
33. Booker T. Washington, "Extracts from an Address at the Unveiling of the Harriet Tubman Memorial," in *Booker T. Washington Papers*, vol. 13, ed. Louis R. Harlan and Raymond W. Smock (Urbana: University of Illinois Press, 1984), 60.

34. W. E. B. Du Bois, *W. E. B. Du Bois on Sociology and the Black Community*, ed. Dan S. Green and Edwin D. Driver (Chicago: University of Chicago Press, 1978), 174.
35. Maya Angelou, *I Know Why the Caged Bird Sings* (New York: Random House, 2009), 7.
36. Ibid.
37. W. E. B. Du Bois, *The Souls of Black Folk*, ed. Henry Louis Gates Jr. and Terri Hume Oliver (New York: Norton Critical Editions, 1999), 97.
38. Cheryl A. Wall, *Women of the Harlem Renaissance* (Bloomington: Indiana University Press, 1995), 142.
39. For example, the porch-talkers shower girls with sugary gifts: "Please let them pay for it. Joe is begged to wrap up all the candy in the store and order more. All the peanuts and soda water—everything!" (67). Charlie Jones even jokes about his own penury: "Gal, Ah'm crazy 'bout you . . . Ah'll do anything in the world except work for you and give you mah money" (67). After Tony Robbins buys his weekly groceries, his wife comes begging for more, and Joe adds the extra meat to their bill (73–74).
40. Black intellectuals identified the Egyptian pharaohs as progenitors of black achievement. See Kevin Kelley Gaines, *Uplifting the Race: Black Leadership, Politics, and Culture in the Twentieth Century* (Chapel Hill: University of North Carolina Press, 1996), 109.
41. In this reading, I build upon the insights of Saidiya Hartman, who argues that "the individual, denuded in the harsh light of scrutiny, reveals a subject tethered by various orders of constraint and obscured by the figure of the self-possessed, for lurking behind the disembodied and self-possessed individual is the fleshy substance of the embodied and the encumbered— that is, the castigated particularity of the universal." Hartman, *Scenes of Subjection: Terror, Slavery, and Self-Making in Nineteenth-Century America* (New York: Oxford University Press, 1997), 123.
42. The food historian Jessica B. Harris observes that "ingenuity was called upon to relieve the forced monotony of the slave diet and inspired whatever creativity could be wrung from a peck of corn and three pounds of salt pork." Harris, *High on the Hog: A Culinary Journey from Africa to America* (New York: St. Martin's Press, 2012), 100.
43. Vincent Woodard uncovers a nineteenth-century association between cannibalism and homoeroticism, which might help to explain this idiom in the porch-talkers' tall tales. Woodard, *The Delectable Negro: Human Consumption and Homoeroticism within U.S. Slave Culture* (New York: New York University Press, 2014), 8–9.
44. This figure holds up to physiological scrutiny. Carnivorism is sodium-seeking; wild animals and humans can "meet their salt needs by eating meat." Mark Kurlansky, *Salt: A World History* (New York: Penguin Books, 2002), 10.
45. Margaret Visser observes that "our desire for salt is little understood; so is our need for it, and so is the reason for the saltiness of our bodies. It is usually thought that we are salty— our blood, our sweat, our tears, our urine, our saliva (the word derives from *sal*, Latin for 'salt'), are salty—because life began in the sea." Perhaps it is not too much of a stretch to see the shared saltiness of the ancient varmint and John the Conqueror as an indication of our primordial past as sea creatures. Visser, *Much Depends on Dinner: The Extraordinary History and Mythology, Allure and Obsessions, Perils and Taboos of an Ordinary Meal* (New York: Grove Press, 1987), 63.
46. See Andrew Warnes on the significance of barbecue across Hurston's oeuvre. Warnes, *Hunger Overcome? Food and Resistance in Twentieth-Century African American Literature* (Athens: University of Georgia Press, 2004), 69–74.
47. Zora Neale Hurston, *Folklore, Memoirs, and Other Writings* (New York: Library of America, 1995), 922–31. Further citations appear parenthetically in the text.
48. Orlando Patterson, *Rituals of Blood: Consequences of Slavery in Two American Centuries* (Washington, DC: Civitas/CounterPoint, 1998), 198–99.
49. See Hortense J. Spillers, *Black, White and in Color: Essays on American Literature and Culture* (Chicago: University of Chicago Press, 2003), 206–207.
50. Hartman argues that pleasure "is a way of redressing the pained constitution and corporeal malediction that is blackness" (*Scenes of Subjection*, 59).
51. Scott invokes the bifurcation that I am trying to get at here when he suggests that "those of us who live in and as black bodies . . . perceive somewhat more clearly the properties of

embodied alienation than those who are unconscious of that legacy and/or living in racially unmarked or 'white' bodies" (*Extravagant Abjection*, 13).

52. For examples, see Charles Ball, *Slavery in the United States: A Narrative of the Life and Adventures of Charles Ball, A Black Man* (1837) (Chapel Hill: University of North Carolina, Academic Affairs Library, 1999), 253–57, 335–37; Octavia V. Rogers Albert, *The House of Bondage, or, Charles Brooks and Other Slaves* (1890) (Chapel Hill: University of North Carolina, Academic Affairs Library, 2000); "Dirge of St. Malo," *Century Magazine* 31 (1886): 814–15; and "15 Negroes Are Shot Down," *Montgomery Advertiser*, August 1, 1910, in *100 Years of Lynchings* by Ralph Ginzburg (Baltimore: Black Classic Press, 1962), 69–70. One folk tale called "King Buzzard," collected in 1928, stages an encounter between "an African American man out in the woods at night—a scene redolent of slave escape and rebellion"—and a "red-eyed buzzard," who turns out to be "an African chief who sold thousands of his fellow Africans into slavery only to be enslaved himself" and who, in death, was punished by taking "the form of a grotesque scavenger." Jared Hickman, *Black Prometheus: Race and Radicalism in the Age of Atlantic Slavery* (New York: Oxford University Press, 2017), 109.

53. See J. Eric Oliver, *Fat Politics: The Real Story Behind America's Obesity Epidemic* (New York: Oxford University Press, 2006), 66.

54. See Amy Erdman Farrell, *Fat Shame: Stigma and the Fat Body in American Culture* (New York: New York University Press, 2011), 42–45; Sander L. Gilman, *Fat Boys: A Slim Book* (Lincoln: University of Nebraska Press, 2004), 41; Oliver, *Fat Politics*, 67–68; Hillel Schwartz, *Never Satisfied: A Cultural History of Diets, Fantasies, and Fat* (New York: Doubleday, 1990), 152–53; and Peter N. Stearns, *Fat History: Bodies and Beauty in the Modern West* (New York: New York University Press, 1997), 54–60.

55. Ferris, *The Edible South*, 127–28.

56. Ibid., 128–29. "Most families ate little or no fresh meat," Ferris explains, "due to its cost. Instead, they depended on cheap, store-bought bacon, once their own supplies of home-grown pork were depleted in the early spring" (131).

57. See Melanie E. DuPuis, *Dangerous Digestion: The Politics of American Dietary Advice* (Oakland: University of California Press, 2015), 63. In their nutritional studies of the southern pellagra epidemic, Joseph Goldberger and George Wheeler, and Edgar Sydenstricker, realized that the availability of fresh food was as critical to consumer health as income. Alan M. Kraut, *Goldberger's War: The Life and Work of a Public Health Crusader* (New York: Hill & Wang, 2004), 167.

58. Henry Louis Gates, Jr., *The Signifying Monkey: A Theory of African-American Literary Criticism* (New York: Oxford University Press, 1988), 193. In *Hunger Overcome?*, Warnes considers the possibility that Janie has poisoned him with conjure (62–63).

59. Geoffrey Sanborn, *The Sign of the Cannibal: Melville and the Making of a Postcolonial Reader* (Durham, NC: Duke University Press, 1998), 17.

60. Zora Neale Hurston, *Mules and Men* (New York: Perennial Library, 1990), 97. Further citations appear parenthetically in the text.

61. On slavery and the ontology of the thing, see Bill Brown, "Reification, Reanimation, and the American Uncanny," *Critical Inquiry* 32 (2006): 182.

62. Achille Mbembé, "Necropolitics," trans. Libby Meintjes, *Public Culture* 15, no. 1 (2003): 14, emphasis in original.

63. Zora Neale Hurston, *Dust Tracks on a Road* (New York: Harper Perennial, 1996), 65. Further citations appear parenthetically in the text.

64. Spillers sees the flesh and the feminine identification it entails as an opportunity for black men. See Hortense J. Spillers, "Mama's Baby, Papa's Maybe," in *Black, White and in Color*, 228.

65. Adam Ewing's deft reading of diaspora in *Their Eyes Were Watching God* has helped to shape my own thoughts on the subject:

> This invocation of diaspora offers no panacea, but it reveals the stony ground upon which identities are debated, constructed, and enacted. It gives less weight to the flow of ideas, goods, and people traversing back and forth across the Atlantic—across the world—than to those moments when those flows touch down upon the earth and acquire a particular currency. It suggests the point, in other words, at which

diaspora might emerge, under the right circumstances, as a framing device for political consciousness on a larger scale: introducing new vistas to enliven and propel old traditions; gesturing to a shared and fictive past; and pointing towards the light of a glorious future.

Ewing, "Lying Up a Nation: Zora Neale Hurston and the Local Uses of Diaspora," *Callaloo* 31, no. 1 (2014): 131.
66. *White Zombie*, directed by Victor Hugo Halperin (1932; Los Angeles: United Artists).
67. Zora Neale Hurston, *Tell My Horse: Voodoo and Life in Haiti and Jamaica* (New York: HarperPerennial, 2009), 181. Further citations appear parenthetically in the text. Achille Mbembé points out that "discourse on Africa is almost always deployed in the framework (or on the fringes) of a meta-text about the *animal*—to be exact, about the *beast*: its experience, its world, and its spectacle. In this meta-text, the life of Africans unfolds under two signs . . . the strange and monstrous . . . [and] intimacy . . . We can give an account of him/her in the same way we can understand the psychic life of the *beast*." Mbembé, *On the Postcolony* (Berkeley: University of California Press, 2001), 1–2, emphasis in original.
68. Mimi Sheller, *Consuming the Caribbean: From Arawaks to Zombies* (New York: Routledge, 2003), 146.
69. I borrow the term "pericapitalist" from Anna Lowenhaupt Tsing, who uses it to indicate economies and spaces "in which both capitalist and noncapitalist value forms may flourish simultaneously—thus allowing translations . . . [This] economic diversity makes capitalism possible—and offers sites of instability and refusal of capitalist governance." Tsing, *The Mushroom at the End of the World: On the Possibility of Life in Capitalist Ruins* (Princeton, NJ: Princeton University Press, 2015), 301n2.
70. On the Everglades, abundance, and diasporic identity, see Scott Hicks, "Rethinking King Cotton: George W. Lee, Zora Neale Hurston, and Global/Local Revisions of the South and Nation," *Arizona Quarterly: A Journal of American Literature, Culture, and Theory* 65, no. 4 (2009): 79.
71. Frederick Douglass, *Narrative of the Life of Frederick Douglass, An American Slave* (New York: Penguin Classics, 1986), 115.
72. Susan Scott Parrish, "Zora Neale Hurston and the Environmental Ethic of Risk," in *American Studies, Ecocriticism, and Citizenship: Thinking and Acting in the Local and Global Commons*, ed. Joni Adamson and Kimberly Ruffin (New York: Routledge Press, 2013), 22.
73. Martyn Bone, "The (Extended) South of Black Folk: Intraregional and Transnational Migrant Labor in *Jonah's Gourd Vine* and *Their Eyes Were Watching God*," *American Literature* 79, no. 4 (2007): 767, and Ted Steinberg, *Acts of God: The Unnatural History of Natural Disaster in America* (New York: Oxford University Press, 2006), 61. See also Jay Barnes, *Florida's Hurricane History* (Chapel Hill: University of North Carolina Press, 1998), 127–40; Robert Mykle, *Killer 'Cane: The Deadly Hurricane of 1928* (New York: Cooper Square Press, 2002); and Eliot Kleinberg, *Black Cloud: The Great Florida Hurricane of 1928* (New York: Carroll & Graf, 2003).
74. Cindy Hahamovitch, *Fruits of Their Labor: Atlantic Coast Farmworkers and the Making of Migrant Poverty* (Chapel Hill: University of North Carolina Press, 1997), 118.
75. Steinberg, *Acts of God*, 48.
76. One history of the storm gives a particularly pointed example: "After the hurricane a report emerged that numerous black workers had heard the warnings and wanted to evacuate. These workers were met at the depot by an armed officer, who barred the way onboard and informed them that they could not leave unless they had their employer's permission. The blacks would not be allowed to go, he told them, until 'they' were ready to let them go. It is not known who 'they' were, whether individual growers or more likely Southern Sugar, which hired most of the workers in the Clewiston area and was noted for its rather draconian attitude towards the field hands." Eric L. Gross, "Somebody Got Drowned, Lord: Florida and the Great Okeechobee Hurricane Disaster of 1928" (PhD diss., Florida State University, 1995), 374–75.
77. Mbembé, *Necropolitics*, 40; emphasis in original.
78. Ibid.

79. This language recalls Nanny's claim that the swamp creatures, "moccasins and other bitin' snakes" and "panthers prowlin'," did not attack her because of her vulnerability: "But nothin' never hurt me 'cause de Lawd knowed how it was" (18). Similarly, in "High John de Conqueror," Hurston avers that "rattlesnakes never bit no colored folks until four years after freedom was declared" (*Folklore*, 926).
80. See Susan Lurie, *Unsettled Subjects: Restoring Feminist Politics to Poststructuralist Critique* (Durham, NC: Duke University Press, 1997), 66.
81. Drawing upon the work of Cora Diamond and Jacques Derrida, Cary Wolfe argues that mortality is a major source of human(ist) anxiety about species difference, both "the unnerving proximity of life and death" and "the *physical* exposure to vulnerability and mortality that we suffer because we, like animals, are embodied beings." Cary Wolfe, *What Is Posthumanism?* (Minneapolis: University of Minnesota Press, 2010), 72; emphasis in original.
82. Frantz Fanon, *Black Skin, White Masks*, trans. Richard Philcox (New York: Grove Press, 2008), 92.
83. Frantz Fanon, *Wretched of the Earth*, trans. Richard Philcox (New York: Grove Press, 2004), 90.
84. Chen, *Animacies*, 14.
85. On the significance of gardens for enslaved Africans, see Sonya Posmentier, *Cultivation and Catastrophe: The Lyric Ecology of Modern Black Literature* (Baltimore: Johns Hopkins University Press, 2017), 234n12, and Sylvia Wynter, "Novel and History, Plot and Plantation," *Savacou* 5 (1971): 95–102.
86. O. Henry, *Cabbages and Kings* (New York: Bert, 1904), 132.
87. See Cynthia Enloe, *Bananas, Beaches, and Bases: Making Feminist Sense of International Politics* (Berkeley: University of California Press, 1989), 127–29.
88. On the "dizzyingly layered" banana skirt, see Cheng, *Second Skin*, 45.
89. See "When to Gather Fruit," *California Fruit Grower*, September 20, 1913, 4. On modern peach cultivation and shipment, see Susanne Freidberg, *Fresh: A Perishable History* (Cambridge, MA: Harvard University Press, 2009), 133–34, 139, and Thomas Okie, *The Georgia Peach: Culture, Agriculture, and Environment in the American South* (Cambridge: Cambridge University Press, 2017), 120–32.
90. Kathryn Stockton, *The Queer Child, or Growing Sideways in the Twentieth Century* (Durham, NC: Duke University Press, 2009), 97.
91. See Verner D. Mitchell and Cynthia Davis, *Literary Sisters: Dorothy West and Her Circle: A Biography of the Harlem Renaissance* (New Brunswick, NJ: Rutgers University Press, 2012), 145, and Sherrard-Johnson, *Dorothy West's Paradise*, 5.
92. Mitchell and Davis speculate that West's mother may have had an affair with Lewis (*Where the Wild Grape Grows*, 29–30).
93. Mitchell and Davis, *Literary Sisters*, 143–44; Sherrard-Johnson, *Dorothy West's Paradise*, 95.
94. Mitchell and Davis, *Where the Wild Grape Grows*, 38.
95. Marian Minus, "The Fine Line," *Opportunity: A Journal of Negro Life* 17 (November 1939): 333–37, 336.
96. Mitchell and Davis note the importance of "the erotic attraction of transgressive interracial relationships" in the fiction of both Minus and West (*Where the Wild Grape Grows*, 41).
97. Ibid., 36.
98. Audre Lorde, *Sister Outsider: Essays and Speeches* (New York: Random House, 2007), 57.
99. Teresa C. Zackodnick, *The Mulatta and the Politics of Race* (Jackson: University Press of Mississippi, 2004), 20.
100. West leaves Mr. Davies's race unclear. The caterer's assistant is definitely white: "the caterer's man, who had come with the ices and to serve the highballs and hors d'oeuvres, had got over his initial shock that colored people were briefly his betters" (244). West does not give an extended description of "Mr. Davies," except to say that "with the departure of the caterer's man, [he] was now the sole representative of his craft" (254).
101. As a result, West tried to convince Countee Cullen to father her child. Mitchell and Davis, *Where the Wild Grape Grows*, 32.
102. Dorothy West, "Prologue to Life," in *Where the Wild Grape Grows*, 71. Further citations appear parenthetically in the text.

103. Mary Douglas, *Purity and Danger: An Analysis of Concepts of Pollution and Taboo* (New York: Routledge, 1966).
104. Roderick A. Ferguson proposes that "capital produces emergent social formations that exceed the racialized boundaries of gender and sexual ideals . . . capitalist political economies have been scenes for the universalization and, hence, the normalization of sexuality. But those economies have also been the arenas for the disruption of normativity" (11). West's depiction of fruit and fruitfulness represents "the normalization of heteropatriarchy on the one hand, and the emergence of eroticized and gendered racial formations that dispute heteropatriarchy's universality on the other" (11). Ferguson, *Aberrations in Black: Toward a Queer of Color Critique* (Minneapolis: University of Minnesota Press, 2004).
105. See John Soluri, *Banana Cultures: Agriculture, Consumption, and Environmental Change in Honduras and the United States* (Austin: University of Texas Press, 2005), 8–9.
106. Joel Denker, *The World on a Plate: A Tour Through the History of America's Ethnic Cuisine* (Lincoln: University of Nebraska Press, 2007), 48–49.
107. Cleo is internally amused when she watches a maid's "wagging rear": "She longed for the eager audience [her sisters] would have provided, the boisterous mirth she would have evoked when she flatfooted up an imaginary flight of stairs, agitating her bottom. Who did she know in the length and breadth of Boston who wouldn't have cleared an embarrassed throat before she got going good on her imitation?" (44).
108. Sigmund Freud, "Character and Anal Eroticism," in *The Freud Reader*, ed. Peter Gay (New York: W. W. Norton, 1995), 293–300, 296.
109. Hartman writes about the illusory nature of this emancipatory masculinity: "The transubstantiation of the captive into volitional subject, chattel into proprietor, and the circumscribed body of blackness into the disembodied and abstract universal seems improbable, if not impossible" (*Scenes of Subjection*, 123).
110. Mark M. Smith, *How Race Is Made: Slavery, Segregation, and the Senses* (Chapel Hill: University of North Carolina Press, 2008), 13–16.
111. Julia Kristeva suggests that "excrement and its equivalents (decay, infection, disease, corpse, etc.) stand for the danger to identity that comes from without: the ego threatened by the non-ego, society threatened by its outside, life by death." Kristeva, *Powers of Horror: An Essay on Abjection* (New York: Columbia University Press, 1982), 71.
112. Weheliye, *Habeas Viscus*, 32.
113. Hartman observes that "race itself" functions "as a kind of property, with blackness as the mark of object status and whiteness licensing the proprietorship of self" (*Scenes of Subjection*, 119).

INDEX

abjection, 3, 12, 14
   and race, 1, 22, 116, 125, 130, 136, 138, 143, 164–69, 175n62
   and sex/sexuality, 130, 138, 175n62
   and women, 68, 130, 136, 143, 151, 169
abolitionist fiction, 49
advertising, 5, 9, 23–24, 29, 35, 44, 56, 94, 103, 119, 121, 131, 159, 204n90
affect (communicable), 19, 32, 161
affiliation, 5, 7, 8, 9, 14, 27, 75, 89, 90, 91, 98, 100, 103, 109, 127, 143, 146, 154, 155, 166
African diaspora, 26, 27, 170, 113, 179n58
Africanism, 3, 55, 173n29
Afrofuturism, 54
agribusiness, 6, 9, 14, 152, 153, 154, 156, 158, 159, 167
Ahmed, Sara, 12, 129, 133, 203n79
Alaimo, Stacy, 140
alcoholism, 119, 122, 123, 125
Alsop, Joseph, 63, 187n113
Angelou, Maya, 146
animality, 66, 102, 117, 122, 133, 139, 143, 147, 206n22
animals, 14, 47, 66, 126, 143, 144–146, 147, 149, 151, 155, 156, 187n130, 190n37, 206n22, 207n44, 210n81
anti-miscegenation laws, 6
anti-Semitism, 6, 9, 75, 77, 101–102
artificial flavors/colors, 9, 20, 21, 33–34, 37, 112, 134–35, 180n78, 183n48
Asian Americans, 6, 59. *See also* Chinese

Baker, Josephine, 159
Baldwin, James, 40, 41
banana industry, 159, 164
Banana Wars, 9

bananas, 5, 9, 10, 63, 111, 115, 133, 135, 152, 169
   and human flesh, 144, 159, 160, 162
   and imperialism, 159, 168
   olfactory sensations, 12, 159, 168
   and race, 49, 133, 164, 167
   and sex/sexuality, 160, 162
barbarism, 62, 63, 66, 119
Barrès, Maurice, 75
Barthes, Roland, 63
Basques, 76–77, 78, 79, 81, 94
Baudelaire, Charles, 2, 97
Belasco, Warren, 44
Berlack-Boozer, Thelma, 62, 186n103
Berlant, Lauren, 60, 61
Bernstein, Robin, 70, 187n127, 201n38
bildungsroman, 6, 9
biopolitics, 47, 175n57, 193n84
black bodies, 5, 11, 13, 14, 19, 116, 128, 168, 185n71, 207–208n51
   and industrial/manual labor, 10, 24, 152–53
   as sites of pleasure, 148, 155
   and violence, 148, 149
   vulnerability of, 14, 148, 168
black femininity/womanhood, 49, 60, 69
black feminism, 144, 145
Black Lives Matter, 170
black masculinity, 57, 58, 145, 146, 152, 163, 211n109
black nationalism, 44, 56
black readers, 10, 54
blackness, 4, 11, 12, 15, 27, 34, 37, 57, 72, 126, 128–29, 131, 132, 134, 162, 170, 175n59, 176n68, 204n97, 211n113
   pleasures of, 112, 173n29
   stigmas of, 33, 112, 116, 125, 140, 143, 155, 167, 169, 173n29, 207n50

bodies
　commodification of, 36, 142
　feminization of, 31, 124, 129, 136
　racialization of, 3, 6, 7, 14, 19, 29, 30, 36, 116, 129, 130, 135, 136, 142–44, 155, 158, 165, 167, 169, 171–72n7, 180n76
　sexualization of, 31, 36, 142, 183n53
　See also black bodies
Bridgetower, George, 61, 186n98
Brooks, Samuel I. *See* Schuyler, George
Brown, Anna Wiggins, 68, 69
Brown, William Wells, 48

Cage, John, 102
Campbell's Soup, 55
canned food, 9, 106
cannibalism, 7, 17, 52, 56, 57, 126, 137, 146, 147, 148, 150, 169, 207n43
capitalism, 25, 89, 125, 144, 145, 147, 164, 170, 209n69
carbonation, 15, 20, 22, 23, 31, 41
Carruth, Allison, 3, 172n10
Cather, Willa, 97, 186n96
chain stores, 9, 144–45, 158, 164, 168
Chambers, Iain, 133, 203–204n87
Chen, Mel Y., 7, 143, 144, 173n35, 175n62, 205–206n18, 206n22
Cheng, Anne Anlin, 20, 51, 52, 142–43
Chero-Cola, 23, 24, 29
Child, Lydia Maria, 48
Chinese, 7, 136, 163
citizenship, 5, 9, 17, 19, 106
Coca-Cola, 23, 35, 122–23, 128, 155, 178n43
cocaine, 19, 122
Cocks, Catherine, 7
coffee/caffeine, 5, 53, 111, 115, 116, 117–18, 119, 121, 122–23, 124, 200n30, 200n36
Cold War, 9
colonialism, 12, 19, 20, 22, 55, 119, 122, 143, 156, 168, 170, 175n57
communicable affects, 19, 32, 161
consumerism, 22, 106, 118, 120
Cooper, Wayne F., 112
cosmopolitanism, 13, 74, 83, 89, 90, 92, 194n107
Coughlin, Robert, 118
Crane, Hart, 20, 21–22
Crisco, 14, 126
Croly, David Goodman, 42
Crosthwaite, Georgia, 64, 187n115
Cullen, Countee, 45, 160, 210n101
cummings, e. e., 21

Deniker, Joseph, 80, 191n50, 199n12
dialect, 112
digestion, 10, 16, 100, 182n23

disgust, 81, 131, 133, 203n79
　and eating, 2, 12
　and femininity, 136, 137, 169, 203n80
　and race, 11, 116, 128, 129, 133, 163, 169
　and sexual desire/sexuality, 101, 133, 140
Dos Passos, John, 20, 21
Douglas, Katharine Waldo, 77
Douglas, Mary, 12, 172n25, 175n57, 203n79
Douglass, Frederick, 153
Du Bois, W. E. B., 115, 146
duCille, Ann, 57
Dydo, Ulla, 96
Dyer, Richard, 33, 39, 117, 171n6

East, Edward, 115, 116, 118
electric refrigeration, 9, 55, 56
elimination, 16
Eliot, T. S., 4
Ellington, Duke, 19
Ellis, Havelock, 81
eroticism, 1, 2, 36, 49, 52, 102, 113, 131, 140, 175n62
　and botanicals, 52, 97
　and black/brown bodies, 123, 129, 155, 159, 162, 163, 210n96, 211n104
　in black culture, 26, 30
　and eating/being eaten, 1, 2, 17, 42, 71
　and the female body, 31, 98, 124, 130, 135, 136, 138, 160, 162, 163
　and homosexual desire, 79, 81, 143, 160, 161, 163, 207n43
ethnic fetishism, 11
ethnic modernism, 22
eugenics, 5, 7, 20, 22, 36, 43, 45–47, 50, 52–53, 64, 65, 72, 82, 88, 95, 101, 107, 112–16, 118–19, 123, 132, 140, 162, 184–85n68, 185n71, 186n95, 198n162, 200n36, 202n59
euthenics, 10, 184n63
exceptionalism, 59, 61, 142
exoticism, 28, 36, 55, 67, 97, 114, 164
expatriate experience, 8, 9, 74, 75, 77, 91, 94, 96, 108–109, 128
expatriate fiction, 6, 13, 79, 80, 82, 90, 93, 113, 120, 133–34
expulsion, 1, 3, 11, 17, 150

Fanon, Frantz, 12, 37, 156
Fascism, 14, 75, 87, 103, 108
Felski, Rita, 52
feminine ideal, 53, 59, 117, 128, 136, 164
femininity, 28, 57, 102, 116, 124, 126, 130, 134, 136, 137, 138, 143, 150, 163
　See also black femininity; white femininity
feminism, 12, 18, 90, 193n89, 196n134
　See also black feminism

Index

Ferguson, Jeffrey, 46
Ferguson, Roderick A., 211n104
Fisher, M. F. K., 101
Fitzgerald, F. Scott, 5, 8, 120, 122, 127,
    132, 171n6
  and alcoholism, 122, 200n29, 200n51
  Great Gatsby, The, 1, 2, 124, 202n53
  and race, 112, 119, 121, 199n10, 201n52
  Tender Is the Night, 6, 13, 14, 112–13, 114,
    116, 117–27, 129, 136, 202n53, 202n64
Fitzgerald, Scottie, 128
Fitzgerald, Zelda S., 5, 8–9, 14, 112, 120, 127–28,
    130, 140, 169
  Save Me the Waltz, 12–13, 14, 116, 128–37,
    139, 200n25, 203n71, 203n73
  and whiteness, 8, 116, 128
Flanner, Janet, 108
flesh, 102, 131, 154, 162, 207n41
  edibility, 12, 147, 149, 151, 156, 158, 159
  femininity, 98, 129, 133, 134, 136, 140, 159,
    163, 208n64
  racialization, 51, 112, 12, 135, 142, 144, 148,
    152, 169; vulnerability, 147, 155,
    168, 169
Foley, Barbara, 37, 176n7, 178n54
food and technology, 10, 13, 16
formalism, 97, 174n41
Forter, Greg, 79, 81, 198n171
Frank, Waldo, 15, 20, 22, 23
freedom, 29, 149, 153
Freeman, Elizabeth, 99
Freud, Sigmund, 36, 71, 96, 167
futurism, 44, 56

Galton, Francis, 64
gastropathia, 125
Gates, Henry Louis, Jr., 150, 180n94, 181n101
Gauguin, Paul, 4, 172n18, 195n114
gender, 28, 32, 52, 54, 57, 64, 68, 125
  and diet/food preparation, 55–56,
    183n53, 200n30
  industrialization and racial identity, 58, 60, 64,
    67, 70, 163, 175n59, 211n104
  traditional roles, 52, 53, 54, 57
General Electric, 55
General Mills, 55
Gide, André, 75, 189n20
Gilman, Charlotte Perkins, 49, 52,
    182n37, 183n38
gleaning, or the glaneuse, 5, 75, 89–90, 91–92,
    96, 102, 103, 108, 193n88, 193n94
global markets, 143, 144
Global North, 119
Global South, 114, 117, 119, 127, 135
globalization, 79, 88, 111
Gopnik, Adam, 109, 188n1, 198n171

Grant, Madison, 88, 113, 115, 123, 127,
    132, 174n49, 198n162, 199n12,
    199n15, 201n52
Great Migration, 9, 31–32, 168
Greeks, 4, 6, 72, 79–80, 165, 166, 167,
    191n44, 191n46
Grosz, Elizabeth, 130, 131, 203n79, 203n80
Gurdjieff, George, 16, 25

Harlem Renaissance, 6, 19, 20, 144, 160, 177n22
Harper, Frances E. W., 48, 49, 52
Hartman, Saidiya, 12, 207n41, 207n50, 211n109,
    211n113
Hawthorne, Nathaniel, 47, 48, 50, 51
Hegel, G. W. F., 151
Heinz Company, 44, 55
Hemingway, Ernest, 5, 8, 13
  and cultural authenticity, 74, 81
  Death in the Afternoon, 80, 83, 191n47, 192n67
  Farewell to Arms, A, 83, 84–88, 89, 105, 108
  fascination with terroir, 75, 76, 87, 89
  friendship with Stein, 73, 74
  Moveable Feast, A, 73, 190n22
  Sun Also Rises, The, 77–80, 81–82, 89, 104,
    105, 189n12, 191n42, 192n58, 200n30
  "Wine of Wyoming," 103–105, 106–108
Herbert, Robert, 94
heredity, 8, 20, 44, 59, 60, 61, 64, 65, 85, 116,
    127, 184n67
heterosexualism, 143
heterosexuality, 13, 27, 97, 143
Hitler, Adolph, 101
homoeroticism, 79, 81, 207n43
  See also eroticism: and homosexual desire;
    queerness
homosociality, 13, 27, 69, 78, 82
Honig, Bonnie, 90, 194n103
hooks, bell, 4, 172n17
Hughes, Langston, 19, 27, 160
humanism, 40, 143, 152, 153
Hurst, Fannie, 49
Hurston, John, 146
Hurston, Zora Neale, 4, 6, 141, 142, 155, 156
  "Diddy Wah Diddy," 141, 142
  Mules and Men, 150, 151, 156
  Tell My Horse, 152, 156, 209n67
  Their Eyes Were Watching God, 14, 143, 144,
    145–52, 153, 154–55, 156, 167, 168
hydroponics, 13, 43, 44, 45, 51, 52, 56, 58,
    169, 183n48
hygiene, 7, 24, 55, 96, 175n57, 193n84

immigration, 4, 6, 54, 85, 106, 114, 115
imperialism, 9, 10, 159, 167
incorporation, 2, 3, 125, 135, 146

individualism, 2, 9, 26, 143, 147, 164
industrial food system, 5, 9, 10, 40, 45, 115, 118, 119
industrialism, 25, 41
ingestion, 3, 10, 13, 47, 71, 119, 122, 125
interracial desire, 3, 188n135, 210n96
interracial encounters, 3, 19, 31, 37, 144, 165, 172n17
interracial marriage, 62, 160
  See also anti-miscegenation laws
interracialism, 2, 44, 62, 65, 67, 69, 160, 182n37
intoxication, 19, 20, 26, 36, 37, 56, 73, 83, 105, 106, 117, 121–22, 123, 124, 125, 126, 153, 201n51
Irish, 6, 11, 123, 126, 166, 201n52

Jannath, Heba. See Schuyler, Josephine
Jewishness, 6, 13, 75, 77, 89, 91, 92, 102, 103, 110
  See also anti-Semitism
Jim Crow. See segregation
Johnson, Helene, 162
Johnson, James Weldon, 19
Jones, Arnetta, 45
Jones, Mildred, 160
Jordan, David Starr, 94, 186n95
Joyce, James, 126, 127

Keats, John, 117
Kellogg, John Harvey, 118
Kilgour, Maggie, 57
Kipling, Rudyard, 49
Kreymbourg, Alfred, 97
Kristeva, Julia, 12, 203n79, 211n111
Ku Klux Klan, 9, 19
Kurlansky, Mark, 94, 207n44

Larsen, Nella, 1, 2, 44–45
Latin cultures, 75, 85, 110, 114, 119, 124
Lattimore, Marjorie, 38
Lawrence, D. H., 75, 97
lesbianism, 97, 100, 160, 161, 162, 196n134
  See also queerness
Levine, Caroline, 8, 173n26, 174n40, 174n41
Lévi-Strauss, Claude, 63
Lewis, Edith, 160, 210n92
Lewis, Lena Morrow, 61, 186n95
Liebig, Justus von, 47
liminality, 5, 12, 20, 27, 52, 121, 132, 135
Lincoln, Abraham, 42
localism, 13, 81, 82, 83, 92
Logan, William, 11
Lorde, Audre, 161
Lost Generation, 6, 13, 77, 79
Lott, Eric, 12, 32

Lye, Colleen, 8, 174n42
lynching, 14, 27, 148, 149, 206n28

Macfadden, Bernarr, 16, 52–53, 54, 58
Mannur, Anita, 5
Marshall, Thaddeus, 11
masculine ideal, 54, 124, 125, 128, 139
masculinity. See black masculinity; white masculinity
masochism, 14
mass production, 23, 24, 25, 40
masturbation, 160
Mbembé, Achille, 154, 209n67
McKay, Claude, 11, 111, 112, 113, 114, 165
meat, 57, 76, 77, 85, 86, 108, 136, 142, 145, 169, 174n49, 199n15, 207n39, 208n56
  beef/lamb, 53, 62, 86, 115, 126, 165, 168, 186n103
  as diet staple, 59, 150, 207n44
  as metaphor for black men, 147, 148, 152
  pork, 11, 55, 76, 79, 139, 147, 150, 168, 169, 190n24, 207n42, 208n56
  poultry, 11, 142, 152; rawness, 5, 56, 61, 62, 66
meat industry, 87, 88, 118, 150
Merleaux, April, 7, 178–79n55
Michaels, Walter Benn, 4, 32–33, 74, 180n76, 189n4, 189n12
Middle Passage, 23, 148, 168
migrant workers, 6, 143, 144, 152–53, 154, 156
Millet, Jean-François, 90, 91, 93, 94, 193n94
Milton, John, 82
mind-body dualism, 30, 139
minstrelsy, 22, 32, 80, 113, 163
Mintz, Sidney, 25
Minus, Marian, 160
miscegenation, 6, 14, 15, 27, 36, 42, 43, 45, 47, 48, 106, 119, 129, 137, 179n71
Miscegenation (pamphlet), 42, 43
misogyny, 102, 130, 145
Mitchell, Joseph, 61, 64, 65–67, 71, 72, 187n128
model kitchens, 52, 55–56
modernism, 6, 8, 11, 13, 16, 19, 20, 21, 22, 23, 30, 37, 74, 97, 127, 143
modernity, 25, 31, 38, 56, 63, 106, 110, 136
  and industrialization, 24, 25, 113, 204n93
  instability of, 106; and race, 24, 25, 52, 57, 85, 132
Money, Nicholas, 99, 100, 196n141
Monsanto, 9
Monterro, Felipa de. See Schuyler, Philippa
More, Thomas, 83
Morrison, Toni, 3, 6, 173n29
mouth, 71, 137, 139, 156, 204n89
  and eroticism, 140, 160
  and queerness, 13, 78–79

and racialization, 14, 37, 162, 163
and vulnerability, 125, 151
mulatta, 27, 52, 59, 60–61, 70, 72, 182n37, 188n133
   and black masculinity, 57, 58
   as edible, 47, 48, 49, 188n135
   as exotic figure, 30, 67
   and sexual politics, 47, 48
   as tragic figure, 19, 30, 31, 37, 47–48, 51, 60, 67, 72, 182n35, 185n79
Murphy, Alexandra, 91, 193n94
Murphy, W. O., 144, 145
mushrooms, 1, 5, 7, 13, 14, 75, 76, 89, 96–103, 105, 108, 109, 195n122, 196n128, 196n141, 197n143, 197n145

national/transnational identity, 13, 90, 127
nationalism, 9, 40, 41, 78, 85, 94, 175n57, 191n42
nativism, 8, 9, 11, 74, 92, 94, 110, 165
naturalism, 2, 6, 14, 143, 144, 168, 169
Nazism, 67, 94
New Negro movement, 8, 13, 44–45, 50, 58, 69
New Negro womanhood, 13, 44–45, 50, 69
Ngai, Sianne, 20, 34, 35
Niceforo, Alfredo, 84, 85
North, Michael, 4, 202n53
Nowlin, Michael, 126
Nunn, W. G., 50
nutrition science, 3, 10, 69
Nyong'o, Tavia, 43

Okihiro, Gary, 7
one-drop rule, 5, 8, 14, 26, 32
Orientalism, 6, 71, 102, 122

Parrish, Susan Scott, 153
pastoralism, 23, 76, 81, 85, 89, 94, 121
patent medicines, 15, 18, 19
Patterson, Orlando, 148
peaches, 5, 67, 159, 162, 165
peasants, 73–74, 76, 78, 83–86, 89, 90, 91, 92, 93–94, 103, 108, 121, 165, 172n18, 192n74, 195n114, 196n128
Peattie, Roderick, 76
Pendergast, Mark, 122
Perkins, Max, 123
perversion, 81, 101, 113, 137
Pétain, Philippe, 108
Picasso, Pablo, 102, 189n20, 192n58
plantations, 25, 29, 117–18, 152, 153, 154, 168, 205n6
posthumanism, 205–206n18
Pound, Ezra, 20, 21

predation, 17, 117, 130, 147, 148, 150, 151, 152, 154, 155, 187n130
premodern culture, 13, 26, 65, 72, 76, 78, 84, 89, 91, 94, 106
Price, Weston, 10, 58–59
Priestly, Benjamin, 15
primitivism, 8, 10, 28, 32, 54, 55, 59, 65, 81, 94, 161
purity, 12, 46, 59, 63, 88, 124, 172n25, 202n53
   and ethnicity/race, 4, 6, 9, 13, 14, 25, 76, 78–79, 80, 82, 89, 94, 108, 110, 116, 117, 130, 131, 135, 171n6
   and food culture, 3, 23, 44, 45, 53, 56, 70
   and local culture, 96, 110, 192n67
   and primitiveness, 82–83, 114
   and sex/sexuality, 47, 52, 53, 66, 70, 130, 140

queerness, 2, 12, 13, 33, 78, 81, 98, 99, 100, 102, 103, 143, 161, 162, 164, 178n43, 196n139

race suicide, 53, 82
racial agency, 18, 50, 52, 142, 153, 154, 169
racial categorization, 7, 25
   and biologism, 15, 33, 54, 59
   and climatological theories, 7, 75, 88, 113, 114, 116, 125, 128, 199n12
   and food/consumables, 3, 10, 11, 15, 16
   and modernism, 4, 5, 6
   transformations of, 18, 20, 40, 52, 63
racial degeneration, 7, 46, 94, 118, 137
racial difference, 3, 4, 14, 20, 22, 36, 59, 65, 66, 85, 94, 107, 116, 129, 130, 140, 164, 167, 184n67
racial hierarchies, 4, 21, 64, 66, 114, 140
racial indeterminacy, 66, 116
racial intermixture, 11, 20, 42, 44–52, 59, 60–61, 94, 111, 113, 119, 132, 133, 183n43, 185n71
racial isolation, 94
racial transformation, 5, 18, 59
racial uplift, 55, 70, 146
racialized labor, 10, 152
racism, 7, 8, 9, 43, 87, 111, 130, 132, 143, 168, 184n67, 203–204n87
   and binarism, 37, 174n41
   and capitalism, 164, 170
   and skin color, 14, 78, 161–62, 163
   stereotypes, 11, 25, 32, 35, 37, 59, 64, 66, 80, 106
   structural, 14, 149, 150
   See also minstrelsy
raw diet, 5, 10, 12, 13, 14, 45, 46, 53–54, 55, 56, 58, 59, 61–63, 64, 65–66, 70–72, 182n23, 186n103, 187n131

realism, 143, 144
regionalism, 195n118
reproductive control, 52, 53
Retallack, Joan, 108
Ridge, Lola, 21
Ripley, William Z., 80, 88, 94, 113, 190n39, 191n50, 194n113, 199n12
Rose, Francis, 110
Rouff, Marcel, 74
Roy, Parama, 3, 23, 175n57
Rush, Benjamin, 162

Sadler, William, 118
Sailland, Maurice Edmond (Curnonsky), 74
Sanborn, Geoffrey, 150
Sayre, Anthony Dickinson, 12
Schuster, Joshua, 97, 108
Schuyler, George, 5, 8, 10, 12, 46, 49–50, 55, 62, 64, 71, 72, 145
   Black Empire, 13, 43, 52–53, 54, 55, 56, 57, 58, 59
   Black Internationale, The, 13, 43, 45, 50–52, 56, 57, 59, 60
   Black No More, 43, 184n67
Schuyler, Josephine Cogdell, 13, 45, 54, 58, 59, 60, 61, 63, 64, 65, 66, 67, 69, 70, 71, 72, 185n71, 186n95, 187n115, 187n130
Schuyler, Philippa, 13, 44, 45–47, 59, 60, 61–62, 63–64, 65–72
science fiction, 6, 13, 38, 43, 44, 47, 54, 60, 143
Scott, Darieck, 116, 143, 175n62, 207–208n51
segregation, 2, 4, 6, 11
Semple, Ellen Churchill, 113, 192n67
Sergi, Giuseppe, 84
sexual reproduction, 45, 49, 52, 54, 82, 97–98, 101, 106, 119, 129, 142, 159, 162, 164
Shapiro, Laura, 56
Sheller, Mimi, 7, 152
Sherrard-Johnson, Cherene, 50, 59, 183n43
Shotwell, Alexis, 12
Shuttleton, David, 81
Sinclair, Upton, 4, 5
skepticism, 39, 85, 89
slavery, 25, 27, 30, 35, 54, 55, 60, 128, 147, 148, 208n52
   and marriage, 53, 54
   and racial intermixture, 42, 47, 182n35
Smith, Mark, 128
soda fountains, 9, 12, 16, 18–19, 20, 21, 22, 23, 38, 66, 138, 178n45, 179n62
soda industry, 15, 20, 21, 23, 34, 35, 176n5
Southern Sugar, 153, 209n76
southernness, 7, 14, 138, 139
Spellman, Susan, 144
Spillers, Hortense, 12, 59, 148, 208n64
Stein, Gertrude, 5, 7, 8, 13, 74, 77, 81, 100, 108–109, 170
   "Advertisements," 94, 96–97, 103, 195n118
   Civilization: A Play, 100, 101
   fascination with terroir, 75, 76, 108, 110
   friendship with Hemingway, 73, 74
   Geography and Plays, 89, 90, 94
   History or Messages from History, 97, 99, 103
   Lucy Church Amiably, 98, 99, 100, 103, 108, 196n135, 196n136
   mushroom gathering, 75, 96, 97, 101, 102, 103
   Paris France, 103, 109, 110, 188n1, 198n171
   "Scenes. Actions and Disposition of Relations and Positions," 91, 92, 93–94, 96, 103, 108
   "The Winner Loses," 103, 108, 198n167
Steinberg, Ted, 154
Stevens, Wallace, 4
Stockton, Kathryn, 160
Stoddard, Lothrop, 112, 115, 127, 132
stomach, 16, 17, 122, 125, 134, 138, 150, 166, 202n57, 204n89
Stowe, Harriet Beecher, 48
Streicher, Julius, 101
sugar, 1, 21, 23, 25, 108, 111, 112, 154, 178n54, 179n74
   and gustatory pleasure, 115, 116, 131–32, 207n39
   and health, 58, 66
   refinement of, 45, 46, 171–72n7
   and whiteness, 1, 2, 55
   See also Southern Sugar

Talalay, Kathryn, 45, 187n131
teeth, 56, 80, 135, 153, 155
   deadness/decay of, 21, 58–59
   as marker of health/hygiene, 43, 44, 59, 65, 66, 68
   whiteness of, 10, 43, 45, 50, 52, 59
tenant farmers, 146, 150
Terman, Lewis Madison, 65
terroir, 5, 13, 76, 77, 86, 89, 103, 105, 106, 108, 190n24
   and nativism, 74, 75, 87, 110, 192–93n75
   and race, 75, 80, 88
Thomas, Edith Lewis, 160
Tinsley, Omise'eke Natasha, 23, 178n43
Toklas, Alice B., 74, 81, 96, 102, 103, 108, 189n10, 195n117, 198n170
Tompkins, Kyla Wazana, 3, 7, 13, 17, 23, 74, 175n57
Toomer, Jean, 5, 7, 8, 10, 13, 16, 38
   "The Americans," 16–17, 180n89
   Cane, 8–9, 15–16, 22, 23, 25, 26–37, 38, 39, 41, 111–12, 179n65
   "The Flavor of Man," 38, 39, 40
   memoir, 17–18, 38
   Sacred Factory, The, 25, 40
   "Withered Skin of Berries," 25–26, 27, 28, 179n57, 179n74

tourism, 74, 77, 92, 93, 106, 109; and the automobile, 74; and food, 74
Tsing, Anna Lowenhaupt, 96, 195n122, 209n69
Twain, Mark, 67

United Fruit Company, 159, 164
US South, 5, 127, 128, 129, 132, 139, 144, 199n18

Veit, Helen, 7, 184n63, 184n67

Wakeman, George, 42
Wallace, Thurman, 160
Wampole, Christy, 75
Warner, Sylvia Townsend, 97, 98, 101
Warnes, Andrew, 4, 208n58
Washington, Booker T., 146
Weheliye, Alexander, 7, 12, 170, 205–206n18
West, Dorothy, 6–7, 142, 160, 162
   Living Is Easy, The, 10, 14, 143, 144, 145, 158–64, 165–68
   "Pluto," 142, 205n12
   possible lesbianism, 160, 161
   WPA work, 141, 142
West, Isaac, 144
Whalan, Mark, 18, 174n48, 177n22
Wheatley, Phillis, 61
white anxiety, 61, 113
white consumers, 10, 22, 118
white degeneration, 8
white femininity, 117, 123–24, 128, 129, 130, 134, 136, 137–38
white masculinity, 5, 32, 126, 127, 132, 149

White Zombie, 152
whiteness, 1, 2, 8, 23, 33, 34, 39, 41, 43, 44, 53, 65, 77, 81, 112, 113, 126, 127, 130, 135, 143
   and claims of superiority, 12, 14, 43, 44, 46, 129, 134, 137, 139, 148, 166, 169, 170, 172n1
   fantasy of, 14, 72
   and femininity, 117, 134, 136
   instability of, 6, 70, 110, 121, 164
   and masculinity, 82, 126, 123, 125, 150
   as normative, 128, 130, 131
   as spectacle, 1, 171n6
   and stickiness, 9, 133, 137, 139
   vis-à-vis blackness, 11, 116, 128, 129, 176n68, 182n35, 204n97, 211n113
Wilder, Thornton, 102
Williams, William Carlos, 10, 11, 20
Williams-Forson, Psyche, 4
Wilson, Edmund, 114
wine, 86, 104, 105, 110, 111, 119, 120, 124, 139, 140, 192n58
   and gustatory sensation, 56, 76, 79, 87, 104, 112, 116, 130, 133
   and inebriation, 26, 77, 82, 106, 107, 117
   and terroir, 74, 76, 190n24
   and wineskins, 14, 77, 78, 79
Witt, Doris, 4
Womack, Ytasha, 54
Woolf, Virginia, 102

Young Negroes' Co-Operative League, 145

zombie mythology, 153, 154, 155
Zong Massacre, 168

tourism, 74, 77, 92, 93, 106, 109; and the automobile, 74; and food, 74
Tsing, Anna Lowenhaupt, 96, 195n122, 209n69
Twain, Mark, 67

United Fruit Company, 159, 164
US South, 5, 127, 128, 129, 132, 139, 144, 199n18

Veit, Helen, 7, 184n63, 184n67

Wakeman, George, 42
Wallace, Thurman, 160
Wampole, Christy, 75
Warner, Sylvia Townsend, 97, 98, 101
Warnes, Andrew, 4, 208n58
Washington, Booker T., 146
Weheliye, Alexander, 7, 12, 170, 205–206n18
West, Dorothy, 6–7, 142, 160, 162
  Living Is Easy, The, 10, 14, 143, 144, 145, 158–64, 165–68
  "Pluto," 142, 205n12
  possible lesbianism, 160, 161
  WPA work, 141, 142
West, Isaac, 144
Whalan, Mark, 18, 174n48, 177n22
Wheatley, Phillis, 61
white anxiety, 61, 113
white consumers, 10, 22, 118
white degeneration, 8
white femininity, 117, 123–24, 128, 129, 130, 134, 136, 137–38
white masculinity, 5, 32, 126, 127, 132, 149

White Zombie, 152
whiteness, 1, 2, 8, 23, 33, 34, 39, 41, 43, 44, 53, 65, 77, 81, 112, 113, 126, 127, 130, 135, 143
  and claims of superiority, 12, 14, 43, 44, 46, 129, 134, 137, 139, 148, 166, 169, 170, 172n1
  fantasy of, 14, 72
  and femininity, 117, 134, 136
  instability of, 6, 70, 110, 121, 164
  and masculinity, 82, 126, 123, 125, 150
  as normative, 128, 130, 131
  as spectacle, 1, 171n6
  and stickiness, 9, 133, 137, 139
  vis-à-vis blackness, 11, 116, 128, 129, 176n68, 182n35, 204n97, 211n113
Wilder, Thornton, 102
Williams, William Carlos, 10, 11, 20
Williams-Forson, Psyche, 4
Wilson, Edmund, 114
wine, 86, 104, 105, 110, 111, 119, 120, 124, 139, 140, 192n58
  and gustatory sensation, 56, 76, 79, 87, 104, 112, 116, 130, 133
  and inebriation, 26, 77, 82, 106, 107, 117
  and terroir, 74, 76, 190n24
  and wineskins, 14, 77, 78, 79
Witt, Doris, 4
Womack, Ytasha, 54
Woolf, Virginia, 102

Young Negroes' Co-Operative League, 145

zombie mythology, 153, 154, 155
Zong Massacre, 168